THE TERRY LECTURES

CAPTIVE GODS

VOLUMES IN THE TERRY LECTURES SERIES
AVAILABLE FROM YALE UNIVERSITY PRESS

Psychoanalysis and Religion Erich Fromm

A Common Faith John Dewey

Psychology and Religion Carl G. Jung

Belief in God in an Age of Science John Polkinghorne

One World Now: The Ethics of Globalization Peter Singer

Reason, Faith, and Revolution: Reflections on the God Debate Terry Eagleton

Thinking in Circles: An Essay on Ring Composition Mary Douglas

The Religion and Science Debate: Why Does It Continue? Edited by Harold W. Attridge

Natural Reflections: Human Cognition at the Nexus of Science and Religion Barbara Herrnstein Smith

Absence of Mind: The Dispelling of Inwardness from the Modern Myth of the Self Marilynne Robinson

Islam, Science, and the Challenge of History Ahmad Dallal

The New Universe and the Human Future: How a Shared Cosmology Could Transform the World Nancy Ellen Abrams and Joel R. Primack

The Scientific Buddha: His Short and Happy Life Donald S. Lopez, Jr.

Life After Faith: The Case for Secular Humanism Philip Kitcher

Private Doubt, Public Dilemma: Religion and Science since Jefferson and Darwin Keith Thomson

Against Dharma: Dissent in the Ancient Indian Sciences of Sex and Politics Wendy Doniger

A Way of Life: Things, Thought, and Action in Chinese Medicine Judith Farquhar
For a full list of titles in print in the Terry Lectures Series,
visit yalebooks.com or yaleup.co.uk.

[CAPTIVE]
GODS

Religion and the Rise of
Social Science

Kwame Anthony Appiah

Yale UNIVERSITY PRESS
New Haven & London

Published with assistance from the Ernst Cassirer Publications Fund.

Copyright © 2025 by Kwame Anthony Appiah.
All rights reserved.
This book may not be reproduced, in whole or in part, including illustrations, in any form (beyond that copying permitted by Sections 107 and 108 of the U.S. Copyright Law and except by reviewers for the public press), without written permission from the publishers.

Yale University Press books may be purchased in quantity for educational, business, or promotional use. For information, please e-mail sales.press@yale.edu (U.S. office) or sales@yaleup.co.uk (U.K. office).

Designed by
Set in type by
Printed in the United States of America.

Library of Congress Control Number: 00000000000
ISBN 978-0-300-23306-3 (hardcover : alk. paper)

A catalogue record for this book is available from the British Library.

This paper meets the requirements of ANSI/NISO Z39.48-1992 (Permanence of Paper).

10 9 8 7 6 5 4 3 2 1

For Dorothy Emmet,
in loving memory

THE DWIGHT HARRINGTON TERRY FOUNDATION LECTURES ON
RELIGION IN THE LIGHT OF SCIENCE AND PHILOSOPHY

The deed of gift declares that "the object of this foundation is not the promotion of scientific investigation and discovery, but rather the assimilation and interpretation of that which has been or shall be hereafter discovered, and its application to human welfare, especially by the building of the truths of science and philosophy into the structure of a broadened and purified religion. The founder believes that such a religion will greatly stimulate intelligent effort for the improvement of human conditions and the advancement of the race in strength and excellence of character. To this end it is desired that a series of lectures be given by men eminent in their respective departments, on ethics, the history of civilization and religion, biblical research, all sciences and branches of knowledge which have an important bearing on the subject, all the great laws of nature, especially of evolution . . . also such interpretations of literature and sociology as are in accord with the spirit of this foundation, to the end that the Christian spirit may be nurtured in the fullest light of the world's knowledge and that mankind may be helped to attain its highest possible welfare and happiness upon this earth." The present work constitutes the latest volume published on this foundation.

Contents

Introduction: Communion   **1**

Chapter 1. Edward Burnett Tylor: Starting with Spiritsx   **29**

Chapter 2. Émile Durkheim: Society and the Sacred   **67**

Chapter 3. Georg Simmel: The Feelings and the Forms   **99**

Chapter 4. Max Weber: Religious Rationalities   **139**

Chapter 5. Critical and Cognitive Turns   **203**

Epilogue   **227**

Acknowledgments   **249**   *Notes*   **251**   *Index*   **309**

Introduction

Communion

ON THE VERY IDEA OF RELIGION — THE POSSIBILITIES OF
PLURALISM — FROM ANTHROPOTHEISMUS TO OPIUM —
GOING THROUGH A PHASE — THE SCIENCE OF RELIGION —
DEFINING TERMS — LOSING OUR "RELIGION" — THE SOCIAL
CONSTRUCTION OF SOCIETY — NEGATIVE CAPABILITIES

"How's the water?" the old fish asks the young ones, in the modern wisdom tale. They respond with bafflement: "*What* water?" A medium of our existence, it might seem, rises to our consciousness only when it ebbs. That's one explanation for why the so-called classical sociologists, working mainly in the decade before and the decade after 1900, were preoccupied with religion—so preoccupied that the emerging science of society became at the same time a science of religion. In one familiar narrative, the decline of religion was implicated in a social crisis—the crisis called modernity, which intensified in the later decades of the nineteenth century—and sociology was created in order to explore it. Just as secularity made it possible to see religion as a distinct object of study, social dissolution made it possible to see society as one.

But this narrative is incomplete. It fails to explain why these scholars didn't take on religion as merely another phenomenon to be elucidated, but instead decided that the social and religious—as structures, impulses, sentiments, practices—were inextricable categories, each unthinkable outside the other. As a matter of disciplinary history, the concepts of "society" and "religion" were conjoined twins. To be sure, each concept had previous lives outside the modern social sciences. Our social theorists drew on a considerable library concerning religions around the world. Yet this only brings out the difficulty that they had in defining what they were theorizing. In a secular theory of religion, the gods are secret captives of the societies that worship them, but our theorists themselves are captives, too, of their time and place. We cannot transcend our contexts.

In the chapters that follow, I will pursue a sort of conceptual genealogy through a detailed engagement with four thinkers as their thought took shape in the later decades of the nineteenth century. It's conventional to say that these four helped establish the modern social science of religion, but I want to explore what's hidden by that "of": it misleadingly suggests that religion was just one subject among others to which social science applied itself and belies the profound communion between the two. My aim, as will be evident, isn't to solve the "problem" of society or of religion; my principal interest is in excavating a fraught and consequential stratum of intellectual history. Still, attending to the early conceptual commensalism between the social sciences and religion may illuminate both.

ON THE VERY IDEA OF RELIGION

Because I want to remain alert to the fragility of our guiding concepts, it will be worth sketching, at the outset, how religions came to be seen as religions, long preceding the rise of modern theories about how we should think about them. Before the early modern era, for one thing, religion did not believe in religion. That is, what we would designate as religious traditions did not, in the main, conceive themselves as belonging to a class of different but functionally equivalent objects. To write about "religion" was, in this sense, to write as an enemy of religion. Inside my way of life, I know and can explain how the world works; only from outside can you assemble elements of that worldview and call them a religion, to be placed in a vitrine alongside other religions.

In tracing the itinerary of the idea from, say, the Axial Age to the early modern era, our word "religion" can be an unreliable guide, in ways anticipated by Quentin Skinner's classic 1979 essay "The Idea of a Cultural Lexicon." "Religion," *religio*: among the Romans and early Christians, such words referred to rites and ceremonial observances, but didn't connote what we mean by religion. When Cicero, in one of his "Against Verres" orations of 70 BCE, said that the Sicilian governor's actions were "*contra omnes divinas atque humanas religiones*"—"against all divine and human *religiones*"—the word meant something like rules or strictures. Augustine of Hippo, accordingly, warns that the Latin term *religio* refers not only to the worship of God, but also to "the observance of duties in human relationship." For Aquinas, in the thirteenth century, the word refers to monastic life. A fourteenth-century English use of "religions" refers to sects of Christianity.[1]

This book focuses on specific currents within intellectual life in Britain, France, and Germany in the late nineteenth and early twentieth centuries; the voices I'll take up will mainly be ones that were, in some measure, audible to my principals. But, taking a leaf from Skinner, we should avoid crude nominalism; the uncertain conceptual status of religion isn't just a point about a word, an exercise in logomachy. No term in the Bible truly corresponds to our term "religion." Islam, in premodern times, did not conceive itself as a religion, either. In his richly detailed study *Before Religion* (2013), Brent Nongbri observes that the word *islam*, which appears in nominal form only eight times in the Qur'an, is naturally taken to connote submission or obedience, not to name a creed; the participle *muslim*, in turn, designated one who submits. It appears that, in the seventh century, certain Jews could be members of the ummah, while some of Jesus's followers were themselves *muslimun*. Early members of the Christian church, for their part, understood Mohammedans not as followers of anything like a religion but as heretics, pagans, or idolaters.[2]

It was in the seventeenth century that the term, as it circulated in the Latin world of European intellection, came securely to acquire its modern, comparative sense: you see it in the title of Hugo Grotius's *De veritate religionis Christianae* (1627). This emerging conception—the term is pretty much the same in all the major European tongues—was fueled by the fracturing represented by the Reformation (Christian forms of worship were diverse, but it had still been possible to imagine a unified Christendom under submission to a universal Church). It was fueled, too, by new scholarship about the ancient world, and by the imperial conquests of the New World, along with increased engagement with yet other parts of the globe.

The convergence of these forces is emblematized in a much-discussed dream of Baruch Spinoza's. Writing to a friend in 1664—eight years after his excommunication for heresy—Spinoza wrote of a vision he'd had of "a certain black and scabby Brazilian." Even after he awoke, the image kept reappearing, just as vividly, and faded only gradually. Scholars recall that, in the previous decade, a slave rebellion in Pernambuco, then a Dutch-controlled region of Brazil, had returned it to Portuguese hands.[3] Nobody was more aware of the plurality of belief than the era's most consequential heretic, someone whose theory of God, as a substance coterminous with all existence, seemingly made him fit for no religion at all. In the meantime, scholars have identified a shift from an essential Catholic association of religion with ritual to a more Protestant version that foregrounds a state of mind, an attitude of pious reverence or adoration. "Faith," increasingly, can be used as a synonym.[4] To this day, we tend to refer to practicing Catholics and believing Protestants.

THE POSSIBILITIES OF PLURALISM

It will be helpful, at this point, to give a swift, as-I-stand-on-one-foot overview of how religion was theorized from the mid-eighteenth-century to the early decades of the nineteenth century. For here we'll find intellectual touchstones that the principals of this book took for granted as part of a common inheritance. Everyone in their scholarly circles was at least ambiently aware of them.

The concept of religion gained sharper contours during the Enlightenment, because it was a focus of intent scholarly attention—attention that, as you would expect, was not always reverent. David Hume's *The*

Natural History of Religion (1757) told readers that polytheism and idolatry characterized religion in its most ancient form, one that was ubiquitous in ancient times and still held by the savage peoples of Asia, Africa, and America. How does monotheism arise? Worshippers promote one deity over the others, perhaps as "their peculiar patron, or as the general sovereign of heaven," and, to gain his favor, extravagant flattery is directed toward him, eventually arriving at the ascription of infinite power and presence. Yet even when a supreme deity has been erected, Hume says, there's a tendency to lift up subordinates to divine status, as the Catholic Church had done with the Virgin Mary and various saints.[5] The naturalistic perspective was disturbing to many: to explain the rise of credal beliefs while failing to accord a causal role to their reality was (clerics feared) to explain religion *away*.

Religion had Enlightenment allies, too. Gotthold Ephraim Lessing, the exemplary religious rationalist of the age, had a strategy for dealing with the plurality of religious practices and the rise of materialist explanation. There's an "inner truth" within us, he proposed, that is the engine of various religious modalities and that will ultimately guide mankind to an "eternal gospel" not yet within our reach.[6] On this view, a comparative study of religions need not be a study in error; it could be a study in complementary strivings toward a larger truth not yet fully revealed. But even these benevolent approaches might erode the genuine power of faith. The twentieth-century scholar (and Presbyterian minister) Wilfred Cantwell Smith saw in them the replacement of historical communities of belief with the notion of a generic religion; it was a process in which—as another scholarly Smith, Jonathan Z. Smith, writes—religion was "domesticated" and "transformed from pathos to ethos."[7]

From this perspective, religion's most sophisticated and influential defenders in the decades that followed were unwitting fifth columnists of secularity. Consider Friedrich Schleiermacher, who was a housemate, in the late 1790s, of the arch-romantic Friedrich Schlegel (later a son-in-law of Moses Mendelssohn's), and who, with Schlegel's encouragement, published a 1799 volume titled *On Religion: Speeches to Its Cultured Despisers*. For Schleiermacher, "religion" encompasses monotheisms and polytheisms, but was, at its essence, a realm of "intuition and feeling."[8] That feeling—the essence of religion, he later suggested—could be described more specifically: it was "the feeling of absolute dependence."[9] Influenced by Johann Gottfried von Herder, he was a pluralist of a sort: "just as nothing is more irreligious than to demand uniformity in humanity generally, so nothing is more unchristian than to seek uniformity in religion." In his second speech, he admits that defining religion is a daunting task. But in the end, religion's shared goal is "to love the world spirit and joyfully observe its work." For him, accordingly, every faith tradition, including "polytheistic Egypt," contained an intuition or longing for the one in the all.[10] Religion was, in contemporary terms, akin to an application programming interface with the divine; it's just that some APIs were fitter, or closer to the truth, than others. This was someone who hoped to have his pathos and ethos, too.

FROM ANTHROPOTHEISMUS TO OPIUM

If God wasn't in the details, secular scholars might now take the holy writ itself as a historical document. David Strauss's *Life of Jesus Critically Examined* (1835–1836), did just this. Strauss highlighted contradictions and inconsistencies in the tales of the New Testament and argued that these accounts had to be understood as symbolic or mythological renderings that expressed the early Christian community's faith in Jesus, with the various texts reflecting the particular theological agendas of their respective authors and communities. But it was Ludwig Feuerbach who posed the greater test of faith. He had grown up in a devoutly Lutheran family, studied theology at Heidelberg, and then transferred to the University of Berlin. Schleiermacher was teaching there, but Feuerbach switched his course of study to philosophy, attending Hegel's lectures quite religiously. Reading Strauss contributed to his reconsideration of his hero. In *The Essence of Christianity* (1841), Feuerbach ventures something like an anthropology of religion, or what he termed "Anthropotheismus"; human beings can see only what they're equipped to see, and their God is a projection of their vision. (He was religiously too heterodox for an academic career, but his wife had inherited a share of a porcelain factory, and he was able to live as an independent scholar.) Certain Hegelian influences are legible here: a certain conception of self-consciousness and self-alienation, a certain conception of historical development, a certain role for emanation. But for Hegel, our knowledge of God was part of an unfolding process of self-realization—with religion, divided into stages, being itself a stage, as an imperfect representation of the Absolute Spirit.[11] For Feuerbach, God is, decidedly, a purely human creation.

What was religion? It was a question Feuerbach took up with a certain fervor:

> Religion is the relation of man to his own nature,—therein lies its truth and its power of moral amelioration;—but to his nature not recognised as his own, but regarded as another nature, separate, nay, contradistinguished from his own: herein lies its untruth, its limitation, its contradiction to reason and morality; herein lies the noxious source of religious fanaticism, the chief metaphysical principle of human sacrifices, in a word, the *prima materia* of all the atrocities, all the horrible scenes, in the tragedy of religious history.

Where Schleiermacher supposed that the more developed forms of religion brought us closer to the divine, Feuerbach supposed that the less developed forms of religion bring us closer to the truth about human creeds: "the nearer religion stands to its origin, the truer, the more genuine it is, the less is its true nature disguised; that is to say, in the origin of religion there is no qualitative or essential distinction whatever between God and man. And the religious man is not shocked at this identification; for his understanding, is still in harmony with his religion."[12] (I've been quoting George Eliot's careful translation.) After Feuerbach, religion—at least for a formidable educated cadre—became firmly situated as a *something*, not an everything. Studying it, we could learn about human nature and about human relations.

Perhaps we would learn nothing good. Karl Marx was an attentive and enthusiastic reader of Feuerbach—he tried to commission a piece from him for his planned French and German *Jahrbücher*—even though, famously, he thought Feuerbach's analysis fell short in critical ways. It did so because it was insufficiently social. "Feuerbach dissolves the religious essence into the human essence. But the human essence is not an abstraction inherent in each particular individual," Marx writes in his 1845 "Theses on Feuerbach." "In its reality it is the ensemble of social relationships." And so Feuerbach "does not see that the 'religious sentiment' is itself a social product, and that the abstract individual he analyses belongs to a specific form of society."[13]

For Marx, convinced by the mid-1840s that "the criticism of religion has been essentially completed," the struggle against religion was a staging ground for a struggle against a world to which religion had given a "spiritual aroma." Religion may have been a phantasm, but it arose from the cruelty of actual subjugation: "Religious suffering is both the expression of real suffering and a protest against real suffering. Religion is the sigh of the oppressed creature, the soul of a heartless world, and it is also the soul of soulless conditions. It is the opium of the people." He goes on to write that the protest against real suffering must be carried out through the scrutiny of religion: "The criticism of religion is, therefore, the germ of the criticism of that vale of tears whose halo is religion."[14] In this account, Hegel's Absolute Spirit has been inverted and replaced with the materiality of subjugation; religion has been afforded little autonomy beyond that afforded what he mischievously terms "the halo," the *Heiligenschein*. Marx is writing with the clarity of combat. But also with the fixed view of combat: this is religion in the singular, uninflected and undifferentiated.

GOING THROUGH A PHASE

In France, August Comte, the man who, perhaps prematurely, coined the term "sociology" (he would have preferred "social physics," but that had a prior claimant, the formidable Belgian statistician Adolphe Quetelet), had already been approaching the question of religion through an elaborate intellectual edifice. Comte's six-volume *Course of Positive Philosophy*, which assembled a series of texts largely written in the 1830s—then abridged and "freely" translated into English by the intrepid Harriet Martineau in 1853—proposed that the intellectual development of our species began with what he termed a theological stage, in which phenomena were explained as the outcome of magic and supernatural entities. (The stage had the substages that led from fetishism to polytheism to monotheism.) Our development then advanced to a metaphysical stage, which supplanted such spiritual entities with abstractions such as essences, vital principles, and teleology, as well as a consideration of human tendencies. The third stage was the positive, scientific one, given over to systematic forms of inquiry—measurement, observation, statistical evidence, verification—that allowed us to establish the causal laws governing natural phenomena. True science confined itself to "positive facts"—observation-derived data, which, unlike metaphysical speculation, could be positively affirmed. (For Marx, this was the sin of idealism: by focusing on ideas, it scanted the material and historical conditions that shape societies.)

What's striking is that Comte, in his later years, sought to replicate and reform religion in the image of science, devising a Religion of Humanity—complete with a priesthood, prayers, and rituals—devoted to furtherance of altruism and the veneration of humankind. (You can still find positivist Chapels of Humanity in France and Brazil.) Even admirers found this a bit much. In a book on Comte and positivism, John Stuart Mill found "something ineffably ludicrous" in Comte's instruction that his devotional practices be engaged in three times each day for a two-hour period.[15] Thomas Huxley acidly called the Religion of Humanity "Catholicism minus Christianity."[16]

Still, Comte's vision of humanity's movement through progressive phases of understanding was catalyzing for many intellectuals, not least in Great Britain. Among them was Comte's English translator, Harriet Martineau, who began her career as a contributor to a Unitarian monthly. In her *Society in America*, from 1837, she deplored the ascetic form of Christianity she found widespread in the United States (she thought it could not endure, "it is so destitute of all reason") and worried about the way American women had taken to religion, which testified, in part, "to the vacuity which must exist when such a mistake is fallen into." But it was the ascetic strain that disturbed her, not the true spirit of religion: "It brings religion down to be ceremonial, constrained, anxious, and altogether divested of its free, generous, and joyous character." At this point, she thought that the "spirit of Humanity" was the "very sanctum of religion."[17]

In the preface to Martineau's 1853 edition of Comte and in a treatise in the form of a correspondence with Henry Atkinson, *Letters on the Laws of Man's Nature and Development* (1853), she elaborated a worldview in which the laws of the universe would be uncovered through scientific inquiry rather than religious doctrine. And yet she worried about the dangers posed by the discarding of religion. "I believe that no one questions that a very large proportion of our people are now so adrift," she wrote in that preface, alert to a decline in ecclesiastical authority. Fortunately, Comte's system of belief, with its radiant vision of progress, represented "the greatest single effort that has been made to obviate this kind of danger."[18]

THE SCIENCE OF RELIGION

The disengagement from formal religion among intellectuals in the industrializing West—a disengagement that people like Martineau represented and helped spread—had consequences for the way they thought about religions elsewhere. The concept of "world religions," Tomoko Masuzawa observes, took root at a time when European scholars saw nonmodern people elsewhere in the world as in the grips of religion in a way that these scholars were not. At the same time, these religions, to be religions, had to be akin to Christianity: they were vast metaphysical systems interwoven with all aspects of society; they had a sacred scripture of some sort; they had a God or gods. As she observes, the framework required that scholars reprocess a great deal of the cultural and political activities they observed among foreigners.[19] This was a form of pluralism on the universalist terms of the European pluralists.

In the nineteenth-century science of religion, or *Religionswissenschaft*, a discipline that emerged in the 1870s, Buddhism proved a fascinating test case. First, scholars had to deem a set of diverse practices in South, Central, Southeast, and East Asia to be variants of a single thing.[20] An 1844 British study focused on a set of Sanskrit documents and Gautama Buddha as its originary figure; an early "pure" form was to be excavated and distinguished from later corrupted forms. But once the entity had been identified, or confected, the issue of whether it counted as a religion had to be resolved. The Oxford professor of Sanskrit, Sir Monier Monier-Williams, in an 1889 study, insisted it did not: "Christianity is a religion, whereas Buddhism, at least in its earliest and truest form, is no religion at all, but a mere system of morality and philosophy founded on a pessimistic theory of life." At the same time, it was configured on the analogy of religion: there was, as Masuzawa notes, the "extraordinary yet historically genuine person as the founder and initiator of the tradition," and there was some canonical set of ancient texts.[21] (Scripture could be ascribed to Shintoism and Hinduism, even if a founder couldn't be identified.) And soon it was broadly accepted as a religion, even a *Weltreligion*, which is to say, not just a religion in the world but a religion of the world, with universal—transnational, transtemporal—tendencies.

European theorists could have found their categories challenged closer to home. When did Judaism become a religion? Leora Batnitzky, in a fascinating book on the topic, shows that it functioned, in medieval times, as creed, culture, and nationality at once and people weren't in the habit of seeing these things as distinct. She argues that it was, more than anyone, Moses Mendelssohn (Friedrich Schlegel's father-in-law) who invented the idea that Judaism was a religion, assimilating it to a German Protestant conception that, she notes, Judaism didn't quite fit. Lutheranism, Calvinism, Catholicism: these were organized faith practices that appeared to be playing roughly the same role, that could be conceived as separable from the state, even from the emerging notion of a nation-state. But *Judentum*—a word that could mean Jewry, Jewishness, or Judaism—remained tied to ideas of descent and of a nationhood of its own.[22] An ex-Jew, in the sense of one who had given up traditional beliefs or practices, remained a kind of Jew.

DEFINING TERMS

Meanwhile, efforts to define religion persisted with a proselytic zeal, in part because no contender gained wide acceptance. "What, in truth, are the conditions necessary to constitute a religion?" John Stuart Mill asked in his book on Comte. "There must be a creed, or conviction, claiming authority over the whole of human life; a belief, or set of beliefs, deliberately adopted, respecting human destiny and duty, to which the believer inwardly acknowledges that all his actions ought to be subordinate. Moreover, there must be a sentiment connected with this creed, or capable of being invoked by it, sufficiently powerful to give it in fact, the authority over human conduct to which it lays claim in theory." Notice the triune nature of the definition, in which sentiment connected beliefs and actions. Herbert Spencer, writing in 1867, went smaller: what religions all had in common was "the tacit conviction that the existence of the world with all it contains and all which surrounds it, is a mystery ever pressing for interpretation."[23]

A few years later, Edward B. Tylor, as we'll see, proposed a "belief in Spiritual Beings" as the minimum definition that connected religions across the historical stages of development. His ally and sparring partner Max Müller, in an 1873 book, offered a definition that would not have been inhospitable to Lessing and Schleiermacher: religion "is a mental faculty" that, "independent of, nay in spite of sense and reason, enables man to apprehend the Infinite under different names and under varying guises."[24] In an alternative formulation, friendly to the nonbeliever, religion "consists in the perception of the infinite under such manifestations as are able to influence the moral character of man."[25] In *The Varieties of Religious Experience: A Study in Human Nature* (1902), William James (who decided that Buddhism was, strictly, atheistic) expressed impatience with "verbal" disputation, but then offered an account consistent with older Protestant, state-of-mind approaches: *"the feelings, acts and experiences of individual men in their solitude, so far as they apprehend themselves to stand in relation to whatever they may consider the divine."* Evidently worried that his formulation had begged too many questions, he then took up another angle: "the life of religion," taken in the broadest terms, "consists of the belief that there is an unseen order, and our supreme good lies in harmoniously adjusting ourselves thereto."[26] In *The Elementary Forms of the Religious Life* (1912), Émile Durkheim—who sought to include Buddhism, where spirits or gods didn't necessarily play a role—proposed a definition that had the breadth of Mill's but with a social valence: "A religion is a unifying system of beliefs and of practices in relation to sacred things—that is, things kept apart, forbidden—beliefs and practices that unite all those who adhere to them into one moral community, called the Church."[27]

That same year, two other books notably acknowledged the difficulty of the definitional enterprise. In *Themis: A Study of the Social Origins of Greek Religion*, the classical scholar and linguist Jane Ellen Harrison announced, "we shall at the outset attempt no definition of the term religion, but we shall collect the facts that admittedly are religious and see from what human activities they appear to have sprung." Toward the end, she advised, "A definition however illuminating always desiccates its object."[28] In *A Psychological Study of Religion: Its Origin, Function, and Future*, James H. Leuba, a psychology professor at Bryn Mawr, denied that religion could be characterized by any particular emotion or purpose, and eschewed the "little formulae called definitions of religion," but he allowed that its end was to maintain and perfect life, and that it was a functional part of the "struggle for life."[29] In an appendix, he anthologized dozens of proposed definitions, dividing them into intellectualistic, affectivistic, and voluntaristic.

Few were more cautious than Max Weber and Georg Simmel. At the opening of a work on religion, Weber declared, "To define 'religion,' to say what it *is*, is not possible at the start"; he did not promise it would be possible at the end, either. Simmel, sounding like a bruised veteran, urged a retreat from the field of definitional combat: "No light will ever be cast in the sibyllic twilight that, for us, surrounds the origin and nature of religion as long as we insist on approaching it as a single problem requiring only a single word for its solution. Thus far no one has been able to offer a definition of religion that is both precise and sufficiently comprehensive. No one has been able to grasp its ultimate essence, shared by the religions of Christians and of South Sea islanders, of Buddha and Vitzliputzli."[30]

LOSING OUR "RELIGION"

Ensuing generations have not caught Simmel out. Functionalist definitions—many developed in the wake of A. R. Radcliffe-Brown and Bronisław Malinowski, and invariably drawing on Durkheim—typically wave aside the specific requirement of supernatural or superhuman entities. They attended to what religion did: the way it supported social cohesion and control, offered psychological support (especially in the face of crises, including death), marked rites of passage, legitimized social institutions, and so on. For critics, though, waiving that requirement was a fatal flaw: whatever functionalism explained, they thought, it did not explain religion. Religions weren't always sources of social stability; sometimes they were the opposite. Conversely, cultural systems not obviously religious in nature appeared to provide these functions, too. Functionalism was even suspected of tautology, of defining religion by functions that are then used to explain the existence of religion. And then functionalism had little to say about what religion meant to its practitioners.

The anthropologist Melford Spiro, in a paper from 1966 that socialized Tylor's stipulation, decided that religion was "an institution consisting of culturally patterned interaction with culturally postulated superhuman beings."[31] It was another definition published that year, though, that generated a notably vast literature, concurring or contesting. In the essay "Religion as a Cultural System," the anthropologist Clifford Geertz stipulated that religion was "(1) a system of symbols which acts to (2) establish powerful, pervasive, and long-lasting moods and motivations in men by (3) formulating conceptions of a general order of existence and (4) clothing these conceptions with such an aura of factuality that (5) the moods and motivations seem uniquely realistic."[32] An immediate question that arose was whether a formula that included Confucianism and Buddhism and Stoicism could exclude Marxism, forms of nationalism, and so forth. A deeper question, to which I'll return, had to do with the privileged status of the symbolic.

Symbolism has, in the event, had a broad constituency. For the sociologist Robert N. Bellah, too, symbolism was key: "Religion is a set of symbolic forms and acts which relate man to the ultimate condition of his existence."[33] Critics worry that symbolism is too powerful a solvent, dissolving disparate phenomena into a slurry of vague significance. And because, in these models, the status of entities *as* symbols may not be apparent to those who use them, symbolists must continually deny that people quite mean what they say.

Other approaches have arrived, with helpful mnemonics. They may distinguish religion through four C's, if not necessarily the same C's. Creed, cultus, code, and community are the characteristic features, in one version. In another version, we're offered "counterintuition (supernatural agents), commitment (costly sacrifice), compassion (relief from existential anxieties), and communion (emotion-arousing ritual)"— taken to be "cultural manipulations of psychological adaptations."[34] Ninian Smart sought to demarcate religion through what he took to be its seven dimensions (ritual, experiential, mythological, doctrinal, ethical, institutional, and material). All are no doubt useful angles of approach, whether or not the sum of the angles completes a definitional circle.

Evolutionary accounts have evolved their own definitions. Robin Dunbar says that "a minimalist definition of religion might be belief in some kind of transcendental world (that may or may not coincide with our observable physical world) inhabited by spirit beings or forces (that may or may not take an interest in and influence the physical world in which we live)." The philosopher Daniel Dennett, whose work has an evolutionary bent, carefully words his definition of religions as "social systems whose participants avow belief in a supernatural agent or agents whose approval is to be sought."[35] One thinks of the Mumbai gentleman Rohinton Mistry writes about in *Such a Long Journey*, who, all too plausibly, spends his days railing against the Almighty.[36] And doxastic accounts, focused on belief or even the avowal of belief, are mistrusted by those who regard them as artifacts of the Protestant paradigm, and who consider institutions and practices, not beliefs (or simple belief avowals), to be central in many religious traditions.

The Millian move of connecting behavior and belief remains available. One influential sociologist of religion, Martin Riesebrodt, argues that " 'religion as such' isn't an empirically accessible object," but that "religion" can and should be retained, and proposes to define it as a "complex of practices that are based on the premise of the existence of superhuman powers, whether personal or impersonal, that are generally invisible."[37] ("Religiousness," the subjective enlistment of religion, figures large in his account.) But for many scholars, the urgent challenge is to wrest religion from paradigms that are in some combination Christian, or Western, or modern.

Secularity, in the anthropologist and cultural theorist Talal Asad's widely discussed account, is a specific artifact of Western modernity, responsive to certain ideological interests, as is the simultaneous effort to delimit a specific domain as religious. Asad urges us to see religion through an archeology of its shifting conceptions, and to resituate it as something embodied in practices, such as rituals, gestures, and forms of worship, that are not merely symbolic expressions of inner states, but are themselves constitutive of religious experience and meaning. That requires keeping in mind the way that religious practices and discourses are shaped by the material and institutional conditions in which they occur, such as the built environment, economic relations, and political structures. Yet religion—a concept Asad is intent on saving—can sometimes seem merely epiphenomenal in this account, more a product of political and social forces than a shaper of them. Critics have wondered, too, how we were to know that all these very different things, shaped by local forces and features, were all examples of the same thing.[38]

In the past decades, we've had the "family resemblance" and polythetic approaches (I'll discuss these in Chapter 5) that urge us to take the notion of religion as we see it, and give up on any specific list of necessary and sufficient conditions. For certain scholars, though, the religion concept is beyond redemption. Wilfred Cantwell Smith thought that talk of religion conflated too many things not to cause mischief. He considered it Eurocentric, conducive of bigotry, and—of critical importance to him—hostile to piety. "Neither religion in general nor any of the religions," he argued in his classic *The Meaning and End of Religion* (1962), "is in itself an intelligible entity, a valid object of inquiry or of concern either for the scholar or for the man of faith."[39] Why not speak of faith and of cumulative traditions, and jettison religion?

The stakes for other eliminativists are more political. For one recent critic, treating religion as a sui generis object isolates people from their sociopolitical contexts and treats them "not as social, economic, and political beings with certain basic material needs and relations but as essentially believers of creeds."[40] Another worries that religion not only fails to demarcate any cross-culturally coherent category, but also belongs to a broader process of "western imperialism, colonialism, and neocolonialism."[41] The theologian Gordon Lynch, hoping to reform our notions of the sacred, has recently worried that the concept of religion, far from a neutral cross-cultural category, picks out "the kinds of social institution and subjectivity appropriate to modern, liberal, and Enlightened societies," in ways implicated in cultural projects such as colonial domination. He wonders whether the study of religion might be reconceived as "the study of the operations of the discourse of 'religion' in academic thought and other arenas of social life"; or at least "as the study of whatever is constructed as 'religion' in a particular context."[42] Save religion, he proposes, by losing "religion," or at least scare-quoting it into submission.

Other scholars have been scouting for a replacement concept. Daniel Dubuisson, who considers "religion" a nineteenth-century Western product imposed on the anthropology of the non-Western world, suggests, as an alternative, the concept of a "cosmographic formation"—which could be taken as not so much an alternative to "religion" as a superior definition of it. Critics have been unmoved. Riesebrodt prophesied, mordantly, that cosmographic formations and the like can be shown to "have also been 'constructed' through historically specific discourses," and revealed as "instruments in the linguistic battle between classes or cultures."[43]

Shall we content ourselves with talk of religion buffered by a strong sense of its artifactual nature? Jonathan Z. Smith, the celebrated historian of religions, once surveyed four comparative modes of religious inquiry—the ethnographic, the encyclopedic, the morphological, and the evolutionary—and threw up his hands with genial ecumenicism. "Religion is solely the creation of the scholar's study," he wrote, with "no independent existence apart from the academy." But this wasn't the counsel of defeatism. As he later elaborated, the term was created for scholarly purposes and was for scholars to define. "It is a second order generic concept that plays the same role in establishing a disciplinary horizon that a concept such as 'language' plays in linguistics or 'culture' plays in anthropology. There can be no disciplined study of religion without such a horizon."[44]

Let me end my disciplinary survey here. Inasmuch as religion is the creation of the scholar's study, the principals I will discuss in the chapters ahead weren't merely theorists of religions but creators of "religion." As I noted at the start, society, as a subject of inquiry, emerged from the secular study of something called religion, and vice versa. By the same token, "society" is equally the creation of a scholar's study. Indeed, the extent to which contemporary social theory continues to be shadowed by the early explorations of Durkheim, Simmel, and Weber, our classical sociologists, is remarkable. When we think about society, we still use their lenses. And the concept of religion was used to grind those lenses.

THE SOCIAL CONSTRUCTION OF SOCIETY

When did our concept of "society" emerge? What we're looking for is not the "body" model you find in some medieval discourse (the king is the head, the realm the body); nor merely taxonomical (wherever it is that laws and institutions do their work); nor an abstraction that possesses no agency or *all* the agency; nor simply a group of co-located individuals. As an object of study, we can't quite see it in Hobbes and Locke: they spoke of society, even civil society, of the common good and the private good; and yet their social contracts were an undertaking of individuals. We can't quite see it in Rousseau's social-contract model, either, where we're regularly asked to veer between individuals and some abstract and unitary collective. Nor do we quite find it in Diderot or Helvetius.

Something closer to our notion of society is presaged by the luminaries of the Scottish Enlightenment, notably Adam Ferguson, James Dunbar, John Millar, David Hume, Francis Hutcheson, and Adam Smith. In their writing, society is more than a group of co-located individuals. In Ferguson's *Essay on the History of Civil Society*, it was an assemblage that evolved according to internal forces, shaped by the division of labor, property relations, and so on. Ferguson, insisted, too, on the group as a unit of analysis: "Mankind are to be taken in groupes, as they have always subsisted. The history of the individual is but a detail of the sentiments and the thoughts he has entertained in the view of his species: and every experiment relative to this subject should be made with entire societies, not with single men." Smith, famously, compared society to a mirror that allows the human creature to comprehend what he is. Dunbar deemed society "the free and legitimate offspring of the human heart"; Hutcheson was sure that society was "enjoined by the Law of Nature." Hume was convinced that "man, born in a family, is compelled to maintain society from necessity, from natural inclination, and from habit."[45]

Yet "society," for our Scotsmen, is an essentially static entity. It's the cumulative result of individual action shaped by human nature and historical circumstance, and set to proceed through orderly stages. What we don't find is anything like an analysis of group processes and interactive dynamics; we don't have social structures with a logic and causal powers separate from individual agency.

Thinking about "the social" gained a particular charge in the first half of the nineteenth century. To paint with a broad brush, the French Revolution had shown the power of social forces to shape history, while the Industrial Revolution was creating new forms of social interdependence and conflict. And though it's simplistic to see the models of society that were promulgated in the penumbra of revolution as reactive or reactionary, some of them, in some part, clearly were so.

Comte, an enemy of Enlightenment individualism, supposed society to be bound by natural-law-like regularities, such that it could be studied much as we studied the natural world, which is why he was so drawn to "social physics." Society was greater than the sum of its parts, but precisely the way an organism is; a unified whole, it evolved in a quasi-biological and determinate way. With respect to the social upheavals of his day, it could be said that Comte thought he had proposed a cure—a protocol for a radiantly peaceable mode of coexistence. Robert Nisbet, the sociologist and historian of sociology, was onto something when he provocatively suggested that Comte's was a medievalist conception of society: "Into its veins Comte pumped the blood of Positivism, replacing Catholicism, but he leaves us in no doubt of his admiration of the structure of medieval society or of his desire to restore its essence."[46] Normatively and empirically, Comtean society was idealized out of recognition.

In the meantime, the "social question"—with urbanization, too often, leading to pauperization—posed the specter of fragmentation and instability. Society as a cohesive force becomes salient when cohesion falters. What about Karl Marx's model of society, then? His model, while stadial, was certainly not static. In the century's most influential critique of bourgeois society, he had identified, in the capitalist mode of production, a fundamental antagonism between the bourgeoisie and the proletariat that could be resolved only through revolution. Society was not simply an aggregate of individuals, but a complex totality structured by historically specific relations of production, that is, class relations. He grants that individuals constitute one another—and that this was true even in our early, herd-like social consciousness, when society was agonistic and riven by contradictions, not functionally integrated or equilibrating. "It is not the consciousness of men that specifies their being, but their social being that specifies their consciousness," Marx wrote.[47]

At the same time, his view was still very much a nineteenth-century one, wedded to unabashed social evolutionism and historical determinism, with crisply demarcated developmental stages. (Among the classical sociologists I focus on, you'll find *abashed* social evolutionism.) More than that, Marx's materialism mirrors the idealism it opposes, abstracting away from cultural particularity to expose universal laws of historical progression. Social superstructures—legal systems, politics, culture, morality, metaphysics, corresponding to "definite forms of social consciousness"—emanate from the economic base. The social, in this model, is demoted to bondsman, captive to the dictates of the economic. In the mode of an old-school natural scientist, too, Marx's language is not of tendency but of necessity (even as the necessitarian language has, itself, a theological resonance). Finally, the soteriological vision of a stateless and classless communist society—in which the division of labor and attendant forms of differentiation were erased, along with all local loyalties, was scarcely recognizable as a human society at all. The sociologist Donald MacRae declared, understandably, that Marx "neither was—nor in an important sense intended to be—a sociologist."[48] The canons of disciplinary history rule out such a peremptory judgment. But his theories do sideline the forms of social inquiry that our principals wanted to explore.

Marx's near-contemporary, Herbert Spencer—who, in writing of sociology, took up Comte's coinage, though not his political program—

was intent on severing sociology from socialism. But his depictions of society do not easily slot into the modern program, either. His writings variously emphasized society as a unity, society as a system of organs, and society as an assemblage of atomistic individuals. It must be said that another way in which Spencer was not a modern sociologist was the extent to which he was committed to racial hierarchy, envisaging serried ranks of humanity marked by differences in capacity. He even bruited a notion of progress as propelled, in part, by ongoing race war, "a continuous over-running of the less powerful or less adapted by the more powerful or more adapted, a driving of inferior varieties into undesirable habitats, and, occasionally, an extermination of inferior varieties."[49]

Still, the "social turn" of the nineteenth century, it should be clear, was under way before our pioneers of sociology started their work. Debates involving Young Hegelians other than Marx contributed; so, as we'll see, did the *Völkerpsychologie* of Moritz Lazarus and Heymann Steinthal and then of Wilhelm Wundt, as well as the psychological "ethnology" of Theodor Waitz—to begin a long list. But in the writings of our later sociologists, the salience of the social coalesced. In Weber's metaphor, ideas can create worldviews that, like a railroad switchman, reroute collective trains of thought—especially when social, economic, and cultural conditions are aligned.

Sociology was a product of an age that experienced fracture, social dissolution, and, yes, anomie, and that was marked by much fretting about whether these developments were the cause or consequences of the erosion of religious. Simmel rightly mocked the temptation to think that problems exist for the sake of being solved. But because modern sociology arose amid not only a crisis in religion but also a crisis in society, its first steps were to devise theories about what each thing was. These overlapping conceptions of society—as a dynamic complement of representations, norms, sentiments, constraints, ideals, authority, and so on—then emerged as a field of study and as a mode of explanation.

There were other terms in contention: for Tylor, "culture or civilization" was the thing to be studied. But "society" had sticking power. When Prime Minister Margaret Thatcher, in a 1987 interview, said "there is no such thing as society," she was arguing with exactly this range of conceptions.[50] So it's telling that her next sentence started to walk back the provocation: "There is a living tapestry of men and women and people and the beauty of that tapestry and the quality of our lives will depend upon how much each of us is prepared to take responsibility for ourselves and each of us prepared to turn round and help by our own efforts those who are unfortunate." (With Penelope-like determination, policy mavens are always trying to weave and unweave that living tapestry.) Society, the sociologists saw, was exactly what put us in a position to try to understand entities like society; it was an unappeasable god that had created us, could support us, would outlive us, and, though it would always surpass our mortal efforts to theorize it, it might reward our efforts to do so.

NEGATIVE CAPABILITIES

I've suggested that religion becomes an object of study once we can conceive a space away from it, just as social dissolution encourages scholars to study the forces of social cohesion and refine their conceptions of society. In Edward Burnett Tylor, Émile Durkheim, Georg Simmel, and Max Weber, we see a larger disciplinary toolkit emerging from their years of wrestling with religion. Durkheim, Simmel, and Weber are conventionally regarded as among the disciplinary architects of sociology. They were born within six years of each other and did their major work between the 1890s and the 1910s. But I've chosen to start with the earlier figure of Tylor, typically seen as the founder of cultural anthropology, because his work provided a substrate for everyone theorizing about religion thereafter, helping to naturalize religion as an appropriate subject for an increasingly scientific age. Beyond that, Tylor, more than anyone, was the scholar who, from a resolutely nonreligious perspective, resituated religion as a product of human rationality. (In ways I'll discuss later, much contemporary work on religion by evolutionary and cognitive psychologists is essentially neo-Tylorian.)

Still, some readers will wonder why I've chosen these social theorists and not others. In truth, not a few sociologists these days chafe against the notion that their discipline, with its universalizing ambitions, might be thought to be established in significant part by figures who seem so specific to a European intellectual milieu. Some will be disquieted by the fact that this work is still taught as foundational or that the field can still seem raptly in conversation with these scholars. Some would highlight, as more recent textbooks do, the remarkable work of Harriet Martineau, Charlotte Perkins Gilman, W. E. B. Du Bois (whose intellectual formation was the subject of a previous book of mine), or, indeed, Beatrice Potter Webb—a figure who loomed large in my own family lore, being my mother's great-aunt Bo. "I hope you slept well," my mother said to her one morning when, as a girl, she was staying with the Webbs in London. Aunt Bo glowered and set her straight: "I *never* sleep." Vital disciplines don't sleep either; they toss and turn. Some contemporary sociologists, accordingly, promote an engagement with more far-flung figures. Why not say that our subject is "social thought," and enlist as forerunners intellectuals from other parts of the world? A few, pledging to decolonize their field, talk of "Southern Theory," even at the risk of enshrining another tidy distinction between North and South.

In truth, disciplinary canons are always in the process of being reshaped. For Talcott Parsons, after all, Pareto and Marshall were as important to sociology as Durkheim and Weber were. In *Introduction to the Science of Sociology*, a mammoth 1921 compendium edited by the Chicago stalwarts Robert E. Park and Ernest W. Burgess, you'll find Durkheim and Simmel to be well represented (along with many names now little known), while Weber is scarcely mentioned. Even granting the particular intellectual matrix I sought to explore, my argument could surely have unfolded through other thinkers.

I focus on these four thinkers for a couple of reasons. First, they are, as I try to make plain, *representative*—they emerge from an expansive but historically specific intellectual seedbed. Second, their work was not only methodologically self-conscious but also disciplinarily *influential*. Tylor's magnum opus was a touchstone for almost any academic thinking about religion in this era. Durkheim, not least through his *L'Année sociologique*, helped entrench certain paradigms and templates that helped shape British (and American) anthropology and sociology.

Simmel, taken up first by the Chicago School, helped fertilize interactionist perspectives, as well as later work in humanistic sociology. Today, any discussion of rationality is likely to bring up categories from Weber.

By way of analogy, one could no doubt adjust the philosophical canon so that Hume and Kant were no longer the familiar names for sets of positions and the spotlight fell, instead, on Christian Wolff, Adam Ferguson, F. W. J. Schelling, and J. F. Herbart. One certainly can, as I do in my classes on global ethics, bring in thinkers from continents around the world who represent intellectual traditions outside the traditional canon. But if we're interested in the history of a disciplinary conversation, we can't lightly set aside decisions of longstanding about whom we argue with and through.

I'll also take care to show these thinkers not as disciplinary godheads but as historical subjects, embodied and situated within—which is to say captive to—social, economic, intellectual, and personal contexts. I'll sometimes be going "off-road"—away from the stuff you find on a syllabus and into lesser-known writings—because I want to convey a developmental sense of how our principals came by the thoughts for which they are known. (I take responsibility for translations where no translator is noted.) My hope is to capture at least some sense of the voices they were contradicting, modifying, amplifying, extending. Their ideas did not arrive via some scholarly version of ensoulment. What the Germans call *Biografismus* is the fallacy of reducing the thought to the thinker; but we all exist in and through history, and a reciprocal fallacy is, as Franz Rosenzweig insisted, to deny any connection between the way we think and the lives we live.

One consequence of these shaping historical circumstances is seen in the fact that our principals are men—critics of patriarchy, in the main, but also, inevitably, participants in it. They had intellectually formidable women in their lives and weren't oblivious to the multiple barriers that did so much to keep women sidelined from the institutional forms of intellectual life. They would have supported reforms allowing women to compete on a more equitable basis, but the injustice wasn't, so to speak, top of mind for them. Not a great deal is known about Anna Fox, Tylor's wife of nearly six decades; nor about Louise Dreyfus, who was

Durkheim's, for three decades. But Gertrud Kinel, Simmel's wife for a little less than two, published her own philosophical writings under the pseudonym Marie-Luise Enckendorff, including a short book about religion that greatly impressed Weber. And Weber's wife, née Marianne Schnitger, had more of a public profile than he had for most of his career; she was Germany's leading feminist intellectual, published significant books about the social and legal status of women, and, though impeded from pursuing an academic career of her own, had written a doctoral thesis (on Fichte and Marx). To study society does not remove you from society.

The disciplinary pioneers I write about aren't the only ones shaped by the currents and the contingencies of history. You have been, too, and so have I. A quirk of biography no doubt explains why I wanted to write this book in the first place. Much of my life has been spent in and around religious traditions. I have feasted at Eid al-Fitr with my Muslim cousins, celebrated Seders at home with my in-laws, recited a Sanskrit mantra as I meditated alone, and attended a nuptial mass conducted by a cardinal. In my childhood, I sang in an Anglican school choir in England, went to Sunday school back home in Ghana in an interdenominational church (dressed in my Sabbath finery), and murmured "Now I Lay Me Down to Sleep" in prayer each night before I retired. My weekly recitation of the Nicene Creed was quite sincere, even if I always had difficulty understanding how Christ could be of "one substance with the Father"; the words had some extra-semantic resonance. Like millions of people, I have experienced the inward peace that comes from meditation—the sense of oneness with everything that is spoken of in contemplative traditions from around the world; but I have felt that sense of communion, too, at the end of a long season of training, rowing with my fellow oarsmen in perfect concord on the Thames near Henley, when my body was working as hard as it ever has. Then, as in the daily meditations of my teenage years, I felt with the Blessed Julian of Norwich, who lived six centuries ago, that "all will be well and all will be well, and all manner of things will be well." As a child, I gained security from a gold cross that hung on a chain around my neck, which had been blessed by a spirit that spoke through the mediumship of a modest Scottish postman, who also reassured me by transmitting benevolent messages from my long-dead English grandfather.

And because much of my childhood was spent in Kumasi, in Ghana's Ashanti region, I followed my father in pouring libations to our ancestors, who were once as real to me as the God whose presence I felt when I prayed. We would offer spirituous beverage, in particular, to the founder of my father's lineage, the warrior Akroma-Ampim. *Nana Akroma-Ampim, bɔgye nsa nom*: Akroma-Ampim, our elder, come take this alcohol to drink. We would honor, too, our formidable great-grandmother Takyiwah, or her brother Yao Antony, for whom, like Akroma-Ampim, I was named. Mind you, my father was an elder in his Methodist Church and considered himself a good Christian; but as a proud Asante man, he also shared the "traditional" beliefs of the world where he grew up. If he dreamed, it meant that his *sunsum*—a spirit of consciousness—was traveling the realm; when he died, he believed, something would leave his body and join the ancestors, to be given offerings on occasion. He joined in practices related to Nyame, the sky god, as well as to Asase Yaa, the earth goddess, and to other spirits of diverse kinds. There were ritual practices and prayers, and professional priests and shrines of varying degrees of authority and various scopes of jurisdiction. (When he visited friends in, say, Sierra Leone, he expected that, just as the people were different there, so the gods would be: alternate technologies of the divine.) The same would have been true of his grandparents—of the Asante people in the mid-nineteenth century. But it would never have occurred to his ancestors to define themselves as belonging to a tradition compounded of ritual and belief.[51] Those things we now call "Asante religion" were a constituent of everyday life; there is no word in nineteenth-century Asante-Twi (as in most of the world's languages until recently) to translate our word "religion."[52]

In many developmental accounts of religion, "primitive" persons traffic in magic, while civilized ones participate in complex and ecclesiastical forms of worship. In early religion, the whole world is enchanted; in advanced ones, a sphere of sacred doings is carved off from the sphere of everyday reality. Lucien Lévy-Bruhl had seen a gulf between the primitive and the civilized *mentalité*, and, although scholars no longer talk this way, they often posit a crevasse between two forms of life that correspond to those he was concerned with. But as a child, I moved between a world where witches had to be warded off and ancestors appeased and a world where Anglican priests led you through the sacraments and the Creed; I detected no crossing of an intellectual crevasse, no transfigured *mentalité*. Neither was it clear that these were even rivalrous systems, competing for the same tasks. For my English kinfolk, religion seemed mainly to be something you did on Sundays; for my Asante kinfolk, interactions with spiritual entities were fluidly part of everyday activities. These were, in each place, things people did together, but not necessarily for similar reasons. I saw—I lived—continuities and discontinuities that my peers mainly did not. I had questions.

I still do. Should one believe in "religion"? Are we too quick to talk about the social construction of things without a sense of how the social has been constructed? In the chapters ahead, we'll circle the conceptual ouroboros I pointed toward at the start: how religion gave definition to the social sciences that gave definition to religion.

CHAPTER 1

Edward Burnett Tylor

Starting with Spirits

MR. TYLOR'S SCIENCE — A FORTUNATE INFIRMITY — SOUL SURVIVORS — CALL IT ANIMISM — IN DREAMS BEGIN RESPONSIBILITIES — SPIRIT MATTERS — MAKE ROOM FOR GOD — THE MÜLLER REPORT — THOUGHTS AND DEEDS — THE UNBELIEVERS — NATURAL SUPERNATURALISM — THE EXILE OF AFFECT — MARGINALIZING MORALITY — TWO CHEERS FOR INTELLECTUALISM — THE SECOND REFORMATION

MR. TYLOR'S SCIENCE

To credit Sir Edward Burnett Tylor with having founded the discipline of anthropology is to describe both institutional and intellectual developments. Tylor, the first person Oxford University hired to teach anthropology, lectured on the subject when he became keeper of Oxford's University Museum, in 1883; was appointed reader in anthropology the following year; and received Oxford's first chair in anthropology, in 1896. The key anthropological fact here is that anthropology, though previously a realm of knowledge, had not yet been an academically credentialed field of study. Both Tylor and Oxford were pioneers here.[1] It's to Tylor, more than anyone else, that we owe the idea that anthropology is the study of something called "culture," which he defined as "that complex whole which includes knowledge, belief, art, morals, law, custom, and any other capabilities and habits acquired by man as a member of society."[2] The Oxford professor Friedrich Max Müller, renowned as a scholar of Sanskrit and comparative philology, expressed a widespread view when, late in the nineteenth century, he called the emerging discipline "Mr. Tylor's science."

The magnum opus on which Tylor's career was chiefly based was titled *Primitive Culture*. Because we shall be spending much of this book in the company of European intellectuals at the turn of the twentieth century, I should warn readers that we'll need to get used to their use of words like "savage" and "primitive," and to their condescension to "lower races" from other societies around the world. (When I describe their views, the scare quotes around such terms will often be tacit.) Tylor, in seeing these living contemporary cultures as reflections of the human past, was representative of the thinking of his place and time, whereby every society could be placed somewhere on a scale from a savage antiquity to a civilized modernity. Civilization was a process, not a state; and societies were largely advancing (with occasional setbacks) in the same direction.

But we should not make the mistake of condescending to him for his condescension. Tylor was a powerful creative thinker, one formed, as we all are, by the world he lived in, but able sometimes to see further than most of his contemporaries. In consequential ways, as we'll see, Tylor argued powerfully for the fundamental rationality of "primitive man," and for profound continuities between their ways and ours. Even as he drew on the older language of hierarchy, his was a fundamentally integrative project.

From the remove of our times, it's difficult to convey how influential Tylor's work was in its day. It's can also be difficult, from that remove, to make out what was distinctive in Tylor's thought and what was not. And so it will be helpful to situate the fellow in his own time and place, beginning at the beginning.

A FORTUNATE INFIRMITY

Tylor was born in 1832 in Surrey, to an affluent Quaker family; his father had a brass foundry in the parish of Camberwell, south of London.[3] At the time, Quakers—members of the Society of Friends—

were a rather small confession in England, numbering perhaps sixteen thousand. But, in part as a side effect of their exclusion from certain professions, they were well represented in the world of business. (Quaker-founded companies that survive today include Barclays, Cadbury, Carr's, Clarks, and Lloyd's.) After attending a Quaker school, Tylor duly joined the family business at sixteen, working as a clerk for seven years.

He never attended college. As a Quaker, he would have been unable to obtain a degree from England's most ancient and august universities. (Only after the Universities Tests Act, in 1871, was the requirement of an Anglican oath lifted.) Still, there were fine alternatives; many Quakers attended Scottish universities, which, unlike Oxford and Cambridge, didn't require a profession of Anglican faith. And University College London (first called London University) had been founded in the 1820s—by, among others, John Stuart Mill's father, James—as a secular alternative. Tylor's health was frail, however, and he may well have feared that his life would be short. In 1855, at the age of twenty-three, Tylor was provisionally diagnosed with tuberculosis and sent abroad, for the good of his lungs. Robert Ranulph Marett, a self-described epigone of Tylor's and the next occupant of that Oxford chair in anthropology, wrote that Tylor was among those who "have had to thank the ills of the flesh for moving them to seek the fruits of the spirit."[4]

On an omnibus in Cuba, Tylor met a fellow Quaker, Henry Christy, a collector of Paleolithic specimens and a member of the Royal Geographical Society, who invited him to join him on an expedition to Mexico. Spending time in Mesoamerica, covering broad expanses on horseback, Tylor was impressed by what he called "the evidence of an immense ancient population, shown by the abundance of remains of works of art."[5] His adventures left him with a lifelong fascination with societies seemingly remote from his own.

Returning to England in 1857, he met, at a Quaker meeting, Anna Fox, whose family had long owned a large textile mill in Somerset. They married the next year. "E. going on with 'Anahuac,'" she wrote in an 1859 diary entry.[6] "Anahuac"—the Aztec name for Mexico—was the title of his extensive account of his Mexican journey, which was published in 1861. Taking pen to paper seems to have suited him; an 1860 chalk portrait of Tylor, by the Maltese artist George Bonavia, shows him with clear blue eyes and sleek brown hair, his beard full but far from unruly. There's no hint of the ill health that sent him on his travels.

In the book, Tylor does not write much about religion, though he did offer a few rather snarky observations about the malign role played by the Catholic Church. He conjectures that the Spanish conquest of Mesoamerica had a bad effect on the character of the people there—that "the religion brought into the country by the Spanish missionaries concerned itself with their belief and left their morals to shift for themselves." He doubted that Christianity produced any improvement for the Mexicans. He was able to observe that the priests had the greatest influence among women, the poor, and the less educated. The higher-status men were skeptical, "after the manner of the French school of freethinking," while the young male dandies showed up to the fashionable churches on Sunday to stare at the ladies. The poor mestizos and Indians, by contrast, were "zealous churchmen, and spend their time and money on masses and religious duties so perseveringly that one wishes they had a religion which was of some use to them." As for the dogmas: "They hear them and believe in them devoutly, and do not understand them in the least." They received the new mysteries, he insisted, in the very same spirit as they had received the old mysteries of their heathen past.[7] It must be said that his cheerful disdain for Catholicism was far from unusual for someone of his background. Many British Protestants, and especially Dissenters like Tylor, were inclined to regard Catholicism, with its "Mariolatry" and saint worship, as not truly monotheistic and, indeed, perilously close to paganism.

SOUL SURVIVORS

The work that followed, and that won Tylor his international influence, was the product not of more fieldwork but of long labor in the library. What first established him as a figure in a field known variously as ethnology and as anthropology was the book he published in

1865, *Researches into the Early History of Mankind and the Development of Civilization*. It has become an article of faith among Tylor adepts, starting with Marett, that the work has nothing to say about religion.[8] This is quite wrong. Although Tylor is sparing in the use of the word, he rehearses theories about its origins. As he writes early on of the savage: "The belief that man has a soul capable of existing apart from the body it belongs to, and continuing to live, for a time at least, after the body is dead and buried, fits perfectly in such a mind with the fact that the shadowy forms of men and women do appear to others, when the men and women themselves are at a distance, and after they are dead. We call these apparitions dreams or phantasms, according as the person to whom they appear is asleep or awake, and when we hear of their occurrences in ordinary life, set them down as subjective processes of the mind." But those are modern habits of mind, he cautions. "We do not think that the phantom of the dark Brazilian who used to haunt Spinoza was a real person," he notes. The less civilized would see things differently. In fact, the "separation of subjective and objective impressions," Tylor ventured, "makes the most important difference between the educated man and the savage." And so the Dayaks take dreams to be real occurrences—they're convinced that, in sleep, their soul sometimes leaves their body and travels far away—while the "Finnish races" think that the spirits of the dead can bring harm to us through our sleep.[9]

Generalizing, he diagnoses primitive forms of engagement with the spirit realm as arising from a "condition of mind which we of the more advanced races are almost outgrown." This condition of mind is explored in a chapter on "Images and Names." Tylor starts by inviting us to see that "the idol answers to the savage in one province of thought the same purpose that its analogue the doll does to the child. It enables him to give a definite existence and a personality to the vague ideas of higher beings, which his mind can hardly grasp without some material aid." The Christian missionary, teaching these heathens the "doctrines of a higher religion"—"a belief in a God so far beyond human comprehension, that no definition of the Deity is possible to man beyond vague predications"—will regard an idol as a specimen of folly and devilry. "But the student who occupies himself in tracing the early stages of human civilization, can see in the rude image of the savage an important aid to early religious development." And here we approach what Tylor then considered a profoundly important law of primitive thought.[10]

An objective connection, Tylor says, is like that of a mathematical function: if y is a function of x, it changes when x changes. An object and its image, we know, do not relate in this way. While that is common sense to the educated European, Tylor writes, it is an instance where accumulated experience and long education have brought them "not only to reverse the opinion of the savage, but commonly to think that their own views are the only ones that could naturally arise in the mind of any rational human being." In fact, "man, in a low stage of culture, very commonly believes that between the object and the image of it there is a real connexion," and that one can "communicate an impression to the original through the copy." A whole host of primitive superstitions—idols, effigies, verbal taboos—arise from this assumption. Indeed, Tylor concludes, "It is not too much to say that nothing short of a history of Philosophy and Religion would be required to follow them out."[11]

CALL IT ANIMISM

Through the early 1860s, Tylor had immersed himself in work by August Comte, Herbert Spencer, John Stuart Mill, and German scholars such as Moritz Lazarus and Herman Steinthal, pioneers of *Völkerpsychologie* (more on that later); as well as Theodor Waitz, whose six-volume study *Die Anthropologie der Naturvölker* was just appearing. Tylor absorbed David Hume's *Natural History of Religion*, which he would describe as "more than any other work the source of modern opinion as to the development of religion."[12] And then—possibly not unrelated to his scholarly immersions—there were his own religious renegotiations. The author of *Anahuac* seemingly wrote as a man of faith, one with a particular sectarian mistrust of the Catholic Church. If the author of *Researches* does not draw a thick line between primitive religion and religion proper, there may be a personal reason for this: he was in the process of losing his own. The historian Timothy

Larsen, consulting the monthly meeting records of the archives of the Friends House, of London, has found that Tylor and his wife resigned their membership in the Friends in the summer of 1864.[13]

A sketch of Tylor's basic theory about the origins of religion appeared in an 1866 article he published in George Henry Lewes's *Fortnightly Review*, titled "The Religion of Savages." The savage tendency to impute spirits to ordinary objects reflected a conception that "fit with the ordinary phenomena of dreams and waking hallucinations"; there was the body and there was the phantom, the spirit. "Now inanimate as well as animate objects appear to us in dreams, and we find accordingly that in savage theology what we call animals and what we call things may have souls alike," he elaborates. Already, he situated these assumptions as the savages' efforts at explaining the phenomenal world: "The very assertion that their actions are motiveless, and their opinions nonsense, is itself a theory, and, I hold, a profoundly false one."[14]

What to call this doctrine? The word "spiritualism" had already acquired another meaning. ("The modern spiritualism, as every ethnographer may know, is pure and simple savagery both in its theory and the tricks by which it is supported," Tylor wrote.) What about "fetishism," which had been introduced by Charles de Brosses in 1760, as the earliest stage of religion, and indicated the savage's perception that all things were animated by a life force akin to his own? In truth, what Tylor had in mind was very like de Brosses's fetishism, but Tylor thought that the word should be properly reserved for objects used in witchcraft. He appropriated a term that had been deployed by the vitalist Georg Ernst Stahl, best known for introducing the doctrine of "phlogiston." And so, Tylor wrote, "The theory which endows the phenomena of nature with personal life might perhaps be conveniently called Animism." Here was the primordium of all religion, and the engine of its destined collision, the one Comte had seen, with scientific understanding: "Upwards from the simplest theory which attributes life and personality to animal, vegetable, and mineral alike," Tylor wrote, "to that which sees in each department of the world the protecting and fostering care of an appropriate divinity, and at last of one Supreme Being ordering and controlling the lower hierarchy—

through all these gradations of opinion we may thus see fought out, in one stage after another, the long-waged contest between a theory of animation which accounts for each phenomenon of nature by giving it everywhere a life like our own, and a slowly-growing natural science which in one department after another substitutes for independent voluntary action the working out of systematic law."[15]

IN DREAMS BEGIN RESPONSIBILITIES

Tylor's enormously influential *Primitive Culture* (1871)— its interweaving of ethnography and theory marking it as the first modern work of anthropology—elaborates this idea, and draws, too, on some thoughts he had rehearsed in his *Researches*. What is not new is its stadial assumptions of social evolution—as when he refers to a belief "extending through savage, barbaric, classic, oriental, and mediaeval life."[16] Culture, for him, was fundamentally progressive; he was interested in "primitive culture" because it was human culture at its earliest stage of development. (The 1873 German translation of his book was entitled *Die Anfänge der Cultur—The Beginnings of Culture.*) As he notes toward the book's start, "The thesis which I venture to sustain, within limits, is simply this, that the savage state in some measure represents an early condition of mankind, out of which the higher culture has gradually been developed or evolved, by processes still in regular operation as of old."[17]

Social evolutionism of this sort was, by then, a highly evolved discourse itself. For Rousseau, "the savage is a hunter, the barbarian a herdsman, civil man a tiller of the soil"; Adam Ferguson had marked a similar distinction between the "savage" and the "barbarous" (only barbarians were acquainted with property) in *An Essay on the History of Civil Society* (1767), the tract that introduced the new term "civilization" to British readers. Tylor, at this point, wasn't particularly interested in the details of such stages: he made no systematic distinction between the savage and the barbarian.[18] Still, if this is your general thesis about culture, your account of religion will start with the "savage" stage, looking among contemporary "savages" for a reflection of how religion arose and operated in the earliest human societies. *Primitive*

Culture's subtitle brings this out: "Researches into the Development of Mythology, Philosophy, Religion, Language, Art, and Custom." The book begins with a discussion of this evolutionary framework, exploring through it the nature of magic, the development of language, and the invention of arithmetic. Only after nearly three hundred pages does Tylor turn to issues that are central to the study of religion; but these take up the rest of the nearly thousand pages of this two-volume work.

Tylor's great contribution to the social science of religion is one we met when it was still a child: his theory of animism. And my, how it has grown: a chapter entitled "Animism" is followed by six more entitled "Animism (continued)." He would pile up the examples. Although Tylor was the person who introduced talk of the "diffusion" of culture, the hypothesis plays a very secondary role in his work; the congruences he turns up mainly testify, he thinks, to the uniformity of human nature. Oddly enough, Tylor doesn't turn to a systematic account of animism until chapter 11. What we might think of as religion shows up long before this, however, in particular in three chapters on mythology. There Tylor writes of the earliest phases of culture—which he saw represented in the present in many contemporary societies in every continent from Lapland to New Zealand—that its denizens live in an enchanted world: "To the lower tribes of man, sun and stars, trees and rivers, winds and clouds, become personal animate creatures, leading lives conformed to human or animal analogies."[19]

How did they become persuaded of this? Tylor, picking up on a claim he'd introduced in his *Researches* and developed further in his "Religion of the Savages" essay, maintains that they were simply trying to make sense of their experience. In his view, the existence of a soul, which survives the death of the body, scarcely needed argument: "Plain experience is there to teach it to every savage; his friend or his enemy is dead, yet still in dream or open vision he sees the spectral form which is to his philosophy a real objective being, carrying personality as it carries likeness." And so "the ancient savage philosophers," contemplating the entity that made the difference between a living body and a dead one with the entity that appeared to them in dreams and visions, combined them into an "apparitional-soul." That soul, though connected to the body, was also separable from it. The idea of spirit beings naturally arose, for once you had detachable people spirits, it was a small step to impute spirits to trees and other entities. We have now entered "the gateway into a complex region of belief." Indeed, he writes, "the conception of the human soul is the very 'fons et origo' of the conceptions of spirit and deity in general." It's in the final chapter of the first of the two books of *Primitive Culture* that he turns to his theoretical account of animism, describing what he sees as the core of religion. Here he offers his first and famous "minimum definition of religion," as "the belief in Spiritual Beings."[20]

These spiritual beings are entities that are thought to be able to affect the material world and our lives here and hereafter; they can be pleased or displeased by our actions, in a way that leads "sooner or later to active reverence and propitiation"—to worship.[21] The ontological belief is primary; the placation a reasonable response to it. In extending souls into the wider world, we generate naturally a system of quasi-social relations beyond the world of living human beings. Tylor's evolutionary framework leads him to argue that societies elaborate the basic scheme in various directions, producing, in what he called the "higher stages" of culture, more sophisticated elaborations of it.

SPIRIT MATTERS

If we're interested in the religion concept, some immediate issues suggest themselves. One is that "superstitions," such as the belief in ghosts, may not arise in anything like a straightforwardly religious context. What should we say about a culture where magic—witchcraft, say—played a role but where spiritual beings as agents did not? Marcel Mauss and Henri Humbert, in an account they published in 1904, proposed a simple contrast between magic and religion: magic was private; religion was public. Religion upholds the norms of a community; magic often subverts them.[22] By contrast, Tylor, like Comte and others, thought that the primitivist traffic in magic preceded the formulation of gods.

Nor is it clear how Tylor's "minimal definition" accommodates Buddhism, at least in its elite forms, where belief in spiritual beings isn't central or required. Tylor recognizes that, at the very least, some Buddhists do not appear to believe in the human soul, which obviously makes difficulties for a theory that proposes that religion begins by extending the idea of the soul out into the nonhuman world. So he rather squirms out of the situation: even if Buddhists "refine away into metaphysical subtleties the notion of continued personality, they do consistently and systematically hold that a man's life in former existences is the cause of his now being what he is, while at this moment he is accumulating merit or demerit whose result will determine his fate in future lives."[23] This is, as litigators say, nonresponsive: if the mechanism of karma does not involve spirits, then Buddhism is not a Tylorean religion. Many forms of Jainism pose similar problems, as do some varieties of Shintoism, depending on how you shade "spiritual beings."

There are also ethnographic reasons to doubt Tylor's assumption that the functions of the life force and phantasm—the first making a body alive; the second providing the sensory experience of dreams—are naturally combined into one entity (as, indeed, there are reasons to doubt many of his claims about "primitive" culture). Weber, as we shall see, thought the evidence here suggested otherwise. My Asante ancestors kept the functions distinct: each person's body was associated with two distinct spiritual agencies—the *ɔkra* was responsible for the distinction between the living and the dead, the *sunsum* was the entity that travels in dreams and returns as a ghost. (It is this "phantom" that thinks and acts.) Similar configurations occur in other West African cultures. Still, the case fits with Tylor's idea that there are two distinct questions to ask—about the life force and the phantom.

A bigger question: If religion is to be defined in terms of spirits, how are we to define spirits? What qualifies an entity for the status of spirit? Look through the hundreds of pages of Tylor's compendium of examples, and you'll find that his "Spiritual Beings" are a motley crew. Many followers of Taoism and Shinto believe in ancestral spirits, as I did when I was young, along with almost everyone I knew. The Romans had their *manes*, spirits of the underworld, spirits of the dead; and their household gods, the *lares* and *penates*; but many Romans also believed in nature spirits, nymphs and satyrs, as well as in Jupiter and

Venus and the other Olympians, and the hundreds of gods named in the *indigitamenta*, the priestly lists of gods. The Māori, on the other side of the globe, have Maui, who played a leading role in Tylor's book (long before he played a leading role, alongside Moana, in the Disney film named for her); but they also have a sky god and an earth goddess, and gods of the sun, the sea, and the stars, of peace and war, all beings with evocative names: Ranginui and Papatūānuku, Tamanuiterā, Tangaroa, Rehua, Rongo, and Tu. They have nature spirits as well, which are identified, for example, with trees, lakes, or mountains.

Members of the major monotheisms have their own spirits. Many Jews have believed not just in Yahweh but also in golems, creatures made from animated mud; Christians traditionally believe not just in Christ but also in the supernatural agency of demons and saints. According to Justin Martyr, the second-century Christian apologist, demons were spawned by the Nephilim, giants who were themselves spawned by human women who had seduced the sons of God; the pagan gods existed, then, but were demons. Lactantius, a Christian adviser to Emperor Constantine I, in the fourth century, warned that Roman household deities were demons, too: "Since these spirits are light and incomprehensible, they insinuate themselves into the bodies of men, and secretly working on the inner organs, they vitiate the health, incite sicknesses, terrify the thoughts by dreams, and disturb the minds with madness."[24] Orthodox Muslims believe in Allah, of course, but also in jinn, of whom only one is well known in the non-Muslim world, as the genie of Aladdin's lamp. And in all the Abrahamic traditions you will find people who worry about ghosts and have faith in angels, as hundreds of millions of people in Europe, Asia, Africa, and the Americas, north and south, still do. If, as Tylor thinks, all these are ways of believing in spirits, and spirits are so diverse, don't we need to say something about what, conceptually speaking, they all have in common?

Tylor's preliminary answer to this question marks a distinction between souls of individual creatures—which he takes to be the prior and most elemental idea—and other spirits, extending to potent deities.[25] So how does an anthropologist identify in an alien culture a conception of the soul, an entity that animates humans and other creatures? Under the influence of Descartes, you may be tempted to suppose that spirits like these must be immaterial. But Tylor's examples show that spirits don't have to be immaterial, or even invisible. You can see (even if you cannot grasp) a shadow. And when they do elude our senses, spirits can interact in other ways with the material world. Indeed, Tylor gives a compendium of cases from around the world of traditions in which the soul is represented as a material substance. So, for instance, "the Tongans imagined the human soul to be the finer or more aeriform part of the body, which leaves it suddenly at the moment of death; something comparable to the perfume and essence of a flower as related to the more solid vegetable fibre," and the Siamese "conceive of souls as consisting of subtle matter escaping sight and touch, or as united to a swiftly moving aerial body."[26] To be able to escape the body is not to be immaterial, which is why ghosts can act in the physical world, even though they can also sometimes pass through walls.

The extension of souls goes far beyond their ascription to animals and plants, which, like human beings, can pass from life to death, and so may need a life force to explain the difference. For many things, including artifacts like knives or spears, can have spirits, too; and some of the principal spirits, as with the Māori, inhabit lakes and mountains, the sun, and the stars. Demons and deities, then, are of the same essential nature as souls, just as the souls of animals and plants are of the same essential nature as human souls. And because souls can live either independently or in bodies and objects, spirits, too, can live either free or embodied.[27] Tylor cites a couple of lines from Milton's *Paradise Lost* that indicate the pervasiveness of spirits in the many cultures he discusses:

> Millions of spiritual creatures walk the Earth
> Unseen, both when we wake, and when we sleep[28]

Again, Tylor presents this belief in spirits as a perfectly natural response to early human experience of the natural world. "The animism of savages stands for and by itself; it explains its own origin." He gets closer to an account that covers all the thousands of cases he examines in *Primitive Culture*, when—in a passage added to the book's second edition, published in 1873—he writes, "Spirits are simply personified causes."[29]

And once you had populated the spirit realm, you might well make inferences about the afterlife, the experiences our spirits have after our death. "It is a vicious circle," Tylor says about the savage's epistemology. "What he believes he therefore sees, and what he sees he therefore believes." This is true even of the Christian "who beholds the heights of heaven and the depths of Hell."[30] The study of the savage mind, for Tylor, mattered not just as a story of development; Tylor was fascinated by "survivals"—beliefs and practices from our primitive past that persisted into the modern world. (Larsen offers the intriguing suggestion that because the Society of Friends rejected certain conventions—including our days of the week—as surviving paganisms, Tylor would have been trained to think in those ways.) Although the book is titled *Primitive Culture*, it is also an assessment of modern Christianity. And in the end, the most consequential survival was religion itself.

Tylor's savages project agency into myriad things. We could say that they adopted what Daniel Dennett, the American philosopher, has called the "intentional stance," which is "the strategy of interpreting the behavior of an entity (person, animal, artifact, or whatever) by treating it *as if* it were a rational agent who governed its 'choice' of 'action' by a consideration of its 'beliefs' and 'desires.' "[31] It's just that they did so over a much wider range than many of us now think is warranted, and they based their appeal to these quasi-psychological states in the belief that they are the capacities of a sort of spiritual substance. We should recall, in contemplating our ancestors, that we, too, still adopt the intentional stance toward objects, such as our pets and our computers, that are certainly not human. The intentional stance might seem to arise from the primitive personification that David Hume had written about. ("There is a universal tendency among mankind to conceive all beings like themselves, and to transfer to every object, those qualities, with which they are familiarly acquainted, and of which they are intimately conscious. We find human faces in the moon, armies in the clouds; and by a natural propensity, if not corrected by experience and reflection, ascribe malice or good-will to every thing, that hurts or pleases us."[32]) Max Müller himself wrote about the habits of mind—

and certainly of language—by which the sun, the rain, the wind, and so forth were routinely endowed with personhood. Tylor uses the verb "personified" a fair amount himself. So, using the vocabulary of the contemporary philosophy of mind, Tylor's claim is that the core of religion is the adoption of the intentional stance toward the nonhuman world, as mediated by belief in a substance widely instantiated in the nonhuman world.

One thing Tylor's definition did, of course, was connect primitive religion with the religion of Tylor's coevals. You could say that this was part of its cultural task. Indeed, an important respect in which the exposition of the animist model of religion in *Primitive Culture* differs from Tylor's previous versions—quite aside from the obvious ways in which a highly detailed picture differs from a sketch—is a matter of emphasis: the author of that book is particularly intent on showing how close primitive thinking is to our own. (Savages: they're just like us!) When Tylor remarks on how savages personify things, he will go on to discuss the ways that we personify things, too, seemingly without giving it any thought: for instance, "*France* is talked of by politicians as an individual being, with particular opinions and habits."[33] And though Tylor wrote of "lower races," it was civilizational development that made them lower. As he had explained toward the start of the first volume, he found it "both possible and desirable to eliminate considerations of hereditary varieties or races of man, and to treat mankind as homogeneous in nature."[34]

MAKE ROOM FOR GOD

Many readers will think that the core of religious belief is belief not in spirits but in gods. After all, this is presumably what distinguishes religion from atheism: what atheism denies, etymologically speaking, is that there are gods.

Tylor anticipates this objection at the beginning of the first of his seven chapters on animism. He brings up a claim he has encountered that Australia's Aborigines "have nothing whatever of the character of religion" because they "have no idea of a supreme divinity, creator, and judge, no object of worship, no idol, temple, or sacrifice."[35] Tylor, in response, cites authorities for the view that Aborigines believe that smallpox is the work of "Budyah, an evil spirit who delights in mischief," and that they "have definite traditions concerning supernatural beings, Baiame, whose voice they hear in thunder, and who made all things, Turramullum the chief of demons, who is the author of disease, mischief and wisdom, and appears in the form of a serpent."[36] In context, we can see him as claiming that the Aborigines have religion because they have spirits: they don't need gods to qualify.

Although earlier parts of *Primitive Culture* use the words "god" (with and without a capital G), as well as "deity" and "divinity," a theoretical discussion of deities arrives only toward the end of the chapters on animism. That's because gods are, for Tylor, only one of the kinds of spiritual beings that are at the heart of religion. Finally, we're told that people ascribe to their deities not just a soul like theirs, but a form like theirs, and feelings like theirs.[37] The implication is that the deities are the spirits that humans think are most like us. A tree spirit need not have a human form, even if its soul is, in its general operation, like ours. Its concerns are arboreal, not human; perhaps it is incapable of love or fear. But the gods that Tylor discussed in his chapters on mythology—Zeus or Odin or Maui—can be imagined as like human beings; they can take on our form and our feelings, be irascible, love and hate. And, like us, they can have social relations with one other; even have, like us, a kind of politics:

> Among nation after nation it is still clear how, man being the type of deity, human society and government became the model on which divine society and government were shaped. As chiefs and kings are among men, so are the great gods among the lesser spirits. They differ from the souls and minor spiritual beings which we have as yet chiefly considered, but the difference is rather of rank than of nature.[38]

That suggestion (which elaborates a line of argument found in Hume's *Natural History of Religion*) runs in a different direction from the earlier proposal that the divinities are the anthropomorphic spirits. Because now the distinction between gods and other spirits is, in essence, that the former are the aristocrats of the world of spiritual beings.

This creates a problem for Tylor when he turns to the Abrahamic monotheisms—Christianity, Judaism, and Islam. As I mentioned earlier, their followers have frequently recognized a range of spirits; and doesn't a king need courtiers—or, anyway, other spiritual beings—to keep Him company? In the Anglican prayers of my childhood, we joined with "the Angels and Archangels and all the blessed company of heaven" to "laud and magnify His glorious name." What, in this scheme, is the distinction between monotheism and polytheism? Tylor discussed the matter with a measure of delicacy:

> If the monotheistic criterion be simply made to consist in the Supreme Deity being held as creator of the universe and chief of the spiritual hierarchy, then its application to savage and barbaric theology will lead to perplexing consequences. Races of North and South America, of Africa, of Polynesia, recognizing a number of great deities, are usually and reasonably considered polytheists, yet under this definition their acknowledgment of a Supreme Creator, of which various cases will here be shown, would entitle them at the same time to the name of monotheists. To mark off the doctrines of the lower races, closer definition is required, assigning the distinctive attributes of deity to none save the Almighty Creator.[39]

Yet he never tells us what "the distinctive attributes of deity" actually are. He had, after all, little interest in trying to minimize the commonalities between Christianity and an earlier paganism—quite the contrary. (The reference to the Almighty Creator leaves readers to decide whether to stipulate its extra-cultural reality.) His discussions of how deities differed from souls and spirits was also meant to show how deities grew out of souls and spirits. In *The Course of Positive Philosophy*, Comte had written, "If, on the one hand, every positive theory must necessarily be founded on observations, it is equally clear, on the other hand, that, in order to make observations, our mind needs some sort of theory."[40] Tylor's theory helped organize a wealth of examples that were intended not only to explain the origins of religion but also to supply reason to hope that it would be steadily supplanted by natural science and the uncovering of "systematic law."

Primitive Culture is, as we've seen, marked by a strain of not just anticlericalism but a deeper skepticism as well. We could explain the phenomena under scrutiny, he insisted, without positing "supernatural intervention"; he adhered to what Peter L. Berger would call methodological atheism.[41] But for theists, it was troubling that *Primitive Culture* failed to accommodate the possibility that the existence of the divine played any role in the formation of human belief. Alfred Weld, a Jesuit critic of Tylor's, wrote that it was as if "a historian were to discuss the origin of the widespread belief in the exploits of Alexander of Macedon, without touching on the hypothesis that such a conqueror perhaps really did exist."[42] Here the work of Robert R. Marett is illuminating; as Tylor's protégé, he sought not to overturn Tylor's account but to modify it in ways that—among other things—sat better with an ally of religion like himself.

Marett had grown up Anglican, in Jersey, and attended Balliol College, Oxford, in the 1880s, where he studied classics, with a focus on Roman law. But like Tylor, Marett developed a serious illness that caused his life to take a swerve; after he contracted meningitis, he was treated in Switzerland and ended up studying philosophy at the University of Berlin for a year. Eventually, he returned to Oxford, where Tylor was on the examining committee for a prize essay Marett wrote on "The Ethics of Savage Races." Marett, doing his own library research into the rituals of "primitive man," was impressed by reports from the Anglican priest and ethnographer Robert Codrington concerning "mana" among the Melanesian people. *Mana* was a substance that, though not itself physical, had physical powers: it was impersonal but connected to persons and personified beings; was present in all supernatural creatures, but also in special objects and special persons; and was responsible for supernatural powers they possessed.[43] (As we'll see, Weber's notion of charisma drew on this literature.) Marett, generalizing from "mana theory," designated a belief in such generalized powers, controllable to some degree by human agency, as "preanimism" or "animatism," marking it off from the conceptually later stage of animism. In animism, entities had discrete souls or immanent spirits; in "animatism," a general life force infused everything that was not lifeless, something like an electrical current that powers a variety of machines and appliances. What *mana* picked out, Marett thought, was "that positive emotional value which is the raw material of religion, and needs only to be moralized—to be identified with goodness—to become its essence."[44]

How was this more compatible with the forms of religion that Marett cared about? The notion of a unitary force immanent in the world—a presence we register through the emotion of awe as well as through rationality—was, I suspect, better aligned with what Marett thought was the truth; it's what some identify as religious naturalism. There's an aroma of Schleiermacher in Marett's conclusion: "If there be reason, as I think there is, to hold that man's religious sense is a constant and universal feature of his mental life, its essence and true nature must then be sought, not so much in the shifting variety of its ideal constructions, as in that steadfast groundwork of specific emotion whereby man is able to feel the supernatural precisely at the point at which his thought breaks down." In all these imperfect apprehensions, Marett wrote stirringly, "a single impulse may be discerned as active—the impulse, never satisfied in finite consciousness yet never abandoned, to bring together and grasp as one the *That* and the *What* of God."[45]

THE MÜLLER REPORT

If *Primitive Culture* gave God the side-eye, it also shadowboxed with the era's leading mythologist. That would be Max Müller, the German scholar who had arrived in England in the mid-1840s and made his home there, gaining a chair at Oxford in 1868. The son of the beloved poet Wilhelm Müller, he was both a personal ally of Tylor's and a formidable intellectual rival, having already established himself as an influential theorist of religion and its origins. In a book that Tylor had reviewed, *Lectures on the Science of Language* (1861), Müller put forward a much discussed theory that related primitive religion to something like a law of linguistics: when we forget how a term has come to be used metaphorically—or how an attribute has come to name a divinity—we succumb to mythology, which he called "a disease of language."[46]

So, according to Müller, the story in which Apollo (the sun god) pursues Daphne (a nymph who turns into a laurel tree to escape him) can be understood metaphorically as the sun chasing the dawn, which disappears as it is overtaken by the light of day. Müller argued that "Daphne" has the same root as the Sanskrit word for "dawn," and that the myth represents an ancient observation of natural phenomena—the rising sun dispelling the dawn—encoded in narrative form. In a broader pattern, he argued, many myths can be explained as poetic descriptions of natural events that were anthropomorphized and deified by early humans. The primitive inclination toward personification, in turn, reflected how language worked.[47]

In *Primitive Culture*, Tylor's references to Müller largely honor him as an authority, a purveyor of useful examples. But he politely dissents from the "disease of language" thesis. Although he was happy to say that "spirits are simply personified causes," he didn't believe that dead or forgotten metaphors were critical to religious thought. "I am disposed to think (differing here in some measure from Professor Max Müller's view of the subject) that the mythology of the lower races rests on a basis of real and sensible analogy, and that the great expansion of verbal metaphor into myth belongs to more advanced periods of civilization," he writes. "In a word, I take material myth to be the primary, and verbal myth to be the secondary formation."[48] Marett, in a study of his mentor, suggests that this conflict had been generative. Tylor was spared the temptation to throw himself into the mythological approach because the scientific investigation of mythology was already occupied by Müller, "the autocrat of Comparative Philology," who—in a colonial metaphor both facetious and overdetermined—was "notoriously anxious to annex Comparative Mythology as an outlying portion of his dominions."[49] Instead of consulting the mythology manuals for insights, Tylor would consult the ethnography of living subjects.

Müller had his own critique of Tylor's central strategy. In ways resonant with the concerns of a later era, he cautioned against the assumption that contemporary "savages" could represent mankind in its earliest stages. After discussing clashing descriptions of the inhabitants of Tierra del Fuego in his essay "The Savage" (1885), Müller wrote, pointedly, "The idea that the Fuegian was salted and preserved for us during many thousands of years, so that we might study in him the original type of man, is nothing but a poetical sentiment, unsupported alike by fact, analogy, and reason." He went on: "How untenable is the theory which would boldly identify the modern savage with primitive man, and how cautious we ought to be whenever we take even a few hints here and there from degraded tribes of the present day in order to fill out our imaginary picture of the earliest civilization of our race."[50] Tylor and Müller were the most respectful of sparring partners; Müller, in his next sentence, exempts the lessons that might be extracted by those—he mentions Tylor as an example—who study them in a "truly scholarlike spirit." (This wasn't mere tactical diplomacy; Müller helped orchestrate Tylor's appointment at Oxford.) But he was battering at a pillar of the anthropology of religion.

THOUGHTS AND DEEDS

The great weakness of Tylor's account is also its great strength: his central concern is with belief. The approach came to be known, in a coinage of Marett's, as "intellectualism." To its credit, it enabled us to see primitive religion as a rational response to phenomena. To its discredit, it failed to give weight to ritual and practices, and, in general, the communal dimensions of its subject: notice that the book is titled *Primitive Culture*, not *Primitive Society*. That's not to imply that Tylor has nothing to say about ritualized practices. In the final chapter before his "Conclusion," Tylor turned to "Rites and Ceremonies" and discusses discussing such topics as prayer and sacrifice, or "Fasting and other methods of Artificial Ecstasy." But his attention is largely limited to the goals pursued; these activities are essentially transactional. Prayer, which he describes as "the address of personal spirit to personal spirit" is "simply an extension of the daily intercourse between man and man." Tylor sees prayer as above all a matter of making requests for "personal advantage."[51] The paradigm here is not the personal address that begins the Christian Lord's Prayer ("Our Father, who art in Heaven"), not the blessing of His name, which continues it ("Hallowed be thy name"), and not even the hope that "thy kingdom come, thy will be done," but rather the peremptory "Give us this day our daily bread," which comes after all of them.

In many of the examples Tylor discusses—from Samoa to Zululand—prayer is accompanied by an offering, that is, with forms of gift or sacrifice. He sees that, as with gifts between human beings, there is the possibility of offerings that express love or respect without expecting anything in return. Is the gift giving of Christmas, Hanukkah, or Diwali an act of propitiation, aimed at gaining personal advantage? Don't we see it as mostly expressive ("It's the thought that counts")? In fact, Tylor might have offered a general explanation of the existence of ritual and ceremony in our relations with the gods, for in all societies, relations between people are mediated by ritual and by ceremony. He could also have explained the appeal of prayer as offering the rewards of communion with another person. The point is that the animist hypothesis provides much more scope for an exploration of religious ritual and communion with the gods than Tylor actually gives us.[52] But for Tylor, such practice is, in the first instance, motivated by practical interests in the here and now.

In this story, what the religious agent is usually doing is "as directly practical as any chemical or mechanical process." What's more, Tylor says, "doctrine and worship correlate as theory and practice." His view is that, once we understand religious belief, religious behavior will make sense as the instrumental pursuit of goals people already have. He doesn't think of religion, as so many of us might, as giving us things to aim at. This may seem puzzling: after all, it's only the belief that there is a world of spiritual beings beyond this world—an afterlife—that makes people aim at getting there; and only because the gods command it that certain practices are required or forbidden. He does concede that ritual and ceremony involve "expressive and symbolic performances, the dramatic utterance of religious thought, the gesture-language of theology."[53] But these are ways of recording and communicating belief or of swaying the spirits we believe in. The drama, the gesture, are epiphenomena of the beliefs they express.

What about in more advanced forms of religion? Tylor acknowledges a "powerful tendency of civilization" to "arrange worship into mechanical routine." Here, he says, "religion deposits itself in sharply defined shape from a supersaturated solution, and crystallized into formalism. Thus prayers, from being at first utterances as free and flexible as requests to a living patriarch or chief, stiffened into traditional formulas, whose repetition required verbal accuracy, and whose nature practically assimilated more or less to that of charms." He is pleased to note of the rosary that this "calculating machine is of Asiatic invention."[54] But again, the practices are epiphenomenal on beliefs. And some critics viewed the supposition as a dire misrepresentation of religion.

The most eloquent and influential exponent of this thesis was William Robertson Smith, whose own work came to represent a singularly powerful alternative to Tylorian intellectualism. Robertson Smith was a minister in the Free Church of Scotland, a Presbyterian denomination that twice put him on trial for heresy, in 1878 and in 1881, owing to articles he had contributed to the *Encyclopedia Britannica*. (He later became its editor.) An article on the Bible had landed him in the dock by evincing its author's belief that scriptures be subjected to the usual "methods of historical investigation"; a later article, on Hebrew language and literature, suggested that he was unrepentant, and got him into trouble again. He found safe harbor at Cambridge, where he became a professor of Arabic, his predecessor having, by grim providence, been murdered a few months earlier.[55]

Robertson Smith was, as Evans-Pritchard saw, unusual among early anthropologists in not being a free thinker; when he defended himself at his heresy trials, he was defending his standing within the Free Church (and, yes, his teaching position at an affiliated institution). In his view, the Bible—though written by human beings, with the fallibilities of human scribes—was nonetheless written in the penumbra of revelation. Still, if not quite a free thinker, he was a free-ish thinker, one who had immersed himself in the work of science-friendly theologians.

In his *Lectures on the Religion of the Semites*, which appeared in 1889 and would prove to be his most influential single work, Robertson Smith set forth a view of religion antithetical to Tylor's. Whereas Tylor explicated sacrifice as a gift or tribute that a worshiper paid in order to influence a deity, Robertson Smith balked at this contractual individualism, and at the notion that the deity wasn't part of the worshiper's society. Instead, sacrifice was a collective act that united deity and worshipers with one another.[56] Ritual, not belief, was key to the development of religion. Earlier forms of religion had no belief systems, Robertson Smith argued, but "consisted entirely of institutions and practices." The belief-centered approach, he proposed, represented an idiosyncratic legacy of Christianity, especially of Protestantism. "It is a vicious circle; what he believes he therefore sees, and what he sees he therefore believes," Tylor had written. For Robertson Smith, Tylor's beliefs about belief showed that he, too, had succumbed to that vicious circle. As the Scotsman wrote:

> Our modern habit is to look at religion from the side of belief rather than of practice; a habit largely due to the fact that, till comparatively recent times, almost the only forms of religion which have attracted much serious study in Europe have been those of the various Christian Churches, and that the controversies between these Churches have constantly turned on diversities of dogma, even where the immediate point of difference has been one of ritual. For in all parts of the Christian Church it is agreed that ritual is important only in connection with its interpretation. . . . But the antique religions had for the most part no creed; they consisted entirely of institutions and practices.[57]

In ancient Greece, he ventured, certain rites were performed at a temple, and people concurred that it was necessary to do them; but if you asked them why, you'd hear different explanations, and nobody thought it mattered, religiously, which explanation you adopted. In such antique religions, Robertson Smith writes, "Belief in a certain series of truths was neither obligatory as a part of true religion, nor was it supposed that, by believing, a man acquired religious merit and conciliated the favour of the gods. What was obligatory or meritorious was the exact performance of certain sacred acts prescribed by religious tradition."[58] Orthopraxy, not orthodoxy, was of the essence. It is tempting to suggest that, in elevating belief over ritual, Tylor was being faithful to his own religious upbringing among nineteenth-century Quakers, for whom sitting for long periods in silence, awaiting the Inner Light, constituted the dominant liturgical form, the Society of Friends having abandoned the energetic shaking that had given the group its original name. But Robertson Smith's approach is also friendlier to religion than Tylor's in an important respect: it didn't place religion and science on a collision course, as two bodies of inquiry pursuing basically the same set of problems.

The contrast with Robertson Smith brings out another feature of Tylor's account. Rites and rituals are communal activities, and Robertson Smith's religion was a social institution, binding people together. Tylor, particularly at this point, inclined toward individualism—toward how the "savage philosopher" would make sense of the world around him. Having read his Quetelet, to be sure, he was well-attuned to society as something that had lawlike patterns. "There is found to be such regularity in the composition of societies of men, that we can drop individual differences out of sight," he wrote in the first chapter of *Primitive Culture*, "and thus can generalize on the arts and opinions of whole nations, just as, when looking down upon an army from a hill, we forget the individual soldier, whom, in fact, we can scarce distinguish in the mass, while we see each regiment as an organized body, spreading or concentrating, moving in advance or in retreat." He notes Quetelet's ability to make reliable generalizations concerning "the recurrence, year after year, of such obscure and seemingly incalculable products of national life as the numbers of murders and suicides." But group analysis had to be reconciled with the reality that groups are composed of individuals:

> There are people so intent on the separate life of individuals that they cannot grasp a notion of the action of a community as a whole—such an observer, incapable of a wide view of society, is aptly described in the saying that he "cannot see the forest for the trees." But, on the other hand, the philosopher may be so intent upon his general laws of society as to neglect the individual actors of whom that society is made up, and of him it may be said that he cannot see the trees for the forest. . . . Seeing that collective social action is the mere resultant of many individual actions, it is clear that these two methods of enquiry, if rightly followed, must be absolutely consistent.[59]

Still, most of what he says about religion could have been said about Robinson Crusoe before Friday joined him on that fictional island. (And even then, the presence of another person would have added to belief and ritual only the results of their communicating with one another.) He would have more to say about "society" in later work, but in *Primitive Culture*, little happens between the small-scale realm of intersubjective relations and the aggregative, uniform realm of those historical stages.

THE UNBELIEVERS

If Robertson Smith had argued that the belief-centered approach was implicitly Protestant, a more radical line of argument emerged in his wake: that the concept of belief was alien to many of the cultures where we might want to apply it. Max Müller anticipated this thesis when he wrote, "If we take such a word as faith or 'to believe,' it may seem to us very simple and natural; but that the idea of believing, as different from seeing, knowing, denying, or doubting, was not so easily elaborated, is best known by the fact that we look for it in vain in the dictionaries of many uncivilized races." Evans-Pritchard ventured a similar claim. Writing about a people whom he had studied in southern Sudan, he insisted that when the Nuer said, "God is present," they weren't saying "There is a God": "That would be for Nuer a pointless remark. God's existence is taken for granted by everybody." So to say that all Nuer have faith in God is to deploy the Biblical sense of "trust," and not "the modern sense of 'belief' which the concept came to have under Greek and Latin influences. There is in any case, I think, no word in the Nuer language which could stand for 'I believe.' "[60]

The social anthropologist Rodney Needham expanded on their unease. In his *Belief, Language, and Experience* (1972)—it was the book he was proudest of—he complained that ethnographic writing, though replete with references to "belief," paid scant attention to how the term should be interpreted. He had done fieldwork among the Penan of the interior of Borneo; but he could not see how they'd make sense of the proposition "I believe in God." They worshiped a supreme god, Bungan, and did not entertain his nonexistence. In the later formulation of the French anthropologist Jean Pouillon, "It is the unbeliever who believes that the believer believes in the existence of God," since for the faithful, God's presence is not believed but perceived. Needham concludes that "belief is not a discriminable experience, it does not constitute a natural resemblance among men, and it does not belong to 'the common behavior of mankind.' " Thus: "when other peoples are said, without qualification, to 'believe' anything, it must be entirely unclear what kind of idea or state of mind is being ascribed to them."[61]

This argument is useful in encouraging humility; talk of "belief" can carry with it assumptions—about how individuals internalize and assert the truth of certain proposition—that are specific to European intellectual traditions. Particular care is due in the context of religion. Wilfred Cantwell Smith, in *Belief and History* (1977), argued that the notion of believing did not appear in the Bible, and that "the idea that believing is religiously important turns out to be a modern idea." ("A great modern heresy of the Church," in his view, "is the heresy of believing.")[62] The argument has a contrarian allure; but it's easily overdrawn. Belief ascriptions are, in the end, part of what makes human beings intelligible to one another. Eighteen-month-olds, research indicates, ascribe beliefs to others, including false beliefs.

Still, we should be cautious about what conclusions we draw from the word, or its absence. For one thing, Needham might profitably have bracketed "believe in" statements from "believe that" statements. (Pouillon: "If I have confidence in a friend, if I believe in him, will I say that I believe in his existence?") The philosopher Neil Van Leeuwen, drawing from work by Dan Sperber and others, has proposed that factual beliefs operate differently from other beliefs, which he calls "credences." Credences are closer to the imaginative claims we traffic in during play; they may command our hearts, but they belong to a different map of reality than straightforward factual beliefs.[63] In L. M. Montgomery's *Anne of Green Gables* (1908), set on Prince Edward Island in the late nineteenth century, the title character explains to her guardian Marilla that she and a friend had decided to pretend that a spruce grove was haunted, and that she was now scared to walk through it. Marilla is confounded: "Do you mean to tell me you believe all that wicked nonsense of your own imagination?" she asks. The novel provides its heroine a plausible response: " 'Not believe *exactly*,' faltered Anne. 'At least, I don't believe it in daylight.' "

Nor does the vocabulary of the Penan or the Nuer settle very much: if everyone you know speaks the same language, you may not have anything corresponding to my concept of language, but that absence will not impede your linguistic capacities. Like Molière's *bourgeois gentilhomme*, we can speak prose without the concept of prose. A member of the Penan could report that she had believed a mushroom was safe to eat but was mistaken; that she believed someone was a loyal friend but learned otherwise. We typically use the verb "believe" for beliefs that can be revised—that are, in some sense, conditional. What we believe with a hundred percent certainty is, by convention, simply what we know. By speaking of what I "believe" (or "think"), I allow for contingency, for the possibility of being mistaken or challenged; for the possibility of scrutinizing my own and others' propositional attitudes.

Now, certain concepts come with attendant epistemic commitments; if I didn't grasp that cats typically had teeth and fur, you might conclude that I didn't have the concept of a cat. You might reach the same conclusion if, in the presence of cats, I wasn't sure cats existed. The Penan, reared to take for granted the activity of a supreme god, Bungan, could think that a stranger who entertained doubts about the pervasive power of Bungan simply lacked the Bungan concept. Then again, many Penan have become Christian; some of them may have slotted Jehovah in Bungan's place, and others may have relinquished a world picture where Bungan reigned. Could the Penan really be unable to apply their everyday concept of a false belief (as when one warns another that a foraged mushroom isn't, in fact, safe to eat) to spiritual entities? Navigating a world of other people requires the recognition that other people have beliefs, desires, and intentions. Even if we dispute Tylor's thesis that religion is fundamentally a matter of beliefs—and I'll be saying more about the nature of religious belief later—we'll want to retain the background assumptions about propositional attitudes. We may choose to toss out the baby; we do need the bathwater.

NATURAL SUPERNATURALISM

An account of religion that runs on belief and little else raises another question. Tylor is cunning about locating commonalities between the "savage" and the "civilized." He delights in finding likenesses—between, for example, what Zulus and Europeans say when someone sneezes—because his larger project requires that he cognitively promote the savage and demote the modern in the reader's eye, in order to lessen the distance between them. ("The very word 'superstition,' in what is perhaps its original sense of a 'standing over' from old times, itself expresses the notion of a survival.")[64] But suppose that gods and spirits were real and could reliably be deployed and assuaged; would our intercessory practices even be properly described as religious? What qualifies a being or an action as supernatural?

It can't be that something defies attempts to provide a naturalistic explanation. For the savage, Tylor stresses, these *were* naturalistic explanations, or their best effort at them. And moderns, too, live in a world of unexplained phenomena. Why is the sky blue? Long after the so-called scientific revolution, nobody had a clue. Apparently, the explanation involves something called Rayleigh scattering, in a theory first trotted out in the 1870s. Medical technology has always exceeded our collective scientific understanding; consider aspirin and its willow-bark predecessors, used for thousands of years. Only in the late 1970s did scientists start to understand how it worked. How does paracetamol work? Researchers still aren't sure. Recall Arthur C. Clarke's dictum: "Any sufficiently advanced technology is indistinguishable from magic." As individuals, we can't say how power plants work, how air conditioners work, how the Internet works, how our apps do what they do. We don't conclude that these entities are supernatural.

For that matter, the superheroes in our comics and movies regularly violate the laws of nature, but they don't have the quality of the sacred and we'd be hard-pressed to describe civilian interactions with them as religious. Suppose we lived in a world where the basic agents of traditional Christian faith—heaven, hell, angels, and more—didn't require faith to be known. Would this world be a religious one? Ted Chiang's 2001 novella "Hell is the Absence of God" probes just this problem. In the world that Chiang unfolds, God and the angels make regular appearances, often destructive ones; you hear about angelic visitations on the nightly news. After the angel Nathanael appears at a downtown shopping district, "sixty-two people received medical treatment for injuries ranging from slight concussions to ruptured eardrums to burns requiring skin grafts. Total property damage was estimated at $8.1 million, all of it excluded by private insurance companies due to the cause." Of the eight resultant deaths, "three souls were accepted into Heaven and five were not." Hell manifested itself on a regular basis: "you could see Hell as if you were looking through a hole in the floor." And so on. The existence of these creatures wasn't at issue; how you felt about them might be.[65]

Chiang's tale is a thought experiment; we don't live in that world. But it suggests that if these demiurges and their supreme commander really were continuous with the rest of creation, our encounters with them would not be what we think of as religious experience. Hume, in his *Enquiry Concerning Human Understanding*, contrasted two inexplicable events: in one, the entire planet is (we learn from reliable accounts) overtaken by darkness for some period. In another, Queen Elizabeth rises from the dead.[66] Our response to the first, but not the second, Hume writes, is to refine our grasp of the natural sciences in order to try to understand how such a thing happens. That sounds right, and yet Hume doesn't deliver a clear explanation for how the cases differ. The Chiang scenario is different again. Here, we have a belief in spiritual or, anyway, supernatural beings, but something is missing. As we'll see in the next chapters, Durkheim had an answer; so did Simmel.

THE EXILE OF AFFECT

The most obvious response to this challenge, though, is to consider religion's emotional valences. Religious experience, as a category, poorly accommodates an angelic visitation that inspires not awe but annoyance. That Tylor scants the role of intense emotion in religion, though it may reflect his particular Quaker upbringing, will strike many readers as noteworthy, whether they live within one of the many religious traditions of the contemporary world or were raised outside them all.

Primitive Culture makes occasional allowances, to be sure. In the second volume, Tylor grants that "even in savage religion," prayer can be "a means of strengthening emotion, sustaining courage and exciting hope."[67] He recognizes, then, that when we talk to the gods, as when we talk to one another, we are not simply making demands but also experiencing the sentiments that grow out of our relationships. It may be that we can't imagine a profound relationship with a tree spirit (though Keats, who spoke of the nightingale as the "light-winged Dryad of the trees," might rebuke us for this failing), but when we are dealing with the more richly realized psychology of personal gods, our interactions can be personal and not purely instrumental. They won't be devoid of sentiment.

In the second edition of the second volume, at the end of the chapters on animism, Tylor observes that he has kept in view the "intellectual rather than the emotional side of religion." He concedes that even among "the rudest Savages, religious life is associated with intense emotion, with awful reverence, with agonizing terror, with rapt ecstasy." Recognizing this, Tylor admits, "those to whom religion means above all things religion feeling, may say of my argument that I have written soullessly of the soul, and unspiritually of spiritual things." Well, he says, that was his plan, because, as he sees it, the core of religion among primitive people was animism, his great discovery, and "scientific progress is at times most furthered by working along a distinct intellectual line."[68]

So his successor Robert Marett pressed an inevitable objection when, rejecting such "intellectualism," he wrote, "Psychologically, religion involves more than thought, namely, feeling and will as well; and may manifest itself on its emotional side, even when ideation is vague."[69] The generation of anthropologists who followed Tylor often embraced an account influenced by depth psychology: they were interested in how religion captured or was generated by the emotion of "awe," say, or perhaps how religion was a response to emotional stress. Those of a Freudian persuasion might see religion in terms of a psychodrama projected upon the external world. Over the past few generations, many would agree with the social anthropologist Stanley Tambiah—who had much to say about the role of ritual in maintaining social realities and relationships—when he concluded that Tylor "had no feeling for what religion, particularly public, organized, ritualized religion, meant to the worshippers themselves."[70]

But we can distinguish between the nature of Tylor's account and the capacities of his theory. There's no reason to think that the theory of animism—conjuring a world full of spirits that have an emotional palette like that of people—deprives us of the resources to predict and explain the role of emotion in religious practice, since, after all, a great swathe of human emotion consists, precisely, of responses to other people. That Tylor doesn't write much about religious emotion does not mean that his model cannot encompass it. Belief in creatures with minds something like ours provides a quite reasonable basis for an emotional response. Still, for these purposes, one emotion isn't as good as another: if there are characteristic emotions related to religious experiences, we may need more than Tylor's model to explore them.

MARGINALIZING MORALITY

There is another strategic absence in Tylor's treatment of primitive religion. You might have thought that religion played a major role in shaping the ethical life of its adherents—in the enforcement of norms, in their creation, and in their content. Recall Müller's stipulation that religion "consists in the perception of the infinite under such manifestations as are able to influence the moral character of man"—or Marett's notion that the essence of religion was in the moralization of a particular emotional value. Tylor insisted, by contrast, that "savage animism is almost devoid of that ethical element which to the educated modern mind is the very mainspring of practical religion."[71] Notice that Tylor wasn't claiming that his primitive subjects lacked access to moral ideas. He maintains, in fact, that morality is not "absent from the life of the lower races," because human society requires it:

> Without a code of morals, the very existence of the rudest tribe would be impossible; and indeed the moral standards of even

savage races are to no small extent well-defined and praiseworthy. But these ethical laws stand on their own ground of tradition and public opinion, comparatively independent of the animistic beliefs and rites which exist beside them.[72]

Tylor granted that, "in the higher faiths," prayer was "a great motive power of the ethical system, controlling and enforcing, under an ever-present sense of supernatural intercourse and aid, the emotions and energies of moral life." But he did not view it as a reliable guide: "Moralists admit that prayer can be made an instrument of evil, that it may give comfort and hope to the superstitious robber, that it may strengthen the heart of the soldier to slay his foes in an unrighteous war, that it may uphold the tyrant and the bigot in their persecution of freedom in life and thought."[73]

One way of understanding Tylor's position here, the historian Timothy Larsen observes, is as a rejoinder to Victorian critics who thought that free thinking would undermine morality. Alluding to Thomas Huxley's reference to Comte's Religion of Humanity as "Catholicism minus Christianity," Larsen proposes that Tylor's mature perspective could be characterized as "Quakerism minus Christianity." At the end of his magnum opus, Tylor writes that a painful "office of ethnography" is "to expose the remains of crude old culture which have passed into harmful superstition, and to mark these out for destruction." Doing so is "urgently needful for the good of mankind," he declares. "The science of culture is essentially a reformer's science."[74] Looking forward to a post-religious era, Tylor wanted to reassure his readers that they didn't need God to be good.

TWO CHEERS FOR INTELLECTUALISM

Despite its deficits, there was something profoundly generative in Tylor's "intellectualist" approach—notably, in its insistence on the continuities between his savages and his moderns. Many theorists in his own and later generations resisted this. Indeed, as we saw, Tylor was revising an earlier argument of his own, shifting the emphasis from alterity to similarity. Lucien Lévy-Bruhl made the argument that the primitive mind was "pre-logical"; in *How Natives Think* (1910), he complained that Tylor's interpretations of the facts concerning souls was "imposed upon him by his postulate, according to which the mentality of lower races follows the same logical laws as our own thought." Tylor thought both that we were less logical than we might like to think and that those primitives were more so.[75]

As we'll see, Durkheim, Simmel, and Weber accepted important features of the basic paradigm: primordial forms of religion solved problems; our early ancestors were not fundamentally irrational or incapable of reason; there are profound continuities between earlier efforts to grasp some ultimate reality and our own attempts. And though the term "neo-Tylorian" was often a term of reproach in the 1950s (and his universalism remains suspect in much contemporary anthropology, a deeply penitential discipline), today, in other disciplines, it is often a self-awarded distinction. That's because a large body of contemporary thought about religion, often called the cognitive science of religion, can be thought of as a culmination of the approach that Tylor had started in earnest.

A bridge figure here is Edward Evans-Pritchard. He had his differences from Tylor. He had little use for Tylor's stadial evolutionism, or what Evans-Pritchard called "progressionism"; he thought Tylor was wrong about "primitive monotheism" necessarily emerging from polytheism, wrong to think that his primitives routinely confused ideal connections with real ones. He considered Tylor's "dream theory" of how the notion of the soul arose as a "just-so story." Is it really so obvious that when someone dies and you dream of her afterward, she has a divisible phantom life? Must the idea of the soul lead to the idea of spirits? "Generalisations about 'religion' are discreditable," Evans-Pritchard averred. "They are always too ambitious and take account of only a few of the facts."[76]

For all that, Evans-Prichard endorsed Tylor's claims "about the essential rationality of primitive peoples."[77] However they reached their beliefs, those beliefs were coherent and intelligible to anyone who took the time to study their way of life. In religious belief, as in the natural sciences and in folk theories of the world, what we see is the postulation of entities to explain the phenomena of experience. Building out from their understanding of human beings—animated material creatures able to act on physical objects, guided by their beliefs and their purposes—our ancestors projected a theory that was wildly successful in predicting and understanding each other onto a much wider world. In ways explored by a later self-described neo-Tylorian, Robin Horton, traditional religions were in key respects less analogous with Western religion, with its typically attenuated formalities, than with Western science: it was a means of control and prediction, a way of mastering or, anyway, contending with the natural realm. (More on this in Chapter 5.)

Tylor, of course, thought it was a natural feature of human thought to adopt the intentional stance toward things that many modern people would say have no mental states. But human beings have other explanatory schemas available to them. We understand certain events—the breaking of a tree limb by the wind or by a person, say—as a causal process, explicable without appeal to the will or the beliefs or the emotions of the tree, or, indeed, of the wind. If a branch doesn't break when we bend it, we know we must press harder. Everybody understands the push and pull of efficient causality. People also have the idea that some things have functions: that hearts are for pumping blood, knives for cutting. Dennett calls this latter explanatory schema the "design stance," and it, too, is available across societies, precisely because our species is homo faber, the maker of things, and design is one of our characteristic activities.

In the contemporary world, with the rise of a scientific approach, we can give many more detailed causal explanations, allowing for much more successful prediction and control than was possible in earlier societies. Darwinism allows us to explain how functions arise without appeal either to agency or to design. And when things happen in the world around us, we moderns often turn to explanations grounded not in agency (by way of the intentional stance) nor design, but natural causality. Why did our ancestors so often do otherwise?

Recent work in evolutionary psychology and in cognitive psychology has, as we'll see in Chapter 5, extended Tylor's inquiries. Tylor had demonstrated, with an astonishing range and depth of ethnographic materials from the human past and around the world, that a great deal of what we call religion can indeed be understood by seeing it as the projection of agency into the cosmos. Contemporary theorists have their own account of why human beings project agency in this way. Still, in developing the hypothesis that religion is, at heart, a protoscientific belief in spirits, Sir Edward Tylor delineated a template for the scientific study of religion that persists even among researchers oblivious of its ancestry. Call it a survival.

THE SECOND REFORMATION

Primitive Culture made Tylor a name to conjure with. One reviewer asserted that he "has done for the spirit world what Mr. Darwin has done for the animal. All who would not fall behind the best thought of their time, must make themselves acquainted with this book of deep and universal interest."[78] Tylor became a fellow of the Royal Society, served (twice) as president of the Royal Anthropological Institute, and was awarded an honorary degree by Oxford, in 1875, in a prelude to his notable career with that institution. Helping his discipline find its lodgings in college classrooms was his 1881 textbook *Anthropology: An Introduction to the Study of Man*.[79] The book included a chapter devoted to the topic of "Society." He wrote that "controlling forces of society are always at work even among savages, only in more rudimentary ways than among ourselves," noting that "public opinion is already a great power, and the way in which it acts is particularly to be noticed." If religion wasn't the handmaiden of morality, he suggested here that society might be, inasmuch as personal actions that benefited society, rather than the individual, were those we saw as moral:

> Whereas the individual man is too apt to look to his own personal interest and the benefit of his near friends, these private motives fall away when many minds come together, and public opinion with a larger selfishness takes up the public good, encouraging the individual to set aside his private wishes and give up his property or even his life for the commonwealth. . . . To a great extent it is evident that customs have come into existence for the benefit of society, or what was considered so.[80]

Tylor's institutional successes were considerable but circumscribed; at Oxford, his unavailing efforts to make anthropology a diploma subject had, he believed, been stymied by the theologians and the "classical men."[81] (Only under his successor, Marett, could students get a degree in it.)

If his skepticism on religious matters was not pugnacious, it was far from muted. "How many years must pass before it shall be expected of every theologian that he shall have studied the development of religious ideas in the world before he reasons about them?" he wrote in an 1875 letter to the *Times*. "Such a time will come, and with it the time when a theologian's education will necessarily include an elementary knowledge of the laws of nature. On these two steps will follow the second Reformation in England, and it will be greater than the first." The language was fraught; Larsen notes that T. H. Huxley referred to his scientific campaign against religious orthodoxy as "the new Reformation."[82]

The fact that Tylor also became a member of the Athenaeum Club indicated that his heterodoxies did not greatly trouble the establishment. He played tennis; he wrote satiric doggerel about the errant assumptions of the theologians; he gained followers. It was no doubt to his benefit that he had what could later be called a certain charisma. "To look as handsome as a Greek god, to be as gentle at heart as a good Christian should, and, withal, to have the hard, keen, penetrating intelligence of the naturalist of genius—this is to be gifted indeed; or, as they would say in the Pacific, such as man has *mana*," Marett wrote of him.[83] An 1890 piece in *Harper's*, by the journalist and suffragist Ethel M. Arnold, tells us that Tylor is "one of the most delightful of all the scientific men of the day," and reports a young man's remark, after a conversation with Dr. Tylor: "He is the *simplest* 'great man' I have ever talked with!"[84]

In those days, Tylor was working on a book, which he planned to call *The Natural History of Religion* (in homage to Hume) and would expand on lectures delivered at the University of Aberdeen starting in 1889. He sought to establish more directly that all religions, however "evolved," were rooted in savage animism. (He also added "demons" as a category that followed the soul in animistic ontology.) If Tylor failed to complete the work—he labored over it until at least 1901—it might have been in part because of certain scholarly complexities he found himself immersed in; but it may also have been related to a slow fading of his cognitive faculties that appears to have begun in the late 1890s, and was pronounced by 1904, although he did not officially resign from Oxford until 1910. By the time he was knighted, in 1912, there was some question as to whether he was even aware of it, which means that he may have been blissfully oblivious to the arrival of the Great War a couple of years later. In an obituary that marked his death in early 1917, *Nature* politely remarked that his death had come "after a twilight of seven or eight years and a few days' illness."[85] The founder of intellectualism, to the distress of his students, had long outlived his own intellect.

The battles over Tylor's legacy continued after his death, with younger readers variously attempting to refute and refine the basic picture. Precisely because his tough-mindedness, rigor, and range were unexampled, his work could scarcely be set aside. But for our purposes, what matters is that he helped to set the stage—to clear the stage, it could be as fairly said—for the social theorists who followed. Although their perspectives were not his, it mattered enormously that he set out to define religion in terms of human subjects and to analyze religion in terms of what it provided them. And it mattered that his inquiry could draw from the study of mythology, from empirical psychology, from archeology, from history, and even from theology, while remaining distinct from all these disciplines. By showing what could be achieved by melding exhaustive empiricism with sophisticated theory, Tylor invited others to join the expedition.

CHAPTER 2

Émile Durkheim

Society and the Sacred

EMANATIONS FROM THE DIVINITY — YOUNG MAN FROM THE PROVINCES — A GERMAN INTERLUDE — A SOCIAL ANIMAL — EVERYTHING SOCIAL WAS RELIGIOUS — RITUAL REVELATIONS — LINES OF DEMARCATION — TOTALIZING TOTEMS — PUTTING PSYCHOLOGY IN ITS PLACE — BLURRED LINES — HOMO DUPLEX

EMANATIONS FROM THE DIVINITY

In his last major book, Émile Durkheim set out to provide a systematic account of early religion: how it arose, what role it played, and, in a larger sense, what it meant. Because these were the central questions of Tylor's *Primitive Culture*, it was almost obligatory that, early in *The Elementary Forms of the Religious Life (Les formes élémentaires de la vie religieuse)*, Durkheim would both credit and attack his enormously influential precursor. "First of all, it must be acknowledged that the theorists of animism have rendered an important service to the science of religions and even to the general history of ideas by subjecting the notion of the soul to historical analysis," he wrote. Yet Durkheim denies that the experience of dreaming would have invited elaborate explanation, for "familiarity readily puts curiosity to sleep." It was, rather, the survival of the social collectivity, far beyond the lifespan of any of its members, that demanded resolution. The hypothesis of a double seemed, to Durkheim, a poor explanation of our dreamed experience, anyway. He was inclined to wonder whether "the souls of men, far from having been the model on which the gods were imagined, were not conceived, from the beginning, as emanations from the divinity."[1] He complains, too, that the Tylorians proceed as if religion were an indivisible entity, whereas it is really made up of myths, dogmas, rites, ceremonies—separable elements that relate in certain ways.

But Durkheim's most definitive complaint was that the theory of animism suggests "religious beliefs are so many hallucinatory representations." It cannot be that "systems of ideas like religions, which have held such a considerable place in history, and where peoples have always drawn the energy necessary to live, are merely webs of illusions." Chemistry is a science because it analyzes something that has an independent reality, and the same must hold for a science of religions. And yet if people endorsed the animistic theory, "they could not help but sever themselves from the errors whose nature and origin would thus be revealed to them," Durkheim wrote. "What kind of science is it if its biggest discovery is proving its own subject matter to be an illusion?"[2]

This is Durkheim at his most dialectical; the objective reality he imputes to religion is, as we'll see, remote from the reality that the religious would impute to it. *The Elementary Forms of the Religious Life*, which boldly ventures its own definition of religion, was the culmination of a lifetime's engagement with the topic. It runs through all of his work, in ways often overlooked, like a golden thread. In the picture he developed, religion embodied a society's awareness of itself as a society; it made a society legible to itself, crystallizing its values, norms, ideals, and structures. As he honed his thought over the years, we can see the main implements of his methodological approach arising from work in the vicinity of religion. The subject was, for him, singularly generative, albeit sometimes of contradiction.

YOUNG MAN FROM THE PROVINCES

Tylor, who had a plausible disciplinary claim to being the founder of anthropology, was raised a Quaker in an Anglican society; David Émile

Durkheim (1858–1917), who had an equally plausible disciplinary claim to being the founder of sociology, was raised Jewish in a Catholic one. Growing up in Épinal, in the Lorraine region of northeastern France, he was the son, grandson, and great-grandson of rabbis. The Durkheim household was, as you'd expect, an observant one, and he was expected to carry on his father's vocation. He learned Hebrew, attended synagogue, had a bar mitzvah, and became acquainted with the Talmud.

Although many of France's Jews came from the Lorraine region, the Jewish community in Épinal was tiny—his father had to take on more than one congregation to make ends meet—and fit his later description of a "small, compact, and coherent society with a strong feeling of self-consciousness and unity." David Émile was a schoolboy when, in 1870, Prussia's forces defeated those of the Second French Empire; Prussian soldiers occupied his hometown for two years. Some blamed France's defeat on the Jews (as Durkheim wrote amid the Dreyfus affair, a scapegoat always comes in handy at such times), and Durkheim was acutely aware of his religious community as a site of both external sanctions and internal bonds. "Never does the believer feel himself so strongly drawn towards his co-religionists as in time of persecution," he wrote in his first book.[3]

Yet his parents raised no objections when he found himself drawn to secular learning and set his sights on the École Normale Supérieure. He was sent to board in Paris, where he attended the lycées that could prepare him for admission; after a couple of false starts, he was finally able to matriculate in 1879. There, possibly under the influence of such classmates as Jean Jaurès, a lifelong friend who was later a leader of the French Socialist Party, and Henri Bergson, who would become a renowned philosopher of vitalism and an intellectual opponent, Durkheim lost his faith. At the same time, he gained membership in a community that was as cloistral and intense as that of his childhood. The École was not a house of worship, but for the *normalien* it was a forcing house energized by intimacy, discipline, and a sense of discovery. Jaurès later described it as "animated sometimes by a marvelous effervescence of ideas." Durkheim swiftly acquired a reputation among his classmates for argumentative force and intellectual gravity; he was nicknamed the Metaphysician.[4]

Some of the faculty members, notably Émile Boutroux, a philosopher known for his efforts to establish a rapprochement between science and religion, had a lasting and acknowledged influence on him. Boutroux, Durkheim said, taught him that every science "has its own principles."[5] The insights of sociology need not be cashed out in terms of psychology, those of psychology in terms of biology, those of biology in terms of chemistry, and so on. He had, then, been trained to resist methodological reductionism in all its forms. Other influences were inescapably part of the intellectual milieu, not least August Comte and the neo-Kantian philosopher Charles Renouvier. Comte's great insight, Durkheim would write, was that the social laws were like the laws of nature and could be discovered by similar means; yet, in Comte's writing, the science was presented as a completed project while its foundation had scarcely been laid.[6] The positivist's progressionist scheme, which called for the elimination of psychology along with metaphysics, was widely seen as dogmatic and empirically undernourished—a celebration of scientism that was itself unscientific. Comte, then, was the intellectual prophet who had both introduced the term "sociology" and brought it into discredit.

Renouvier's work was, in part, a corrective to Comte, and Durkheim immersed himself in it. He later wrote to a friend, "If you wish to mature your thought, devote yourself to the study of a great master; take a system apart, laying bare its innermost secrets. That is what I did and my educator was Renouvier."[7] Work such as Renouvier's *Science de la morale* (1868–1869) tended to naturalize, or socialize, Kant. For Renouvier (as for the positivists), there was no noumenal realm, only a phenomenal one, but he faulted Comtean positivism for failing to recognize that the scientific study of the world had to encompass "psychic facts"—such mental phenomena as experience, feelings, desires, intentions. At the same time, a quasi-Kantian ethics could be seen to arise, step by step, by contemplating the dynamics that would arise in the most elementary of societies: you'd start with promises, which gave rise to contracts, and then generate a sense of justice reflecting the prerogatives and duties spawned by those contracts. Renouvier could be read, then, as saying that moral rules arose from social rules. In his account, moral principles weren't inborn (aside from the fact that they're predicated on our disposition to live in groups); they had a social basis, directed by a unitary social logic. Durkheim enlisted specific terms of Renouvier's, notably "representative functions" (*fonctions représentives*), to help explain the social functions of religious thought and activity; in Renouvier, too, you can find a precursor to Durkheim's notion of society as a set of "living consciousnesses, organisms of ideas."

Herbert Spencer belonged in the category of the inescapable as well. In *Social Statics* (1851), the essay "The Social Organism" (1860), and in his *Principles of Sociology* (the first volume of which appeared in 1876), he elaborated a theory of social evolution characterized by an increase in the division of labor. Within early, "military," societies, cooperation was secured coercively, and despotism played a major role. Within later, "industrial societies," marked by civilizational complexity, coercion waned and individualism waxed. Spencer also advanced a modified version of Tylor's intellectualism. Primitive humans, seeking to understand phenomena beyond their control or comprehension, and failing to grasp the distinction between subjective experience and the objective world, were inclined to believe that their spirits persisted after their deaths. Such spirits came to be deified and worshiped; natural forces came to be personified. But Spencer put forth a more sociologically attuned account of subsequent developments: in early, military-type societies, "the political head and the ecclesiastical head are identical" (the chief, descendant of a god, is the god's chief propitiator). As the structures of society grew in complexity, so did ecclesiastical structures. Durkheim—we learn from Marcel Fournier, Durkheim's most exhaustive biographer—started reading Spencer in 1881 and 1882, in his last two years at the École; he wasn't alone. Bergson recounted that the students were then split between Kant and Spencer.

Perhaps because Durkheim was struggling with ill health, he did not perform well in his *agrégation*, his leaving exams; after he graduated from the École Normale, in 1882, he spent the next several years teaching philosophy in provincial high schools. An intellectual infusion arrived when, in 1886, Durkheim headed north for a semester, having been awarded a scholarship from the Ministry of Public Education to visit a few German campuses.

A GERMAN INTERLUDE

One way the sojourn affected him was in his preparations for it. He read up on various German intellectual eminences he didn't personally meet, not least the historical economists and "lectern-socialists" Gustav Schmoller, Adolph Wagner, and Albert Schäffle—critics of the individualism they saw in the Manchester School of economics. Schäffle was already known for his *Bau und Leben des sozialen Körpers (Construction and Life of the Social Body)*, an effort to coordinate the life sciences with the social sciences, which appeared in four volumes between 1875 and 1878. Social cohesion wasn't mainly the product of instincts or even traditions but of specific clear ideas (*idées claires*, in Durkheim's rendering). Durkheim's long essay on it, from 1885, was his first published work. It brought out Schäffle's view that society, far from being reducible to an aggregation of individuals, instead shaped its members, and had its own interests.[8]

Durkheim visited the universities at Berlin and Marburg, but more significant was his time spent in psychologist Wilhelm Wundt's laboratory in Leipzig. Wundt's *Ethik: Eine Untersuchung der Thatsachen und Gesetze des sittlichen Lebens* (*Ethics: An Inquiry into the Facts and Laws of Moral Life*) appeared the year of his visit, and many of Wundt's intellectual habits would have been to Durkheim's taste: his exhaustive empiricism, his anti-reductionism, his recognition of the social as a singular force. Durkheim, in his late twenties, was still collecting his intellectual gear, and yet the continuities between his responses in this decade and his later positions are striking. Writing about Wundt's *Ethik* at length, in 1887, he commended the psychologist for stressing the importance of early religion in societies, and tracing how it issued rules of conduct and generated systems of ideas and ideals that would later establish an independent existence. Wundt recognized that religious thought restrained human egoism and inclined people toward sacrifice and impersonal ideals.[9] Wundt had also shown that individualism was the product, not the predecessor, of social development.

Other features of Wundt's argument were less congenial. Wundt insisted—in ways aligned with Tylorian intellectualism—that much of primitive mythology wasn't properly religious; it was more like science, concerned with explaining the natural world, and not necessarily imbued with the feelings of the ideal and the exalted. He also held, as Renouvier did, that morality was, ultimately, unitary. Durkheim thought that there were "as many ethics as there are social types"; Wundt thought that there was one set of moral ideals toward which all societies developmentally converge. "It is no more right to conceive of religion as emerging from morality than morality from religion," Durkheim cautioned. "In the beginning, law, morality and religion were combined in a synthesis from which is it impossible to dissociate the elements." More to the point, "Does one not see people venerating in their gods the worst of human vices?"[10]

Still, Wundt had very clearly established morality as a subject for socially oriented and empirically informed inquiry. And he had firmly countered the temptation to reduce society to its individual participants: "Collective phenomena do not come from individuals to be spread through society; they rather emanate from society and are then diffused among individuals."[11] Durkheim's later concept of "social facts," set out in his *Rules of Sociological Method*, has roots in Wundt's discussion of mental representations, *Vorstellungen*.

A SOCIAL ANIMAL

Durkheim himself encouraged the erroneous idea that he did not write seriously about religion until after 1895. What one finds is that, in the late 1880s, he honed his own thoughts concerning society and religion against the whetstone of other theories. In 1886, writing about, and against, Spencer, Durkheim argued that the true sociologist "will give little attention to the different ways in which men and peoples have been able to conceive the unknown cause and the mysterious foundation of things," but rather "discard all these metaphysical speculations and will see in religion only a social discipline." He will resist secular triumphalism, too, and recognize that religions come under attack only when they cease to ensure the equilibrium of their societies. Spencer's book would have been entirely different, Durkheim wrote, had it concerned itself with the sociology of religion more than glancingly. Doing so might have saved Spencer from his misapprehension that free and rational inquiry was coming to supplant religious faith.

"A prejudice does not dissipate because it has been discovered to be irrational," Durkheim writes, epigrammatically, "but is discovered to be irrational because it is in the process of dissipating." Religion begins with faith—"that is to say, with any belief accepted or endured without discussion"—but belief in God is just one kind of faith; belief in progress is another. And in important ways, faith expands in a scientifically advanced society: "the more the field of knowledge and action expands, the more there are things that we must believe by authority." Lacking a true sociological understanding, Spencer mistakenly supposed that the role of custom, prejudice, and authority was in decline. "As long as there are men who live together, there will be among them some common faith," Durkheim wrote. "What one cannot foresee and what only the future will be able to decide is the particular form under which this faith will be symbolized."[12] (Four years later, he wrote that the *liberté-fraternité-egalité* principles of 1789 are "believed in not as theorems but as items of faith," arising from "a religion, which has had its martyrs as well as its apostles.")[13]

In Durkheim's intellectual trajectory, antagonism and influence cannot be disentangled. Consider his combative critique of Alfred Fouillée, the author of *La Science sociale contemporaine* (1880). Fouillée—whose work stressed mutual dependencies, society as an organism, and *âme social*, or social spirit—used the term *idées-forces* to designate activated systems of ideas that guided humanity and that might, as he wrote in the book, be "veiled under the myths of religion."[14] Durkheim's *représentations collectives*, which we'll encounter later, are Wundt's *Vorstellungen* seasoned with Alfred Fouillee's *idées-forces*. (William James mocked them as "idées-farces.") Intellectual propinquity can breed enmity; the two debated each other for years, starting with Durkheim's skeptical review of a book Fouillée had published about social property and democracy, in 1885.

It's significant, too, that Durkheim took up the term "anomie" in the course of an 1887 critique of a book about religion, or, more precisely, about the coming eclipse of religion. For it was the young philosopher Jean-Marie Guyau—a stepson of Alfred Fouillée and, by self-description, a sociologist—who introduced anomie as a sociological concept. In Guyau's *L'irréligion de l'avenir*, anomie referred not to a modern malaise but to a challenge posed by the emerging social order. In his account, religion—consisting in mythic explanations, a dogmatic creed, and bodies of ritual practice—originates in the human sense of sociality and dependency. But as society advanced, Guyau argued, the old rites and myths were increasingly supplanted by scientific inquiry and explanation. Standards of conduct could no longer be drawn from transcendental truths or religious instruction but had to come from within; anomie, for Guyau (who introduced the term in Greek), was a mode of autonomy. Religious and moral anomie would result when external laws of conduct faded away, and freedom of thought was supreme.

Durkheim, who was clearly drawn to the word (though he would give it the opposite spin, taking anomie to be a condition of pathology and, as he wrote later, "the contradiction of all morality"), criticized Guyau's understanding of religion as excessively "rationalist." Whereas Guyau ascribed shifts in religious belief to intellectual reflection, Durkheim insisted that religion is responsive to the practical needs of society, so that changes in the nature of religious belief arise from changes in the structure of society. He also took issue with the part of Guyau's origin story of religion that implicates the human desire to know and explain; Durkheim, at this point, accepted only that sociability gave rise to religion.[15] For Guyau, "religion is a universal *sociomorphism*," and "the religious feeling is first of all the feeling of dependence." Here, he comes closer to Durkheim's perspective. But Guyau, critically, veers from it: "religion is a *physical, metaphysical, and moral explanation* of all things by analogy with human society, in imaginative and symbolic form. In short: religion is the *universal sociological explanation of the world, in mythical form.*"[16] Other aspects of Durkheim's critique were further developed later: Guyau looked for a successor to religion, and, more broadly, to moral traditions, in which the external constraints of sanction and obligation fell away; for Durkheim, sanction and obligation were part of what makes social rules moral ones.

These were, intellectually speaking, Durkheim's years of hunting and gathering, although one senses an intelligence that knew what it wanted to hunt and to gather. Other resources arrived: in 1887, the year he published at length about his anti-individualist Germans, he got married, to Louise Dreyfus, who came from a prosperous Parisian Jewish family, and he accepted a lectureship at the University of Bordeaux. There his position was "Chargé d'un Cours de Science Sociale et de Pédagogie"—he had requested the "Science Sociale" part. (In his inaugural lecture, he commended Schäffle's *Bau und Leben* for recognizing that "society is not a simple collection of individuals but an entity which has its own life, consciousness, interests, and history," and for making plain how "narrow and feeble" Spencer's construction of society was.)[17] A particularly important colleague of Durkheim's at Bordeaux was Alfred Espinas, who had helped arrange his position, and whose significance to sociology Durkheim always heralded. Espinas claimed to have submitted the first doctoral thesis in sociology, although, as with Durkheim, it is difficult to be formally credentialed in a discipline you are trying to establish. Perhaps because of their personal ties, Durkheim was happy to credit Espinas's *Des sociétés animals* (1877) as having advanced his discipline. It's a curious book, with long chapters about group behavior among insects and fish. Reading it from a Durkheimian perspective, one is struck by its use of "conscience collective" (a term that otherwise sympathetic reviewers quarreled with, and that Durkheim put to use in his own first book), and, perhaps more significantly, of the tricky term "représentation." Espinas aimed to show, by studying a series of social groups in the animal world, "that representation, which is to say a psychological phenomenon," soon comes to be "the preponderant cause of association." It's not just that the individual, rather than being a pre-social entity, arises from the social one, but also that "individual animals which make up a society tend to form, through the exchange of their representations and the reciprocity of their mental acts, not only a more or less concentrated consciousness, but one that is also apparently individual."[18] A collective consciousness comes into being.

 Durkheim could fondly regard Espinas's volume of protosociobiology as raw material, but Ferdinand Tönnies's *Gemeinschaft und Gesellschaft* (often translated as *Community and Society*), released in 1887, must have occasioned some anxiety; it must have seemed to encroach on territory Durkheim had thought would be his. In an 1889 review, Durkheim, always besotted by binaries, readily conceded the distinction between the *Gemeinschaft* and the *Gesellschaft*: *Gemeinschaft* was the small-scale and intimate community, held together by "organic" bonds and exhibiting a high level of religiosity; *Gesellschaft* was the larger-scale, more articulated society, typified by the advanced division of labor. For Tönnies, this shift from folk culture to the state bureaucracy, from the village to the city, was marked by a "complete reversal of intellectual life": "Previously, all was centred around the belief in invisible beings, spirits and gods; now it is focalized on the insight into visible nature. Religion, which is rooted in folk life or at least closely related to it, must cede supremacy to science, which derives from and corresponds to consciousness." Durkheim would have considered such intellectualism, in which religion functions as a proto-science, misguided. But his review homed in on another line of critique. While Tönnies held that the *Gesellschaft* was held together by the "entirely external impulsion of the State," Durkheim held that the "life of the great social agglomerations is just as natural as that of small aggregates"—it is "neither less organic nor less internal."[19] It would take a book to lay out the correct view, he maintained—a book that he was already in the midst of writing.

EVERYTHING SOCIAL WAS RELIGIOUS

In 1892, Durkheim presented his doctoral thesis, "De la division du travail social," which appeared in book form the following year. In his schema, the earlier, small-scale forms of society were characterized by "mechanical" solidarity or "solidarity by similars"—for example, shared beliefs and traditions; the more advanced, large-scale forms of society were characterized by "organic" solidarity. It's possible to wonder whether Durkheim deliberately sought to invert Tönnies's vocabulary, so that his model would not be taken for a mere variant of its predecessor.[20] In broad outlines, the account aligns with other precursors in certain respects while diverging in others: like Spencer, Durkheim saw modern society as marked by a specialization of tasks, a retreat of traditional religion, and a stronger sense of individuality.

Solidarity was organic inasmuch as it represented the sort of coordination that bodily organs collectively display: complex mutual dependencies bring together the engineer, the baker, the teacher. Yet the picture is also distinctly Durkheimian. As societies evolve from mechanical to organic forms of solidarity, their "collective representations" change accordingly, as do their *consciences collectives*. They become more abstract (a belief in the law or in social equality, for instance), but contribute shared values and symbols that promote social cohesion.[21]

The clearest index of where a society stood among these shifting modes of solidarity was the role of religion. In arguments presaged by his earlier essays, Durkheim insists that "religion is something essentially social." More than this, it imposes the sanctions and obligations that constitute our sociality and curtails our egoism: "It exercises constraint over the individual at every moment. It obliges him to observe practices that are irksome to him and sacrifices, whether great or small, which cost him something. . . . The religious life is made up entirely of abnegation and altruism."[22] Customs forged within religious life persisted in some form for so long that we could forget their connection to religion.

There's nothing auxiliary about religion's role here. If *The Division of Labor in Society* isn't exactly about the genesis of society, in the manner of Rousseau, it's because it has no theoretical space for pre-social persons. The book *is* about the development of society from its simplest stages to its most complex. And what role does religion play for early man? That's the wrong question, Durkheim says, for it implies some zone of activity that is not religious, and there isn't one:

> At this time religion includes everything, extends to everything. It embraces, although in a very confused state, besides religious beliefs proper, ethics, law, the principles of political organisation, and even science, or at least what passes for it. It regulates even the minutiae of private life. Thus to state that religious consciousnesses are then identical, and that this identity is absolute, is implicitly to assert that, except for those sensations that relate to the organism and states of the organism, every individual consciousness is roughly made up of the same elements.

Hence there was, in such communities, no real gap between the individual and the collective consciousness.[23]

A few generations later, some sociologists would see industrial modernity as creating a conformist and culturally homogeneous culture. Durkheim saw the opposite. He was convinced that "the farther we go back in history, the greater the homogeneity." As societies advance, religions become less totalizing, less repressive; Christianity, reproached for its intolerance, was less intolerant than its precursors. "Everyone would acknowledge that the Christian religion is the most idealistic that has ever existed," Durkheim writes. "Thus it is made up of very broad and very general articles of faith much more than of special beliefs and well determined practices. This explains how it came about that the birth of free thinking within the Christian religion took place relatively early on."[24]

But what did we mean by "religion"? Durkheim, in his first book, wasn't ready to offer a definition. ("At the present time we do not possess any scientific conception of what religion is.") He *was* ready to dismiss various definitions on offer: "It has often been stated that at any moment in history religion has consisted of the set of beliefs and sentiments of every kind concerning man's links with a being or beings whose nature he regards as superior to his own. But such a definition is manifestly inadequate." Consider, he says, the raft of prohibitions—dietary, sartorial, and otherwise—that Judaism imposes upon Jews, regulating their conduct with one another and with non-Jews, and conjuring "a sphere of action" that "thus extends far beyond man's communication with the divine." And, anyway, "there exists at least one religion without a god," by which he meant Buddhism. The phenomenon had, in any case, to be understood as constitutively collective. "The sole characteristic that is apparently shared equally by all religious ideas and sentiments is that they are common to a certain number of individuals living together," he writes. "Moreover, their average intensity is fairly high. Indeed, it is invariably the fact that when a somewhat strong conviction is shared by a single community of people it inevitably assumes a religious character."[25]

And yet—here Durkheim is aligned with many of those he criticizes, including Spencer and Guyau—"if there is one truth that history has incontrovertibly settled, it is that religion extends over an ever-diminishing area of social life. Originally, it extended to everything; everything social was religious—the two words were synonymous. Then gradually political, economic and scientific functions broke free from the religious function, becoming separate entities and taking on more and more a markedly temporal character. God, if we may express it in such a way, from being at first present in every human relationship, has progressively withdrawn."[26]

Everything social was religious: the significance of this equation shouldn't be missed. Throughout his career, Durkheim's central concern was to establish society as an independent object of study—one not epiphenomenal on social psychology or anything else. So it's significant that Durkheim had, in the long book that marked his arrival on the intellectual stage, decided that the constitution of society could be understood only through religion, and, equally, that the constitution of religion could be understood only through society. Of the two big volumes that bookended his career, one emphasized the former proposition, the other emphasized the latter.

Durkheim's second book, *Rules of Sociological Method*, which appeared in 1895, introduced adjustments to the theory. It's in this work that he introduces his notion of *faits sociaux, or* "social facts"—social facts being, in effect, social forces that were to be understood in their independent reality. The imperative was to "treat social facts as things," he wrote. "A social fact is identifiable through the power of external coercion which it exerts or is capable of exerting upon individuals," he explained, but he swiftly qualified the assertion, for social facts can equally be "ways of functioning," and "collective ways of being." To say that religion was a social fact did not mean it was a static one. Once more, he depicted religion as a contracting domain: "we have been able to show that the present weakening of religious beliefs and, more generally, of collective sentiments towards collective objects, is utterly normal; we have proved that such weakening becomes increasingly marked as societies evolve toward our present type."[27]

Although he drops any discussion of the *conscience collective*, he makes more extensive use of *représentations collectives*—emotions and tendencies that arise not from individual states of consciousness but from "the conditions under which the body social as a whole exists." These *représentations* must be understood as affective as well as ideational: "What a gulf, for example, between the feelings that man experiences when confronted with forces superior to his own and the institution of religion with its beliefs and practices, so multifarious and complicated, and its material and moral organization!" He also returns to the notion that religion is socially elemental: "Sociologists and historians tend increasingly to come together in their common affirmation that religion is the most primitive of all social phenomena. It is from it that have emerged, through successive transformations, all the other manifestations of collective activity—law, morality, art, science, political forms, etc. In principle, everything is religious."

Durkheim, citing Tylor among others, writes that the comparative study of religion had established "that social phenomena could no longer be deemed the product of fortuitous combinations, arbitrary acts of the will, or local and chance circumstances. Their generality attests to their essential dependence on general causes which, everywhere that they are present, produce their effects. These effects are always the same, endowed with a degree of necessity equal to that of other natural causes."[28] Religion was a social fact, entraining collective representations that had to be, in his formula, treated as a thing. But what exactly was this thing?

RITUAL REVELATIONS

Durkheim claimed that in 1895 he had a "revelation" (surely choosing the scripturally inflected word mischievously), gaining "a clear view of the capital role played by religion in social life." As he explained in a letter, "It was in that year that, for the first time, I found a means of tackling sociologically the study of religion. It was a revelation to me. That lecture course of 1895 marks a watershed in my thinking, so much so that all my previous research had to be started all over again so as to be harmonised with these new views. . . . It was due entirely to the studies of religious history which I had just embarked upon, and in particular to the works of Robertson Smith and his school."[29] His equation of religion and society, in their elementary forms, was unaffected. In truth, the development of his thought, after 1895, was more additive than subtractive—he alighted on a new dichotomy, a new definition, a new account of religion's genesis, nature, and function.

Why was it Robertson Smith who awoke him from his dogmatic slumbers? Essentially, because, as we saw, Robertson Smith inverted Tylor's intellectualism. In Tylor's account, animism, religion in its simplest and earliest form, was a way of making sense of experience. In the classical Greek formula, they were theories that "saved appearances"—that meshed with observed phenomena (such as seeing your dead father while you slept). These elements built on each other, in often self-ratifying ways, and the creeds sponsored rites, rituals, ceremonies. Robertson Smith, again, thought that this belief-centered Tylorian approach was all wrong, a distortion induced by assumptions made by advanced Christian churches. But Robertson Smith had a subtler point to make as well. In ancient societies, he argued, "the gods had their part and place in them equally with men. The circle into which a man was born was not simply a human society, a circle of kinsfolk and fellow citizens, but embraced also certain divine beings, the gods of the family and of the state, which to the ancient mind were as much a part of the particular community with which they stood connected as the human members of the social group." Robertson Smith thus arrived at "the principle that the fundamental conception of ancient religion is the solidarity of the gods and their worshippers as part of one organic society."[30]

Tylor, Spencer, and many others had basically supposed that religion had played an explanatory role that was to be taken up by science, because the two were rival ways of representing the natural world. Religion was an illusion, a misstep to be corrected. Durkheim had, since his twenties, chafed against such accounts; he maintained that religion had a social role to play, too. But Robertson Smith helped him cleave his position from theirs more sharply. Start with the thought that, in ancient religions, deities weren't seen to stand outside of society but to be an integral part of it. Where did that *représentation collective* lead?

LINES OF DEMARCATION

Two essays from 1898 give us clues. One was "De la définition des phénomènes religieux," published in the journal *L'Année sociologique*, which Durkheim established that year, and which became the center of a veritable *Gemeinschaft* of sympathetic scholarship. Here Durkheim introduced a dualism that was to be central to his *Elementary Forms of Religious Life*: "The sacred distinguishes itself from the profane by a difference not simply of quantity but of quality.... The line of demarcation which separates these two worlds comes from the fact that they are not of the same nature, and this duality is only the objective expression of that which exists in our *représentations*." We respond differently to beings whose existence we learn about through ordinary empirical means and those whose existence is described to us through myths and dogmas, and "this division of things into sacred and profane... is the basis of any religious organization."[31]

Durkheim's emphasis on the disjunction between sacred and profane may have reflected urgings from his nephew Marcel Mauss; it resonated, too, with features of Robertson Smith's account. But what catches the eye is how the essay that introduces the dichotomy was also quick to complicate it. Science, Durkheim acknowledged, is also made up of representations, including collective representations, but those are not "expressly mandatory"; it may make sense to believe them, but we're not morally bound to. And then, having established the contrast, Durkheim noted that there are things intermediate between the two realms, citing "the common beliefs of all kinds, relating to apparently secular objects, such as the flag, the fatherland, some form of political organization, some hero or some historical event, etc. that one must call religious." He continued, "Public opinion does not willingly tolerate anyone contesting the superior morality of democracy, the reality of progress, the idea of equality, just as the Christian does not allow his fundamental dogmas to be questioned. The fatherland, the French Revolution, Joan of Arc, etc., are sacred to us all."[32]

Then there's the 1898 essay "L'individualisme et les intellectuels," in which Durkheim, responding to an anti-Dreyfusard polemic, made the case for individualism as the religion of the future. In his books *Division* and *Rules*, society and religion were, in their origins, as one; modernity could be gauged, then, by the withdrawal and segregation of religion. Yet he was now complicating that vision.

Since the essay wasn't intended as a scholarly contribution—it was published in a monthly literary and political magazine—a bit of social context will be helpful. Although Captain Alfred Dreyfus was convicted of treason in 1894, the intense phase of the Dreyfus affair started a few years later, after the military was seen to have suppressed evidence implicating another culprit, and lodged new charges against Dreyfus. Zola's "J'accuse" had appeared in January of 1898; a month later, the Human Rights League was established, with Durkheim among its founding members. By September of 1898, the director of the military secret service admitted to having forged a document that incriminated Dreyfus. For anti-Dreyfusards like Charles Maurras, protecting the institution of the army took precedence over the picayune matter of whether or not Dreyfus was innocent; the intellectuals, a treacherous and self-important cadre, had succumbed to a cult of individualism. So the argument went.

In "Individualism and the Intellectuals," Durkheim sought an alternate way of understanding both religion and individualism. What if individualism—not the self-centered utilitarian conception, but the post-Kantian one of the *droit de l'homme*—was itself at the center of something that could be called religious? This form of individualism at least "seems to those minds who aspire to it to be completely stamped with religiosity," he wrote.

> This human person (*personne humaine*), the definition of which is like the touchstone which distinguishes good from evil, is considered sacred in the ritual sense of the word. It partakes of the transcendent majesty that churches of all time lend to their gods; it is conceived of as being invested with that mysterious property which creates a void about sacred things, which removes them from vulgar contacts and withdraws them from common circulation. And the respect which is given it comes precisely from this source. Whoever makes an attempt on a man's life, on a man's liberty, on a man's honor, inspires in us a feeling of horror analogous in every way to that which the believer experiences when he sees his idol profaned. Such an ethic . . . is a religion in which man is at once the worshiper and the god.[33]

The religion—"la religion de l'humanité"—centered around the advocacy of human rights and the protection of human dignity, and in this way effects the sacralization of the individual. It is, indeed, the only belief system that can "ensure the moral unity of the country." Durkheim saw Christianity as having laid its groundwork (for in Christianity, "the very center of moral life was thus transported from the external to the internal," elevating the individual to be "sovereign judge of his own conduct"). But this emerging religion of humanity would succeed it.

How could someone who had insisted on the priority of the social make this case? By insisting that the individual was not a cause of society (as Rousseau wrongly thought) but rather—as Durkheim had maintained since the 1880s—a product of society. Individualism, properly understood, was "the glorification not of the self but of the individual in general," driven not by egoism but by "sympathy for all that is human, a wider pity for all sufferings, for all human miseries, a more ardent desire to combat and alleviate them, a greater thirst for justice."[34]

Once again, if people are social beings, their egoism must, at some cost to them, be constrained; the sacred plays that role. So does society, as a system of *représentations*—encompassing the values, norms, ideas, and sentiments that attach individuals to something beyond themselves. Comte's "religion of humanity" had been ridiculed; now Durkheim was boldly proposing one of his own.

TOTALIZING TOTEMS

By 1900, Durkheim was giving a lecture series, at Bordeaux, on "The Elementary Forms of Religion." In 1902, he gained a grander academic appointment, at the Sorbonne, and relocated his family (his son André-Armand was born that year) and his intellectual life to Paris, as he'd long hoped to do. That intellectual life now had an institutional cynosure, in *L'Année sociologique*.

In building an intellectual community around this journal, Durkheim was no cult leader, hunting for heresies. But he could be described as a fisher of souls. In this, he was increasingly assisted by

Mauss, always on the lookout for talent. The librarian at the École Normale pitched in as well, directing some of the school's best and brightest in Durkheim's direction—including Antoine Bianconi (who studied West African societies), Jean Reynier (who had expertise in Christian and Hindu asceticism), and Maxime David (who, under Durkheim's supervision, wrote a thesis about group marriages in Australia). Most precious to Durkheim, after Mauss, was Robert Hertz, a *normalien* who took the *agrégation* in 1904, and met with Edward Tylor and James George Frazer in England. Durkheim, worried that Hertz's brilliance was not matched by intellectual focus, took his career in hand; Hertz came to specialize in religious sociology, making a study of funerary rituals. All of these scholars published in the *Année* and many helped edit it. Later there was the emerging incandescence of Durkheim's own son, André, who matriculated at the École Normale at the age of seventeen and proved a brilliant student.

"Sociology is nothing if it is not the science of societies considered concurrently in their organisation, functioning and development," Durkheim wrote in 1903.[35] His developing conviction was that society had a blueprint, and that it was inscribed in the realm of the sacred. But to make his arguments plausible, he sought to ground them in a deeply researched, focused body of ethnographic evidence concerning Australian Aboriginal totemism. *The Elementary Forms of the Religious Life* (1912), his last major work, starts there because it was (he thought) the most primitive religion, in the sense both that it is found in communities with the simplest form of social organization and that none of its features needed to be explained as the result of earlier religions. Hence the subtitle of the original French edition: *Le système totémique en Australie*.

Durkheim's intellectual ingenuity is displayed in the account he offers of Australian totemism as his paradigm of early religion. The essence of totemism, in Durkheim's view, is the identification of the clan with a plant or animal—the totem—and the development of ritual practices around an emblem of that organism, which becomes the most sacred kind of object. If my clan is the clan of the kangaroo, then an abstract symbolic representation of kangaroos, carved on a piece of wood, is, for me and the members of my clan, hemmed about with the prohibitions due such a sacred emblem. Indeed, Durkheim even suggests at one point that the totem *is* this emblem, first and foremost.[36] Next most sacred will be kangaroos themselves and other members of the clan: for these people are kangaroos, too, and, in certain contexts, they will engage in kangaroo-like behavior. Among the taboos will be harming or eating the kangaroo (except within a specific ritual context), and marriage within the clan (and possibly with members of other descent groups associated with it).

Durkheim's most complete explanation of the relations between the clan, the clan animal, and the emblems is this: "Totemism is the religion not of such-and-such animals, or such-and-such people, or such-and such representations, but of a sort of anonymous and impersonal force that is to be found in each of these entities, though without being totally identical with any of them. None of them possesses that force totally and all participate in it." (He had been impressed, as you might suppose, with Codrington's writings about *mana*.) As he goes on to say, "Individuals die, generations pass and are replaced with others, but this force remains forever real, living and like itself. To use the word in a very broad sense, the force is the god that each totemic cult worships."[37] And all these things—the clan animal or plant, the emblems, the force that unites them—are surrounded with taboos, because contact with this force, this god, poses dangers for those not specially prepared for it. Durkheim likens this force to electricity: dangerous to handle, pervasive, powerful.

He thinks these ideas originated in a special kind of social experience in which the Aborigines gathered to dance and sing together in what is now usually called a corroboree. (Such ceremonies had different names in the many Aboriginal languages.)[38] In the course of the rite, they experienced what Durkheim called a collective effervescence, the sort of energy generated in periods of revolutionary collective action—he offers the Crusades and the French Revolution as examples—that enhances the individual power of those who participate in it. The religious idea seems to grow from these contexts of social effervescence.[39] What the Aborigines are responding to is the experience of social union: this is one, immediate sense in which religion is *about* society.

In a number of respects, Durkheim starts with tenets derived from Robertson Smith: that religion is a (totemic) clan cult; that the god is the clan divinized, a representation of that clan; that totemism is the most elementary form of religions.[40] The appeal, for Durkheim, is plain: a specific community, a special sense of the sacred, and a specific commitment to something spiritual in nature. But what explains its persistence? If religions survive for long periods as social institutions, they must have got something right. It is, he tells us, "an essential postulate of sociology that a human institution cannot be based on error and lies. If it did, it could not survive.... There are, therefore, in essence, no religions that are false."[41]

This immediately tells us one thing about religions: they are, or at the very least, they must include, the kinds of things that can have a truth-value. And the obvious candidate for the possession of truth-values are propositions, the things we assert and believe. Durkheim's postulate is, prima facie, a provocation. After all, many familiar claims made in the name of one religion seem at odds with claims made by others. Christianity and Islam disagree about whether Muhammad is a prophet. How can both be true? That would only be a problem, though, if Durkheim had claimed not that *religions* must be true, but that every claim made in the name of a religion must be true; and this he would certainly have denied. Still, one thing that almost everyone in the world agrees about is that most religions are wrong about something really important. Polytheists, like my Asante ancestors, think monotheists and atheists are mistaken: each pays the other the courtesy of thinking the same about the others. In what sense can they all, nevertheless, be true?

The truth of religion, for Durkheim, does not lie in the assertions and beliefs of its adherents. Durkheim, unlike Tylor, takes the literal meaning of religious claims to be one of the least important aspects of their role in explaining social behavior. Tylor had defined religion in terms of the supernatural; Durkheim protested (near the start of *Elementary Forms*) that the very idea of the supernatural was a modern one, predicated on a conceptual contrast with a law-governed natural order of things, a contrast that was of recent origin.

We can best understand Durkheim's view if we start with what he thinks is distinctive of religious belief. The answer is superficially straightforward: religious beliefs, in societies both simple and complex, are in some sense *about* the division of the world of ideas and of things into two classes, the sacred and the profane. "Beliefs, myths, dogmas, legends are representations or systems of representations that express the nature of sacred things, the virtues and the powers that are attributed to them, their history, their relations with one another and with profane things," he writes. But such representations are just one of the two main kinds of religious phenomena. The other is ritual: behavior governed by the strictures concerning how one should relate to sacred things.[42]

The sacred is to Durkheim what animism for Tylor: the key to unlocking the door to religion. And, indeed, *mana* and magic both figure as examples of the sacred. Durkheim is keen to point out that his theory explains why you can count Buddhism as a religion, even though it has no soul and no gods: precisely because the Four Sacred Truths are, indeed, sacred, so are the practices that derive from them, which makes them instances of ritual.[43] But it is also crucial to Durkheim's view that these beliefs and rituals play a role in binding those who share them into the moral community that he calls a church.

The first chapter of *The Elementary Forms* offers this well-known definition: "A religion is a unifying system of beliefs and of practices in relation to sacred things—that is, things kept apart, forbidden—beliefs and practices that unite all those who adhere to them into one moral community, called the Church." (Note that the definition leaves out a crucial element of his theory of religion: sacred objects represent or symbolize social facts, which is why they're sacred.) He notes that in saying "the concept of religion is inseparable from the idea of a church," he is indicating, as he so often had, "that religion has to be something profoundly collective."[44] When Bronisław Malinowski reviewed Durkheim's book, not long after its publication, he observed that for Durkheim, "the distinctive characters of social and religious phenomena practically coincide."[45]

In the theory that Durkheim favors, "religion ceases to be some inexplicable hallucination and gains a footing in reality. We can, in fact, say that the believer is not mistaken when he believes in the existence of a moral power on which he depends and from which he receives what's best in himself: this power exists, it is society." He goes on to write that religion's principal objective

> is not to give man a representation of the physical universe; if that were its essential task, one could not understand how it could have endured, since, in this respect, it is scarcely more than a tissue of errors. But, above all, it is a system of ideas by means of which individuals represent to themselves the society of which they are members, and relationships, obscure but intimate, that they have with it. This is its primordial role; and though it is metaphorical and symbolic, this representation is not unfaithful.[46]

Previously, we surveyed various concepts that were circulating during Durkheim's intellectual formation—concepts that he took up or took issue with. Here, at last, we have a thesis that seems both an organic outgrowth of his earlier preoccupations and a genuinely original formulation.

PUTTING PSYCHOLOGY IN ITS PLACE

Durkheim was resolutely opposed to using postulates about individual psychology to explain the existence of totems and taboos. Consider his refusal to treat an instinctual aversion to incest as an explanation for the incest taboo.[47] Rather, he thought, the incest taboo developed because of the fundamental incompatibility between the nature of family relationships (of parents to children and sibling to sibling), on the one hand, and the sentiments associated with sexual relations, on the other. As he pointed out, you could not explain the existence of incest taboos in their actual details as a reflection of a universal psychological tendency, since the incest taboo took different forms in different societies. In the Aboriginal world of totems, for example, you could not have sexual relations with any fellow member of your clan—anyone with whom you shared a totem. In Asante, where I grew up, you could marry the child of your father's sister but not the child of your mother's sister. The official explanation of the Asante ban on sex with members of one's matriclan—the group of people with whom one shares descent in the maternal line—is that you are all of the same "blood," since your blood comes, in Asante conceptions of the human person, from your mother.

Durkheimian sociologists would look elsewhere and see this talk of blood as being the result—not the cause—of the incest taboo. And they would point to the fact that in traditional Asante families, children don't live with both parents; they live with their mother and her siblings, along with the children of her sisters. Our Durkheimian sociologists would also have taken notice of the fact that in Twi, the Asante language, the most natural word to use to refer to one's brothers and sisters, which is *nua*, is the same as the word for one's mother's sister's children. To refer specifically to your siblings, you have to say "nua, from the same belly." Once you have developed this system and the belief in common blood, you will have reason to avoid marriage with anyone in your matriclan—those with whom you share descent in the female line from a common ancestress.

Durkheim's chariness about invoking individual psychology didn't mean he denied that an individual *had* a psychology. He wasn't disputing that institutions were made up of people whose psychological states could be enlisted to explain their behavior; nor did he dispute that the institutions were, in an important respect, made up of their interactions. Every truth about organizations, we can agree, is made true by individual people doing things. The collective rituals exist because people make and do things. And what they make and do determines what form the ritual takes. So a story about individual agents *must*, in some sense, underly every truth about institutions.

To see that this fact establishes less than we might hope (or fear), we need the useful distinction between ontological individualism—the claim that *organizational facts are made up of facts about individuals*, so that, in particular, if all the individual facts are the same, the organizational facts can't be different—and methodological individualism, which is the claim that *we must always be able to give explanations of social facts in terms of facts about the individuals composing them*. Notice that methodological individualism doesn't follow from ontological individualism, any more than the fact that every organism is made up of atoms interacting according to natural laws means that we cannot give biological explanations—in population biology, say—that don't mention atoms at all. The general point is that there are social facts: that is, stable generalizations that we don't know—and don't need to know—how to derive from the aggregation of individual behaviors. And, Durkheim argued, there are stable relationships between one social fact and another, which is why sociology has a subject. Your individual human mind, in turn, is in part a product of its interactions with others in a society that was already up and running when you arrived. Since what an individual believes and desires is shaped by experience in that society, what people believe and desire always depends, in part, on the nature of their society. Since societies differ, people are likely to end up wanting and believing different things.

Incest taboos are certainly a concrete illustration of the power and limitations of Durkheim's model. Societies, Durkheim says, have developed incest taboos delineated in terms of particular relationships defined by ancestry. Those with whom sexual relations are forbidden are those with whom we have a kind of relationship that would be undermined by our having sex with them: sex with an opposite-sex parent or sibling would impose on our relationship with them a set of sentiments that would damage our relationship with the other members of the group in which we have grown up. But this is not the explanation given by members of the society themselves. So why do societies invent the elaborate structure of totem and taboo, of matriclan exogamy, rather than simply settling on the rule that you cannot have sex with people who belong to the household in which you grew up? And even if the incest taboo serves the function of keeping two important kinds of relationships distinct, how did it come about that the incest taboo was developed to serve that function, especially since people don't acknowledge that this is the reason it exists?

A similar objection can be raised against Durkheim's claim that totemism *expresses* facts about social relations because it grows out of the particular social experience of the corroboree. The whole system is fantastically more complex than is necessary to achieve the effect of stabilizing the ritual, even if we accept that the ritual does serve as a kind of social glue, bringing people together regularly in an institution where they can experience the rewards of "collective effervescence," and become a "moral community," bound to one another by obligations and entitlements.

Such gaps, though, are surely inevitable in historical accounts. Human institutions may need to be useful to survive, but there is never a unique solution to the problems that they solve. And one universal human tendency is to elaborate theories and practices, giving new twists and turns to old patterns. We can believe that totemism, the religious system whose elaborate structures Durkheim sought to explore and explain, solves certain problems in the social life of Australia's diverse Aboriginal peoples, while denying that every feature of that system must serve some purpose, and while being confident that myriad other systems would have met the need.

BLURRED LINES

Although Durkheim's analysis of religion could negotiate away certain challenges, other difficulties were harder to dodge. His most pointed attack on Tylor, recall, was that a naturalistic account of a belief in the supernatural undermines that belief. As he had complained, "What kind of science is it if its biggest discovery is proving its own subject matter to be an illusion?" But how could a religion survive the argument that it functions, with some accuracy, to represent one's society and one's relation to it? That makes religion "true" in a way that matters only to a sociologist. For Durkheim, the symbolic content of religious beliefs and practices—in other words, what these beliefs and practices *express*—is the deep truth of our social relations, our profound dependence not on something outside the human world but on our own societies. Though they may encode this dependence, however, they are not understood by the practitioners to do so. So while Durkheim protested that the Tylorians thought religion was mostly untrue, Durkheim makes the truth of religion something that the religious do not know.

And how do I know that Durkheim's account *is* true? Durkheim is perhaps drawn to totemism because it seems to illustrate the thesis with special clarity: clan, totem, the divinization of society through the repertory of the sacred. Later research has complicated and corrected various ethnographic details on which Durkheim relied. But the most important of his mistakes is surely the belief that totemism is "the most primitive and the simplest religion it is possible to find."[48] Robertson Smith had laid out this view in his *Kinship and Marriage in Early Arabia* (1885), but there is little reason to think that the earliest forms of something we might recognize as religion were like the system of ritual and belief that the Aborigines of Australia (or certain Tribal Nations of North America, whose totems he also discussed) had developed over a long history by the time Europeans first came upon them. It is true that Durkheim says it doesn't matter whether or not totemism was once universal.[49] But he does take it to be representative of the oldest and simplest forms of religious life.

There's also the question of whether the contrast between the sacred and the profane can be sustained in the way that *Elementary Forms* asks. Here was Durkheim's official explanation of what the sacred is: "Sacred things are those that are protected and isolated by prohibitions; profane ones, those to which these prohibitions apply, the latter having to keep their distance from the former. Religious beliefs express the nature of sacred things and the relation they enter into, whether with each other or with profane things." Religious rituals, in turn, are forms of behavior governed by the rules, not least taboos, that regulate how human beings should behave in relation to the sacred.[50]

But many anthropologists balked at segregating the sacred and the profane. Evans-Pritchard, in his consistently penetrating and occasionally pettish *Theories of Primitive Religion* (1965), considers Durkheim's dichotomy between sacred and profane to be discredited by the ethnographic evidence: "Far from being cut off from each other, they are so closely intermingled as to be inseparable." (He recalls the Azande stations that were meant to provide portals for tributes to ancestors, but that were often just useful for propping your sword against.)[51] Durkheim himself had made this point in his earlier work, citing the drear prohibitions of kashrut, and, more generally, the distance between the organized modern church and the elemental experience of awe. Nor is the demarcation easily applied in other areas where he thought it must. For Durkheim, for example, morality is derivative of religion and so of the sacred, but plenty of our "thick" moral concepts are both normative and descriptive—we have no difficulty blending moral and nonmoral explanations and, in fact, struggle not to.

And then, Evans-Pritchard contends, there's a methodological awkwardness in the effervescence thesis: "Fundamentally Durkheim elicits a social fact from crowd psychology." Now, social facts are supposed to be, as Evans-Pritchard observes, "traditional, general, and obligatory." Language is a good example: it has a history we don't fully comprehend; everyone in a closed society participates; and its character isn't just up to us. But effervescence doesn't look like that; it's something that a group of individuals experience together, a transporting experience of communion, yes, but one that we can make sense of as an individual experience. Language, law, religion: those social facts or forces are irreducibly social in a way that effervescence isn't. A trippy loss of individuality is something that an individual can, as we say, "own." As for the larger argument that religion arose to represent society to itself? Evans-Pritchard thought it was a brilliant and poetic just-so story. "It was Durkheim and not the savage," as he'd previously written, "who made society into a god."[52]

HOMO DUPLEX

Writing in *Scientia* in 1914, Durkheim issued a sort of addendum to his *Elementary Forms*. He saw a factual basis for "the old formula, Homo duplex." In fact, he maintained, "our internal life has something like a double centre of gravity. On the one hand, there is our individuality, and, more especially, our body that is its foundation; on the other, everything that, within us, expresses something other than ourselves." Echoing a point he had made about Wundt a quarter century earlier, he tells us that we are, as a result, always at odds with ourselves: "Our joys can never be pure; there is always some pain mixed in with them, since we cannot simultaneously satisfy the two beings within us." And religion, he suggested, provides a natural way of representing this internal tension. The soul is always considered sacred, the body profane, and the duality is congruent with the "double existence that we lead simultaneously: one purely individual, which has its roots in our organism, the other social, which is nothing except an extension of society."[53]

The essay picks up on themes that appear earlier in his work, but it also foregrounds certain inconsistencies. If the individual is a product of society, why does Durkheim insist on characterizing the social by its "exteriority to individual minds," by its "coercive action"? Where is this pre-social individual rooted in our organism? The philosopher Alasdair MacIntyre proposed that Durkheim was hobbled by the way that his thought "remains bound by the categories of the very atomistic individualism that he sees himself transcending." That's because individualism is, at essence, a tendency to "frame all questions according to an ostensible antithesis between the individual and the collective." Even if you championed the collective, you adhered to the categories of individualism, reifying these figments: "We see one another as egoistic individuals estranged from a moral collective in many situations, and, seeing and being seen in this way, we often act as if Durkheimian sociology were the truth about society." MacIntyre suspected that Durkheim's social theory supplied "one more dramatic script for the social theaters of an individualist culture."[54]

An alternative approach would say that the story of the individual does not compete in the same explanatory space as the story of the society. But Durkheim could not decide whether the egoistic individual of utilitarianism was a misconceived artifact of an erroneous theory or was an actual mode of human existence, in which we are driven by our sensory appetites. The boldest claim in Steven Lukes's magisterial five-decade-old intellectual biography of Durkheim remains rather persuasive: that, in their form, all Durkheim's dichotomies—individual/society, profane/sacred, psychology/sociology, sensual appetites/moral rules, pathological/normal, anomie/integration—were effectively one.[55]

Durkheim's models, it should be admitted, always struggled to accommodate conflict. He was sympathetic to socialism (nearly everyone in his *équipe* was, usually with greater warmth), but not to class struggle. He believed in the *patrie*—or, more precisely, he believed in believing in the *patrie*—but he also thought that Europe's fatherlands were bound to coalesce into larger units. He believed in social progression, despite himself, and when war broke out, in the year that he published his dualism essay, he was unprepared for the malign collective effervescence that spilled across the map. He threw himself into propaganda efforts (a study of Heinrich von Treitschke was the basis of a study of the German national character), while his protégés threw themselves into battle.

Durkheim saw the conflict as between civilization and barbarism; he celebrated French victories, anticipated the collapse of the Austro-Hungarian empire, and convinced himself that "the geography of Europe will be redrawn on a rational and moral basis." Hertz, a student of mortuary rites, had written to his wife, at the start of the hostilities, that he was reluctant "to let my brain be addled and to use the war as an excuse for hating everything German, and for loathing Wagner and Nietzsche." Now he was writing to her, from the front, "As a Jew, I feel that the time has come to give *a little more* than I owe." But he was, to the last, a Durkheimian sociologist. The war was, he said, "a fantastic experience of collectivism."[56]

The religion of inhumanity had swept over Europe. Then the reports came in; the best and the brightest of the *Année* circle, fallen on the field: Antoine Bianconi, Maxim David, and then Jean Reynier. When Hertz, dearest of them all to Durkheim, died in battle on April 13, 1915, Durkheim visited his wife, who read aloud his letters to her. In mid-December, Durkheim stopped receiving letters from his son, André, who had been killed in the front lines in Bulgaria, although his father was not officially informed until late February. In an obituary for him, Durkheim wrote that André had "a sense of self-abnegation that naturally and painlessly prepared him to make sacrifices. . . . And so, he quite simply did the things that put an end to his life."[57]

Durkheim never quite recovered. He described his grief in clinical terms: "Basically, I have to convince myself that what has happened is real, so as to ensure that I do not go on seeing two contradictory images that are in conflict with one another." The therapy for this "greatest evil that besets men" had seen no advancement. There was, he wrote to Mauss, a wound:

> The wound is localized; it is clean, and I am keeping an eye on it. What comes out of it is fresh blood, and it bleeds all the time. It opens up 10 or 20 times a day—I really can't say how many times—and bleeds a little. That is a good description of my position.[58]

His health declined swiftly. Marcel Mauss wasn't alone in thinking that the son's death brought about the father's, two years later. Émile Durkheim was buried in the *Israëlite* section of the cemetery at Montparnasse in 1917. A Hebrew inscription—an acronymized passage from 1 Samuel 25:29 found on Ashkenazi graves around the world—was chiseled, in the customary way, onto his tombstone: *May his soul be bound up in the bundle of the living.*

CHAPTER 3

Georg Simmel

The Feelings and the Forms

FLESH WOUNDS — BERLIN BOY — THE SOCIAL SYLLABUS — DIFFERENTIATING BEINGS — GENEALOGY OF MORALS — THE MAGIC WORD — STRANGER AMONG US — THE REIGN OF RELIGIOSITY — REACHING FOR THE ABSOLUTE — THE THREAT OF SOCIOLOGY — VITAL SIGNS — AXIAL ROTATIONS

FLESH WOUNDS

It's a commonplace of intellectual history that Georg Simmel, though less known than Durkheim and Weber, was equally among the founders of sociology. What set him apart was an acute and subtle historicism; he was alive to the contingencies of time and place, aware that many things we take for granted are the deliverances of a particular past. So it's appropriate to reflect that, if an assailant's bullets had been slightly better aimed, he would not have played that role at all. Simmel, avowedly wary about defining religion, nonetheless ventured that what all religions shared was a story about surviving death, about how our souls might persist after our bodies gave out. In this respect, religion was the answer to the problem posed by our mortality. In a startling episode that took place when Simmel was still in his twenties, the problem must have been borne on him with particular force.

The episode was, at the same time, a story about money, a subject he would soon be writing about. Rentiers need rent collectors, and Simmel, who had been effectively adopted by the businessman Julius Friedländer, was charged with administering some of the man's properties in Berlin. Among its tenants was a certain Guggenbüchler, who manufactured and traded bronze goods, and had evidently fallen on hard times; his rent was two quarters in arrears. On the morning of October 30, 1886, Guggenbüchler called on Simmel at his home on Landgrafenstrasse, and, as they spoke outside, asked whether he could maintain his residence if he made good on his arrears. Simmel told him that he could, but that he would also be responsible for the legal fees that had been incurred.

"I can't pay it," the tenant said. "Everything is finished." He pulled out a revolver and started firing. As the twenty-eight-year-old academic fled, one bullet struck him in his left shoulder; another pierced his hat and grazed his head. Guggenbüchler then made himself scarce, while Simmel proceeded to make himself abundant, presenting a paper on the "psychology of money" a couple of years later and then influencing a generation of social theorists.[1]

"If sociology succeeds in developing itself into an autonomous individual science, then its future historian will have to celebrate Simmel as its founder," wrote Alfred Vierkandt, who later held the first chair in sociology at the University of Berlin, in a review of Simmel's eight-hundred-page magnum opus, *Soziologie*. The uncertain disciplinary status of sociology and Simmel's conditional role as a progenitor are both significant in this declaration. It's possible to simplify the matter of credit by specifying further the kind of sociology associated with him; some see Simmel as anticipating the symbolic interactionist school, the Chicago school, or conflict theory. More broadly, Simmel has been called the founder of the "humanist version" of sociology. Evidently, the trajectory of a discipline is subject to ballistic analysis, too.[2]

But whereas Durkheim was intent on entrenching sociology as an intellectual paradigm and an academic discipline, Simmel sought to probe and problematize its status. What *is* society, and what are its conditions of possibility? What, if anything, made sociology a separate field of inquiry? Unlike Durkheim, he never held an academic position that described him as other than a philosopher, and he sometimes declared himself puzzled that his readers abroad took him as a sociologist. In truth, he was like one of those confluences where differently angled rivers and watercourses meet with an explosive churning. His thought productively encompassed contending intellectual currents—historicism and neo-Kantianism; psychologism and anti-psychologism. Again and again, he sought to use the riddle of religion to sort through the riddle of society as well as vice versa. And a central part of his analysis was something that played a notably limited role in both Tylor and Durkheim's work: the emotional dimensions of religious beliefs and practices—the "religiosity" that he took to be prior to religion itself.

BERLIN BOY

Simmel and Durkheim were born within weeks of each other, in the spring of 1858, and Simmel survived Durkheim by less than a year; like Durkheim, he was of Jewish ancestry. In other respects, they were a study in contrasts. While Durkheim grew up in the provinces in materially modest but religiously rich circumstances, Simmel's situation was the opposite. Sociologists interested in the sociology of their profession take note that Simmel emerged from the *Besitzbürgertum*—the affluent and property-owning stratum of the bourgeoisie. He was an urban sophisticate from birth, reared within an only perfunctorily religious household in a posh neighborhood of Berlin. Durkheim was, by temperament, an ascetic who didn't quite see the point to the arts (his wife, who had enjoyed playing the piano in her youth, took it up again only after his death); Simmel was an aesthete, who loved and wrote about music, painting, and sculpture. Both of Simmel's parents had converted to Christianity, though different kinds. His father, a merchant, had become a Roman Catholic on one of his journeys to Paris in the 1830s; his mother's family had converted to Protestantism, and Georg himself was baptized Protestant. But religion, for the Simmels, was evidently more a matter of convenience than conscience. His father—whose enterprises included a candy business that became the well-known Felix & Sarotti chocolate brand—died when Simmel was sixteen.³ That's why Georg, the youngest of seven children, was taken in hand by his guardian Julius Friedländer, a successful bookseller and music publisher (he acquired and modernized what became the Edition Peters), and eventually came into a small fortune. The man best known for *The Philosophy of Money* was no stranger to money.

It would be easy, perhaps too easy, to map Simmel's religious dislocations onto features of his later sociological accounts, in which individuals are at once within society and without it, and in which tensions arise between the self-fulfilling impulses of the individual and the demands of a society. His upbringing appears to have been largely secular; but as he knew well, you didn't have to practice Judaism to be considered a Jew. Simmel was thirteen when Jewish emancipation was extended throughout a united Germany, in 1871. Most Germans and many Jews themselves would still have conceived of Jewish people as being members of a nationality or descent group (*klal yisrael* was what rabbis called the collectivity) as much as practitioners of a creed.

And so the specific character of Simmel's religious identity posed difficulties for others, and sometimes for himself. Observant Jews often regarded the *getaufte Juden* (baptized Jews) with disdain or resentment, while many Christians continued to see baptized Jews (a category that included many prominent Jewish academics, from Max Scheler to Husserl) as alien, in ways that Simmel later touched on in his essay "The Stranger." Simmel, who as an adult disavowed any religious allegiances, never claimed to be other than Jewish; he enjoyed telling Jewish stories to his son, and, when his future father-in-law, a gentile, asked if he was a Jew (*Sind Sie Jude?*), he replied, "My nose gives it away unmistakably." When a medieval historian at the University of Berlin, Dietrich Schäfer, sought to block Simmel's appointment to a chair at Heidelberg, he wrote to a government official that Simmel was "an Israelite through and through, in his outward appearance, in his manners, and in his way of thinking." Klaus Christian Köhnke, in his invaluable intellectual biography *Der junge Simmel*, says that, given the way others would type him, Simmel often left the house as a German and returned as a Jew.⁴

At the same time, Simmel scarcely wrote about himself as Jewish and never saw himself as representing Jewish opinion. When he once remarked to Martin Buber, who had been a student of his, that "we are a curious people," Buber made note of the first-person plural, simply because it was so unusual. Simmel dismissed Zionism and saw an ongoing process of mutual acculturation between Jews and their European compatriots. ("Europeans and Jews are locked in a tight cultural embrace. They are inseparable.")[5] His interest in the Bible was merely anthropological.

Simmel's interest in Berlin, by contrast, ran through his *kishkes*. Leaving home for college was a trip he could make on foot. It was in the summer of 1876 that Simmel matriculated at the University of Berlin—then formally known as Friedrich-Wilhelms-Universität zu Berlin, and now as Humboldt-Universität zu Berlin. There his instructors included the historians Theodor Mommsen and Heinrich von Treitschke, the ethnologist Adolf Bastian, and the philosophers Moritz Lazarus (who lectured on psychology) and Heymann Steinthal (who was also a philologist and Old Testament scholar, not to mention Lazarus's brother-in-law and collaborator). In 1881 he received a doctorate in philosophy for a thesis concerning Kant and the nature of matter. (An earlier thesis on the evolutionary origins of music was rejected.) His "habilitation" thesis, necessary for securing an academic position, concerned Kant and spacetime, and initially ran into difficulties, but with the support of Wilhelm Dilthey, among others, was accepted. A further delay arose, it seems, because during the subsequent oral examination Simmel was rudely dismissive toward a professor who floated a theory about a neuronal seat of the soul. But once again Simmel's supporters prevailed, and in 1885—the same year that Durkheim visited the campus—he joined the faculty as a *Privatdozent* (lecturer) in philosophy.[6]

THE SOCIAL SYLLABUS

Simmel's social turn—taking up the challenge of theorizing human collectivities—was the act less of a rebel than of a sophisticate. His key influences, in his student years, were scholars oriented toward collectivist models. An array of such approaches—from Spencer's "social statics" to Taine's "milieu theory"—had emerged and gained traction since the 1860s; they were trendy at the University of Berlin. Simmel gives a clue to the intellectual milieu in which he had been marinating when he avowed that Moritz Lazarus (who was unusual in being a full professor and an unconverted Jew) and Heymann Steinthal had been singular influences on him. The two were founders of a would-be discipline we've encountered before: *Völkerpsychologie*. (How to translate *Völkerpsychologie* was soon a matter of vigorous dispute: folk psychology, ethnic psychology, social psychology, psychology of peoples?) Lazarus had introduced the term in 1851, and, with Steinthal, founded the journal *Zeitschrift für Völkerpsychologie und Sprachwissenschaft*, in 1860. The aim was what they sometimes called a "mental ethnology"—a supraindividual study of behavior, values, inner life. In demarcating their object of study, they enlisted an older term, the *Volksgeist*, associated with *Gesamtheitsgeist* (group spirit), and they made mention, too, of the *Geister* of "religious communities, of social estates, of scientific and artistic schools, and others indeed." The two were very clear that the *Volksgeist* was something that people had fashioned and that fashioned people. But Lazarus and Steinthal were vigorous anti-reductionists: what existed in the relation between and among persons could not be reduced to a mere aggregation of individuals.[7]

"Psychology teaches that people are entirely and in their essence social [*gesellschaftlich*]," they wrote in 1860, in the first volume of their new journal. "No human being has become what he is purely from himself but only under the determining influence of the society in which he lives." The two envisaged a sort of metadiscipline that could draw from empirical psychology, ethnology, philosophy, philology, and history. "Is not a community like a moral and legal person?" Lazarus wrote later. "And does it not fulfill all the human, moral, and political interests just like an individual, and in a manner indifferent to the particular people now belonging to it?" The individual could be understood only as an entity embedded in society. Lazarus noted that while individuals are united in an ecclesiastical community, people tend to discharge their moral responsibilities "without knowing that in their actions they are doing something for society; and with a religious attitude, individuals position themselves before their God without recognizing it as having any social significance in it. Morality and religion appear as purely private matters." Yet, he notes, this is far from the case. He observes that Protestantism seems to favor individualism, Catholicism a greater sense of social unity; and yet in Catholic Italy, religious individualism developed freely, while certain Protestant sects, such as the Brüdergemeine Herrnhut (also known as the Moravian Church, or Unitas Fratrum), created "the highest degree of community."[8]

In an alternative world, this would-be discipline might have supplanted sociology. It clearly left an imprint on at least one of its founders; for one thing, an important concept of Simmel's, the notion of *Verdichtung* (condensation, compression, crystallization), was first introduced by Lazarus. "I will never forget that, above all others, you forcibly directed me to the problem of the supra-individual," Simmel wrote to Lazarus, in 1894.[9] But where Lazarus and Steinthal ran into trouble was in placing argumentative weight on vague-seeming concepts like *Volksgeist* and *Volksseele* ("folk spirit" and "folk soul"). It was a period in which neo-Kantians (whose subject-centered approach wasn't readily reconciled with the social turn) were preoccupied with "how do you know?" questions; a period in which every discipline was to come equipped with a theory of knowledge. *Völkerpsychologie* was seen to come up short in this respect. Toward the start of his first book-length publication about sociology, Simmel specifically, if implicitly, quarrels with the model, even though it presaged many of his own positions.

One reason was probably his exposure to Wilhelm Dilthey, who joined the University of Berlin in 1882, and, the following year, published his influential *Einleitung in die Geisteswissenschaften*, which has been published in English as *Introduction to the Human Sciences*. It was this work that gave currency to the term *Geisteswissenschaften*, in the context of an argument about the relationship between the natural sciences and humanistic knowledge. How best to translate *Geisteswissenschaften* has been contentious, too; *Geist* means mind, psyche, spirit—but was it the instrument of inquiry or the object of inquiry? *Wissenschaft* is tricky, too: as a term for a systematic body of knowledge, it is typically translated as "science," but would perhaps be more aptly rendered in modern English as "scholarship" or "study" or "discipline," inasmuch as it encompasses both humanistic and natural-scientific knowledge.[10] Dilthey, who had been a friend of Lazarus's, faulted *Völkerpsychologie* for emulating the methods of the natural sciences in doing the work of the humanities.

What's easy to overlook is that Dilthey's *Introduction to the Human Sciences*, subtitled "an attempt to lay a foundation for the study of society and history," was, in broad terms, also a chronicle of the rise of secularism. It told of how mythical thought in Europe gave way first to religious thought—which Dilthey characterized as mythical thought amalgamated with metaphysics and self-reflection—and then to scientific modes of thought. Religion was insusceptible to scientific attack, in Dilthey's view, because it "points to inner experience"; he maintained that *"religious life is the permanent substratum of intellectual development and not a passing phase in man's mental life."* He took from Schleiermacher and from Max Müller the notion that religious states of mind involved a consciousness of dependence and the experience of a higher being independent of nature. And to get at religious life, we were to attend to the undeniable presence of *Erlebnis* (lived experience) or *innerer Erfahrung* (inner experience, in a reflective and cumulative sense of "experience").[11]

Dilthey's celebrated contrast between *Verstehen* and *Erklären*, understanding and explanation, arose in this context. The natural sciences aim to explain (*erklären*) natural phenomena by identifying general laws and causal mechanisms, developing—by means of observation, experimentation, and quantitative analysis—knowledge that is objective, context-independent, and universal; the human sciences (our *Geisteswissenschaften*) set out to understand (*verstehen*) human phenomena in their peculiar historical and cultural contexts. *Verstehen* requires knowledge of subjective human experience, arrived at through interpretation, self-reflection (*Selbstbesinnung*), and re-living (*Nacherleben*: by which we seek imaginative access to another's lived experience). It called for efforts to understand motives, intentions, and meanings from the inside.

Where did psychology fit in? That depended on what you meant by psychology. Dilthey, in his middle period, inked a very thick line between descriptive, analytic psychology and empirical, explanatory (*erklärende*) psychology. The first was the humanistic kind; the second was the naturalistic kind. In his *Introduction*, Dilthey wrote, "The human being as a fact which precedes history and society is a fiction of genetic explanation. The man whom sound analytical science studies is the individual as a component of society. The difficult problem which psychology has to solve is this: analytical knowledge of the universal characteristics of this man."[12]

Dilthey's *Introduction* took aim at *Völkerpsychologie*: wasn't *Volksgeist* a mystification, a hypostasis of an indeterminate abstraction? (The term *Volksgeist* was given currency by Hegel; Herder, with whom it has long been associated, did not use it, but did refer to "Geist des Volkes" and "Genius der Völker.") Such concepts were "as useless for history as the concept of living force is for physiology." Dilthey was equally harsh about what passed as sociology. He took aim at the "science of society" as Lorenz von Stein had conceived it, where society was a way station between the state and the individual; he also took aim at sociology as Comte, Spencer, and Mill conceived it. We were to be wary of the rage for generalization. Dilthey accuses Comte of founding his sociology on "crude naturalistic metaphysics." He bemoans the "monotonous and tiresome prattling of the words induction and deduction" in Mill's ventures into the human sciences. We should mistrust a "science of systems of culture and external organization of society." (Among the culprits he singled out was the "system of natural religion" promulgated in the seventeenth and eighteenth centuries.) Discussing the rise of a science of society in France and in Germany, he suggests that the question of whether a special science of this sort is likely to be fruitful—of whether "staking out a science of sociology" was justified—was akin to the "the question whether a knife lying before me is sharp or not. One has to cut." Sociology, in his view, was not a "true science." At the same time, Dilthey saw value in comparative linguistics, in anthropology ("no exact scientist ignores the link with anthropology anymore"), in approaches to the social sphere that were alert to the specificity of time and place rather than those that sought to abstract themselves from "historico-social reality."[13]

Gustav Schmoller, a leading light of the (younger) "Historical school" of economics, was another inescapable presence for Simmel. He did not study with Schmoller, but the economist, who had joined the University of Berlin in 1882, was effectively a patron of his;

Simmel published eight papers in the senior scholar's *Jahrbuch*. Much in Schmoller's general orientation would have been welcoming to Simmel's emerging study of society. Schmoller was among those skeptical of abstractions that were unmoored from the specifics of historically grounded institutions. In 1889 and 1890, Schmoller published a pair of essays in which, championing a sort of methodological holism, he described how the division of labor would emerge from a cohesive society but eventually pose a threat to that cohesion, through the creation of social classes—requiring institutions to mediate these tensions. (Here, he parts ways with Durkheim.) Drawing on Albert Schäffle, he later argued that the "social organ" can be considered, from the outside, as a unity, and "from the inside as a structured plurality."[14]

The arguments advanced by Lazarus (1824–1903), Dilthey (1833–1911), and Schmoller (1838–1917), to place them in birth order, represented three distinct conceptions of social science, as Köhnke notes.[15] They did not coexist harmoniously; they had different ways of addressing now familiar problems—what later theorists would know as the structure-versus-agency problem, say, or the problem of reflexivity (people shaping norms that shape people). But what mattered more, for our purposes, was simply that they were attempting to theorize society into existence, and persuading Simmel to try his own hand at it.

DIFFERENTIATING BEINGS

As a *Privatdozent*, Simmel was paid not by the university but by the students who attended his lectures; fortunately for him, his lectures were popular. At first, they focused on philosophy, especially ethics, but in time he took on sociological topics not taught elsewhere at the university. In 1890, he married the intellectually formidable Gertrud Kinel, who was baptized Catholic and reared Protestant, and who, three decades later, published the book *Über das Religiöse (About the Religious)*. A number of scholars, discussing Simmel's early work, hastily suppose that he went through a "positivist" phase; the term is loosely flung around. In fact, he had been carefully inculcated into hostility toward positivism from his student days; that he occasionally referred to Spencer, or offered conjectures about origins (to be taken, he warned, as perhaps no more than methodological fictions), did not make him a positivist, in any meaningful sense of this multivalent term.[16] What we find instead, in his writings from this decade, is a boldness of argumentation not yet quite weatherproofed against philosophical concerns about social evolutionism, hypostasis (wrongly treating theoretical constructs as if they had an independent substance or essence), and the like.

Simmel's earliest major contribution to sociology, his 147-page tract *Über sociale Differenzierung* (*On Social Differentiation*), was published in 1890 in Schmoller's series *Political and Social Science Research*. (Tönnies gave it a polite but mixed review; Durkheim added a reference to it in the second edition of his *Division of Labor in Society*.) Although Simmel would later complicate and qualify various of its claims, the book contains basic tenets found in his mature thought. There's the dynamic relationship between society and the individual, taken as both product and producer of society; the link between the growth of a society in scale and complexity and the increasing specialization of roles within it; the difficulty of new content, new thoughts, being subsumed into old, solidified forms, or categories.

The title anticipates Durkheim's *The Division of Labor in Society*, which appeared three years later, and some of its themes presage Durkheim's. Simmel and Durkheim agree (as Tönnies and Spencer had before them) that the small, primitive group is characterized by a much higher degree of solidarity and uniformity among its members than later, larger ones. Simmel even says, in a para-Durkheimian way, that the early church community was an area in which "the social structure as such came easily into consciousness."

And yet Simmel's emphasis is, in some respects, the reverse of Durkheim's in *The Division of Labor in Society*. For Simmel, a person is "a differentiating being" (*ein Unterschiedswesen*).[17] Whereas Durkheim foregrounds the social entity, Simmel is especially interested in how individuality emerges as collectivities increase in scale and complexity. A person who's a member of multiple, intersecting circles becomes more individuated through a combinatorial process: that is, when you're a node on more and more intersecting circles, you're less and less like anyone else. Our persistent individualities amid our commonalities are what draw Simmel's notice. Because we are social creatures, the measure of our individuality varies with our community. The social organism, Simmel maintains in a striking metaphor, requires a certain amount of nutrition, such that in smaller communities—exemplified by the early church—more is demanded of each member, while in larger ones the burden of providing nourishment is lightened by being more widely distributed, and the demands on each member are less, permitting more individuality.[18]

Once again, the evolution of society is the evolution of religion—but with a twist. Simmel argues that in the early church, community life was entirely permeated by the "religious idea," but when it spread to the masses, a necessary measure of profanation was inevitable. To perpetuate and stabilize itself at scale, religion was obliged to spawn secularity: "The unity of religion and life broke down into a secular and a religious status, a differentiation within the sphere of the Christian religion that was absolutely necessary for its continued existence, if it was to transcend its original narrow boundaries."[19] Only by breaking away from "undifferentiated togetherness," he thought, was it possible for a larger group to coexist within a religious framework. The division of labor, then, arose within a context where the labor was often spiritual. Even in early times, he says, the church sustained a division between the spiritual aristocracy and the *misera contribuens plebs* (the poor plebeians who contribute). In his mischievous gloss: "The priesthood of the Catholic Church, which mediates the believer's relationship to heaven, is just the result of the very same division of labor that constituted the post office as a special social institution for mediating the citizen's relationship to distant places."[20] When small dissenting groups break off, in turn, they may distinguish themselves by offering an unmediated relationship with the Almighty.

A few other points of emphasis in the book are worth attention. One is that Simmel recognizes the way that a religion may serve as the basis of a collective identity precisely to the extent that it meets antagonism from without. When a group faces another, hostile one, we should expect an increase in internal solidarity. (France, he observes, essentially owes its sense of national belonging to its wars with the English.) At the same time, he sees religion as a relationship with what members conceive as some higher Other, a "third element" that strengthens the collectivist cohesion among members—if we all have a connection to Christ, we all have a connection to one another. Hence, Simmel writes, "the immeasurable socializing effect of religion rests fundamentally upon the shared relationship to the highest principle."[21]

Finally, it's notable that even in his earliest engagements with religion, Simmel doesn't lose sight of *feeling* as a dimension of the phenomenon. The "specific feeling" of dependency that characterizes our relationship with the divine is, in ways Simmel would later elaborate, the experience of our dependency on society. Simmel was mindful of Schleiermacher's famous phrase: *das schlechthinnige Abhängigkeitsgefühl*—that feeling of absolute dependence.[22]

And how were we to study such experiences? Dilthey, in his *Introduction to the Human Sciences*, had argued that *Verstehen*, via introspection and self-reflection, could give an individual access to the structures of society inasmuch as our minds were socially formed. Simmel's 1892 book *Die Probleme der Geschichtsphilosophie: Eine erkenntnistheoretische Studie* (*The Problems of the Philosophy of History: An Epistemological Study*), returned to these issues in ways tinctured by Dilthey, evoking *Nachbildung*, the re-creation, of another's mental processes. Simmel posed the question of how we could have access to the experience of others unlike ourselves: the lover, if we have not loved; the hero, if we were a coward. For to some extent, we can—we can understand Caesar, Simmel wrote, without being Caesar; we can understand Luther, without being another Luther.[23] Was this a social or psychological insight? Durkheim, from early on, was intent on expelling psychology from the temple of sociology; the subtitle of Simmel's book, *Soziologische und psychologische Untersuchungen* (sociological and psychological studies), proposed that we split the difference.

GENEALOGY OF MORALS

The "religious idea" suffused Simmel's first great tome as well. *Einleitung in die Moralwissenschaft* (*Introduction to the Science of Morality*), which seems to have been the product of many years' work, came out in two volumes, in 1892 and 1893, together weighing in at nearly nine hundred pages. Discussions of the church feature prominently throughout. It's a critique of moral realism so thoroughgoing that it tips into conventionalism; his method is often sociohistorical, sometimes implying the functionalism then associated with Spencer. Moral norms are merely social regulations. Hence: "As far as the relation of religion to morality is concerned, one can say that it is moral to follow the commandments of God, because in general every group constructs its God in such a way that He commands what it recognizes as socially beneficial."[24]

Accordingly, Simmel writes, "Christianity, the religion of the poor and oppressed, developed suffering into an ideal" whereas the happier Greeks "saw nothing ethical in enduring suffering." (Simmel was likely already working on this study when Nietzsche's *On the Genealogy of Morals* was published, in 1887.) From the point of view of the individual, religion appears to prescribe the moral laws for us, but, Simmel maintains, from the point of view of the species, the opposite is true: we prescribe those moral laws that religion has to recognize. As the creator of the universe, Simmel argues (and here he is not far from Feuerbach), God is only an "analytical expression," a name for the presumed cause of the world in which we find ourselves; as the creator of the moral law, God, in turn, is given the role of absolutizing our own legislations. And so, Simmel contends, "The deeper essence of religion, insofar as it is a teacher of ethics, lies in the fact that God is the personification of the community as legislator for the individual." When the devout claim that God gave them the strength to obey the moral laws, Simmel sees "the intensification of the same psychological process that is also responsible for the projection of moral lawmaking onto God." What to make of the seeming contradiction "in the commandment to act in accordance with the will of God, while the will of God already determines every event in the world by itself"? This is, Simmel writes, in one of his most penetrating insights, "a difficulty of which the concept of freedom is more an expression than an exit."[25]

Through various case studies, Simmel traces a relation between socio-religious trends and ethical ones. For example, the shift from the ancient Hebrews' henotheism (Schelling's term for having special veneration for a god while not denying the existence of other gods) to ontological monotheism tracks with the emerging Christian belief in the equality of men before God, which in turn is based on the concept of the personal immortal soul and generates the political ideal of equality. He sees a similar shift from in-group egoism to altruism in the development of Jewish charity from something extended to members of your tribe to something extended to outsiders as well.[26] Again he aligns social and religious behavior, depicting moral norms as arising from the internalization of external compulsion.

Expanding on his discussion in *Differenzierung*, he writes:

> There is a profound analogy between attitudes toward society and attitudes toward God. Above all, the sense of dependency is crucial here; the individual feels bound to something more general, higher, from which it flows and into which it flows, to which it devotes itself, but from which it also expects elevation and redemption . . . I have no doubt that all these feelings, which meet in the concept of God as in a *focus imaginarius*, can be traced back to the relationship that the individual has to his species, on the one hand to past generations who gave him the handed-down main forms and contents of his being, on the other hand that which lives with him. . . . We are dependent on society as it expands in time and as it expands in space.[27]

Returning to the point in the second volume of *Einleitung in die Moralwissenschaft*, he tells us that an individual's relationship to God is often just "a symbol" of his relationship to the social community. The thesis that our relationship to God symbolizes our relationship to society has some proximity to Durkheim's thesis that religion is how a society represents itself to itself, but is less removed from the register of psychology. "The humility with which the pious person confesses that God is to be credited for all he is and has," Simmel argues, can justly be transposed to "the relationship of the individual to the community. For man is not absolutely nothing compared to God, but only a speck of dust, a weak but not completely insignificant power."[28] By the same token, the individual, though a product of society, is not without a separate creative power, however attenuated.

A regular case study is the Catholic Church's success in creating a universal religion—by its universalist doctrines and by its ability to interpose itself between the individual and God, thus appealing, as he had earlier written, "in the strongest degree, to the social element in man." Its most strenuous followers are people conscious of having sinned, because for them "the individualistic principle has proved so inadequate" that they seek the security and tranquility afforded by "agreement with the community."

The socialist view of the individual as merely epiphenomenal (a view Simmel did not share) is itself presaged by religious discourse: "Just as, according to the strict religious view, the individual is only a vessel of God's grace or wrath, so, according to the socialist view, he is a vessel of effects emanating from society." He sees this in the special bond that sinners feel toward the Catholic Church: "the social nature of man" gives rise to an impulse to shelter the fragility of individuality in the comforts of community, a shelter that the church offers. "The religious form is, in innumerable ways, just a way of clothing a sociological content."[29]

As such, it served as a binding agent. Religion "has brought us social cohesion, has developed forces in us that . . . remain valuable and effective when their religious content and vehicle have long since become obsolete and decayed." Anticipating (and perhaps correcting) aspects of Durkheim's work on anomie and suicide, he continues, "This is shown with great clarity by the fact that the moral statistics are always more favorable for the religious minority within larger groups. So, to cite just one example of many, the Catholics in Prussia and the Protestants in Bavaria have the better moral statistics, both with regard to illegitimate birth and crime, suicides, and childrearing." For minorities, in Simmel's account, will have a more active and moralizing religious community. (Durkheim, by contrast, considered Catholicism inherently more communitarian than Protestantism.)

But Simmel also is more inclined to attend to conflict than Durkheim; he stresses that religion plays a role not just in social cohesion but also in social antagonisms, and, again, that the first can be reinforced by the second. A community is bound to rise up against the individual who rejects its values, its thoughts and norms, and this community's "ethical hatred,"

Simmel maintained, "only disguises itself in the religious belief that it is the specific content of this deviation that drives the persecution of heretics." Here he's writing, a little incautiously, as if religion merely supervened on the thought and will of a society. But a Feuerbachian insight hovers: "man paints himself in his gods, in the double sense that he can be deduced indirectly from them and is directly depicted in them." And Simmel remains characteristically alert to emotional impetus, the way feeling advances to thought. "A crowd will gather in and through primitive feelings much sooner than through more abstract intellectual functions," he had observed earlier. He relished a late seventeenth-century Quaker's description of a congregation overtaken by an ecstatic phenomenon, "such that its members were unified into one body."[30]

As we've seen so often, sociology emerges as a perspective on secularization—about both the retreat and the persistence of religion. The conceptual history of "religion" is the history of being able to see it from a distance, in an owl-of-Minerva-flies-at-dusk manner. Insofar as secularism is the founding subject of sociology, then, we won't be surprised to find that Simmel accepted modernity as a period of secularization: "Faith is dying more and more, and criticism is destroying unbiased devotion to traditional ideals of a political, religious, and personal nature." The eclipse of faith and absolute ideals has resulted, he suggests, in the "feeling of life's emptiness and worthlessness"—a feeling that he took to be a hallmark of modern culture.[31]

All this may sound like a version of what Charles Taylor calls the "subtraction story"—secularism as merely the subtraction of religion, rather than as the emergence of a humanist counterprogram. Yet Simmel had already noted all manner of reactions and forms of resistance.[32] As we'll see, too, he would later explore the ways in which religious content could take nonreligious forms.

THE MAGIC WORD

Simmel's *Einleitung in die Moralwissenschaft* can sound more baldly relativistic than the work that followed; over the next decade, he became increasingly influenced by certain neo-Kantian thinkers, especially those from what came to be known as the Southwestern school. He was a philosopher, and a philosopher of sociology, even before he was a sociologist. Methods and their conceptual integrity were a big concern of his. The potency of the natural sciences, *Naturwissenschaften*, was everywhere in evidence, and, indeed, part of the standard story about secularization. But was sociology best positioned among the other forms of systematic knowledge—namely, the humanistic kind, or what Dilthey taught people to call the *Geisteswissenschaften*? What sort of *Wissenschaft* was sociology anyway?

Wilhelm Windelband, in a famous 1894 lecture "History and Natural Science," criticized what had become the usual distinction drawn between *Naturwissenschaften* and the *Geisteswissenschaften*. As he noted, the terms make it sound as if the first is about nature and the second about mind, when, in fact, much of psychology (say, Hermann Ebbinghaus's research on the forgetting curve) seemed to fall more naturally in the first category and many instances of the second (archeology, say) had little to do with our mental processes. Previous theorists, he contended, had failed to explain how the realms differed. If Dilthey thought that the difference between two realms corresponded to the difference between understanding and explanation, *Verstehen* and *Erklären*, Windelband found Dilthey guilty of psychologism and relativism—two great sins for the Southwestern school.[33] Instead, Windelband invented the word "idiographic" to describe the way in which humanists pay attention to *particular* past artifacts. Whereas natural scientists are mainly interested in what he called the "nomothetic," the lawlike, as in laws of nature, a humanist might attend to an artifact for precisely what's singular about it.

Simmel's conception of sociology straddled the two realms; his conception of the two realms, in turn, straddled Windelband's and Dilthey's conceptions of how those realms differed. Simmel sought to attend to the particularity of social phenomena but in a way that was alert to patterns that recurred through different contexts. If a field called "sociology" had been founded by a founder of positivism, Simmel's task, in his early work, was to wrest it from that positivist armature and bring it firmly into the realm of reflective inquiry and *Verstehen*. (Durkheim assigned himself the same task, as we saw, but approached it differently.) At the same time, the Southwestern theorists—which basically meant everyone around Windelband—had a habit of casting everything as an epistemological problem to be sorted through, and Simmel, a Kant scholar himself, was susceptible to it. Although chemists seemed to make progress without a big "theory of knowledge" in tow, sophisticated students of the human sciences allowed themselves no such latitude.

Simmel was preoccupied with two other fixtures of Kantian and post-Kantian thought as well. One, already in evidence, was the form-and-content binary. Kantians distinguished, in the manner of the *Critique of Pure Reason*, between the wash of raw sensory input and the forms of our mental apparatus—innate concepts or categories through which we apprehended, structured, and organized that content. Some of these mental structures relate to quantity (the concept of a single entity; the concept of many such entities); some to relation (for example, cause and effect); and some to modality (possibility or necessity). But the neo-Kantians broadened the notion of form to encompass dynamic, changing principles of organization; form could be historically and culturally contingent.

A related notion was the synthetic a priori. This combined two distinctions. The a priori, as opposed to the a posteriori, didn't depend on knowledge we gleaned from our encounters with the external world. A synthetic truth, as opposed to an analytic truth, was something that wasn't true by virtue of its meaning (a bachelor is an unmarried man), but that conveyed information. For Kant, our intuitions could give us truths that were a priori but informative (thus synthetic, rather than analytic): the truths of arithmetic and geometry and metaphysics. Moral thought too, involved synthetic a priori propositions. Moral laws involving autonomy and duty, say, weren't tautological but neither were they derived from experience. Neo-Kantians were concerned to identify new a priori principles and eject pretenders.

The potency of this approach, for Simmel, was reinforced by his longstanding correspondence with the philosopher Heinrich Rickert. A student of Windelband's, Rickert was also the son of a journalist and parliamentarian who had helped establish the Verein zur Abwehr des Antisemitismus (the Association for Defense against Antisemitism). Perhaps it isn't surprising that Rickert bridled at the relativist notion that morality was nothing more than a supercharged social convention. Starting in his 1892 volume *Der Gegenstand der Erkenntnis* (*The Object of Knowledge*), which he expanded and revised throughout his life, Rickert focused on the issue of validity, or *Geltung*; and having developed a sophisticated account of the objectivity of values, he chastened Simmel for the lack of one. The point isn't that Simmel accepted Rickert's account; it's that he engaged with it. In 1898, Simmel wrote Rickert that he could "only stick to my relativism if it is also able to solve all the problems posed by absolutist theories."[34] As we'll see, the relation between the absolute and the relative became central to his evolving theories of religion.

But Rickert also had much to say about the methodologies appropriate to the natural sciences and the human sciences, and about how the realms could be demarcated. In his 1899 book *Kulturwissenschaft und Naturwissenschaft*—"Cultural Science and Natural Science," cultural science (or scholarship) being his cunning alternative to *Geisteswissenschaften*—he offered an updated version of his teacher's nomothetic/idiographic distinction, while polemicizing against the crude historicism that refused to accommodate objectivity, transhistorical truths and values.[35] Concepts in the natural sciences (gravity, say) would be based on the observation of regularities; concepts in the cultural sciences might be based on values and general concepts (like freedom) that could transcend specific contexts. The classic Kantian account of the "form" imposed by the cognitive faculties of the mind upon the "content" of our empirical exposures could, Rickert thought, be usefully extended to the disciplinary level. In the natural sciences, which were value-free, content would be empirical phenomena, and form would be the principles or laws that arise from observation. But in the cultural sciences, the form provided by a historian's "value concepts" could be imposed on the vastness of individual historical events. For our social understanding of the world is not just a passive reflection of external reality. Instead, it is actively shaped by our values, which determine what is meaningful to us.[36]

Simmel was—like his neo-Kantian friends, foes, and frenemies—eager to transpose the critical Kantian distinctions to other realms. Although the Kant story was about the individual and the individual's cognitive categories, supraindividual entities might have their own versions of these things. Hence what Simmel sometimes calls the "social *a priori*," the basic, structuring categories of social consciousness, such as *Vergesellschaftung*, a term that Kurt H. Wolff, sidestepping the developmental connotations of "socialization," usefully translated as "sociation."[37]

A careful dance between historicism and apriorism winds through Simmel's early pronouncements on sociology. In his essay "The Problem of Sociology," published in 1894, he announced, "The science of human beings has become the science of human society." And so "in the realm of religion, as in that of economic life," he wrote, "we find a tendency to refer each single fact back to the historical condition, the needs and efforts of the entire society concerned." But he had qualms about any talk of society as an organic whole. He posed the "riddle, 'What is Society?' " and remarked, "certainly it is not a unified being which lends itself readily to apt definition, but rather consists of the sum of all those modes and forces of association which unite its elements."[38] Once secularity had made religion legible—after the existence of the not-religious had enabled the religious to come into view—we could grasp how religion, too, was an interplay between content and form.

"For a while, sociology appeared to be the magic word that promised salvation to all the mysteries of history and practical life, ethics and aesthetics, religion and politics," Simmel warned in an 1895 essay. A more modest approach was possible; sociology could be understood, for instance, as "as the investigation of the forms in which people socialize, and which demonstrate the same essence and development through all the diversity of purposes and contents around which societies crystallize."[39]

STRANGER AMONG US

In the meantime, Simmel's career was beset by a difficult fit between the content of his intellectual interests and the forms of academic life. He remained at the level of private lecturer, ineligible for a university salary, for an unusually long period. In 1898, the faculty put him up for a promotion, but professorial appointments required the approval of the Prussian minister of education, who—perhaps sensing some ambivalence, and perhaps having been privately lobbied—demurred. Only in 1901 was Simmel advanced to the intermediate rank of *außerordentlicher Professor*, extraordinary professor, which normally provided a salary but not the status required to supervise doctoral theses. (The minister denied Simmel a salary, in any case, perhaps in light of his private income.)[40]

At Berlin, he was never advanced further. Why not? For one thing, the university was generally disinclined to promote from within. For another, some of his colleagues were reluctant to see another Jew on the faculty. This was a moment and a milieu in which antisemitism was not a private vice to be publicly disavowed; for the likes of Treitschke, it was a rallying cry. (While many movements have been named by their enemies, the term "antisemitism" had been coined by an outspoken proponent, Wilhelm Marr.) The philosopher Ludwig Klages, a graphology enthusiast, once interpreted a handwriting sample of Simmel's as revealing a "flatness of the inner life under cheap rhetoric and unimaginative hairsplitting"—conveying a cluster of specifically antisemitic tropes.[41]

Simmel himself was inclined to blame Dilthey, who, though he approved of Simmel's anti-positivist approach toward social theory, evidently had mixed feelings about Simmel's disciplinary program and wasn't eager to see him promoted.[42] And, of course, Simmel *was*, disciplinarily, somewhat eccentric. He was not the author of a foundationalist "closed system" of the sort neo-Kantians prized. Some feared—with support from his book on the science of ethics along with his *Philosophy of Money* (1900)—that he was inclined toward relativism. Some found him personally insufferable. He could hit up patrons (this was a particular complaint of Schmoller's) with a fusillade of requests—he sent dozens of letters to the legal scholar Georg Jellinek at Heidelberg telling him how he could be helpful. Simmel could be rude to his seniors and condescending to his peers; he seldom bothered to feign humility. "Simmel's arrogance becomes more and more tasteless," Rickert complained to his (Jewish) protégé Emil Lask in 1902. "He actually cannot pass an opportunity without hinting to me how much he towers above me."[43]

That Simmel had gained a name outside the academy—he wrote frequently for the newspapers—was no help. Nor was the fact that his politics in the early 1890s had leaned toward socialism (later he was informally aligned with the Social Democrats), and that he wrote for socialist journals. (The left-wing paper *Der sozialistische Student* praised him for his openness to historical materialism.) He had several times taught a course titled "Social Psychology, with Special Reference to Socialism" that raised eyebrows at a time when some in the government and beyond saw "red professors" as a menace.[44] In short, his collegial relationships often fell short of collegiality.

For all that, Simmel remained a popular teacher and proved an influential one; among his students were Karl Mannheim, Ernst Bloch, György Lukács, and Martin Buber. Off campus, he and his wife were champion salonistes. Over the years, they entertained such guests as Rainer Maria Rilke, Stefan George, Edmund Husserl, Lou Andreas-Salomé, and the Webers. The poet and philosopher Margarete Susman described the conversations there as "floating in an atmosphere of intellectuality, charm, and tact." (She was also taken with the Persian carpets, the Buddha figures and other specimens of Eastern art, the grand piano covered with an embroidered Chinese fabric, the Rodin sketches on the wall, and the characteristic smell of "exquisite apples and very fine cigarettes.")[45] Abroad, he was acquiring a name abroad as a sociologist. The debut issue of Durkheim's *L'Année sociologique*, in 1896, contained an essay of Simmel's.

Two years later, he published his first full essay on religion, "A Contribution to the Sociology of Religion," which appeared in the *Neue Deutsche Rundschau* (and which incorporates passages from his *Einleitung in die Moralwissenschaft*). It opens, in words I quoted in the Introduction, by acknowledging a definitional perplexity: "Thus far no one has been able to offer a definition of religion that is both precise and sufficiently comprehensive." Religion, he observed, had to be distinguished from "mere metaphysical speculation or from belief in ghosts." Yet nobody had specified an "ultimate essence" shared by "the religions of Christians and of South Sea islanders." The "multiplicity of psychological motives ascribed to religion," in turn, fit certain models and not others. The question, on one level, was of belief: should we believe in religion as something more than a verbal artifact?

Simmel did. "We must insist that no matter how mundanely and how empirically the origin of ideas about the supramundane and the transcendent is explained, neither the subjective, emotional value of these ideas nor their objective value as matters of fact is at all in question." The reference to objective value may have been a neo-Kantian concession; the stress on "subjective, emotional value" was distinctively his own. Dissenting from those influenced by Tylor, he denies that there is a single answer to the question of origin. Still, he insists that religious ideas could never have gained such power unless they had been "the formulas for or embodiments of previously existing relations for which consciousness merely had not yet found a more appropriate expression."[46]

His most powerful move was to separate the religious impulse from religion proper. Just as we understand art by understanding aesthetic experience in everyday life, we could seek to "discover in all kinds of nonreligious relationships and intentions certain religious qualities that, as they become independent and self-sufficient, come to be 'religion.'" If we're searching for a "genetic explanation"—one that retraces the stages of origination and development—we'll want to attend to "religion before it becomes religion"; to the fact that religious feelings manifest themselves in all sorts of nonreligious contexts. "Only with extreme intensity and specificity does religion appear as an independent sector of life, as an area with boundaries of its own."[47]

THE REIGN OF RELIGIOSITY

Religiosity (*Religiosität*), Simmel's central analytic concept here, invariably "contains a peculiar admixture of unselfish surrender and fervent desire, of humility and exaltation, of sensual concreteness and spiritual abstraction." Under what circumstances are such feelings elicited? "Many human relationships harbor a religious element," Simmel tells us, and he points to "the relationship of a devoted child to his parent, of an enthusiastic patriot to his country, of the fervent cosmopolite to humanity; the relationship of the worker to his insurgent class or of the proud feudal lord to his fellow nobles." In all these relationships of communal identity, he finds a "common tone" (*gemeinsamer Ton*) that can be described only as religious. The subject feels included in "a higher order—an order which, at the same time, is felt to be something inward and personal."[48]

If *Ton* can suggest a musical metaphor, Simmel also described the quality of religiosity with the term *Färbung*—coloring or tint. Because the "separation and materialization of religion" draws on what he called the "coloring of so-called religiosity," he thought that "religion conceived as an independent phenomenon is a derivative thing."[49] For Windelband's teacher Hermann Lotze, such secondary qualities as tone or tint ("secondary" because, in the classic Lockean distinction, they exist only by dint of human consciousness) belonged to the holistic structure of reality, interconnecting the subjective and objective. Simmel, who liked to think beyond dualities, would devise another approach toward transcending this one.

It's still the case that, in this feelings-first account, the story of society is a religious one, and the story of religion a social one: "The faith that has come to be regarded as the essence and substance of religion is first of all a relationship *between human beings*; for this relationship is a matter of *practical* faith." Faith in God, Simmel contends,

> has an analogy in how humans become part of society: we do not by any means base our mutual relations on what we know conclusively about each other. Rather, our feelings and impressions articulate themselves in certain representations that can be described only as matters of faith; these, in turn, have an effect on practical conditions. We illustrate a specific psychological reality, hard to define, when we "believe in someone"—the child in its parents, the subordinate in his superior, the friend in a friend, the individual in the people, the subject in his sovereign. The social role of this faith has never been investigated, but this much is certain: without it, society would disintegrate.

Faith in God is thus akin to the acceptance of our dependence on and constitution by society. It's an act of assent quite different from assent to propositional knowledge: "When I say, 'I believe in God,' the assertion means something entirely different from the statement 'I believe that light is diffused through ether' or 'The Moon is inhabited' or 'Human nature is immutable.' It not only means that I can accept the existence of God even though it is not fully demonstrable, but also implies a certain spiritual relationship to Him, a surrendering of affections to Him, an orientation of life toward Him."[50]

A whole constituted by separate elements, he says, is something we see in the family, the clan, the state. For "what does unity signify, but that many are mutually related, and that the fate of one is felt by all?" More than that, the way a society was organized would be mirrored in the form of the divine: if the family was the main social unit, Baal could be a father, his subjects his children; when the society aggregated unrelated groups, Baal had to be enthroned as a king. Monotheism, then, arose when the tribal unit was all-controlling.[51]

Again, that wasn't to say that a religion was tethered to the circumstances that give birth to it. Religion "consists of forms of social relationships that, when separated from their empirical content, become independent and are projected on substances of their own." In this respect, religion "represents in substance that which regulates the group life in form and function—indeed, to a certain extent, consists of the materialization of that quality." Inasmuch as the unity of society consisted in the aggregation of the reciprocal interactions (*Wechselwirkungen*) among its members, religion, Simmel held, "is the purest form of unity in society, raised high above all concrete individualities." (Our consciousness of collectively constituting a unity is "actually the entire existing unity in question," he later wrote about society.) In the idea of the divine, "the manifoldness and the contradictoriness of things" find "coherence and unity—whether the absolute unity of the one God or the partial unities of polytheism pertaining to particular provinces of reality."[52]

Morality represents one kind of coherence and conformity. Relations between an individual and the group that would be characterized as "moral," Simmel says, are effectively crystallized in the individual's relationship to God: "The compelling and punitive gods, the loving God, the God of Spinoza who cannot return our love, the God who gives or takes away both the directive to act and the strength to follow it—these are precisely the signs through which the ethical relationship between the group and its members unfolds its energies and oppositions."[53]

Simmel sometimes depicted religiosity itself as an amalgam of subjective and objective aspects. He evidently thought that Durkheim and his *équipe* had shied from the "concrete reality of the factual content of faith." They preferred to contemplate religion as a public institution and scanted the individual experience of faith. They failed to see that religiosity—as an individual phenomenon, distinct from collective transport—is not a deliverance of religion; religion is the deliverance of religiosity. Religion's effects, in turn, come from its "persistent ability to draw a given item of religious data into the flow of the emotions."[54]

In a 1902 essay on the epistemology of religion, Simmel proposes that the "great categories of our inner life"—such as "being and duty, possibility and necessity, willing and fearing"—can be compared to "the multiplicity of musical instruments, each with a different timbre [*Klangfarbe*] on which one can play the same melody." Simmel, who learned as a child to play both violin and piano, insists that religiosity is one of those categories that has its own particular timbre.[55] The slipperiness of the form-and-content distinction is evident: is religiosity content that gets structured by the forms of actual religions, or is religiosity a social category that structures experience of another sort? *Form* and *Inhalt*, form and content, often switch places in these arguments. Very often Simmel writes as if religiosity represents a set of inner feelings and dispositions that can subsume and unify a variety of experiences and that gets expressed through the form of particular religious systems. Sometimes, he conceives religiosity as a form through which individuals relate to the transcendent—as a social category giving shape to the content of their experiences. Later, as we'll see, he turns this equivocation into a provocation: religion as a zone between the objective and the subjective—as a way of mediating between the relative and the absolute.

REACHING FOR THE ABSOLUTE

Simmel's evolving thought found fullest expression in *Die Religion*, which was published in 1906 as a slender monograph, or long pamphlet, in a series edited by his pupil Martin Buber, then reissued in revised form in 1912. ("I am sending you a little booklet"—*ein kleines Büchelchen* was his double diminutive—"which is a down payment on a debt that I probably won't be able to pay in full; given everything else that must be addressed first, I likely won't be able to take on a comprehensive treatment of religious problems," he wrote to Rickert in February 1907.)[56] The work was dedicated to Margaret Susman and to Gertrud Kantorowicz, a brilliant former student who had become an assistant of his, and it ran to seventy-odd pages of text. In those pages, Simmel returns to the notion that religion, like society, takes disparate elements as constituent parts of a whole (say, "the kingdom of God"). Again, affect plays an active role: "the dynamics of group life are borne up by the momentum of religious feeling and are projected beyond the materials and agents of those dynamics into the transcendent sphere," such that God can be seen as the "absolutization of sociological unity."[57] Clearly, Simmel's perspective remains remote from the Tylorian model of religion as an explanatory, proto-scientific mode; and remains at some distance, too, from Durkheim's division of existence between sacred and profane, from his ideational view of religion as the direct embodiment of society's shared consciousness, from his focus on religion's role in maintaining and expressing societal cohesion.

For even though Simmel depicts religion as the "materialization" of the qualities that regulate social life, he is intent on keeping in view individual experience and the intricacies of social interaction. "The life of society consists of interactions between its elements," which "come about as a result of certain interests, purposes, and urges, which make up what one might call the fabric of society: the existence of individuals in social groups, with all their indifference and affection, mutual support and conflict." All this is inscribed in religious life. It's precisely because Buddhism, in his view, "entirely lacks a social dimension"— its "ideal is that of the monk's existence"—that Buddhism is not a religion.[58] Others had denied that Buddhism was a religion because it lacked a divinity; Simmel's objection was that it lacked sociality.

He was increasingly wary of social evolutionism. "I will not attempt to deal with the methodological problem of whether 'religion' as such may be regarded in any way as a concrete subject that 'develops' from fetishism and ancestor worship to Christianity," he wrote, and he warns against the temptation to think of one's own faith as "the top of an upward progression leading toward it." He no more believed in " 'imperfect' religion" than in "imperfect artistic styles": phenomena that are perfectly religious are perfect religions, he says, just as trecento art is as perfect as later art. He introduced "the sequence *religiosity— social phenomenon—objective religion*" but appended the warning that this was "not intended, of course, as a temporal sequence." He had been chastened by the neo-Kantians on this score.

He explored further how the ideal of human equality had been generated by the idea of equality before God, of equality in salvation. As he had proposed in his *Einleitung in die Moralwissenschaft*, we were to see this development against the background of the particularist gods of self-contained groups (such as the ancient Hebrews). Such a group wouldn't be pleased by the idea that its god should become the god of others; it would prefer to keep its god to itself, and not dilute its ownership claims. The revolution represented by Christianity, then, was "its denial of the existence of all gods other than its own, not only for itself but universally." Moral universalism was a logical consequence.

But why did religion come into existence at all—why, as Simmel framed the question, "does group unity have this tendency to cloak itself in the form of transcendence and to equip itself with emotional qualities of a religious nature?" He conjectured that society itself could be perceived by individuals "as some kind of miracle," with inheritances like law, language, and custom regarded as "the product of this mysterious unity." And then there is the affective power of religiosity itself: man puts the divine into the sphere of the absolute in order to "match the profundity of religious inspiration within his soul."[59]

All this talk of feeling was, for certain critics, a serious demerit. The eminent theologian Ernst Troeltsch, in a 1907 essay on the philosophy of religion, declared Simmel's theory to be "pure psychologism."[60] Simmel would have contested the point, because he saw the social and the psychological in dialectical relation. For him, the distinction between individual and society is itself a social artifact; both terms are theoretical entities, idealizations that enlighten only when we remember their fictional status.

Troeltsch wasn't the only grumbler, but there were other things on Simmel's mind that year. Gertrud Kantorowicz, the co-dedicatee of his *Büchelchen* and secretly his lover, had traveled to Bologna to give birth to their daughter, who was baptized Angela Bolzano. Simmel had recently published an essay on secrecy and could speak about the subject with the authority of *Erlebnis*. Our relationships with others, he observed in this essay, depend on our knowing something about them, but there's no such thing as "complete reciprocal transparency." Besides, relationships of an intimate character lose their charm unless they also involve "distance and intermission." Nor should the "ethically negative value of lying" lead us to overlook its "positive sociological significance." Indeed, Simmel argued, "Discretion is nothing other than the sense of justice with respect to the sphere of the intimate contents of life." He was devoted to his wife and cherished their shared existence; he was also in love with Kantorowicz and would remain so. This tension was, like other tensions he theorized, unresolvable. In a footnote to the secrecy essay, he ventured that the faith one person might have in another, however unjustified, was a kind of religious faith.

"Just as no one has ever believed in the existence of God on grounds of proof, but these proofs are rather subsequent justifications or intellectual reflections of a quite immediate attitude of the affections; so we have faith in another person, although this faith may not be able to justify itself by proofs of the worthiness of the person, and it may even exist in spite of proofs of his unworthiness," he wrote. "This confidence, this subjective attitude of unreservedness toward a person, is not brought into existence by experiences or by hypotheses, but it is a primary attitude of the soul with respect to another."[61]

THE THREAT OF SOCIOLOGY

That intimacy may require distance even in the religious context is a point made in Simmel's 1908 magnum opus, *Soziologie: Untersuchungen über die Formen der Vergesellschaftung* (*Sociology: Investigations into the Forms of Sociation* would be a fairly precise rendering). In order for religion to be able to form societies in more expansive circles, God had to be located at some distance from the believers. He writes:

The, as it were, immediate proximity with believers where the divine principles of all totemistic and fetishistic religions, but also the old Jewish God, are located makes such a religion quite unsuited for ruling wide circles. The incredible height of the Christian concept of God first makes the homogeneity of the heterogeneous before God possible; the distance from him was so immeasurable that the difference between human beings is thereby dissolved.

Abstraction sponsors the egalitarian ideal. He conjectures that the Catholic Church succeeded in creating a world religion only because it put God beyond individual reach, interrupting the immediacy of the individual's communing with the Almighty and putting itself in the middle. Having done so, the church is eventually vulnerable to direct-access heresies promised by certain forms of Protestantism; yet such forms of communing, as they expand, will themselves grow routinized and institutionally mediated. Meanwhile, some version of secrecy or information control attends hieratic operations. Illustrating the point that people are never entirely subsumed by their social roles, Simmel brings up the example of a Catholic priest. "His ecclesiastical function completely envelopes and engulfs his individual self," disguising the complicated relation between his social being and his not-social being. The religious person may feel "fully embraced by the divine essence, as though one were nothing more than a pulse beat of divine life," yet the embrace wouldn't be meaningful if the person hadn't retained a distinct sense of self. In this respect, the individual "can never stand in a union without also standing outside it."[62]

But Simmel knew that a social role itself can involve standing at a distance from others; his *Sociology* contained an influential discussion of "the stranger." The dynamic was certainly playing out in his professional life. In 1908, the same year this book came out, he found himself angling for a professorship in philosophy that Heidelberg University was trying to fill; Max Weber and others lobbied for Simmel to be considered, and the faculty recommended his appointment. But ministerial consent was not forthcoming. Evidently the grand duchess Luise von Baden, who had extensive behind-the-scenes influence, shared her view that Simmel's religious opinions were worrisomely "relativistic."

Then there was the notoriously antisemitic report that the medievalist Dietrich Schäfer, a protégé of Treitschke's, sent to the education minister. It contained plenty of character assassination, and horror voiced at all the women and Jews whom Simmel's lectures attracted, but Schäfer also comes out with a telling complaint: "It is, in my opinion, a disastrous error to put 'society' in the place of state and church as the decisive organ of human coexistence."[63] Note the scare quotes around the word "society" (*Gesellschaft*). From Schäfer's perspective, human coexistence could and should be parsed in terms of persons, the church, and the state; granting society an ontological status and an explanatory role would downgrade church and state to being historically contingent products of social forces. To speak of society, in other words, was to accelerate secularization.

Was Schäfer right? One version of the secularization thesis saw the dominion of science, which provided materialist explanations for the world's wonders, as eroding that of religion. Tylor hoped this would happen; Durkheim believed that it was happening. Simmel proposed (in line with what Dilthey had proposed much earlier) that a modus vivendi was possible under certain conditions: "If religion is not a set of claims but a certain state of being—which is precisely what enables it to interpret and judge empirical phenomena—then it can be no more disproved by science than can any other state of being. It becomes refutable, however, as soon as its images of things . . . become rigidified into a system of knowledge that somehow imitates the thought processes of science."[64]

Yet what if the graver threat to religion was sociology itself, providing an explanation for the existence of religion in which its truth claims played no role? "It has been said that man does not have religion because he believes in God," Simmel had written, "but because he has religion as an attitude of the soul, consequently he believes in God."[65] The duchess could not have found this reassuring.

Increasingly, in these years, Simmel is thinking about how this subjectivity, this mood of the soul, relates to religion as a set of empirical phenomena. He invokes a tension between subjective culture and objective culture, which he sometimes depicts as a clash between content and form, even life and form. Subjective culture relates to lived experience (*Erlebnis*), to the individual capacity to absorb and create cultural entities. Objective culture takes in the forms of law, morality, art, economics, and so on. Perhaps influenced by Marx on commodity fetishism, Simmel describes "objective culture" as a production of sociation, something that has undergone crystallization or condensation (*Verdichtung*), using the term the way Lazarus had. But you can hear the murmurs of the neo-Kantians, too. Form, in this collectivized sense, is far from the prefab mental furniture that featured in Kant's *Critique of Pure Reason*; it's an objective thing that we fashioned. What Simmel, in his 1911 essay "On the Concept and Tragedy of Culture," called the paradox of culture is that individuality can only be fulfilled through the external forms of objective culture, but is also constrained by them. Meanwhile, religiosity (which he had glossed as "a quality of spiritual being, *the religious life process*") had to go out and secure a form from elsewhere that was merely a crystallization of itself.[66] The paradox of culture followed us to our holiest communions.

So religiosity is seen to congeal into "objective religion," while religion is "perhaps only the subjective reflection on the reality of that sum total" of human relations.[67] Writing about Hans Vaihinger's *The Philosophy of "As If"* (1911), Simmel argued that we were accustomed to dividing our knowledge as either subjective or objective, and that we needed to attend to a "third layer which cannot be divided into those two, but is rather a self-sufficient synthetic unity of them."[68] The religious process, in his account, exemplifies this sort of thirdness: religiosity is a condition of possibility for religion; it is a feeling and an attitude; it organizes experience, while it is itself organized into other objective forms. Dilthey, also writing in 1911, offered a similar relay circuit. Religion, he argued, takes the form both of the religious experience and the various objectifications of it; "experience always remains subjective: objective knowledge of religion is made possible only by the re-experiencing (*Nacherleben*) of it."[69] Yet Simmel sometimes put aside this subjective/objective distinction, using the unadorned term *Kultur* to name the dialectical zone in which individuality and reified social forms meet. His friend Margarete Susman chose her words carefully when she later remarked that in both his thought and his life, "culture" was a "almost a religious concept."[70]

In another essay from 1911, Simmel made a bold proposal: "the problem of religion today would be solved if people were to lead religious lives: not lives which are lived 'with' religion, but which are religious in their very essence and which certainly are not 'derived' from religion—that is, out of consideration for some object external to religious life." Even if truly religious people were to be "robbed of their God through rational criticism," Simmel thought, "they would retain within them not only the source from which He originated, but also the metaphysical value that He represented." The language here presages Charles Taylor's argument about "fullness," something readily enjoyed by the religious while "exclusive humanism must find the ground and contours of fullness in the immanent sphere, in some condition of human life, or feeling, or achievement." In this spirit, Simmel insists, "A religious person is never left with nothing, for he has a fullness of being."[71] It's just that this fullness of being, though religious in coloring and tone, need not take the form of religion.

The structural congruence of religion and society remains, for Simmel, inescapable. As the Simmel scholar Volkhard Krech remarks, "the sociological discourse about 'religion *and* society' makes no sense."[72] Society is the absolute, is God; sociability corresponds to religiosity; and just as the hegemony of religion, as we knew it, has been challenged, so the hegemony of society, in its earlier, more cohesive state, has been challenged. Modernity and urbanization weakened older communal bonds and led to an increase of individuality while depersonalizing social relationships and further fragmenting social identities.

Except, of course, new forms of sociality, new social orders, and new social bonds would emerge, just as post-religious forms of religiosity would. Life would find a way.

VITAL SIGNS

In 1914, after three decades of teaching at Berlin, Simmel was hired away by the University of Strasbourg, finally securing a full professorship. Easing the appointment was the character reference from Gustav von Schmoller (he had been awarded the nobiliary particle "von" in 1908). "Of course, there is no denying his Jewish background," the great man wrote, but "he belongs to the decent wing of Jewish academics." Still, Strasbourg—an Alsatian outpost that became part of Germany after the Franco-Prussian War and would be returned to France after the Great War—was far, in every sense, from Berlin. "If I accept it (which I have not yet decided), it will not be with a light heart," Simmel wrote a theologian friend about the offer.[73] But once he relocated, he buoyed himself, as usual, by taking on a dizzying number of projects, including a short introduction to sociology and a book on Rembrandt.

Philosophers in their fifties typically devote themselves to ringing variations on their earlier theories, but Simmel—perhaps because he was not burdened with a big system to defend; perhaps because the intellectual milieu was shifting—swerved into his own version of *Lebensphilosophie*, "life philosophy."[74] It was an orientation in which experience was the ultimate reality, and life was the only absolute, with no purpose beyond the purposes that human beings created for themselves. As such, it spoke to his concern with subjectivity, with the color and tone of religious experience, with self-transcendence. And though Dilthey's later work had helped crystallize the movement, Simmel was no less influenced by Henri Bergson. The French semi-vitalist was casting a spell on him, as he did on so many.

"I have been working quite a lot on Bergson lately and I have to say that I am extremely impressed by his epistemological concepts," Simmel had written earlier to Husserl. They were not concepts that would have suited the neo-Kantian crew. In *L'évolution créatrice* (1907), Bergson wrote that our intellect compassed not only conceptual and logical thought but also more nebulous powers of intuition that expand in the "very direction of life," so that "theory of knowledge and theory of life seem to us inseparable."[75] (Simmel encouraged Gertrud Kantorowitz to translate the volume into German, and her version appeared, as *Schöpferische Entwicklung*, in 1912.) In December 1908, Bergson wrote to Simmel to thank him for sending him a copy of *Die Probleme der Geschichtsphilosophie*, which he was finding "deeply engaging, both for the ingenuity of its insights and the originality of its guiding idea, which is of the first importance." He agreed that there was a certain affinity between their work. "One reason for this affinity may be that we both tend to distinguish, in fact, between what is directly presented by experience and what the mind adds to it to meet practical requirements," Bergson went on. "I, for my part, place great trust in raw, immediate experience, free from the frameworks into which action forces us to place it."[76] Both men's intuitions, it seemed, were moving in "the very direction of life."

By 1914, of course, the conflicts between the great powers were moving in the very direction of death. Simmel, like most German intellectuals, was initially supportive of the war. Durkheim, as I mentioned, would produce a pamphlet on the German "mentality," which he found exemplified in Treitschke, evoking a nationalist ideology that refused to bind the state to treaties, that saw the state as antagonistic to civil society, and that took the expansion of power to be the state's sole duty. This was not Simmel's view. The war, he was convinced, boded spiritual renewal. He hoped for a new Germany, and for a new Europe, one oriented toward something nobler than money. The war promised, in short, a restoration of *fullness*. On August 9, he wrote to Margarete Susman:

> It's a whole new experience when a people, 65 million strong, from the Kaiser down to the proletarian's child, is faced with the question of whether to be or not to be. Everything I experienced up to this date as distress now seems flimsy and insubstantial in comparison. There is no space in the present moment for any mention of individual fate. But I believe that, as a result, the force of the people will be deployed in a way that global history has yet to experience. . . . If we survive this war, we will in a radical sense be new men.

Two weeks later, he wrote her about feeling "the heat of the whole cultural world's destiny as entirely personal—no longer as a part, but as both absolutely insignificant and at the same time as the bearer of the whole and of each fragment."[77] Patrick Watier, a Simmel scholar who was a sociologist at Strasbourg, rightly describes the tone as religious. Writing to Marianne Weber, on August 14, 1914, Simmel groused that Lukács, his old student, "speaks of militarism all the time," and explained that "for us it is precisely a question of liberation from militarism." Militarism, in peacetime, is characterized by its "self-conceit," he said, and "liberation would strip this away to produce a form and a means for the total exaltation of life."[78] Mammonism was the true enemy. Writing in November, Simmel disputed Bergson's claim that Germany had cynically disregarded treaties in invading Belgium, and insisted that, on the contrary, "German life has been cleansed of cynicism." Mass mobilization meant the assertion of a collective will that offered a way to leave self-interest behind and experience transcendence, securing an absolutized social unity. It would be an almost religious effervescence. And so a man who had literally dodged a bullet in his twenties persuaded himself of the merit in sending millions of such men to dodge many such bullets.

His lambent faith eventually succumbed to the horrors of empirical reality. In March 1915 he published "The Idea of Europe," in which he mourned the loss of the "spiritual structure" inherent in this idea. The idea of Europe mattered to every cultured person, and did not conflict with national allegiances; he expressed hope that Germany would eventually find its way back to Europe. When "The Idea of Europe" was reprinted in 1917, he made changes: he ascribed the war to "the delusion and criminal frivolity of a minority of men across Europe," and looked forward to a reconciliation. That hope was hard to sustain. In a letter from May 1918 to Gertrud Kantorowicz, he despaired: "How long will this insane suicide last? . . . Everything the war seemed to promise has long since disappeared." The only victor, he believed, would be America.

In "Der Konflikt der modernen Kultur," a lecture he gave and published in 1918, the last year of his life, Simmel declared, "It can be counted among the deepest inner difficulties of numerous modern people that it is impossible to further protect the religions of church tradition, while at the same time the religious drives continue to persist in spite of all 'enlightenment.' This is so since religion can be robbed only of its clothing but not its life." The tone is strikingly unlike his earliest writings on the topic; he is not sneering but seeking. As for religiosity:

> Is it a being, not a having, is it a form of piousness which is called belief whenever it deals with objects? Now, however, religiosity is similar to life itself. It does not aim to satisfy extrinsic needs, but

searches instead for continuous life in a deeper sphere in which it is not yet torn between needs and satisfactions. . . . Life wishes to express itself directly as religion, not through a language with a given lexicon and prescribed syntax. One could use an apparently paradoxical expression and say: The soul can find faith only by losing it. To preserve the integrity of religious feeling, it must shake off all determined and predetermined religious forms.

He formulated a new iteration of a familiar difficulty: "life can express itself and realize its freedom only through forms; yet forms must also necessarily suffocate life and obstruct freedom." There is "a tempting way out of this dilemma," he suggested, "in the cultivation of the religious life as a thing in itself, the transformation of the verb 'to believe' from a transitive 'I believe that . . .' to a purely intransitive 'I believe.' " Yet he wondered whether the religious impulse could ever be satisfied with blessing the ups and downs of ordinary life or whether it ultimately requires an object. Either way, he mused, the power of belief is part of our soul's constitutions; and, because life will always transcend mere form, the conflict between the two is a chronic one. Mordantly, he added, "It is a philistine prejudice that conflicts and problems are dreamt up merely for the sake of their solution."[79]

Some of those conflicts and problems, of course, arise from prejudice. From the perspective of history, Simmel's earlier work on how religious identities were interactively affected by in groups and out groups, by real and projected hostilities, would prove disastrously relevant to German political culture, amid a resurgence of racialized forms of religious identity. His son, Hans, an internist, was sent to Dachau in 1938—Gertrud Simmel, who had been urging him to flee, took her own life some months earlier. Although Hans managed to make his way to Britain and then to America, his health had been damaged and he died in 1943. Gertrude Kantorowicz was apprehended while trying to cross the border to Switzerland, and died in Theresienstadt in 1945. Her daughter with Simmel, who embraced her ancestral Judaism, moved to Palestine, and became Channah Kantorowicz, had died the previous year, following an accident. Simmel's diary and much of his *Nachlass* was evidently seized by the Gestapo and have vanished from history.[80]

AXIAL ROTATIONS

Simmel could have foreseen none of this, of course, although some of his most vital, and, indeed, optimistic work was written under a sentence of death. Early in 1918, he learned he had liver cancer and had little time remaining, whereupon he made it his priority to complete his last major work, *Lebensanschauung* (translated as *The View of Life*). He did so, refusing to take morphine for the pain because it would slow his pen. At this point, he had augmented Bergsonian vitalism and *Lebensphilosophie* with a new emphasis on the "axial rotation," the *Achsendrehung*, that was the essence of "spiritual life." The most potent mode of transcendence, he suggested in the book, was the religious mode of taking God as an object of longing and faith:

> Here perhaps more completely than anywhere else has occurred the rotation around forms that life produces in itself in order to give its contents *immediate* context and warmth, depth and value. Now, however, these forms have become strong enough no longer to be defined by these contents, but rather to define purely of themselves; the object shaped by them, corresponding to their no longer finite measure, can now take charge of life.

He wrote, more optimistically than before, of those moments of life, shared or individual, that had a religious character "without being conditioned or defined in the least by a preexisting religion." Here, Simmel thought he had identified the social a priori. Yes, religion was among the forms that life had produced, "but intrinsic to the determination of this form from the outset is the fact that it reaches outward from the vital context through a radical turning to a centering and discovery of meaning in itself—and thus for the first time makes possible the self-supporting world integrated under the idea of religion."[81] How was society possible? This was how. Our relation to God mediates between the relative and the absolute, between reality and ideality. In an aphoristic journal entry, he invoked modality: "Natural science deals with possible necessity—religion with necessary possibility."[82]

For Simmel, in this final phase of his career, the act of seeking is central to the human experience; the questioning and searching matters more than the arrival at a putatively closed system of answers. This emphasis on seeking aligns with his understanding of human existence in the world as inherently fragmentary and filled with tensions. If life is a mosaic of conflicting experiences and desires, then the process of seeking coherence, meaning, and unity becomes a continuous endeavor. The questions we pose, the doubts we have, and the uncertainties we face are all integral to our existence. Our answers, then, are not endpoints; they are waypoints. Whatever answers we find will lead to new questions, further contemplation, and deeper exploration. The cyclical nature of questioning and answering feeds the very dynamism of human existence.

And religiosity, as an a priori faculty, amplifies this process. It drives humans to ask the big questions about existence, purpose, and meaning. The richness of human existence, for Simmel, lies not in the finality of answers but in the perpetual striving for understanding. He criticized Bergson for plumping for "flow" against "fixity" and failing to recognize that the two may constitute a unity. Years before, he had remarked that "religion as such" is a "product of human consciousness and nothing more," in ways consonant with Feuerbach's remark that "consciousness of God is self-consciousness, knowledge of God is self-knowledge."[83] But for Simmel that consciousness was never not social.

Meanwhile, Simmel had come to suspect that the cultural forms of his age were losing their power: "we gaze into an abyss of unformed life beneath our feet. But perhaps this formlessness is itself the appropriate form for contemporary life." His old heuristics were faltering, but new ones now beckoned. All sorts of avenues of thought stretched out before him now; he wished for another twenty years, he told his wife, so that he could explore them.[84] When he died, in September, the war—already the bloodiest conflict in modern European history—was still raging. For Simmel, that philosophy of life, incubated amid the carnage of conflict, had been the one creed that remained.

CHAPTER 4

Max Weber

Religious Rationalities

DIVINE COMPULSION — MEN IN BLACK — THE LIMITS OF HISTORICISM — JUST AS HOLY — AN ETHIC AND A SPIRIT — THE RELIGIOUS AND THE RATIONAL — STUDIES IN *LEBENSFÜHRUNG* — UNDERSTANDING SOCIAL ACTION — RATIONALIZING THE INDIVIDUAL — ORIGINAL *SINN* — FROM ORGY TO SACRAMENT — INTERESTS AND IDEALS — LEAVE THE WORLD BEHIND — THE MAGIC GARDEN — THE PARADOXICAL HINDU — KILLING THE AFTERLIFE — THE GODS AWAKEN — COLLISION COURSE — THE MYSTIC RATIONALIST

DIVINE COMPULSION

"It was like a miracle from God," Marianne Schnitger confided in her diary, in 1893, about a marriage proposal that had just arrived in the mail. It was from her second cousin (or, strictly, first cousin once removed) Maximilian Carl Emil Weber, and the letter lent itself to such a reading. "Read this letter, Marianne, when you are calm and steady, for I have things to say to you that you may not be prepared to hear," it began. "If we understand each other at all, I don't need to tell you that I would *never* dare offer my hand to a girl as a free gift. It is only if I myself am under the divine compulsion of complete, unconditional devotion that I may demand it and accept it for myself." This wasn't your usual letter of courtship. "You do not know me, you cannot possibly," he cautions. "You do not see how I struggle, with difficulty and varying degrees of success, to tame the elemental passions that nature has instilled in me."[1]

What was the character of this divine compulsion? In addition to the elemental passions, there was also the logic of capital accumulation. It was a family tradition. Weber's father came from an affluent family, but as the last of six children, he had to either earn a livelihood or marry one. He did hold a law degree, but what secured his fortunes was his union with Helene Fallenstein, a scion of a Huguenot textile fortune. (Her own father had married another such heiress.) Helene had grown up in a proper Heidelberg mansion known as the Villa Fallenstein, situated on a riverbank and surrounded by a large park, and had the resources to ensure that her family would not suffer deprivation. In 1872, when Max, their firstborn, was eight, the family moved to a spacious home in Charlottenburg—now in central Berlin, but then on its outskirts—that they liked to call the Villa Helene. Four stories high, and with more than a half-acre of gardens, it enabled a routine of salon-like socializing that helped the patriarch's political career: Max Weber, senior, served variously in the Prussian House of Representatives and in the imperial Reichstag, representing the National Liberal Party; as a senior and salaried administrator, he helped administer the Reich and its infrastructure. And he would regularly bring political and academic eminences to their home.

Helene was religiously committed to a luminous creed that was indistinguishable from her socially progressive ideals. Her husband, by contrast, was an essentially secular soul. Young Max—who would have been able to engage with the visiting academics from a fairly early age, given the considerable erudition his teenage letters display—had a largely cerebral connection to religion. In high school, he learned to view Christianity as a historical subject through reading David Friedrich Strauss. But before long he was able to share something of his mother's deep connection with the writings of William Ellery Channing, the eminent Unitarian minister and theologian. In 1884, Max, at age twenty, wrote to his mother that his reading of Theodore Parker and then of Channing (concerning "the infinite value of the human soul") represented the first time in years that "something religious has aroused in me more than an objective interest." Still, Channing's pacifism put his nose out of joint; and he disputed the "chasm" he found in Channing between the divine order and the human order.[2]

If young Max was no more religious than his father was, he had contempt for the contempt with which his father treated it; it was, in his view, an aspect of the insufficient respect his father had for his mother. That same year, he had written to his just-confirmed brother Alfred—who was four years his junior, and was to embark on a similar academic path—a proclamation of sorts:

> Everyone attempts to solve the great mysteries that this religion poses to our spirit in his own way.... The greatness of the Christian religion lies precisely in the fact that it exists equally for every human being, young and old, fortunate and unfortunate, and is understood, albeit in different ways, by all, as it has been understood for almost two thousand years now.... Everything we gather under the name "our culture" is based primarily on Christianity, so that today in the institutions and rules of human society as a whole, in its ways of thinking and acting, everything is connected and dependent on it, so much so that we ourselves are often not even aware of it anymore.[3]

Its influence is so ubiquitous, he went on, that it was as invisible to us as the air we breathe. It's always tempting to find the oak tree in the acorn—to see, in miniature, everything that is to come. We should resist the temptation only in part. Weber was a historicist who was highly wary of historicism, and we would do well to follow him in this.[4]

"*You* wish to write 'personal' books," he once wrote to a colleague. But Weber was convinced that an author's personality "emerges always and *only* when it is *unintended*, when it recedes behind the book and its objective character."[5] If the *Buddenbrooks*-ian aspects of his background aren't irrelevant to his fascination with the so-called spirit of capitalism, the alternating current represented by his parents' attitude toward religion isn't to be ignored, either. He was a social theorist of identity who did not readily identify as a social theorist; he did not always refer to sociology as an author of it and he would have been surprised to be regarded as one of the discipline's progenitors. But much of his work revolved around religion and rationality—which is also to say secularism and irrationality—and even work ostensibly about other topics was woven through with these preoccupations. He was an inveterate comparativist. From a global perspective, religion—which, for him, was about the here and now—explained the different itineraries of the great civilizations; it could be seen as the motor of economic development, or its brake. Unlike Durkheim and Simmel, he made a claim to something like methodological individualism; he was suspicious of holism, certainly in its Herderian or Hegelian flavors, but his individualism cannot be taken at face value.[6]

To trace the development of Weber's ideas is particularly challenging, because after his first proper academic appointment, in 1894, he never published another book during his lifetime. He wrote a great deal, but his writing was brought to print mainly in journals, notably one that he co-edited. In his later years, he embarked on a vast project: he planned to revise and assemble much of his work into a magnum opus, possibly two. But he died before he could complete this daunting task, and his *Nachlass* was assembled into something that was, inevitably, disjointed and repetitive, a palimpsest of prose from different phases of his evolving thought.[7] His best-known work, *The Protestant Ethic and the "Spirit" of Capitalism*, was first published in book form in English, and, throughout the twentieth century, was widely available only in the revised version that Weber had prepared a decade and a half after completing the original.

Yet part of what makes Weber's work on the sociology of religion so fascinating is the sense that it is animated by conflicting impulses. From a theoretical perspective, at least, it can seem as if he believed in religion but wasn't so sure he believed in society. That's not quite right. It's through religion, I've been arguing, that society becomes a disciplinary object. For Durkheim, the content of religion was society; for Simmel, the form of religion was society. But for Weber, in a thoroughgoing way, societies and religions were always plural entities; he was less interested in what faith traditions had in common than in what they didn't. He was a theorist and advocate of the "ideal type" who saw dangers in turning either "religion" or "society" into one.

MEN IN BLACK

Weber's undergraduate years—he left home, in 1882, for Heidelberg University—were intensely social, in the conventional way. He studied law, including the history of German and Roman law, but he also joined a dueling fraternity, the Allemannia, and joined his classmates in their lager-fueled escapades. The scholarship was secondary to the sodality. Returning home for the first time, he was so nicked and coarsened that his mother slapped him on the face.[8]

After a year spent doing his military service (he grumbled pridefully about the hardships, but he took pleasure in brotherly bonds forged across the usual social barriers), Weber studied law in Berlin, while living at home; his parents may have thought his dissipation would thereby be diminished. His mother would arrange for them to spend an hour together reading Channing before he went off to his lectures. (He slyly praised "Channing's entirely original and often magnificent view of the nature of religion—which, incidentally, is hardly to be called Christian.")

A final semester was spent at Göttingen, to prepare him for his law exams. He wrote to his mother, in January of 1886, about trying to bore his way through the Reich Criminal Code in the wake of other distractions, and quoted what he described as the merciless Roman dictum *ultra posse nemo obligatur* (one cannot be obligated to do what one cannot do), offering a gloss of his own devising: "one may stop only when one can no longer go on."[9] It was also from Göttingen, in March, that he found time to write Alfred a long letter that augers significant aspects of his later thought. He recalled how impressed he was by David Strauss when he first read him; but now, not yet twenty-two, he had come to see that certain Straussian concepts require reevaluation. In particular, Strauss's concept of "mythos" (Weber glosses it as "a product of the gradually evolving creative imagination of a poetically inclined people") failed to shed light on the relationship between Jesus as a historical person, who lived and acted within a specific sociocultural context, and the Christ of faith or history—a theological and cultural construct shaped by subsequent generations. The concept was "fundamentally not applicable to the actions of human spirituality and culture." In fact, Weber wrote, the basic Christ story, in the New Testament, is rather stark and poetically sparse. A thirst for knowledge preceded the shaping of religious ideas, he proposed. Accordingly, the notion of myth could not serve as some all-purpose key to understanding. It was misguided, Weber maintained, to liken the myths of Hercules or Persephone to what lived in the hearts of the long-suffering and mostly homeless first Christian communities. These were as distant as a newspaperman's statistically informed reflections on the effects of alcohol on the working class would be from the "immediate experiences and thoughts of someone currently struggling with severe hardship." He went on:

> Many things are similar: if a nanny caps the ink bottle at night and places two matches crosswise over it because she believes that Satan resides in the black liquid and now cannot escape, we laugh about it. And when Luther threw his inkpot at the evil enemy during one of his darkest moments at the Wartburg, one might laugh at that too, but it's a different kind of laughter. And our laughter fades when we think about the witch trials, and yet it's seemingly always the same superstition at play. Each instance touches on a different aspect of the human spirit and thus has a different significance—"One thing does not suit everyone."[10]

This issue of the continuities and discontinuities between folk beliefs and theological doctrine would continue to preoccupy theorists of religion.

Back in Berlin, Weber launched into his doctoral studies, eventually defending a dissertation on commercial partnerships and commercial law in medieval Italy. The usual thumbnail descriptions of the work make it sound rather dull, but the project was not unambitious; he was essentially trying to show how the limited liability corporation, the artificial person that lies behind modern capitalism, arose from premodern structures of medieval commerce.[11] This was followed by the postdoctoral thesis required for a teaching position, which was published in 1891. It concerned, as its title announced, Roman agrarian history and its significance for public and state law.[12] Once again, out of stupefying technicalities—an argument about Roman land measurement protocols for private and public lands—a provocative thesis took shape, this one concerning the development of two status tiers within agricultural labor: slaves and serfs. Of perhaps greater significance, Gustav Schmoller's institute, the Verein für Socialpolitik, assigned him to analyze survey data concerning farmworkers east of the Elbe, where German laborers found themselves competing with Polish and Russian migrants. A report of almost nine hundred pages was published in 1892.

The frat-boy undergraduate had become a rather Stakhanovite scholar, then, by the time he married Marianne in the fall of 1893. The wedding took place in Oerlinghausen, in Westphalia, where the bride's very rich grandfather—who was also the elder brother of Max's father—had a substantial linen factory. (She later inherited a share of the enterprise, Carl Weber & Co.) His relationship to religion remained rather impersonal, albeit liberal-minded in a way that ruled out simple hostility. In a letter to Marianne, from earlier in the year, he complained that the freethinkers of his father's generation were, in fact, narrowly intolerant, that the "dread of the 'man in black' is simply in the blood of our liberals and makes them think that in every pastor there's at least a predisposition to hypocrisy."[13]

Some of it was in *his* blood, too. He considered Catholicism a menace to individual conscience and scholarship, although he thought that Bismarck's anti-Catholic laws, during the *Kulturkampf* of the 1870s, violated rather than affirmed the obligations of the secularized state. He attended meetings of the Evangelical Social Congress in the early 1890s (honoring an enthusiasm of his mother's), but denied that he was of their party. He had ongoing concerns about the close relation between the state and the Lutheran church. Like many liberals, he was outraged when an Army officer, Moritz von Egidy, was kicked out of the military after he published a wildly popular little book, in 1890, calling for a revived Christianity that would shed ossified doctrine and emerge as a religion of love.[14] A Protestantism supposedly devoted to the autonomy of the individual conscience was at odds, he felt, with an alliance between ecclesiastical authorities and a militaristic state.

Weber's academic ascent can seem almost startlingly smooth. After a brief stint as a *Privatdozent* at Berlin, he gained the prize that long eluded Simmel: a full professorship, in his case a chair in economics and finance at Freiburg. There, he made the acquaintance of members of the Southwest neo-Kantians, not least Heinrich Rickert and his student Emil Lask. (Marianne, for her part, studied with Rickert, and wrote a dissertation on Fichte and Marxism, though the absence of an *Abitur* barred her from a formal doctorate.) In 1897, Weber became a professor of economics and finance at the distinctly more illustrious University of Heidelberg, where he quickly became close friends with the liberal theologian Ernst Troeltsch, and where he had his first female student, Else von Richthofen. Yet he let the prize drop from his hands almost as soon as he was given it.

The story of Weber's nervous breakdown in the spring of 1898 ("neurasthenia" was the psychiatrist Emil Kraepelin's diagnosis) has been often told. Marianne's influential biography of her late husband suggested it had something to do with a fierce argument he had with his father. The patriarch's offense was not, as one might assume, neglecting or abandoning his wife, but rather the opposite—encroaching on her vacation away from him and with her children. "We demand that Mama should enjoy the right to visit us alone in peace for four to five weeks a year at a time that is convenient for her," Max, representing the Weber *Kinder*, wrote to him the previous June. "As long as this is not done, any family relationship with Papa is meaningless to us." Joachim Radkau, in his somewhat Freud-flavored biography, maintains that Weber had violently destroyed his parents' marriage. In any case, eight weeks later, on a business trip abroad in August, Weber's father died of heart failure.[15]

What Marianne called a "descent into hell" followed; Max was increasingly afflicted by fatigue and insomnia. They went abroad, in pursuit of convalescence. In August of 1898, he checked into a sanitarium, one that prohibited agitating music (Wagner) but permitted Bach, Mozart, and Schubert. He was treated—with heroin, bromide salts, and the like—but his troubles continued. He was "very unhappy with the Almighty and tormented us by pretty well rebuking the Good Lord," Marianne reported to Helene that winter.[16] He went on leave; then extended the leave. A period of semi-recoveries and full relapses ensued. He was treated for depression and for sexual dysfunction. There were moments when he prepared to resume teaching, but he had also developed a phobia of lecturing. In the summer of 1901, he traveled through Europe, and ended up spending the following winter in Rome, researching church history. In 1903, he officially relinquished his teaching position. He wouldn't resume teaching for fifteen years.

The sociologist Donald G. MacRae wryly ventured that being ill, in that era, was "an alternative vocation for the comfortably off."[17] It's true that the rentier existence he and Marianne enjoyed made it all possible. Yet his suspended academic career wasn't conducted in exile from the academy; nor were these years any respite from research. In fact, the very long leave may have enabled scholarship of a kind that might have fitted only awkwardly within the disciplinary partitions of the day. The first essay Weber wrote as he began to regain his powers of concentration was in response to an academic obligation he had incurred—it was meant to be a contribution to a *Festschrift*. The final result, "Roscher and Knies and the Logical Problems of Historical Economics," which was published in three parts (in 1903, 1905, and 1906), has understandably received scant attention; Weber's biographer Jürgen Kaube calls it "unspeakably dry."[18] But Kaube also recognizes it for what it represents—a convalescent strenuously working his way through a crisis of knowledge. And what's hard to miss is how regularly religious and theological arguments are enlisted to establish points about method.

THE LIMITS OF HISTORICISM

Wilhelm Roscher and Karl Knies were founders of the "older" school of historical economics, and Weber's enormous essay assiduously covers a great deal of disputed terrain. In the section that was completed in 1903, Weber sides with his friend Rickert against Dilthey in the disciplinary characterization of history, critiques the value-ladenness of Wundt's notion of cultural development, offers a verdict on Schmoller's *Methodenstreit* with Menger (a split decision), cites

Simmel's philosophy of history, and commends Emil Lask's book on Fichte. In particular, he deploys the "very gifted" Lask's idea of the "hiatus irrationalis" between reality and the concepts through which we apprehend it, and enlists Lask's critique of Hegelian "emanationism," the notion that the structure of thought emanates from, and mirrors, the structure of empirical reality.[19]

Weber almost marvels at Roscher's unabashed religious commitments, and uses it to discredit a more widespread habit of organicism in political thought. Roscher suggests that the metaphysical soul of the nation is, like the soul of the individual, created by God; Weber uses the arrant naivety of the position against more modern-sounding ones that nonetheless, he suggests, follow a similar logic. In particular, Weber scorns biological analogies (like those favored by the illustrious Karl Lamprecht in *Die Kulturhistorische Methode*), and warns against the way every "organic" theory favors the "hypostatization of the 'nation' as the collective bearer" of certain psychical processes.[20] Weber's defense of individualism has to be seen against this background: he found romantic, Herder-style holism to be hiding within updated, quasi-evolutionary forms of organicism. And so, throughout, the elderly Roscher is less a target than a *reductio*, used to discredit contemporary scholars.

In one instance, though, Weber suggests a way to redeem Roscher's mystification. Roscher thought that "love of God" was a basic human drive, taking up, he maintained, "ideas of equity, justice, benevolence, perfection and inner freedom." The wider our moral circle expands, Roscher surmised, "the more closely the demands of reasonable self-interest coincide with those of *conscience*." How so? Because, in Roscher's view, the divine instinct constrains self-interest. "Thus," Weber glosses, disapprovingly, "the different social driving forces of human beings are conceived as the forms in which a basic religious impulse manifests itself in combination with self-interest."[21]

That's obviously a nonstarter, for Weber. But wait: what happens if you give an empirical, historical account of that "religious impulse"—turn it from a divinely immanent hidden hand of history into a historical object? Some scholars of the older Historical school of economics had argued that self-interest dominates in the private economic realm but that a sense of the common good predominates in public life. The difficulty is that the historicists haven't been historical enough, Weber suggests in a footnote: "A more thorough examination would demonstrate that this distinction is rooted in certain, quite definite, *Puritan* ideas which have been of very great importance for the 'genesis of the capitalist spirit.' "[22] It's almost as if he's advertising a book he had not yet written.

JUST AS HOLY

Undergirding Weber's work on religion as a social force were two very small societies. One, known as the Eranos circle, was an interdisciplinary group of scholars in Heidelberg who met each month to discuss subjects within the field of religious studies. It was convened at the start of 1904 by the theologian Gustav Adolf Deissmann (who had done important work on the Koine Greek of the New Testament) and the classical philologist Albrecht Dieterich (an expert in Greco-Roman religion and mythology). In addition to Weber, other members included the legal philosopher Georg Jellinek as well as the economist Karl Rathgen (a Japan expert) and the historian Eberhard Gothein (author of *Political and Religious Popular Movements before the Reformation*).

The meetings rotated through the homes of each participant. The host would give a talk; the guests would discuss it in a "parliamentary-ordered" way; a meal would be served; and then more freeform discussion was encouraged. (Marianne Weber sardonically wrote, of a later gathering, "Max is in charge of 'Protestant asceticism,' I am handling 'ham in burgundy.' ") The regular meetings ensured that Weber was well acquainted not just with the participants but also with the work that engaged them.

A second small society revolved around the *Archiv für Sozialwissenschaft und Sozialpolitik*. All journals create and are created by a society, and just as Durkheim's *équipe* coalesced around *L'Année*, Weber's intellectual comrades found a port of call in the *Archiv*. In 1903, the economist Edgar Jaffé, who had written a doctoral thesis at Heidelberg on the division of labor in English banking and was then finishing his *Habilitationsschrift*, bought the journal from its proprietor-editor, effectively on Weber's behalf. He may have been encouraged by his wife, Else, née von Richthofen, Weber's former student and current friend. The baroness—Else was the sister of the formidable Frieda, who was later to marry D. H. Lawrence, and a distant cousin of the Red Baron, Manfred von Richthofen—inherited little money with her title. But Jaffé, a *gekaufter Jude,* was something of a merchant prince; he came from a business family with a textile business in Manchester.[23] The relaunched journal would have three editors: Weber, Jaffé, and Werner Sombart—a Marxian economist who was associated with the "youngest" Historical school, and who represented continuity with the previous run. (For the first decade of the new series, Jaffé never published in the journal, while work by his two coeditors appeared regularly.)

The first issue of the new series contained Weber's extraordinary essay "Die 'Objektivität' sozialwissenschaftlicher und sozialpolitischer Erkenntnis" ("The 'Objectivity' of Social-Scientific and Social-Political Knowledge"), which he completed in early 1904. The essay, which effectively outlined a research agenda for the journal, was modestly prefaced with the remark that "those who know the work of the modern logicians—I cite only Windelband, Simmel, and for our purposes particularly Heinrich Rickert—will immediately notice that everything of importance in this essay is bound up with their work." But Weber had an emphatic announcement to make: "The type of social science in which we are interested is an empirical science of concrete reality" (the term he used for that empirical science of concrete reality, *Wirklichkeitswissenschaft,* was the noun Simmel had put to work earlier to describe history).[24] He went on to caution that an economic explanation of social phenomena is never exhaustive—it is "no way more complete than, for instance, the explanation of capitalism by reference to certain shifts in the content of the religious ideas which played a role in the genesis of the capitalistic attitude."[25] That sounds like an implicit disclaimer to his forthcoming *Protestant Ethic and the "Spirit" of Capitalism.* But Sombart, it should be noted, had published the first volume of his *Der moderne Kapitalismus* in 1902, which included twenty pages on *Die Genesis des kapitalistischen Geistes* (*The Genesis of the Capitalist Spirit*).

The gravamen of Weber's essay is that a "one-sided analysis" of cultural phenomena from a particular point of view may be a necessary "technical expedient." Hence scientific analysis of culture or social phenomena cannot be absolutely "objective": they are never independent of our viewpoints, of the way we select and organize knowledge for our "expository purposes." The kind of objectivity we can aim for, instead, is represented by the scholarly ideal of being value-free. "Only positive religions—or more precisely expressed: dogmatically bound *sects*—are able to confer on the content of *cultural values* the status of unconditionally valid *ethical* imperatives," he writes. Accordingly, "the fate of an epoch which has eaten of the tree of knowledge"—he's mischievously using the biblical metaphor to signify secularity—is to recognize "that the highest ideals, which move us most forcefully, are always formed only in the struggle with other ideals which are just as sacred [*ebenso heilig*] to others as ours are to us."[26] Note his language here. Not just as powerful; just as sacred.

Our points of view, in sociocultural analyses, would crystallize into what he called "ideal types"—a term that he borrowed from his Heidelberg colleague Georg Jellinek but made his own. Illustrating their use via generalizations about "church" and "sects," he writes, "An ideal type is formed by the one-sided *accentuation* of one or more points of view and by the synthesis of a great many diffuse, discrete, more or less present and occasionally absent *concrete individual* phenomena, which are arranged according to those one-sidedly emphasized viewpoints into a unified *analytical* construct. . . . This mental construct cannot be found empirically anywhere in reality." He concludes that we will need to determine in each case "the extent to which this ideal-construct approximates to or diverges from reality."[27] To develop an ideal type you must synthesize great quantities of ethnographic and historical material; its value will be visible only once it emerges through the synthesis. But for Weber, there was no dispensing with it.

AN ETHIC AND A SPIRIT

Weber had evidently started work on *Die protestantische Ethik und der 'Geist' des Kapitalismus* (*The Protestant Ethic and the "Spirit" of Capitalism*) in late 1903; the first part appeared in the *Archiv für Sozialwissenschaft und Sozialpolitik* about a year later. The more ambitious second part appears to have been finished by early April 1905 and appeared in the *Archiv* that June. The book is one of the most influential works of sociology ever published. Yet Weber hadn't conceived it as a contribution to sociology, and it wasn't actually prepared as a book until 1920—Weber readied it for publication as a volume in his never-completed project on the economic ethics of world religions, and it was first published as a separate book in English, in 1930. Because most people have read the 1920 version, which was adjusted to accord with his later scholarship and ideas (and to respond, tacitly, to certain criticisms), it's worth trying to keep straight what was and wasn't in the original version.[28]

Weber was writing as a nonbeliever, but, unlike Tylor, he was also writing about religious traditions that were, in some sense, his own. Still, the book maintains an external perspective, beginning with the sort of sociological observation about religion in which religious labels provide an independent variable in defining a social pattern. The pattern in question concerns a topic that does not at first sound terribly thrilling: "the occupational statistics of a denominationally mixed region." But the pattern had received a great deal of attention, especially among German Catholics, and it was this: business owners, managers, and skilled employees were predominantly Protestant. In fact, Weber's work was, in part, an intervention in a social-policy debate. Some Catholic leaders had been agitating for hiring quotas to redress the discrimination they believed they faced. As the historian Thomas Nipperdey writes, many liberals (and Jews, given that the campaign took no interest in any discrimination *they* faced), saw an attack on the ideals of civil neutrality, on behalf of a system of patronage and spoils.[29] What explained the Protestant advantage? The answer had worldly stakes.

Weber moves through a systematic review of a wide range of European societies—Germany, but also Poland, Scotland, England, Hungary, Russia—and rules out a series of possible hypotheses about why this pattern obtains. You might hypothesize, for example, that the answer lies in the greater inherited wealth of Protestants, but Weber tells us that even those Catholic families that *do* enjoy inherited wealth, in Baden, Bavaria, and Hungary, typically make different choices in the education of their children than Protestants do. They favor the classical humanistic education of the grammar school (the *humanistische Gymnasium*) over the technical education provided in the *Realgymnasium, Realschule*, and *Höhere Bürgerschulen*, choices that "may help to explain the low participation rates of Catholics in capitalist business life."[30]

What about the status of Catholics as a minority "excluded from politically influential positions by the dominant group"? Weber counters by pointing out that the opposite pattern holds for other minorities: Poles in Russia, Huguenots in France, non-Conformists and Quakers in England, and Jews all over Europe have in fact "come under *particular* pressure to pursue a business career," precisely because they are excluded from occupations as servants of the state. Thus, he concludes, it cannot be the external historical and political situation that accounts for the pattern; it must be some "distinct internal characteristics" (*dauernden inneren Eigenart*). And so we arrive at Weber's thesis: there is something about the Protestant ethos that conduces to capitalism.

Weber was a thoughtful methodologist, if not always a systematic one, and he tells us that in the development of historical concepts such as the spirit of capitalism, we should not begin with a definition. Instead, our grasp of the concept "must be composed from its individual elements, taken from historical reality," such that "it will not be possible to arrive at the ultimate *definition* of the concept at the outset but only at the *conclusion* of the investigation." Echoing his "objectivity" essay, he writes that what's wanted is a conception that serves "the points of view *which interest us here*"—namely, the understanding of human social behavior. "This is in the nature of 'historical concept-formation,' " he assures us. The analytical concepts that Weber deploys are often complex. Often, too, they are far from precise; he had internalized Aristotle's famous maxim that one should adopt the degree of precision appropriate to the subject—and social behavior shows many patterns but few sharp boundaries.[31] The "ideal type" is what allows Weber to reconcile talk of social forces, institutions, and the like with his vaunted individualism (an expression that "comprises the most heterogeneous ideas imaginable," he apologizes in a footnote). It allows him to write a work with what he considered two troublesome terms in it: *ethic* and *spirit*. A *Wirklichkeitswissenschaft* had to proceed cautiously to avoid the emanationism that dogged earlier theories. He was picking his way through a minefield.

Weber tended to see the spirit of capitalism most clearly expressed in the anglophone world; his exempla start with passages from Benjamin Franklin's "Advice to a Young Tradesman" (1748), urging industriousness and warning against idleness. ("Remember that *time is money*.") But behind all this financial providence is theological providence—the Calvinist belief in predestination. God has chosen some individuals to live with Him eternally; others He has condemned to be forever remote from His presence. During the English Civil War in 1643, Parliament convened a gathering of theologians and legislators in Westminster to revise the principles of the English Protestant church, and, over the next decade, they met to do their work. In 1648, they issued the Westminster Confession, one standard articulation of orthodox Calvinism. Chapter 3, section 3 of the Confession, which Weber cites, states the Calvinist doctrine of predestination in its full and fatal rigor: "By the decree of God, for the manifestation of His glory, some men . . . are predestinated unto everlasting life; and others foreordained to everlasting death."[32]

There was nothing you or anyone else—neither your priest or your prayerful family—could do to change that destiny, and *you did not know what it was*. Only if your life displayed the marks of election did you have some grounds for hope. All the sacraments—the Eucharist, confession, absolution—that had once promised relief and the return to God's favor after the inevitable errors made by a sinful creature; all the hope that came from the possibility that you might be justified by good deeds or saved by faith or the magical power of rituals: all this was gone. Tylor saw in religion a means of shaping one's fate in this world and, in the later, "higher" religions, also the next, even if only by submission. But for the Calvinist, God in all his remote magnificence was absolutely unmovable. The Calvinist could not gain God's favor by asking for it, since, if you *were* among the elect, he had given it to you freely before you had done anything, and if you were not, he had already condemned you.

Weber was cautious about psychology, but in a notably moving passage, he explores the inner state of the Calvinist confronted with the creed's central tenet. "This doctrine, with all the pathos of its inhumanity, had one principal consequence for the mood of a generation which yielded to its magnificent logic: it engendered, *for each individual*, a feeling of tremendous inner *loneliness*," he wrote. "In what was for the people of the Reformation age the most crucial concern of life, their eternal salvation, man was obliged to tread his path alone, toward a destiny which had been decreed from all eternity. No one and nothing could help him."[33]

It might happen that you *displayed* Christian virtues, though. Eternal life was not a reward for virtue, but virtue *was* a sign of election. If you found yourselves drawn to living a Christian life, then you had reason for hope. And here the Lutheran notion of *Beruf*, vocation, was critical. The Confession taught that you could be assured of your eternal election by your "effectual vocation," your *Beruf*, which was reserved for the saved. Weber explained that *Beruf* comes not from the Bible but from Luther's translation of it, and that it was Luther who introduced the modern meaning of the term, as a calling for work that might be nonreligious (except in the sense that all work was for God). Whereas for Catholics the notion of vocation was restricted to ecclesiastic roles, Luther expanded it to everyone, for we all had a calling to work. Weber argues that persons convinced of this truth would naturally seek signs that they were one of the elect, predestined to everlasting life.

What virtues in the callings of everyday life were signs of election? Ascetic Protestantism had an answer: frugality, hard work, and conscientiousness—the virtues that Franklin had commended to the young apprentice. They practiced them not because that would *earn* them a place in heaven (and not, of course, because they wanted to "lay up" for themselves "treasures upon earth, where moth and rust doth corrupt"), but because their presence was a *sign* that they were already guaranteed that place.[34] The practical effect, though, was the same. Calvinist asceticism, valuing ceaseless labor and disdaining profligacy, was a powerful lever.

Weber underlined one of the many ironies of his account. The reformers of Calvinist or Puritan sects were "not the founders of societies of 'ethical culture' or representatives of humanitarian programs of social reform or cultural ideals. The *salvation of souls* and this alone is at the heart of their life and work." Behind capitalism, then, are "purely nonmaterial [*ideell*] motives." Greed, the acquisitive instinct, could be found in all places and periods. Capitalism cannot. By promoting accumulation while inhibiting consumption, ascetic Protestantism favored investment capital. "If that restraint on consumption is *combined with the freedom to strive for profit*," Weber wrote, "the result produced will inevitably be the *creation of capital* through the *ascetic compulsion to save*."[35]

There's a puzzle as to why the predestinarian story took hold so broadly, replacing the older Catholic picture, which offered so much more obvious consolation to sinners—that is, pretty much everyone. And there is something paradoxical about being moved to everyday holiness by the thought that everything is already fixed in advance. Besides, why was it particularly those virtues of frugality and hard work that came to be identified with election? Why wasn't it charity or generosity? But the power of Weber's account didn't require that we share its conclusions. It's like a grand cathedral we admire for its architecture and ornamentation, regardless of our faith.

THE RELIGIOUS AND THE RATIONAL

Weber didn't need to say what made the attitudes that he surveyed religious. All that mattered was that he could apply the label "Protestant" or "Calvinist"—or in his larger category, "Ascetic Protestantism"—to a group of people and associate them with a commitment to certain values and with the behavior that flows from them. But just as Weber had refused to define the spirit of capitalism at the start of the *Protestant Ethic*, he wanted the true nature of religion to emerge in the course of the study, too. In declining to define religion, Weber has left open *which* type of social behavior he is interested in. But he did give us something to go on, for this definition of the project commits him to the sociology of religion as the study of a form of social behavior. Because Tylor had defined culture as including knowledge and belief "acquired as a member of society," he did not need to attend solely to social behavior. Much of the religious behavior that Tylor discussed was indeed the result of socially acquired beliefs, but it could still be practiced on your own.

What interests Weber is social phenomena, behavior that is organized through communities and their shared institutions and concepts.

A second master concept, also scarcely defined, appears throughout the book: rationality. Echoing his "objectivity" essay, he warns, "It is possible to 'rationalize' life from extremely varied ultimate standpoints and in very different directions; 'rationalism' is a historical concept which embraces a world of opposites." In ascetic Protestantism, notably, the notion of *Beruf*, which is "so *irrational* from the point of view of eudaemonistic self-interest," issues in the "*rationalization* of the conduct of life in the world with a view to the beyond," and thus provides an engine for economic rationalization. In a telling footnote, he cautions: "Religious experience as such is, of course, irrational, like *every* experience. In its highest, mystical form it is . . . distinguished by its absolute incommunicability. . . . *Every* religious experience loses substance as soon as an attempt to formulate it *rationally* is made."[36] It would be another decade before he made a concerted effort to rationalize his own idea of rationality.

For Weber, as I mentioned earlier, religion involved doing things together, as a member of a community. The same held for scholarship, he knew, and his work is very much in dialogue with the contentions and findings of previous scholars. It mattered that Weber had read Simmel's *Philosophy of Money*, which would have reinforced his sense that capitalism issued through abstraction, the liquification of desired possessions into a common currency, and gave rise to a domain-specific form of rationalism. "Production, with its technology and its achievements, seems to be a cosmos with definite and, as it were, logical determinations and developments which confront the individual in the same way as fate confronts the instability and irregularity of our will," Simmel had written.[37] The intellectual historian Peter Ghosh shrewdly notes the analogy between Calvin's hidden God, *deus absconditus*, and the hidden and impersonal working of capital, and it was Simmel who had captured that sense of impersonal abstraction.[38] It's possible to hear Simmel's murmurings in other aspects of the project, too. Simmel, in his 1892 *Problems of the Philosophy of History*, a work Weber read and quoted, stressed how motives could become calcified into conventions, pursued mindlessly. Weber illustrated this process in contending that the "Puritan asceticism of the calling, only *without* the religious foundation," could retain its power to sustain capitalism. His choice of Benjamin Franklin, a Deist who was the opposite of ascetic in his personal life, made that clear. And so, Weber wrote, "the idea of a 'duty in a calling' haunts our lives like the ghost of once-held religious beliefs." It's in this way that our outward possessions become a *"stahlhartes Gehäuse,"* a "steel-hard casing" (or as Talcott Parsons translated it, more poetically, "an iron cage").[39]

But whereas Simmel seldom indicated sources for his factual claims, Weber adopts a more modern scholarly mode. He duly cites Werner Sombart's discussion of "The Genesis of the Capitalist Spirit," though he charts a different course. Sombart pointed to a number of factors in the rise of capitalism. One was technical: the rise of double-ledger accounting. Another was a financial crisis caused by the Crusades and the plundering of the Orient in the thirteenth and fourteenth centuries, which presented an opportunity to shopkeepers of the lower orders (in particular, Jewish ones), who were familiar with credit and unencumbered by a canonical proscription on charging interest.[40] The spread of Protestantism among the merchant class, Sombart thought, could be the result of an emerging economic ethos as much as its cause: merchants would have been drawn to a religious language that validated conduct once regarded with social disapproval. Other elements in Sombart's work were more aligned with Weber's project; Sombart had carefully distinguished between craft businesses and capitalism. ("The purpose of a capitalist boot factory is never the manufacture of boots, but always only the achievement of profit.")[41] He stressed that capitalism requires liquidity, the possibility of turning ownership into money, and that it requires, as well, the capitalist spirit—a calculative sense of economic rationality. Weber may have advanced a thesis at odds with Sombart's, but he gained from Sombart's analytic categories.

The most frequently cited scholar in *The Protestant Ethic*—cited sometimes to signal a debt, sometimes to register a disagreement—is the eminent theologian Albrecht Ritschl. What made him inescapable for a social theorist like Weber is that he was associated with "mediation theology," or *Vermittlungstheologie*, which—drawing on Hegel's idea of mediation—aimed at the transcendence of "contradictions," in this case between faith and scientific knowledge. Ritschl complained of theologians who placed undue emphasis on the redemptive aspects of Christianity while giving short shrift to the ethical interpretation offered by the idea of a Kingdom of God, in ways that he elaborated in his best-known work, *The Christian Doctrine of Justification and Reconciliation*, from the 1870s.[42] An attentive reader of Kant, Hegel, Schleiermacher, Lotze, and Dilthey, Ritschl sought to avoid the temptation to produce "either merely a doctrine of redemption or merely a system of morality," but to produce a theology under the constitutive influence of both. And Ritschl insists, in his first chapter, that "two characteristics are perceptible in religious conceptions which must be stated at the very outset. They are always the possession of a community, and they express not merely a relation between God and man, but always at the same time a relation toward the world on the part of God, and those who believe in Him. All religions are social."[43]

Precisely because all religions are social, "when examining the typical individual subject, the complete conditions of fellowship must be taken into consideration from the outset"—this "social character of religion" must always be borne in mind.[44] Beyond Weber's engagement with, say, the theologian's specific claims about pietism (a recreation for the leisured classes, he thought), Ritschl's emphatic situating of religions in the social realm had resonance. Weber, in turn, could insist both on the "profound inner isolation" that marked the Calvinist's relationship to God and on the "superiority of the social organization of Calvinism," for "the *social* work of the Calvinist in the world was only work 'in majorem gloriam *Dei*.' "[45] The socialization of solitude, Weber held, could advance the economic rationality of collective enterprises.

STUDIES IN *LEBENSFÜHRUNG*

At the end of August 1904, Weber crossed the Atlantic, with his wife and with Troeltsch, for a tour of the United States, proceeding to visit twenty-one cities and thirteen states and meet with various notables, including W. E. B. Du Bois (from whom Weber solicited a piece for the *Archiv*) and William James, whose *Varieties of Religious Experience* he had read attentively. He was also introduced to the country's varieties of religious life, and he wrote up his impressions in a piece for the *Frankfurter Zeitung*, which was subsequently expanded into an essay on " 'Churches' and 'Sects' in North America" that appeared in *Die Christliche Welt* in 1906. It wasn't meant to be more than a suggestive sketch. But it reflected his belief that religion had a primary role in shaping national character and in undergirding economic activity. The Americans struck him as less secularized than Western Europeans, with more demanding churchly affiliations. In the United States, Weber wrote, "the most fundamental and universal community, the religious congregation, embraces almost all 'social' interests that take the individual out of his own front door."[46] Church membership served as a social guarantee, a mechanism for ascribing trustworthiness, and, in particular, creditworthiness. You established your bona fides in business transactions through your church membership; and if you were late to pay a debt or came to be seen as spendthrift you might, in turn, find yourself rejected from your church community.

He fleshed out the ideal-typical distinction he had earlier drawn between churches and sects. Whereas a church is an institution ministering to the souls of those born into it, a sect—by which he meant a group small enough that its members knew one another personally—sees itself as an anti-authoritarian "free community" of individuals. (The revivalist spirit of the American sects he saw stood in contrast to the more attenuated ways of the state church in Germany.) The leader of such a congregation gained legitimacy not through erudition but through personality. Although Weber's account is not entirely economistic, it is chiefly concerned with sects as a source of what we might now call social capital.

Weber published relatively little in the next few years, but Ghosh believes that Weber's cumulative revisions of *Protestant Ethic* from 1907 to 1920 had a "centre of gravity" in 1907, which is when he spent considerable energy rebutting criticisms of the work. (Further rejoinders—highly nettled in tone—followed over the next few years.) The task of defending what Weber called his *Hauptarbeit* may have taken a toll; despite having adopted the practice of taking nude midday sunbaths for his health, he experienced a welling sense of nervous depression. He wrote a long report on his "pathological predisposition" for a Heidelberg neurologist; the idea of castration was bruited and rejected.[47] Then again, 1907 was also when Marianne inherited a sizable share of her maternal grandfather's prosperous firm, removing any pressure on Max to earn a salary.

Other tensions remained, some erotic. This was a period when you could find Frank Wedekind's *Spring Awakening* (which had its Berlin debut in 1906) playing in the theaters, and when the sexologist Magnus Hirschfeld's work was widely available; every intellectual now had opinions about sexuality and eroticism. For Weber, of course, these ideas mattered inasmuch as they affected the conduct of life, or *Lebensführung*. Soon, Else Jaffé began spending a good deal of time in the Weber household. (Weber's biographer Jürgen Kaube wonders whether Marianne herself was a little in love with her, and perhaps it's significant that Else named her second child "Marianne.")

Else was certainly untrammeled by the usual marital conventions; in 1907, she had a child, her third, with the psychiatrist Otto Gross, who also had an affair with her sister, Frieda, and then submitted a case study about Else to the *Archiv*. (Weber turned it down.) That same year, Weber wrote Else a long letter, dripping with jealousy and ripping into Gross. The letter made it clear that he was a careful reader of Freud, though he speculated that it might be better if he kept his repressed impulses repressed. On a trip to Italy that the Webers took with the Jaffés in 1909, Max found himself alone with Else in Venice, and Else, in notes she made later, recalled him talking about "the possibility and permissibility of occasional 'adventures,' " with just one carve-out: his brother Alfred, then a professor of economics at Heidelberg. ("I think: 'Easy for you to say!' " she wrote.) By the spring of 1910, Else and Alfred were indeed an item.[48] A long froideur between the brothers ensued. Max viewed Alfred as a libertine but his principal sin, it seems, was a habit of interposing himself between Max and his love interests.

Mina Tobler, a Swiss pianist, came into his life in 1909, via Emil Lask, whose girlfriend she was at the time. Weber found her enchanting ("*so physically* graceful and resolutely strong at the same time") and was wild about her Chopin.[49] Tobler judged Weber the most intelligent man she had ever met, and she told him that she thought he could become chancellor; Weber didn't demur, though he added, "Of course the Kaiser would first have to be killed."[50]

The work on religion continued. In an often-quoted 1909 letter to Ferdinand Tönnies, he wrote, "I am absolutely 'unmusical' in religious matters and have neither the need nor the ability to erect any spiritual 'edifices' of a religious nature within me—that simply doesn't work, or, rather, I reject it. But, on careful examination, I am neither anti-religious *nor irreligious*. In this respect, too, I feel a cripple, like a mutilated person whose inner fate it is to have to honestly admit this to himself, to come to terms with it—so as not to fall into romantic deception—but also (here I find an expression in Mrs. Simmel's profound book very apt) not to pretend to be a full tree when I am merely a tree stump that can still sprout here and there."[51] Radkau suggests that "unmusical" here is a play on Schleiermacher's remarks about the music of religion (he had written that "religious feeling should accompany every human deed like a holy music"); and sees the implication that if he were whole and intact, Weber would be able to partake in religious life. It's also the case that music was enormously important to him; Kaube nicely remarks that Weber, if religiously unmusical, was musically religious. In a letter from 1911, filled with enthusiasm about a concert where Beethoven's cello sonatas were performed, Weber reports that Simmel was in the audience, too, and that "the music visibly spiraled though his body."[52]

In April of 1910, the Webers moved into the Fallenstein villa; the Troeltschs companionably agreed to rent a floor above them. Max and Marianne's *jour fixe*, held there on Sundays, became a basis for what some called the Weber circle. The Simmels paid them a visit, as did all manner of literary luminaries, including Stefan George. By the summer of 1911, Tobler was such a regular at the Weber household that he brought in a piano so she could play whenever she wanted. It's hard to know precisely what *entente* the two Webers reached (Weber's biographers tend to think that theirs was a *mariage blanc*), but the three often socialized together, and Max was open about the time he spent with his *Tobelchen*. He had written mockingly about how experience, and chasing experience, had become a paramount value in German culture; but eroticism as an escape—as part of what, in his most powerful essay about religion, he called the "rejection of the world"—was integral to his own experience in these years.

Eduard Baumgarten, a distant cousin and sort of surrogate son of Marianne's, wrote of a conversation between the Webers in which Marianne said that she couldn't imagine being a mystic and Max replied, "It might even be that I *am* one. Just as I have *dreamed* more in my life than one should really allow oneself, I am also nowhere *entirely* reliably at home. It is as if I could (and wish to) withdraw *completely* from *everything* just as well."[53] He would do so for periods, typically on Easter breaks. While spending much of April 1913 on Lake Maggiore, he read poetry and Thomas Mann's second novel, *Royal Highness*, took a break from various stimulants and opiates, and in responding to a younger colleague, a political economist at Tübingen, refused to be drawn into academic matters—invoking, in more straightforward fashion that he had with his mother, that ethical and legal dictum: *ultra posse nemo obligatur*.[54] One cannot be obligated to do more than one can do.

UNDERSTANDING SOCIAL ACTION

It's notable that around this time Weber started to adopt the Dilthey-associated language of *Verstehen*, understanding, where he had previously used the terms "interpretation" and "interpreting" (*interpretieren*). When a conception of *verstehende Soziologie* emerged in his writing, around 1913, it was clear that *Verstehen* and *verstehen*, the noun and the verb, carried a number of meanings. "One does not have to be Caesar in order to understand Caesar": Weber quoted this line of Simmel's more than once. (Given his larger concerns, it's odd that he skipped the second part of Simmel's sentence: "nor does one have to be another Luther in order to understand Luther.") But you did have to try to see the world from Caesar's perspective—to understand a deed in terms of what it meant to the doer. This discipline of *Verstehen* also helped clarify points about religious practice. In "Über einige Kategorien der verstehenden Soziologie" ("On Some Categories of *verstehende* Sociology") published in *Logos* in 1913, he introduced a few new coinages:

Subjectively rational instrumental [*zweckrational*] action and action "correctly" oriented toward objectively valid goals ("correctly rational" [*richtigkeitsrationales*]) are two very different things. An action that the researcher seeks to explain may appear to them to be instrumentally rational in the highest degree and yet be oriented toward assumptions held by the actor that are totally invalid to the researcher. Action oriented toward conceptions of magic, for example, is often subjectively of a far more instrumentally rational character than any non-magical "religious" behavior. This is because, in a world increasingly divested of magic [*Entzauberung*], religiosity must increasingly take on (subjectively) irrational meaning relationships (ethical or mystical, for instance).[55]

The emphasis on *Verstehen* also supported an emphasis on the analytic term "social action" (*soziales Handeln*)—an action that is subjectively meaningful to the actor and is informed by an awareness of how others will behave.[56] If a "social fact," for Durkheim, was in some way external to the individual, a "social action," for Weber, was to be explained as a dynamic involving the individuals involved. For all Weber's reservations about Dilthey (concerning, for example, the nature of the *Geisteswissenschaften*) and Simmel (concerning interaction and sociation, *Wechselwirkung* and *Vergesellschaftung*), social-action theory enabled him to take aboard what he found valuable in both. Weber, of all people, certainly did not disdain the quantitative aspects of the discipline, but he knew that it was not enough to count; what one chose to count, and the meaning of those counts, were never simply given. *Verstehen* encapsulated, usefully, a critique of positivism.

At the same time, it bolstered his defense of individualism. As he wrote in that 1913 essay on sociological categories, "The object of discussion, 'Verstehen,' is ultimately the reason that interpretive sociology (as we have defined it) treats the single individual and his action as its basic unit, as its 'atom.' "[57] We had to grasp what something meant for a person, not simply what function we might take it to have served. Weber's insistence on what Joseph Schumpeter dubbed "methodological individualism" might seem curious for someone known as a founder of sociology. What to make of it?

RATIONALIZING THE INDIVIDUAL

Individualism or individuality (the distinction isn't lexically marked in Weber's texts) mattered to Weber in more than methodological ways.[58] Simmel had distinguished between an eighteenth-century individualism that was bound up with equality and a nineteenth-century individualism that was bound up with difference.[59] Both made a claim on Weber. In an intellectual biography, Fritz Ringer suggests, plausibly, that Weber prized "cultural individualism," in a tradition that linked Wilhelm von Humboldt and J. S. Mill, and that aligned Weber with the difference-focused individualism, even as—ever the liberal democrat—he valued equality-focused individualism as well.

As for the atom of analysis? We've already seen that some version of this dance between the individual and society—the individual as an artifact of society, and society as composed of individuals—plays out in the work of each of our social theorists. None derogated individuality as such. But Weber was particularly concerned that unreflective forms of organicism were still circulating in intellectual life and thought that his historicist colleagues had sometimes fallen prey to it. He may also have felt, resentfully, that he had been lobbied—by the practitioners of *Völkerpsychologie*, by political economists of the Historical school, by the philosophical likes of Simmel—to stress the social origins of the self, as a product of the interactive and reciprocal influences that individuals had with one another. Obstinately, he didn't wish simply to fall in line.

Still, a meaningful methodological individualism quickly runs into difficulties. Some are epistemological. You can be confident about social patterns without knowing anything about the individuals involved or their psychologies. Why did crime rates drop, or suicide rates rise? Even if a social pattern holds in virtue of the individuals involved, we don't need to know (and perhaps cannot know) about those individuals to know about the social pattern. And the prospect of cashing out in individual terms something like the purchasing power of your dollar, or mark, would be daunting. How useful is the psychology of individuals in explaining why a Rembrandt costs vastly more than a Ruisdael? Other difficulties are ontological. Social institutions may involve more than persons. Perhaps a chapel is its building as well as its congregation. The full explanation of social exchanges may involve technologies and material entities—say, the existence of contemporary ATMs, or a nineteenth-century postal service (which involves horses and paper-based technologies). Cognition itself may, in a range of cases, be a supraindividual process.

How much rides on this? Comparing Weber and Durkheim in this respect, what one finds is a difference in theoretical emphasis, not a substantive disagreement about reality. In the end, Weber mainly wrote about social groups as collective entities, organized around ideal types—the key bridge, for him, between individuals and cultures. Durkheim's holism was more individualistic, and Weber's individualism more holistic, than is often assumed.

Weber's focus on rationalization reinforced his individualism but was also complicated by it. "Rationalization" is a word he uses to cover a number of processes; not just a commitment to means-end calculation but also the systematization of belief; a decline in magical appeals to "mysterious, incalculable forces" (disenchantment); and the growth of "value-rationality" (*Wertrationalität*), which entails an increasing focus on maximizing a narrow range of personal goals prized for themselves.[60]

And those processes are just the major ones. It should be noted that *Rationalisierung, Rationalismus, Rationalität*—rationalizing, rationalism, rationality—were terms he used with the same basic import. What that import was, however, might not be obvious. Surveying Weber's writing on ascetic Protestantism and modern capitalism, the sociologist Rogers Brubaker thought he had identified sixteen meanings of "rational," which he summarizes as "deliberate, systematic, calculable, impersonal, instrumental, exact, quantitative, rule-governed, predictable, methodical, purposeful, sober, scrupulous, efficacious, intelligible and consistent." In Weber's thought, he maintained, substantive rationality, which takes account of the value of actions and objectives, was regularly at odds with instrumental, procedural rationality.[61] A narrowly defined class of technical problems, where there's no clash over ends, can have an objectively determined rational solution; but social tensions invariably involve just such clashes. Whatever value conflicts we have within us are bound to be amplified on the collective level.

Around this time, another ideal type starts to shape what we can now confidently call Weber's sociology of religion. This was effectively announced in his letter to his publisher, Paul Siebeck, at the very end of 1913, in which he describes a work that would encompass "all the major religions of the world: a sociology of the doctrines of salvation and religious ethics."[62] He knew that the concept of the "salvation religion" (*Erlösungsreligion*) had already been explored in various ways by theologians, historians, and philosophers. But its importance, for Weber, is also related to his thesis that religion was a primary vehicle for rationalization—including the rationalization of ethics.

ORIGINAL *SINN*

The liberal theologian Otto Pfleiderer, a professor at the University of Berlin and someone Weber had read since at least his undergraduate years, made the force of the concept plain. In *Religionsphilosophie auf geschichtlicher Grundlage* (1878), he proposed that the religions of Moses, Zarathustra, Confucius, and Muhammad were "law religions," while Buddhism and Christianity were "salvation religions" (*Erlösungsreligionen*). In a law religion, the authority of God was in some sense external; you submitted to it, but you did not recognize it as inherently good and rational (*gut und vernünftig*). In an 1873 book about the future of religion, Eduard von Hartmann was getting at something similar when he wrote about Protestantism, "moral autonomy takes the place of moral heteronomy."[63]

Hermann Siebeck, in an 1893 textbook, connected *Erlösungsreligionen* to the shift from natural religion to "revealed" religion.[64] In natural religion, wrote Siebeck, a philosopher at Giessen, we turn natural forces into gods and appease them to fend off evil, by which we mean external danger; but when God is understood not as a deliverer from evil but as a redeemer from evil, we see that our entanglement with the world poses internal evils as well as external ones, and in this way "the idea of God serves to negate the world." Troeltsch, in a 1901 lecture, seemingly elaborates this point: salvation religions are able to sever men inwardly from the whole of existent reality, even from the nature of their own souls, in order to conform reality with divinely empowered men. Thus they provide the whole of existent reality not only with an example of those values that overcome the world and constitute its only worth but also with the sure hope of victory and of living for a higher world.[65]

The notion of the salvation religion was key to Weber's efforts to rationalize the concept of religion itself, which begins in earnest in *Typen religiöser Vergemeinschaftung* (*Types of Religious Communities*), a treatise he worked on between 1913 and 1914. The caveat it starts with reprises his earlier caveat about the spirit of capitalism: "To define 'religion,' to say what it *is*, is not possible at the start of a presentation such as this. Definition can be attempted, if at all, only at the conclusion of the study."[66] (Spoiler alert: definition is not attempted at the conclusion of the study, either.)

But he adds this hint, intimating the importance of *Verstehen*: "The external courses of religious behavior are so diverse that an understanding of this behavior can only be achieved from the viewpoint of the subjective experiences, ideas, and purposes of the individuals concerned—in short, from the viewpoint of the religious behavior's 'meaning' " or *Sinn*. He notes that the "most elementary forms of behavior motivated by religious or magical factors are oriented to *this* world." Second, religiously or magically motivated behavior is "relatively rational behavior, especially in its earliest manifestations. . . . Religious or magical behavior or thinking must not be set apart from the range of everyday purposive conduct, especially since even the ends of the religious or magical actions are predominantly economic."[67]

Tylorian intellectualism surfaces here, splashily: that's why the earlier forms of religion are especially rational—the this-worldly, transactional structure is up front. Later, human beings might have better explanations for phenomena; in early days, magical or religious hypotheses explain the phenomena as well as anything available. But just because we moderns might consider some technique irrational doesn't mean that it was irrational to earlier religious actors. (Here again he is aligned with Tylor, who had insisted that those who "give their minds to master the general principles of savage religion" will realize that, to a high degree, "they are consistent and logical" and, indeed, "essentially rational.")[68] A distinctively Weberian addendum is the claim that the objectives of religious actions are predominantly economic; these actions aren't undertaken simply to satisfy curiosity. They're not—as Durkheim and Simmel suggest, in various ways—symbolizing, crystallizing, or making intelligible the nature of society. They're advancing economic goals. Is *homo religiosus* ultimately *homo economicus*?

The broader project was taking shape: *The Economic Ethics of World Religions*. Weber told Rickert, in the summer of 1913, that he would be sending him a "systematics of religion," and in it his agenda was plain. While Durkheim and Simmel sought to explain how the religious emerged from social processes (or how the religious impulse was part of the social one), Weber wanted to focus on those features of the overall structure of religion that were "decisive for the shaping of practical conduct of life in its differences from other religions."[69]

Not everything in the sphere of religion related to what Weber called "social action"; contemplation or solitary prayer did not. Religious behavior, to qualify as religious, had to be "oriented to the past, present or expected future behavior of others," which is how he defined social action.[70] (To be sure, such actions could be conditioned by intra-religious features that weren't themselves action-guiding.) At the same time, religious communities could act for nonreligious reasons, perhaps related to status, domination, or economic pursuits. Such things could, indeed, affect the subjective meaning of religious conduct. There could be historical and political influences on religiosity; a religious affiliation could be determined by your class or estate. And so on. Always, religion had to be understood as a human enterprise.

Although Weber, like so many sophisticated thinkers of his era, was leery of crude evolutionism, he wasn't going to abandon stadial accounts altogether, and his "Religious Groups" opens with a carefully composed section on "The Origins of Religion" ("Die Entstehung der Religionen"). It shows that he had already immersed himself in the history, ethnography, and archeology of such regions as India, China, Russia, and the Middle East. He had read his Tylor, his

Marett, his Müller, and the broader syllabus of religious scholarship he had started in his teens. We start with magic, in a state of "pre-animistic naturalism" (*Naturalismus*); he's able to take for granted a widely accepted account of this phase. As we saw in the chapter about Tylor, Marett thought that Tylor's categories could be refined: "animatism," in which the world of objects, plants, and creatures was seen as "animated," might precede the notion of spiritual beings. Weber, splitting the difference, and drawing, as Marett had, on the model of *mana*, says that "at the outset, 'spirit' is neither soul, demon, nor god, but something indeterminate, material yet invisible, nonpersonal and yet somehow endowed with volition." Its presence in a host endows it with its "distinctive power."[71] And whereas Tylor characterized as "religious" all traffic with spiritual beings, Weber mainly defers to those who reserved the term "religion" for a stage that follows primordial magic.

But little rests on these details. The basic story here is consonant with Tylor's, including Weber's invocation of "naturalism," one of his distinctive contributions to the discussion. Although he doesn't define the term, it's plainly a way of emphasizing (consistent with earlier accounts of "natural religion") how the "magical" connected seamlessly with everyday forms of causal interactions: "Rubbing will elicit sparks from pieces of wood," Weber writes, and that is "as much a 'magical' effect as the rain evoked by the manipulations of the rainmaker." In the state of primordial naturalism, he's suggesting, there wouldn't even have been a separate category of the magical. People simply lived in a magical world. He's effectively more Tylorian than many of those who would amend Tylor, stressing that the doctrine of religious grace, in all its forms, is "already present *in nuce*" in the very earliest forms of religion ("lately termed 'pre-animistic' "), and stressing the "survivals" on the level of contemporary folk beliefs. ("To this day, no decision of church councils," he writes, "has succeeded in deterring a south European peasant from spitting in front the statue of a saint" blamed for wrongly withholding a favor.)[72]

Weber's most consequential contribution, in this work, is his introduction of the term "charisma" as a quality that might be found in certain persons (necromancers, magicians), but also certain objects, like that statue. Charisma began, of course, as a technical term in Jewish and Christian thought, referring to the gifts of God's χάρις, his grace, as in Saint Paul's first letter to the Corinthians, where they are listed: wisdom, knowledge, faith, the gifts of healing, miracles, prophecy, the discerning of spirits, and a capacity to speak and understand many languages.[73] Yet Weber seems first to have used the word in a letter, from 1910, about the poet Stefan George, who had visited the Webers at the Villa Fallenstein and who struck Weber as the leader of a sect. George's devotees, mainly young men, craved his approval and were cast out of his circle if they contravened his commands. Weber didn't quite see the allure himself, but he did identify the "extraordinary gift of grace" that his followers imputed to him.[74] In Weber's thinking about religion, as you might suppose, he seems first to have seen charisma as the personalization of magic. People who belonged to the oldest of professions, the *Zauberer*, the magicians, have charisma. They are regularly capable of achieving ecstasy, which is the distinctive human state that both represents and mediates charisma. (Weber's sociology of political authority conceives charisma as an extension of the magically underwritten authority of prophets and heroes.)

Soon, the semantic expansionism we've seen in other favored terms of his took over. Charisma was to be found not just in specially gifted persons but also in objects, and in offices; it could be defined negatively as something that resists rationalization.

FROM ORGY TO SACRAMENT

For all Weber's seeming deference to the individual, he was fascinated with collective forms of self-transcendence, the sporadic merging of consciousness. The primordial form of religious association, he now decides, is "the orgy," *die Orgie*, an occasional form of shared ecstasy, perhaps induced by narcotics and music. In using the term, Weber is mindful of the Greek term ὄργια, which referred to the rites and ceremonies associated with mystery cults, and of the Latin *orgia*, which continued its connection to the ritualistic, encompassing feasting and dance. But yes, the erotic element was also present, and sometimes dominant.

How do our gods arise? In time, the general spiritual essence posited by the pre-animists becomes differentiated, in ways congruent with the differentiation of roles within a society; we get specific and individuated spirits, including the human soul, which may be further differentiated (so that the soul that leaves you during dreams isn't the same as the soul that survives your death). The really important shift involves abstraction, moving us away from naturalism: "magic is transformed from a direct manipulation of forces into a *symbolic activity*."[75] That's because the realm of souls, demons, and gods is accessible through the mediation of symbols. Once, the primitive would tear the heart from his victim's body, convinced that in doing so he actually acquired powers inherent in the organ. But now the community has developed the more metaphorical or analogical mode of "mythological thinking." (Weber remains within the basic Tylor paradigm here; Tylor had told his readers that "magical arts in which the connexion is that of mere analogy or symbolism are endlessly numerous throughout the course of civilization," and, in speaking of "direct symbolism," implicated a role for indirect forms of symbolism.)[76]

Another Weberian emphasis is on the diverse nature of religious phenomena: "The details of the transitions from pre-animistic naturalism to symbolism are altogether variable." He similarly insists on the diverse nature of religious ontology: a god may be the power emanated by a great hero after his death (a deified hero); or a relatively abstracted entity without a name and connected exclusively with a specific, sporadic event. The ordering of gods, souls (he cautions that not all religions accept the soul as an entity independent of the body, citing Buddhism as such a counterexample), and demons in relation to people "constitutes the realm of religious behavior." Now life is influenced not just by tangible things and events, he writes, but also by those intangible things and events that carry meaning.[77]

In time, magical acts that are seen as successful are to be repeated exactly. Even within religions that have "undergone rationalization," Weber contends, deviations in symbolism are less tolerable than those in dogma. ("Thus, the question whether the sign of the cross should be made with two or three fingers was a basic reason for the schism of the Russian church as late as the seventeenth century.")[78]

Like his predecessors, Weber finds that certain early religions could also transcribe features of the societies in which they arose. If the gods of the heroic age recorded in Homer were the product of a "knightly culture," the Romans favored religious practices characterized by formalism, with "tested cultic formulae"; there were a vast number of gods with uncertain jurisdiction, but with the numina to be kept satisfied. The result was a sacred jurisprudence, with sacred law the precursor to "rational juristic thinking." What mattered, among the Romans, wasn't sin, penitence, or salvation; what mattered was maintaining correct etiquette. They were, in turn, averse to religions of the "orgiastic" type.[79] (In a roughly concurrent account, "The Economic Ethics of World Religions: An Introduction"—his *Einleitung*, in the usual shorthand—Weber wrote that "rationalized religions" have "sublimated the orgy into the 'sacrament.' ")[80]

Throughout this chronicle of the origins of religion, political and social formations are inextricable from religious practices and beliefs. Weber eschewed reductive emanationism as well as what would come to be known as functionalism, but he thought that having an ancestor cult made the family a more cohesive force. With a religiously undergirded confederation—as between the Jews and the Midianites—a covenanted, contractual relationship might arise. Weber thought that the "promissory character of Israelite religion . . . is found nowhere else in such intensity."[81]

Other distinctions were carefully noted. Some gods were spatially anchored; others moved with their followers. (Yahweh partook of both qualities: he resided in Sinai but influenced from afar.) And "monolatry" had led the Israelites not to monotheism but to "religious particularism."[82] Invariably, he was attuned to the rational dimension of doctrine: purely pragmatic factors may explain why a particular god attains primacy. That is, you might form a political association under a god who appears to be particularly reliable. This god will then be aggrandized, gaining new capacities. In this way, most religions had a tropism toward monotheism—a tropism that, he thought, had been thwarted in *Alltagsreligion*, everyday religion, except for in Judaism, Islam, and Protestant Christianity. That's because people had a need for the concrete and near-to-hand icon, the prospect of magical manipulations that were lifted out of hand by the big transcendent god.

In a fascinating passage, Weber proposes that the development of one form of religious rationality could come at the expense of another form of religious rationality:

> Every aspect of religious phenomena that points beyond evils and advantages in this world is the work of a special evolutionary process, one characterized by distinctively dual aspects. On the one hand, there is an ever-broadening rational systematization of the god concept and of the thinking concerning the possible relationships of man to the divine. On the other hand, there ensues a characteristic recession of the original, practical and calculating rationalism. As such primitive rationalism recedes, the significance of distinctively religious behavior is sought less and less in the purely external advantages of everyday economic success. Thus, the goal of religious behavior is successively "irrationalized" until finally otherworldly non-economic goals come to represent what is distinctive in religious behavior.[83]

Contrast the transactional logic of offering a burnt sacrifice or a propitiating dance in return for rain with, say, the highly interior ambitions of Pietistic Lutheranism centered on devotional experience, a Christ-centered existence, an inner struggle with sin. Other writers thought that systematization of belief was an important form of rationality, and Weber concurred; it's just that the results were irrational from the calculative, means-end perspective of the agent appeasing a spirit for a particular reward. One form of rationality (the systemization of doctrine) eroded another form of rationality (your prayers will not bring rain or the other material goods that magic or magicians secured).

But could the pursuit of noneconomic, nonmaterial goals—interests related to values and ideals—be rational as well? Weber equivocated but eventually decided that it was. After all, he himself was regularly making trouble, for himself and others, in order to defend his honor. Once, when a young docent at the university published a polemical letter to the editor in a local newspaper that was implicitly about Marianne and a meeting of women's groups she had convened, Weber devoted a vast amount of time and energy hounding his newfound adversary— and then, when the press reported that he had cited his health to evade a duel demand, he spent an enormous amount of time and energy to uncover and ruin the source of those reports. Later, having been asked by his publisher to take on a new edition of the late Gustav Schönberg's handbook on political economy, and learning that an academic at Kiel, who was a student of the original editor and evidently felt he should have been his successor, complained that Weber was betraying Schönberg's legacy, Weber challenged the man to a duel with sabers. His antagonist requested a delay until the end of his teaching semester, though, at which point Weber lost interest— it wasn't a thing to do, he said, after your blood had cooled.[84] It was a rational assessment of the value of irrationality, or possibly vice versa. He would coin the term *Wertrationalität* to describe a substantive rationality oriented to an actor's values or ideals.

INTERESTS AND IDEALS

As he dwelled more on the nature of salvation religions, Weber expanded the domain of the religiously rational. Recall Hermann Siebeck's point about what happens when God is understood "not as a deliverer from evil but as a redeemer from evil." If interests are motivators of action, why quarantine "ideal interests"? The prominent legal scholar Rudolf von Ihering, who had earlier advanced this distinction between ideal and material interests, saw legal rules arising from practical purposes or motivations; institutions, in turn, serve to provide rewards (or penalties), and those rewards could include "power, influence, honor, prestige." In his scheme, the laborer seeks to satisfy material interests, gaining food and shelter; for the scientist or poet, by contrast, material rewards are secondary, while ideal interests are primary.[85] Striving for enlightenment, status honor, or (possibly) otherworldly salvation are ideal interests—although the overcoming of death might be seen as a material interest, too.

Ideal interests were highly mediated by institutions, by culture, whereas material interests were bound to be generic: food, sex, shelter. The distinction arises in Weber's skeptical response when Sombart sought to explain capitalism, a specific historical development, partly in terms of an acquisitive instinct (*Erwerbstrieb*): it was, Weber had objected, a fallacy to invoke a constant to explain a variable. (Revising his *Protestant Ethic*, he referred to "modern" or "rational" capitalism to distinguish it from other forms of capital-accumulating activities.) The point, again, was just that greed was ubiquitous; modern capitalism was not. It arose in response to nonmaterial interests.

And then, to understand how religious forms of normativity, the *Sollen*, operate in the here-and-now, we need to come to grips with moral edicts as a religious effluent. Morality itself represents the rationalization—the systematizing—of shaggier forms of value and belief. How does religion secure its moral authority? Perhaps by creating the realm of the moral in the first place. The prophets of Israel could blame the people's misbehavior for God's evident displeasure; and so, once universalized, transgressing against the will of God "is an ethical sin which burdens the conscience, quite apart from its direct results." The evils that befall us are the consequences of sin, "divinely appointed inflictions," to be remedied by piety. This may seem close to magic worship, but Weber claims that "a systematization of these ethical concepts may ensue": we move from the rational wish to see to one's own pleasures by pleasing god to a "view of sin as the unified power of the anti-divine (diabolical)," with goodness "envisaged as an integral capacity for an attitude of holiness." In ways that track the shift that Otto Pfleiderer and Hermann Siebeck described between law religion and salvation religion, we come to yearn to be "good for its own sake." Piety becomes sublimated into "the enduring basis of a specific conduct of life." Not every religion has completed this journey. You wouldn't find it in Greco-Roman antiquity; they lacked prophet-lawgivers. Nor was it part of China's religious heritage, because, he wrote, "the ethics of Confucianism lack the concept of radical evil."[86]

When it comes to the larger work that Weber had in mind, more than a little guesswork is required. He drafted outlines and revised them.[87] It was going to have volumes, or sections, on the religions of China, India, ancient Judaism, Islam, and perhaps three on Christianity (versions of the first three were written). The ostensible aim was to show how differences in economic development track with differences in religion. Why had capitalism emerged only in the West? As he wrote in that *Einleitung*, "Interests (material and ideal), not ideas, dominate the actions of people. But: the 'worldviews' created by 'ideas' have very often acted as switchmen, determining the tracks along which the dynamics of the interests in action continued to move."[88]

Inevitably, his research turned up far-flung fascinations for him. He wasn't simply testing his *Protestant Ethic* thesis by comparative analysis; far from it. His pages thrum with a sense of revelation as he pursues a range of questions. How did religiously sponsored social ethics affect individual personality? How did religious doctrine relate to social orders, and vice versa? One thing that set Weber apart from Durkheim, it has often been remarked, is that Weber, like Simmel, took an interest in something Durkheim tended to soft-pedal: conflict. And, of course, he would soon find himself in a world rife with conflict.

In August 1914, Weber felt that the just-arrived war was something wonderful; days later, he had to offer his condolences to his publisher, Paul Siebeck, whose son had died "the most beautiful death that fate has to offer us," as Weber assured him, in sacrificing himself "for the existence of our state and our culture." Writing to Tönnies in the fall, Weber would venture that the war is "great and wonderful despite all its horrors." He himself took a post in the Heidelberg medical commission, with responsibility for a number of medical hospitals. The post lasted until September 1915, when he was released and returned to his work on religion. A month earlier, when his brother Karl, a professor of architecture at Hannover, died on the field at age forty-four, having defied his doctors by volunteering to serve, Max told his mother that Karl had met a "beautiful death."[89] And then, in Galicia that May, Emil Lask, the finest of the late neo-Kantians, fell.

To Weber, such sacrifices all seemed essential; theirs was a nation with its back to the wall. In June of 1915, he wrote to Robert Michels (an esteemed colleague who, as a Social Democrat, was nearly unemployable at a German university and found a position in Italy) that the paramount thing was "that Senegalese Negroes and Gurkhas, Russians and Siberians, not enter our country and decide our fate."[90] Unlike Simmel (and, indeed, unlike Troeltsch), Weber did not produce anything that truly qualified as war propaganda, at least in print. "I am only happy when I am back with the things that transport one far away from the present," he later wrote Mina Tobler. "Because everything connected with the present is somehow gloomy and pulls at the iron ring one feels has been placed around one's chest, head, and neck."[91]

LEAVE THE WORLD BEHIND

Weber's most probing essay on religion, "Zwischenbetrachtung: Stufen und Richtungen der religiösen Weltablehnung," was published in the *Archiv für Sozialwissenschaft und Sozialpolitik* in December 1915. The title has been variously rendered in English as interim (or intermediate) considerations (or reflections) and first arrived in English with just a version of its subtitle: "Religious Rejections of the World and Their Directions." The lack of a snappy title should not deter readers; Karl Jaspers was right to describe it as "a key piece in his philosophical thinking."[92] It is Weber's most important piece of writing on religion as such, because it brought a harder edge to a slowly evolving analysis. At the same time, it unmistakably bears the mark of writing done in wartime, by someone with spasmodic yearnings to escape the iron ring of present exigencies. If *The Protestant Ethic* was about the surprising worldliness of a dominant creed, this essay would show how the rejection of worldly affairs had a religious valence as well.

Weber's essays typically begin with an apology, and "Zwischenbetrachtung" is no exception. He acknowledges that he is reducing the "immensely multifarious" nature of his subject by means of "expediently constructed rational type," hewing to such consistencies as can be extracted from practice and doctrine. And his two great ideal types here are the "polar concepts" of mysticism and asceticism. Asceticism refers to conduct adopted by a submissive devotee in compliance with divine will; mysticism is a state of possession, in which you are not a tool but a vessel of the divine. Asceticism is an activity within the world; mysticism a flight from the world. The contrast can be blurred in practice (if the ascetic focuses only on her inward state or if the mystic remains in the worldly orders), but it can persist even through various disguises.

Throughout this book, I've been focusing on the social character of religion and the religious character of society, as our theorists have construed it. Weber's fascination with religious rejections of the world, which is to say, of society, sounds like a rebuttal to this line of thought. A closer look will suggest otherwise. The possibility of rejecting society creates the possibility of embracing society. The essay is actually his most complex engagement with religion as an instrument of *Vergesellschaftung*.

Weber's argument proceeds by carefully identifying the ways that religion is in tension with everything that *isn't* religion. When prophecy creates a social community, Weber tells us, a religious ethic of fraternity supplants the primacy of familial bonds. Two basic principles obtain: "the dualism of in-group and out-group morality" and, within the in-group, the precept of reciprocity. You extend hospitality and financial support to your brethren in need, for "your want of today may be mine of tomorrow." A "communism of loving brethren" arises; in time, the ethic expands to a universalist brotherhood: love even for one's enemies, succor to all in distress. This ethic is obviously at odds with the logic of the economic sphere, which is "oriented to money-prices which originate in the interest-struggles of men in the *market*." The immanent laws of capitalism, especially in its rational and impersonal form, Weber says, can't be reconciled with the religious ethic of brotherliness (*Brüderlichkeit*): "No genuine religion of salvation has overcome the tension between their religiosity and a rational economy." The paradox, of course, is that rational asceticism creates the wealth it rejected. One means of escaping this tension, Weber says, is via the Puritan ethic of vocation: the universalism of love is renounced and worldly labor is routinized into a means of serving God and testing one's state of grace. Ascetic Protestantism is, Weber now sees, no longer a real salvation religion at all.[93]

Then there's the conflict between universalist creeds and the world's political orders. That conflict can take place on the level of education: the priesthood seeks to monopolize the education of youth. But trouble lay ahead. In Weber's view, every "unbroken" religion must, at some point, "demand the *credo non quod, sed quia absurdum*—the 'sacrifice of the intellect.'" And, of course, the world of natural causality and religion's stipulated universe of "ethical, compensatory causality" are at odds. "Science has created this cosmos of natural causality and has seemed unable to answer with certainty the question of its own ultimate presuppositions," Weber writes. "Nevertheless science, in the name of 'intellectual integrity,' has come forward with the claim of representing the only possible form of a reasoned view of the world."[94]

Just as profound is the clash between religious and political ethics. On the one hand, the God of love; on the other, the state that (in Weber's classic formula) claims "a monopoly of the *legitimate use of violence*," the state that has a bureaucracy devoted to meting out punishments for infractions, that must safeguard the internal and external distribution of power. Weber supposed that the strained relationship between religion and politics would be even more acute when both were "completely rationalized." A rationalized religion has systematized its doctrine and practices, has adopted a methodical form of theology, has erected a formal organization with a clear hierarchy and rules and administrative procedures, and has placed emphasis on understanding as well as on avowals of belief. The evolved state has, for its part, achieved legitimacy and promulgated an ethos of its own, a quasi-credal sense of citizenship. Religious ethics and political imperatives are then bound to clash. (There are echoes, here, of Weber's youthful objections to Channing and his pacifism.) "Resist not evil," the Sermon on the Mount counsels; but the state, Weber reminds us, asserts the opposite: "You *shall* help right to triumph by the use of *force*, otherwise you too may be responsible for injustice." At bottom, churches can't be happy with the compulsion to engage in secular wars on behalf of political authorities. Different churches may adopt different stances on the matter, Weber concedes, but that's because they inhabit a world of compromises and pragmatic alliances.[95]

There was also the fact that war—as a mass phenomenon, breaking down social barriers—achieves a religious effect that religions achieve only in "heroic communities professing an ethic of brotherliness." Everyone dies of something, but not everyone dies *for* something. The soldier facing death on the battlefield has a calling, a *Beruf*; he has died in a sacrificial and sacralizing context. Yet for a brotherly, universal religion, the "consecration of death in war must appear as a glorification of fratricide."[96] And the only solutions are, on the one hand, Puritanism (which concludes that violence may be used to promote godliness in a barbarous world) and, on the other, the radical antipolitics of mysticism.

The mystical experience, he says, is "the most irrational form of religious behavior."[97] Notice he says *behavior*, not belief: mysticism is a practice. Why so irrational? Because formally, substantively, and instrumentally, it resists being tamed by reason. It's incompatible with routinization, systematic analysis, and utilitarian payoff. Whereas asceticism involves systematic discipline, mysticism involves emotional ecstasy, a sense of losing oneself in an immediate encounter with the transcendent, an experience that is spontaneous and beyond control. Asceticism lends itself to a high degree of organization, rules, precepts, intellectual attention to ethical conduct. Mysticism remains individualistic and antithetical to organization. It is devoted to experience beyond intellectual comprehension; it concerns the ineffable.

The allied force of eroticism, too, is at odds with the brotherly ethic of the salvation religions, Weber insists. (And yes, eros was straining his own brotherly ties, as he found himself drawn again toward Else Jaffé, now Alfred's lover.) "Originally the relation of sex and religion was very intimate," Weber says, revisiting the topic. We had magic orgiasticism, which survived into sacred harlotry; but later priesthoods worried that sexuality was "dominated by demons." Weber says it's no accident that "prophetic religions, as well as the priest-controlled life orders," have "regulated sexual intercourse in favor of *marriage*," with eroticism sublimated into, say, the chivalric romance—the troubadour love of medieval times, centered on the "lady," the wife of another man. In love, there's the boundless giving of self, a communion that transcends the I and the Thou and comes to be interpreted as a sacrament. (The lover "knows himself to be freed of the cold skeleton hands of rational orders.") And the ethic of brotherliness is, Weber maintains, antagonistic to all this, for the sensation of earthly salvation competes with the "devotion of a supra-mundane God." What lovers have and what worshippers have, in their highest forms, stand in a "mutually substitutive relation." For the lover, rejecting passion is blasphemous; "the erotic frenzy stands in unison only with the orgiastic and charismatic form of religiosity."[98] Every true lover, Weber suggests, partakes in mysticism, a sacramental vision so at odds with society that social religions devote a great deal of energy trying to subdue it.

In the essay "Zwischenbetrachtung," then, religion is in tension with various aspects of society that functionally or intellectually compete with it. Nonreligious faiths and functions arrive to match its deliverances. The catch is that those deliverances are so wildly various. Weber's pluralism hits hard: the heterogeneity of religion, illustrated by the binary of asceticism and mysticism, stands as a rejoinder to a host of easy generalities. Religion is everything—and its opposite.

THE MAGIC GARDEN

Weber's *Wirtschaftsethik der Weltreligionen*, his *Economic Ethics of the World Religions*, was now well under way. The series was to open with his study—which he'd begun in 1913 and serialized in the *Archiv* in 1915—of Confucianism and Taoism (*Konfuzianismus*; a revised version of which was published in English as *The Religion of China*). Here he took pains to show how the major religious cultures in China were unlike those of the West. It mattered enormously, he thought, that Confucianism has no salvational objective, and lacks a metaphysics, unlike the religious practices that underwrote Western rationalism. (Let me offer here the explicit disclaimer that in discussing Weber's writings about these and other "world religions," I'm not positing their accuracy: far from it.) The ostensible rationale was to test the Protestant ethic theory through a comparison with other civilizations, but, as I've suggested, this does not begin to explain the detailed texture of description and analysis. His comparative study of religious modes and their economic influences was a larger inquiry into the human enterprise.

The treatise on China is actually more focused on economic development than the two later installments are, and it was expositorily useful that Chinese religions were, in his accounting, particularly remote from the Abrahamic traditions. Bluntly, Christianity is a religion of striving and process: it has a soteriological vision. Chinese religious rationalism, by contrast, is devoted to adjusting oneself to life as it is. Politics, as Weber affirmed elsewhere, was always the art of the possible, but what's possible was often determined by the act of reaching beyond current possibilities. Confucianism—and in what he viewed as its folk-religious companion, Taoism—was ultimately a mode of reconciliation to present reality. The relationship between the two creeds, allied in their traditionalism, are sometimes complementary, sometimes rivalrous. But the yoking was itself the social formation that mattered. (It is apt that the later book version was titled *The Religion of China*, not *The Religions of China*.) Nor was this policy of adjustment any kind of defeatism or pessimism; on the contrary, it represented an optimism about the perfectibility of persons and of society through our own exertions.

There was no original sin, for Weber's Chinese; no need for redemption. Taoist mysticism might bring the individual to greater enlightenment, but it did not seek to change the world, which was not a fallen one and did not need saving. Confucian rationalism, like Taoist irrationalism, was antipodal to Christianity, especially ascetic Protestantism, then. No satanic force of evil; no struggle for salvation. No cause to be greatly bothered about the beyond. Whereas wrath was a key attribute of Yahweh, the Chinese notion of heaven was suffused with tranquility and reason. And these faith traditions were an artifact of a particularly longstanding and highly bureaucratic polity: "The unshaken order of internal political and social life, with thousands of years behind it, was placed under divine tutelage and then considered as the revelation of the divine." But a creed of adjustment wasn't going to fuel capitalist strivings. "Patrimonial bureaucratization" was powerful; there were merchants, including rich merchants; but pure market capitalism was "rudimentary." Officials invested their money in land, not commercial ventures. Weber cites a Taoist injunction: "Do not introduce innovations."[99]

The calculative rationality of the coin-counting Chinese shopkeeper remained an individual attribute; it didn't spawn "those great and methodical business conceptions which are rational in nature and are presupposed by modern capitalism."[100] What hindered this critical turn from the profit-minded individual to the profit-minded business enterprise? Remember that, in Weber's account, asceticism promotes business enterprise by extirpating petty acquisitiveness—the large, rational enterprise requires long-term investment, postponing the extraction of cash. Confucians believed in self-control, but with a different agenda (essentially, negative, Weber thought), one having to do with dignity and how one is perceived by the group.

Another point of contrast was China's "systematic rationalization of magic." Medicine was animistic; land features could be "geomantically significant"—a rock of the right shape could protect an area from malign demons; and everyday Taoism saw the world as rife with spirits and demons, manipulable by formulas and talismans.[101] Why did magic persist? The magicians had a vested interest in maintaining their profit opportunities. But more than this, Weber conjectures, the mandarins, however much they disdained Taoist irrationalism, wanted magic to persist because they recognized belief in magic as "part of the constitutional foundation of sovereign power." Asked about putting an end to the belief in magic, he reports, a member of the literati replied, "Who will hinder the emperor from doing as he pleases when he no longer believes in omens and portents?"[102]

How, he asks, should we compare "Confucian rationalism—for the name is appropriate—and what is geographically and historically closest to us, namely, Protestant rationalism"? He offers "two primary," albeit interrelated, "yardsticks" for religious rationalism in general. One is divestment from magic. The other is the extent to which each kind of rationalism has "systematically unified the relation between God and the world and therewith its own ethical relationship to the world." While ascetic Protestantism had largely eliminated "magical manipulations," Confucianism had preserved the "magic garden" so central to the Taoists.[103] But Confucianism excelled in the second function, that of systematically unifying the relation between Heaven and earth. Confucianism held our world to be "the best of all possible worlds," proclaimed human nature to be "disposed to the ethically good," and had arrived at an ethical system radically different from that of the West.[104] As against those who thought that the West had achieved a higher level of rational development, Weber offered an explanation of differences in economic development that wasn't about the presence or absence of rationalism; it was about the type of religious rationalism that obtained. In the end, "Confucian rationalism meant rational adjustment to the world; Puritan rationalism meant rational mastery of the world."[105]

The shaping of ethical norms, in the Chinese system, was a feature of Chinese rationalism that drew his scrutiny. The Chinese did not sharply distinguish sins from offenses, whether they were committed against individuals, hierarchies, conventions, or ceremonial etiquettes. (" 'I have sinned' corresponded to our 'I beg your pardon' in violating a convention.") Here was an "unbridgeable" gap with the religious ethic of the West. Whereas Protestantism merely accommodated social hierarchy, as "pertaining to the creatural," Confucianism hallowed it, as well as the interpersonal relations entailed by it.[106]

What's more, Confucianism discouraged expertise, professional specialization: the broadly educated generalist gentleman, the beau ideal of dignity, was "not a tool," which meant that (with obvious economic consequences) the specialist could not be truly dignified. In one of his most arresting passages, Weber saw consequences for the construction of self: "A well-adjusted man, rationalizing his conduct only to the degree requisite for adjustment, does not constitute a systematic unity but rather a complex of useful and particular traits. . . . Such a way of life could not allow man an inward aspiration toward a 'unified personality,' a striving which we associate with the idea of personality. Life remained a series of occurrences."[107]

Reflecting on the vast civilizational arcs that Weber draws, one may wonder whether his model itself entails a kind of providentialism. For all the disclaimers and qualifications, we are left in no doubt: the socio-ethical consequences of a religion effectively determined a society's economic development. And because commercial enterprise was social, there was nothing an individual could do about it. Chinese religion, for Weber, was both the projection of a remarkably stable social order and the means of its perpetuation. You would not embark on a project titled *Economic Ethics of the World Religions* if you did not think that religions shaped economies.

But why did Weber suppose that Confucianism *was* a religion? We would learn the meaning of "religion" not at the outset but at the journey's end, he had promised in "Religious Communities"; but his practice was to address the matter through instantiation, never through definition, and one can wonder whether Confucianism really was an instance. Yes, early Confucianism touched on elements that we'd customarily consider religious, but its centering concept of "tian," which we usually translate as heaven, can plausibly construed as cosmological, involving a force that was, though anthropomorphic, also naturalistic. (Some scholars propose that it was a general term for the phenomenal realm; another proposal suggests that it mediates a moral economy, where nonmoral outcomes are distributed in ways responsive to moral worth, while accommodating "contingency," which marks a disruption in those allocations.)[108] Inasmuch as rationalized "religion," for Weber, involved a form of transcendence that is neither magic nor merely mundane, Confucianism doesn't readily fit into this categorical cabin.

Does it matter? Arguments about why scientific and industrial advances hadn't arrived in China ("the Needham question," as it later came to be known, for the historian of science and sinologist Joseph Needham) were already well under way when Weber was writing, and Weber meant to show how a religious ethic shaped China's historical path and its society's character.[109] Yet if "religion" just is the name of China's practices, values, and beliefs, it cannot be enlisted to explain them.

THE PARADOXICAL HINDU

Weber's next treatise, on religion in India, was rather warmer in tone. Some of this may have had to do with his friendship with a certain Hermann Graf Keyserling, a voluble and, it seems fair to say, charismatic figure who had traveled widely in India. He stayed with the Webers for four days, in the fall of 1912, and Weber found him spellbinding. He was, Marianne wrote to Else, "a spiritual nomad and wanderer, who channels all religions and civilizations and possibilities through his mind." As his later writings made clear, Keyserling believed that Indian wisdom lay not in repressing erotic desire but in fulfilling it.[110] (He cited Freud on the corrupting effect of repressed desires.) Weber's work on religion in India, in turn, does not scant tantrism and orgiastic ritual; he evidently took a rooting interest in the thought that Indian elites, unlike their counterparts in China, did not succeed in extirpating these traditions entirely.

Die Wirtschaftsethik der Weltreligionen: Hinduismus und Buddhismus appeared in three parts in the *Archiv für Sozialwissenschaft und Sozialpolitik* in 1916 and 1917.[111] Weber acknowledged a difficulty early on. In politically unified China, it was possible to offer generalizations (however hedged) about systems of popular beliefs; the emperor himself was assigned a role in them. But "Hinduism" was worrisomely composite. The term "Hindu," he says, was used first by Muslim occupiers, the Mughals, to refer to the subcontinent's unconverted, and "Hinduism" had only recently been adopted by Indians themselves, while the English had come to use it for the religious complex the Germans often called "Brahmanism." And yet (unlike many scholars) he proceeds as if it is the name of a singular entity—a "Hindu system" that was an "almost irresistible social force" as it spread from a small region in the north to comprise a populous subcontinent, propagated in opposition to foreign salvation religions and to indigenous animistic folk beliefs. The spread of the system had, he said, legible social consequences: in the course of Hinduization, various "tribes" became transmuted into castes, the ritually pure and the ritually impure. But beyond a concept of the transmigration of souls and the concept of compensation through karma, what did the system consist of?

"In truth, it may well be concluded that Hinduism is simply not a 'religion' in our sense of the word," Weber admits, considering its accommodation of local beliefs, and he notes that some of its representatives are emphatic on this point.[112] Yet the issue does not long detain him. He had already decided that there were five world religions, and that Hinduism was one. It was simply lax with respect to the details of belief and highly pluralistic with respect to the (often exacting) details of its performances. Every Hindu was also a member of a particular sect; and the dharma, the ritualistic duties, of a Hindu varied with, among other factors, the person's social position and caste.

In his usual manner, Weber situates the creeds with respect to the sociology of their elites and followers. He had already cautioned, "It is not our thesis that the specific nature of a religion is a simple 'function' of the social situation of the stratum which appears as its characteristic bearer, or that it represents the stratum's 'ideology,' or that it is a 'reflection' of a stratum's material or ideal interest-situation."[113] But while he promised not to reduce one to the other, neither did he think these things were unrelated.

And so the orthodoxy of the Brahman priestly caste, Weber says, sought to eliminate ancient orgiasticism, for a shortcut to transcendence like that was bound to undermine the priests' role as ritual intermediaries. But remnants remain in the Vedas; for instance, "the great priestly soma-sacrifice was originally a cult-tempered intoxication orgy." What's more, "ritualistic copulation in the fields as a means of securing soil fertility and the lingam cult with its phallic hobgoblins, the *gandharvan*, are very ancient in India." At least a few forms of these, Weber reports, persist in "popular religiosity." For certain forms of mysticism, orgiastic and otherwise, played a critical role—communion gained through "an accentuation of the power of irrationality." As he summarizes the situation, the sacred impulse in India was either orgiastic in character and anti-rational, or rational in methods but irrational in goals.

For all the power of mysticism in Hindu culture—especially the contemplative, gnostic mysticism favored by the Brahmans—Weber was convinced that, "technically, Indian asceticism was the most rationally developed in the world." The Brahmans, in his view, were a magician caste, entangled in the magical asceticism from which it originated. This asceticism was, to be sure, remote from the Christian varieties: "The ascetic aspired to power over the gods. He was able to force them; they feared him and did his bidding."[114] After all, the Hindu gods were no more virtuous than we were; just more powerful.

One consequence of Hindu pluralism was an absence of ethical universalism, of any notion of natural right. There's no ethical God, no struggle with radical evil as a life project. Echoing his claim in the China treatise, Weber insists, in turn, that the "Asiatic intellectual" would find something philistine in the Western fixation on the idea that one's conduct expresses one's "personality."

But what about karma? The transformation of Brahman asceticism from "magical to soteriological ends" was a complex process. Yet Weber didn't see Hinduism as a salvation religion. For one thing, "individuals could sojourn in Heaven only for a finite time for finite merits." The world is a wheel of meaningless recurrence, and to see beyond that wheel required the " 'emptying' of consciousness of worldly relations."[115] It's possible to read Weber's account—highlighting an absence of a unified ethical framework, a failure to fully extirpate orgiastic traditions, and an interpenetration of mystical and ascetic traditions—as recording putative deficits in India's religious culture compared to the West's; it's also possible to read him as highlighting these features in order to challenge Western ideals of ethical uniformity.

Recall that yardstick of a religion's rationality that Weber described: "the degree to which it has systematically unified the relation between God and the world and therewith its own ethical relationship to the world." Broaden the point to any creed we embrace and suppose that our rationality can be measured by the coherence of our values and convictions. By this measure, Weber was an anti-rationalist. His favored metaphor for the plural nature of human values was "polytheism."

You could see the jostling array of values in his personal conduct. Consider how he severed ties with his brilliant friend Ernst Troeltsch. The two had been intellectual and personal intimates for many years; Weber was the godfather of Troeltsch's son. Then, late in 1914, an Alsatian litterateur and pacifist who lived in Heidelberg (and who now planned to move to France: his children, rabid German nationalists, weren't speaking to him) wanted to visit French prisoners in a military hospital that Weber was in charge of, and Weber agreed. Troeltsch, learning of the Alsatian's plans, secretly arranged for a soldier's escort to accompany him. Weber, though certainly imbued with the nationalist spirit, found himself outraged at what Troeltsch had done. It struck him as repugnantly chauvinistic—so much so that Weber ended Troeltsch's tenancy at the Fallenstein Villa.

These were the years when Weber, once rather phobic of public speaking, emerged as a stirring orator. In various public addresses, he told audiences that the war was being fought for the nation more than for the state, took swipes at both the Social Democrats and the Pan-Germanists (*Alldeutsche*), rejected annexationist war aims, and declared that Germany's future as a self-determining entity with a say in global affairs was at stake.[116] He surmised that Germany would become democratized after the war, that soldiers would have to be fully enfranchised. There was the usual mixture of sense and nonsense in these lectures. But his ability to express an elevated form of nationalism could be transfixing; as a speaker, he seemed to gain charisma. A newly hortatory tone was entering his public voice. Call it the prophetic.

KILLING THE AFTERLIFE

The role of the prophets is central to *Das antike Judentum* (*Ancient Judaism*), the last installment Weber produced for his *Economic Ethics of the World Religions*. Although his research for it had begun around 1911, it appeared in several parts in the *Archiv*, between 1917 and 1919. (It is incomplete, despite its considerable length; even more chapters had been planned.) The treatise is informed by Weber's earlier studies of India and China: he discusses Jews as a "pariah" people—the term originally referred to a Tamil Nadu caste—and compares the tribe of Levi with the Brahmins. Once again, we get his two yardsticks of rationalization: how much the religion has purged itself of magic, and the level of systematic coherence it has achieved in defining the connection between God and the world, and in defining its own ethical stance toward worldly matters.[117]

But where the work on China and India had to address why capitalism had failed to take root there, he could have different foci when he was writing about ancient Judaism. The creed of the Israelites was, after all, a precursor to Christianity—it could usefully adumbrate aspects of ascetic Protestantism. (As he'd written in his *Einleitung*, Judaism "contained the historical pre-conditions decisive for understanding" Christianity and Islam.) The comparisons he attended to, instead, were with the Israelites' neighbors. So the rationalization of religious ethics performed by the Jewish priests—a rationalization that had produced Deuteronomy, a "compendium of Levitical teachings"— was contrasted with the absence of such systematization in Egypt and Babylon.[118]

Once again, the rationalization of religion involved a war with *die Orgie*. The cults of Baal were given over to "sexual orgiasticism" and "sexual promiscuity," and when these activities started to contaminate the Yahweh cult, advocates of pure Yahwism fought against them. Here, Weber detects what would later be dubbed schismogenesis—the shift of behavior, even the formation of an identity, as a means of differentiation. A deep antagonism toward Baal orgiasticism, Weber believes, explains the Israelite policing of eroticism, which extended to the taboo on "any physical divestment"—a fear of nakedness. Weber thinks that the sin of Onan, similarly, was rooted in an antipathy toward "certain Molech orgies" that involved the sacrifice of semen.[119]

A similar strategy of differentiation even explains the scanting of the afterlife in ancient Judaism. The prophets, determined to maintain the purity of the creed and to entrench the holiness code, inveighed against dealings with the Egyptians: it could lead to an accommodation with those Egyptian gods of the dead. The afterlife would be shunted aside precisely because it was such an Egyptian fixation.[120]

Weber, as we'd expect, has an intricate account of how social structures show up in religious legend and beliefs. He stresses demilitarization in the development of Judaism. The patriarchs are not mostly depicted as warriors; they're pacifists. They're humble, not heroic; wily, not brave. And all this can be connected to the influence of the small shepherds, breeders, and socially oppressed peasants—in short, to demilitarized herdsmen in alliance with farmers. In one passage (and in one tradition), control over the city of Shechem is gained by deceit and violence; in another, Jacob peaceably buys it. The "warrior's sense of honor and the herdman's utilitarian pacifism" both leave their mark on scripture, because both had their constituencies. Yet, again, you couldn't simply infer the influence of warriors from warrior tales. In a passage that spoke to the circumstances of its composition, Weber writes that images of Yahweh's heroic feats grew bloodier as their celebrants grew more remote from the military life—"just as today, in all countries, we find the highest measure of war thirst among those strata of literati who are farthest from the trenches and by nature least military."[121]

By the same token, the prophets can too readily be appropriated to our own political ethos, as radical democrats *avant la lettre*. Weber, implicitly taking issue with one established line of argument, insists that the prophets never saw themselves as advancing any social political program. They're certainly not champions of democratic ideas. Certain Levitical socio-ethical decrees and duties of charity favor the "little people" and led the prophets to berate the great, but these were derived strictly from religious imperatives.[122]

At the same time, Weber recognizes that—objectively, not subjectively—the prophets *were* political, and "above all, world-political demagogues and publicists." Yes, all they cared about was the fulfillment of Yahweh's commandments. Still, by effectively demoting worldly authority (they seldom referred to kings), the rich and powerful, and the obligations of subjects to their rulers, weren't many of the prophets also elevating an ecstatic tradition largely in opposition to priests? These prophets were, Weber thinks, bearers of personal charisma who rejected "office charisma" as a qualification for teaching. Eventually, though, "the increasing bourgeois rationalism of the people integrated in the relatively pacified world, first of the Persian kingdom, then of the Hellenic, had given the priests the opportunity to suffocate prophecy."[123] Rationalism, once again, had strangled the ecstatic.

THE GODS AWAKEN

In the fall of 1917, as Weber made plans to return to academic life, he gave a lecture in Munich of lasting significance, titled "Scholarship as a Vocation" (*Wissenschaft als Beruf*). The religious valence of "vocation" isn't limited to its title; religion, as a historical phenomenon and as metaphor, is its powerful subtext. "It is the fate of our times, with its characteristic rationalization, intellectualization, and, above all, the disenchantment of the world, that the ultimate and most sublime values have receded from the public sphere, either into the otherworldly realm of mystical life or into the brotherliness of direct relationships between individuals," he pronounces. "Disenchantment" is, at any rate, the usual rendering of *Entzauberung*: the term has been more fastidiously translated as "de-magic-ification." Weberians have been captivated by the phrase, but it plainly means more to us than it did to Weber, who used *Entzauberung*, in this sense, fewer than a dozen times.

"Only within the smallest circles of fellowship, from person to person, in pianissimo," Weber goes on, do we find something "pulsating that corresponds to the prophetic pneuma that once swept through great congregations like a firestorm, welding them together." A monstrosity would result if one tried to conjure new religions without a new, genuine prophecy, he warns. Prophecy from the lectern, finally, will "create only fanatical sects but never a genuine community."[124] He is summoning the sonorous tones of prophecy to warn against prophecy. And it isn't merely the twilight of central religious authority that he describes; it's a faltering of community. He declares that John Stuart Mill was right to venture that "if one proceeds purely from experience, one arrives at polytheism."[125] It might be a delusion to suppose we could stifle it for long.

"The grandiose rationalism of an ethical-methodical conduct of life, which sprang from every religious prophecy, had dethroned this polytheism in favor of the 'one thing that is needful'—and had found itself, in the face of the realities of external and inner life, forced into those compromises and relativizations that we all know from the history of Christianity," he pronounces. "But today it is the religious 'everyday.' " Has a new civic creed of secular rationalism arisen? Would we see something like Durkheim's human-dignity-focused religion of the future? On the contrary, Weber contends: "The many ancient gods, purged of magic and so in the form of impersonal forces, rise from their graves, strive to gain power over our lives, and resume their eternal battle among themselves."[126]

Isaiah Berlin's students would later come to speak, in a neighborly sounding way, of value pluralism, but Weber had something less irenic in mind. And in case anyone fails to appreciate the stakes, he depicts the enmity between French and German civilization as an arena of clashing values, clashing gods. Some, unwilling to confront the situation, will return to the church, engaging in the ultimate "sacrifice of the intellect" (the religious resonance is clear in the original, which puts the phrase in quotes: *Opfer des Intellekts*). Worse is the temporizing of those who lack courage to make their ultimate standpoint clear and who ease their way with "feeble relative judgments." He recalls a passage from Isaiah, a watchman's song: "The morning cometh, and also the night: if ye will enquire, enquire ye: return, come."

Weber closes: "The people to whom this was said have asked and persevered for more than two millennia, and we know their harrowing fate. From this, we want to learn the lesson: that longing and persevering alone are not enough, and we must do differently: get to work and meet the 'demands of the day'—both humanely and professionally. This is straightforward if everyone finds the demon that holds the threads of their life and obeys it."

"Scholarship as a Vocation" contains Weber's most moving, beautifully composed, and impassioned sentences. He is not merely writing *about* religion; he has written something very like a religious text. Obedience to our demons—compliance with our personal destiny, our own thread-holding Fates—arrives like a divine compulsion, akin to the one Weber invoked in his tempestuous proposal of marriage to Marianne.

That same fall, Troeltsch, having been asked whether Alfred or Max should be offered an economics chair at Bonn, wrote a letter that depicted Max as a bundle of contradictions. Troeltsch (who properly acknowledged their personal estrangement) doubted that Max was a natural-rights democrat, and couldn't reconcile his seeming relativism with his moral obduracy. "He sides with 'victims of persecution' at every opportunity and does so with excessive vehemence," Troeltsch wrote. "A strong hatred of the Prussian system and the person of the present monarch is also at work here. Yet his grounds for democracy etc. are always historically relativistic and practically oriented. . . . I have never understood how this relativism squares with his moral intransigence."[127]

Leo Strauss wondered about it, too, in a much-discussed lecture he delivered in 1949, which was later revised and published as part of his *Natural Right and History* (1953). He argued that Weber, though "the greatest social scientist of our century," could never navigate out from an ethical absence. Troeltsch had come to indict Weber for decisionism; Strauss evidently concurs. The reason Weber insisted that the social sciences be value neutral, Strauss contended, is not that he thought there was a fundamental opposition between Is and Ought, but that he didn't think we could have genuine knowledge of the Ought. There are many values, often in conflict, and social science could only clarify their relations and conflicts. Strauss believed that Weber's view leads to nihilism, an account in which any preference, however evil, is as legitimate as any other before the "tribunal of reason." So, for example, Weber isn't able to point out that the interpretation of Calvinism that fueled the capitalist spirit was a *corruption* of Calvin's theology; he merely says it is a working out of the theology. Weber imagined he could distinguish between cultural values and moral imperatives, Strauss says, but he always suspected that one was as subjective as the other. "He was certain that all devotion to causes or ideals has its roots in religious faith," Strauss maintains, "and, therefore, that the decline of religious faith will ultimately lead to the extinction of all causes or ideals."[128]

Strauss's reading of Weber is sly and often penetrating; it is also unpersuasive. Else Jaffé was onto something when she wrote to Alfred that, unlike him, Max shared her belief in transcendent values. The awakening gods would, Weber prophesied, strive to dominate us—far from envisaging the extinction of causes or ideals, Weber anticipated an escalation in the clashes within us and among us. Strauss ignores a point that Weber had made as long ago as his letter to his newly confirmed brother Alfred and had stressed in his *Protestant Ethic*, where he described the way a "duty in a calling" persisted beyond its theological origins and "haunts our lives like the ghost of once-held religious beliefs."[129] In the realm of social norms, something birthed by religion may gain in strength when it has left the crèche far behind.

COLLISION COURSE

Weber, who had wondered whether he was a mystic, not only theorized about the tension between rationality and ecstasy but lived it as well. He was certainly ecstatic—indeed, it can fairly be said that the German nation was briefly gripped by a collective *Ekstase*—when Russia's forces began to collapse that fall. In December of 1917, Russia officially withdrew from the war, and, with the Brest-Litovsk treaty in March, it ceded to the Central Powers great swaths of territory it had occupied—the Baltic provinces as along with Ukraine, Poland, and Belarus. Weber argued that Germany should position itself as a supporter of the smaller nationalities. (The puppet regimes that Germany established belied any such hopes.) Meanwhile, he became an increasingly insistent voice for democracy, calling for an expanded franchise and an empowered parliament, and for direct election of the president. Shouldn't the returning soldiers have the right to vote and help decide a nation's destiny? He could fill auditoriums. (In a letter from June 1918, he wrote Marianne about speaking before packed halls, with audience members forced to stand by the walls—though, characteristically, he did not fail to mention having heard "the wonderful Schubert quintet, brilliantly played."[130]) He also contributed pieces to the *Frankfurter Zeitung*, a liberal paper. The champion of value-free scholarship had never insisted that politics be value-free.

The end of the war was jolting and bewildering. Six months after the elation prompted by Russia's withdrawal, Germany was suing for peace. Throughout November, leftist insurgencies were forming and claiming power, often with little resistance. Kurt Eisner, an intellectual, journalist, critic, and (non-Marxist) socialist revolutionary, notably mounted a revolution in Bavaria, overthrowing the local monarchy and proclaiming Munich the capital of a socialist republic, a free people's state. When Weber wrote of charismatic authority, a major exemplar was William Gladstone; Eisner's charisma was acknowledged, as a concession to "value-free sociological analysis," but sneered at, Eisner being the "type of *littérateur*" who is "overwhelmed by his own demagogic success." And then Edgar Jaffé, of all people, was invited to serve as the finance minister of the People's State of Bavaria. Weber, whose own efforts at securing a political office went nowhere (he'd run that fall for a Reichstag seat, representing the newly formed German Democratic Party), was no doubt confounded. After Eisner was assassinated, in early 1919, he declared that the killer should get the death penalty—but only so that the assassin could enjoy an honorable martyrdom.[131]

A sense of honor had long been a great strength, and weakness, of his. Now, in the weeks before Weber accompanied the German delegation to Versailles, he told General Erich Ludendorff, Germany's chief wartime strategist, to turn himself over to the Allied officials as a prisoner of war, ennobling his service through heroic sacrifice; Ludendorff thought the ungrateful rabble weren't worthy of such a sacrifice. He would go on to write his memoirs, like so many officers. But

Weber, pointing to the example set by Asian military officers, thought Germany's commanders would have done better to take their lives than to write about them.[132]

By early 1919, the tendresse between him and Else had flared into a torrid affair. She and her husband both lived in Munich, but kept separate apartments; and she never quite broke things off with Alfred Weber, who still sent attestations of his love for her. But the relationship with Max became central. His enchantment with Else, reversing Eduard von Hartmann's formula, was marked by a shift from autonomy to heteronomy. She was, in his intoxicated letters, a witch, a devil, a wild cat, a "despotic mistress" and "slave owner," but also the "goddess of love," whom he abjectly served. He joked that he might add a footnote to the section about eroticism in his *Zwischenbetrachtung*, reading: "Improved after a more careful study of the facts."[133] The main thing, as Kaube observes, is that Max Weber, now in his mid-fifties, was writing, sometimes once a day, the first passionate love letters of his life. After consulting with Marianne, he passed up a more lucrative and less demanding offer from Bonn to take a chair in economics and social science at Munich. At a farewell party for him at Heidelberg, Schubert lieder were performed, and, according to a historian who was present, Weber responded most impressively, crediting his wife for rescuing him from his period of affliction. Explaining the move, Marianne wrote to Helene that Else was a draw for them both.[134] Meanwhile, communists and anarchists seized power in Bavaria, which became a Soviet Republic for a few weeks in April.

In time, Weber had to testify on behalf of Otto Neurath (later famous, or infamous, as a founder of logical positivism and the Vienna Circle's "unity of science" movement), who was in the dock after his stint running the central economic planning office for Bavaria's Soviet government.[135] Weber, as his relations with Robert Michels, Werner Sombart, and György Lukács made clear, did not let ideological distance create personal distance.

Marianne's star continued to rise, as perhaps the foremost feminist intellectual of her era in Germany and as a tireless organizer. Early in 1919, she became an elected delegate for the Baden German Democratic Party at the Constitutional Convention; in October, she was made the chair of the League of Women's Associations. The Webers resumed their *jours*, even though their guests in Munich weren't necessarily of the caliber they had been accustomed to. Still, Max made the acquaintance of Thomas Mann, and the two evidently hit it off: Mann recorded in his diary that Weber "proved to be the good, skillful, and lively speaker that he is considered to be," while Weber, writing to Tobler in January 1920, said he thought that he and his wife should see more young people and writers like Mann. Mann would later draw on Weber's writings about ancient Judaism for his tetralogy *Joseph and His Brothers*.[136]

When Weber's sister Lili, a war widow, killed herself in April 1920—she had been abandoned by her lover, the headmaster of a progressive school—Weber saluted her for her courage; he saw no point in persisting under just any circumstances. "Lili's action seems to me ever more surely the only justified one. And: beautiful."[137] Whereas French theorists like Durkheim saw suicide as a social failure, a symptom of anomie, many German intellectuals felt the pull of that Goethe-Wagner tradition of romanticizing suicide. Indeed, Max, Marianne, and Else had seen *Die Walküre* the evening before Lili's suicide. To insist that life was of value in itself, he said, was a "Christian indignity." Lili left behind four children; while Max poeticized, Marianne took them in and made plans to adopt them. ("And so I am 'Father,' " Max wrote to an in-law, not altogether happily.)[138]

THE MYSTIC RATIONALIST

Weber's grand project was one he was working madly on when he died, though perhaps it never could have been completed. In the version of the Nordic legend of Valhalla that made its way into his beloved Ring des Nibelungen, Wotan promises a pair of giants the goddess Freia, with her immortality-sustaining apples, if they build Valhalla—never intending to make good on the promise. Then he is compelled to turn over a power-conferring ring he has stolen from a dwarf as a replacement offering to the giants, with the pursuit and possession of the ring (rationalization? industrialization?) ultimately leading to the destruction of the gods. Weber anticipated their resurrection.

The new edition of *The Protestant Ethic* was completed; the treatise on Judaism was not, but, in his final days, he dedicated it to Else Jaffé anyway. His core concerns, religion and rationality, consumed much of his time: he was pursuing his truest *Berufung*. And yet neither could ever be systematized. Like religion, rationality was something that he happily anatomized but didn't try to capture with an all-encompassing definition. Rational activities were activities toward some purpose, but beyond that? As we saw before, he distinguished between subjective forms of rationality (in which respect magic and physics might be equally rational, being directed in a deliberative way toward appropriate ends) and, say, *Richtigkeitsrationalität*, correctness-rationality (where an action was regarded as more appropriate if its desired outcome was likelier to happen). He took least interest in objective, "rational"-sounding interpretations of rationality, because these obvious interpretations were the ones he sought to complicate.

It's both understandable and commendable, then, that scholars have devoted enormous exegetical labors to teasing out, much more finely, all the different valences of Weberian rationality. And yet, in taking on that challenge, they are, in a sense, working at cross purposes with Weber. Most of the time, Weber declined to mark which conception of rationality he had in mind; he just wrote about rationality, unmodified. Why? Our line-drawing efforts to rationalize Weberian rationality can show insufficient regard for his rationale. Weber didn't hesitate to produce sentences that drooped with qualifications like an overdecorated Christmas tree. So we can't ascribe his habits of usage, as some have, to carelessness.[139] He could have used different words entirely (systematization, calculative optimization—the neo-Kantians would have had offerings), and sometimes he did, referring to purposive conduct or the calculation of interests. More typically, he found it usefully provocative to use "rational" in ways that clashed with customary narratives of modernity, in which secular forms of knowledge emerged from earlier irrationality. But he returned to that one word, principally, because he thought that all these significations were tied together within the master concept: they were dimensions of something whose comprehension we were still in the process of achieving. In an essay meant as a *Vorbemerkung* (preliminary remark) to his planned *Collected Essays on the Sociology of Religion,* Weber writes that just as there is the rationalization of scientific research, there is the " 'rationalization' of mystical contemplation." For "rationalizations have occurred in the various arenas of life in highly varying ways and in all circles of cultural life."[140] Slice up his concept of the rational—perhaps with subscripted numerals—and the significance of such claims would drain away.

A subtler grip on the rational—in its individual and its social valences—would give us a subtler grip on the irrational, or so Weber was convinced. The instrumental and value-based dimensions weren't detachable; through culture, efficiency could itself become a value, something prized for its own sake; an individual's goals were bound to be shaped by the values and social ethics of larger structures of rationality. ("The concept of culture is a *value* concept," he wrote.)[141] We missed something important, he concluded, if we disaggregated the concept and lost the larger semantic abode. In Weber's form of polytheism, the gods of rationality had various powers and pursuits, but they all gathered in Valhalla.

Joachim Radkau, in his thousand-page biography, suggests that toward the end of his life Weber found religion—of a sort. Weber thought scholarship should be value-free, in this account, because the values that moved him were sacred. The influence on him of *Lebensphilosophie* could be felt, as he wrote of things "full of intense, strong life." On the other hand, he was drawn to Siegmund's remark to Brünnhilde, in "Die Walküre": "Greet Wotan for me, greet Valhalla for me, but of Valhalla's loveless pleasures you need tell me no more." That is, Siegmund was willing to face death but had no interest in its promised rewards; only his sister-bride mattered to him.[142] For Weber, Wagner was the "great wizard," the *Hexenmeister.* On his final Easter vacation—which the Webers spent at Else Jaffé's country house in the pastoral Bavarian village of Irschenhausen—he read the text of *Die Walküre* aloud to Marianne and Else.

"Indeed: one cannot live 'against God' in the day, one can only seek out that Tristan-realm—and then die 'against him,' when it is time and He demands it," he wrote Else a little later. "Above all: I can truly live against another person only in the truth, and that I can and may do so is the ultimate necessity decisive for my life, higher and stronger than any god." In Radkau's interpretation, Weber's God isn't so much a source of values as a force of nature.[143] For all of Weber's mistrust toward naturalism, though, we should not insist on an absolute partition between the realms of value and of nature.

He had remarked on the rationalization of the practice of mysticism; could there be something like a mysticism of rationalization? He never believed that the sway of religion could be magicked away; he described himself not as godless or disengaged, as his father had been, but as remote from God.[144] Indeed, Weber's fascination with mysticism recalls a passage from Robert Musil's novel *Man Without Qualities*, in which the titular Ulrich (prompted by the horrid proto-Nazi Hans Sepp) reflects: "While faith based on theological reasoning is today universally engaged in a bitter struggle with doubt and resistance from the prevailing brand of rationalism, it does seem that the naked fundamental experience itself, that primal seizure of mystic insight, stripped of religious concepts, perhaps no longer to be regarded as a religious experience at all, has undergone an immense expansion and now forms the soul of that complex irrationalism that haunts our era like a night bird lost in the dawn."[145] Weber's notion of rationality was so expansive that it could seem to encompass everything people did, but experience itself—mystical, ecstatic, or otherwise—remained on a plane apart.

On June 4, 1920, students at Munich were told that Professor Weber had to cancel the lecture owing to a cold. Pandemics have no hard stop: he had, it seems, belatedly contracted the influenza that had already claimed tens of millions of lives. He lingered for another ten days, attended by Marianne and by Else. In that letter to Else about dying "against God," he had cautioned: "Rest assured, He will pick a time." On June 9, Marianne wrote to Else, "Fate has blessed me abundantly through Max—he himself, out of his abundance and strength, generously granted me every joy that I wanted. . . . Never forget that I deeply approve of your relationship and that everything good in me can rejoice in it." Biographers puzzle over the reciprocal nature of these small circles. Jürgen Kaube suggests that Marianne, in her relationship with Helene, Mina Tobler, and Else Jaffé, "always tried to integrate all these members of the worship community with one another." The survivors remained close. Decades later, Marianne would essentially die in Else's arms, as, later still, Tobler would.[146] Weber had theorized that self-aware actors, through actions that were intelligible to themselves, created societies; so often opaque to himself, Weber had created one of his own.

In his final days, Weber alternated between the language of rationality and that of mysticism. Recalling that, during his illness two decades earlier, he had "struggled with the good Lord," he insisted, "if this were a real pneumonia, I would draw up the balance sheet of my life." But soon the doctors decided that his pneumonia was very real, and deeply seated; talk of such accounting gave way to something else. For a day or two, Marianne evidently measured his condition by the songs he sang. When things took a turn for the worse, he sang what seems to have been a snatch from Schubert's setting of poetry by Wilhelm Müller, "Die schöne Müllerin." In the song, and poem, in question, "The Beloved Color," the beset narrator says, "the quarry I'm hunting is death . . . / Dig me a grave in the meadow, / Cover me with green grass."[147]

Then delirium set in and more than once Marianne detected a "veiled farewell." Religion was, for Weber, both a subject and an agent of rationalization, something that could make values concrete and systematic. But he would never make the mistake of turning rationality, in whatever form, into a religion. Life was something you experienced, even as it ebbed, and religion could speak to experience, as rationality did not. He strained, despite his professed unmusicality in the key signatures of religion, to hear the chords and remain open to the transcendent. *Wir werden ja sehen, was nun kommt*, the great theorist of religious rationality said, after hopes for recovery had dissipated: "We'll just see what comes next."

CHAPTER 5

Critical and Cognitive Turns

SKEPTICS OF SECULARITY — RELIGION AND RESONANCE — COSMOPOLITAN RELIGIOSITY — A CRITIQUE OF SECULAR REASON — RATIONAL CHOICES — COGNITIVE SCIENCE GETS RELIGION — THE GREAT ENABLERS — SCALING UP

So far I've been telling origin stories—braided with origin stories of their own—about the social science of religion. In particular, I've explored how the idea of social science arose in dialogue with the idea of religion, explaining itself in the effort to explain religion. As a genre, origin stories are thought to have enduring significance, which is one reason we tell them. And these? It might have been that these heated discussions from over a century ago long since ashed over. Our inquiry could still be significant as a matter of conceptual archaeology, but no more than that; it could be as remote from the contemporary discipline as the history of chemistry is from that discipline today. Yet sociology is not like chemistry: it remains, to an extent that is surprising (and sometimes deplored), in dialogue with its ancestral ghosts. In this chapter, I'll look at some present-day argument that in various ways elaborate, repudiate, and resonate with the arguments proposed by the subjects of my previous chapters.

Some strains of contemporary sociology are, to simplify, given over to quantitative modeling; some are adjacent to evolutionary biology; some are interpretive, historical, and humanistic. What I find striking is that an engagement with our old debates can be found across these methodological divides. First, I'll give a hearing to recent critics of secularism—as an ideal as well as an empirical characterization—who, via interpretive sociology, approach the issue of whether society depends on religion. Then I'll delve into contemporary work that aims to advance the scientific understanding of religion, and that makes specific claims about religion as an existence condition for society. You'll notice that the principals of my previous chapters will remain in view, if from new angles. We can learn something about our social-science ancestors by studying their progeny.

The Critical Turn

SKEPTICS OF SECULARITY

For some sociologists, the importance of religion is not measurable by variables such as rates of economic growth or crime; it involves matters of transcendental values and ultimate meaning, experiences that expand the boundaries of our subjectivity. That's why their orientation could be described as interpretive or critical. These sociologists interrogate our multiple modernities—an approach that qualifies them as "social critics"—and worry that we have failed to understand the ongoing significance of religion or religiosity. Many suggest that religion has provided specific deliverances that we relinquish at our peril: it plays a role, they say, in sustaining a humane social and political order.

These thinkers often define themselves against Jürgen Habermas's focus—especially in classic writings from the 1960s to the 1980s—on the capacity of reason and critical discourse to shape democratic societies. Habermas, who took secularization to be part of the broader process of modernization, conceived the public sphere as a zone where private individuals could come together to discuss matters of public interest in a rational-critical debate. The religious were welcome so long as they checked their convictions at the door, the way Old West saloons required customers to part with their guns. This was neutrality on secular terms, which, for critics, was no kind of neutrality at all.

The social thinkers hold both that, as an empirical matter, secularization hasn't really entrenched itself, as the story of liberal modernity proposes, *and* that secularization is at odds with human flourishing. Instead of treating religion as bad science, we should view it as an experiential mode, a form of self-transcendence. Consider the work of Hans Joas, who is, aptly, Ernst Troelstch Professor for the Sociology of Religion at the Humboldt University of Berlin—and directs the Max Weber Center at Erfurt, Germany. Joas, a practicing Catholic who has been active in the Catholic debates in Germany over ecclesiastical reform (collectively known as the Synodal Way), believes that the pressing question is whether we can or should dispense with "the experience articulated in faith." In his view, the traditions and institutions of religion help us overcome "the centering of our experience on ourselves."[1] They provide the fullness that Simmel evoked.

Such talk of self-transcendence has an illustrious pedigree: it's presaged, in various ways, in Rudolf Otto's *The Idea of the Holy* (1917) and its theory of "the numinous"—characterized by the sense of the uncanny, alterity, awe, and grace that we experience in and through our interaction with a "numinous object" (a mountain, a poem, a shrine), and by the self-submergence or self-surrender he called "creature feeling." It has precursors, too, in Simon Weil's later notion of attention, conceived as an effort to direct the mind toward a particular object, idea, or person, and away from the self, and a practice in which, by eschewing our ego and desires, we open ourselves to understanding and compassion. Readers of Iris Murdoch, too, will recognize a version of what she called unselfing. Shared forms of self-transcendence, in turn, qualify as what Durkheim called effervescences, and, as Joas is aware, can have negative as well as positive effects.[2]

Earlier, I described Dilthey separating psychology in its humanistic, experiential sense from psychology as an experimental discipline in the natural sciences: he sought to set *Verstehen* apart from *Erklären*. In the confrontation of believer and nonbeliever, Joas sees a similar disjunction. If we reduce religious experiences to "psychological phenomena," something is lost. Much social science of religion, in his view, has been marred by a failure to engage with religion on its own terms. Weber was undone, Joas thinks, by focusing on the consequences of religious systems, rather than on the systems themselves. Durkheim fares better, in evoking the loss of self that points toward "forces of sociality that are interpreted as sacred." But Joas faults him for supposing that a replacement religion was to be found in a doctrine of individualism and human dignity that, although based on the sacredness of the individual, lacked *cultus*, a community of the faithful, and self-transcendent experience.[3]

A better approach, Joas and others suggest, involves recognizing human rights—the sacralization of the person—as part of an essentially Christian tradition. The values embedded in talk of human rights originate in, and gain their emotional power from, a religious worldview; sever the discourse of human rights from its rightful genealogy and something politically important is lost. In *The Power of the Sacred*, he expresses optimism that "a sphere is opening up" in which the religious and the nonreligious "can articulate their experiences and assumptions and relate them to one another." The flourishing of the political realm, such social theorists argue, requires the sustenance of religion.[4]

RELIGION AND RESONANCE

And in liberal democracies where religion has been sidelined? A healthy democratic culture, we're warned, becomes diminished. Hartmut Rosa, a younger German sociologist in the interpretive tradition (who, among other things, is the director of the Max Weber Center at the University of Erfurt), worries that our society has become aggression-driven, resource-exploiting, alienated, and overtaken by a concern for speed, efficiency, and instrumental rationality, all trends that have debased the political realm. He is best known for his theory of "resonance," which comprises a complex mixture of affect, agency, connection, and transformation. In his magnum opus *Resonance: A Sociology of Our Relationship to the World*, we learn that the titular concept involves a sense of being in tune with the world (including its human inhabitants), of being touched and moved by it, and of being able to respond to it in a meaningful way. It requires a certain degree of openness, vulnerability, and a willingness to be transformed by encounters with the other. Although Rosa's account of resonance draws from Durkheim, Simmel, and, extensively, Weber, it is distinctively affect-centered. Resonance isn't just (as we'd say these days) a vibe; but it is nothing without that vibe. Like Joas's self-transcendence—and similarly resonant, one might say, with those earlier notions of the "numinous," "attention," and "unselfing"—it can arise through our encounter with a range of objects, creaturely and otherwise. (The book includes a discussion of Schubert's *Die Winterreise*, the second of the composer's two song cycles set to poems by Wilhelm Müller.)[5] Rosa wants social institutions to promote resonance, although, of course, this invites the application of instrumental rationality to something meant to elude its grasp; as when, at my high school, transcendental meditation was taught as a form of mental wellness.

A democratic culture, he has argued more recently, needs a listening heart, and "the churches in particular have command of narratives, of a cognitive reservoir, of rituals and practices, and of spaces where a listening heart can be practiced and perhaps also be experienced." Echoing a concept (*Beruf, Berufung*) that Weber did so much with, he writes, "We have to let ourselves be *called*." Religion "has a reservoir of ideas and an arsenal of related songs, gestures, spaces, traditions and practices that give a sense of what it means to let oneself be called, to let oneself be transformed, to be in resonance," he writes. "If society loses *this*, if it forgets *this* form of relational possibility, then it is over and done with."[6]

Even if we diminish and demote the sphere of the secular, though, we still have to think about how to construct a society that accommodates both the religious and the nonreligious. Here, Habermas is an illustrative figure. For over the past three decades, his views about religion and secularity have shifted, in empirical and normative ways. Religious communities, around the world but even in the "advanced" West, proved more persistent than he had perhaps anticipated; the normative idea that religion should be confined to the private sphere has seemed ever more untenable.

In his 2001 lecture "Glauben und Wissen" ("Faith and Knowledge") and in his 2005 collection *Zwischen Naturalismus und Religion* (*Between Naturalism and Religion*), Habermas continues to insist that religious communities must adapt to the principles of a plural, democratic society, but he also suggests that such a society can learn from religious traditions. In what he calls a "post-secular" society, religion can contribute ethical resources to public discourse; it can, for example, motivate social solidarity and moral behavior that the nonreligious can value. At the same time, he tells us in that lecture, religious arguments must be "translated" into a language that is accessible to all citizens. John Rawls, in *Political Liberalism* (1993), had made a similar-sounding stipulation: religion was not to be excluded from the public sphere, but its arguments had to abide by the principle of public reason within an "overlapping consensus," offering reasons that could be accepted by other citizens, regardless of their personal beliefs or comprehensive doctrines of the good. Yet Habermas, engaging with Rawls, envisages a more reciprocal process, in which the burden of communication is not entirely on the religious; both religious and secular reasons may be transformed through dialogue, in ways compatible with a secular and democratic society. Fixing the always "fluid" boundary between secular and religious reasons, he writes in "Faith and Knowledge," ought to be "understood as a cooperative exercise that requires each side to adopt the perspective of the other."[7]

In his *Between Naturalism and Religion*, Habermas advocates a "post-metaphysical" approach that recognizes the limits of both scientific and religious knowledge. Distinct functions can be played by each, he says. Science is concerned with empirical and theoretical knowledge about the natural world, aiming for universal validity through objective methods. Religion, by contrast, provides a moral and existential orientation, addressing questions of meaning, value, and purpose that transcend empirical verification. He notes that the meaning of concepts such as "autonomy," "individuality, "emancipation," and "solidarity"—though they have Greek and Roman forebears—were deeply shaped by "Judeo-Christian" traditions.[8]

Habermas proposes a truce in which science recognizes that it cannot answer questions of moral value or existential meaning, while religion must not contradict empirical knowledge or scientific understanding of the world. By recognizing these mutual limits, science and religion can be seen as complementary, rather than conflictual, each offering insights and understanding that the other cannot provide. The state should be neutral with respect to the worldviews of its citizens, and (he is careful to acknowledge) embracing the worldview of the secular is not neutrality. Discussing, inter alia, Kant, Habermas therefore recommends a "saving appropriation" that not only retains important values (such as human equality; but perhaps even the concept of personhood) carried by the Judeo-Christian tradition but respects their origins.[9] (Indeed, there's a sense in which secularism itself was a religious deliverance, given that the separation between church and state was secured chiefly by nonstate religions.)

The contours of this argument are familiar: Ernst Mach, Windelband, Simmel, Weber, and others articulated versions of it, and so did various liberal theologians of their day. "If religion is not a set of claims but a certain state of being—which is precisely what enables it to interpret and judge empirical phenomena—then it can be no more disproved by science than can any other state of being," Simmel had argued.[10] To be sure, the truce imposes a far heavier tax on religion than on science; religion becomes a realm of value and ultimate meaning, while being severed from its empirical claims. A religionist will still have grounds to complain that this is religion on the terms of secularism—that religion itself is being secularized.

COSMOPOLITAN RELIGIOSITY

But some sociologists think that something like this is happening anyway, with the cult of the individual taking on religious or "spiritual" form. The late Ulrich Beck, perhaps Germany's most influential social theorist after Habermas, argues that the sacralized individual has itself hardened into a steel-like shell. In particular, he sees "institutionalized individualization" as an ideological constraint, a form imposed on us. (He cites Durkheim's remark about individualism as a religion in which "man is at once believer and God.") Secular Europe has become rife with "a God of your own" creeds, DIY belief systems that are hostile to materialism and to the traditions of the church. (Beck writes, impishly, "Religious illiteracy spreads like a plague and atheists cannot even remember which God they no longer believe in.") Amid a decline in church attendance, we see a rise in magical thinking, possibly under the banner of "wellness," while "Amnesty International may be understood as a modern church dedicated to a God of its own making."[11]

Much of this account can be read as an extension of Simmel's "conflict of modern culture" arguments. But Beck sees, as Durkheim and Weber had, that this individualization arises from a long process within the Christian tradition (the post-Reformation invention of a "caring" god, the Protestant autonomy of the individual conscience, and so on). It was religion that had built this modernity; that had pioneered globalization; and that had (out of its own pressing interests) promulgated tolerance. The values of secular humanism were bequeathed by religion, then. And in an era of multiple secularities, the challenge was finding our way to the right form of modernity, globalization, and tolerance.

In making his case, Beck charts three phases of modern religiosity. The first phase is anti-modern, exemplified in all those reactive fundamentalisms. The second is postmodern, and issues in those relativist, individualized, "find your bliss" credos. And the third? This phase he saw arising (provisionally) from what he calls a "second modernity," and it was one that he welcomed. It would reject both reaction and relativism and usher in a "cosmopolitan religiosity."

This form of religiosity saw the world as it was. We are, after all, "a crazy patchwork of identities." We went wrong when, in the name of religious freedom, we sided with a medley of monoculturalisms, institutionally "integrating" religious communities through their putative leaders. The "communitarian" philosophers wrongly gave priority to the preservation of "pure" identities over "an insight into the realities of multiple, interwoven identities." What Beck called for, rather, was a vision "based on the actually existing historical impurity of the world religions: the recognition that they are intertwined, that they are both other and the same."[12]

For this reason, he urges that we distinguish between "religion" and "religious"—between the noun and the adjective. The noun, he thinks, "organizes the religious field according to an either/or logic"; the adjective, according to "a 'both/and' logic." Being "religious" doesn't presuppose that you're a member, or not a member, of some specific group; instead, it signals a particular attitude toward existential questions about humanity.

Beck took up the issue with a certain prophetic tone. A cosmopolitan religiosity would allow for the "coexistence of different, frequently contradictory world perspectives and value systems in a space where they directly interact." And we needed a cosmopolitan religiosity because climate politics was cosmopolitan, a matter of worldwide survival. (Beck had made his name as a "risk society" theorist.) Like Weber, Beck saw a return of the gods; he worried about what sociologists' methodological secularism could blind them to, notably the "remystification of reality."[13] Still, many sociologists who quarrel with the secularization thesis, including Beck, aren't exactly untethered to secularity: they are arguing for religion or religiosity because it would make good things happen, not because it would make us good.

A CRITIQUE OF SECULAR REASON

To explore a far more radical critique of the secular, we'll want to step outside the disciplinary ambit of sociology. John Milbank, in his contentious classic *Theology and Social Theory: Beyond Secular Reason*, from 1990, challenges the secular foundations of contemporary social theory, arguing that sociology and similar disciplines operate within a framework that inherently marginalizes or misunderstands religion. For Milbank, a founder of the left-leaning and avowedly postmodern Radical Orthodoxy, "sociology is only able to explain or even illuminate religion, to the extent that it conceals its own theological borrowings and its own quasi-religious status." In his brilliantly polemical way, he urges us to recognize that " 'scientific' social theories are theologies or anti-theologies in disguise."[14]

To help us see the water in which we swim, he offers a conceptual genealogy of his own. In medieval Christian culture, the "secular" didn't exist; the "saeculum" was the not-yet-redeemed interval between fall and *eschaton* (the end of the world and final judgment). And so the secular had to be imagined, put into theory and into practice. His detailed account arcs through Machiavelli, Montesquieu, the Scottish Enlightenment, and the political economists of the nineteenth century, finally delivering the liberal and positivist discourses hidden beneath the rise of sociology.[15]

What emerges in his account is a malign metaphysics—effectively religious in character—that posited a social world naturally propelled by conflict and coercion, predicated on an ontology of scarcity and competition. By contrast, Milbank is convinced that Christianity embodies a conception of peace based on "the *sociality* of harmonious difference." The Christian imagination is "the imagination in action of a peaceful, reconciled social order."[16]

Milbank's caustic view of sociology recalls Leo Tolstoy's. In 1902, the same year Durkheim was lecturing on the elementary forms of religion, the Russian novelist-turned-sage published a parable titled "The Overthrow of Hell and Its Restoration." It's a dramatic dialogue between Beelzebub, who has just awoken after centuries of slumber, and various of his devilish followers, who are delivering the good news about how, long after Jesus arrived with his teachings and his sacrifice, Hell was now being repopulated. Part of why this was happening, he learns, was that the so-called church had set about to distort Jesus's teachings; another part is the preachings of war-mongering nationalists. Beelzebub still has questions, though: What prevents truly learned people from seeing through clerical distortions and reinstating the teachings of Jesus? The explanation comes from a "matte-black devil in a robe, with a flat, sloping forehead," who speaks "in a quiet, measured voice." He's the impresario of intellectual hindrances, and a big one turns out to be sociology: he persuades people that all religious teaching "is a delusion and superstition and that they can learn how to live from a science I have invented for them, called sociology, which consists in studying how differently bad people have lived in the past."[17] Beelzebub is delighted by the news.

Milbank asks us to entertain the idea that "sociology has always been, by definition, primarily sociology of religion, and that it has been constituted, as a discipline, by a theory of secularization, or of 'normal religion.' " Marx, in Milbank's view, was wrongfooted by both humanism and positivism: cultural processes, in Marx, are deemed "religious" only in contradistinction to some "imaginary naturalistic norm, a new 'natural law' of humanity," so that freedom and peace will emerge naturally, with the abolition of what's holding them back, while the Marxist critique of Christianity is situated within a "quasi-religious" metanarrative.[18] We're to see Simmel and Weber, in turn, as hobbled by a neo-Kantian identification of religion with the personal and the subjective, even if it was operationalized through public processes of ritual and routinization. Durkheim, for his part, is described as having been hobbled by his equation of the social and the religious, and by artificially separating the sacred and the profane. Milbank even ventures that "all twentieth-century sociology of religion can be exposed as a secular policing of the sublime."

But while Milbank means to address secular social scientists as well as theologians, much of his account will be difficult to accept for people who are imaginative outsiders to the premodern, all-encompassing Christendom he posits. Although his account of the peaceful social order accords with Ernst Troeltsch's "ideal of a humanity based on spiritual freedom and fellowship, in which tyranny, law, war, and force are unknown," he fails to recognize, as Troeltsch did, that there had been alternative versions of this ideal, such as in Stoicism.[19] And precisely because Christianity took shape, doctrinally, under conditions of conflict—conflict with a Jewish priesthood, with Hellenic and Roman authorities, and so on—the serene countenance Milbank sees requires an amputated account of its beliefs and practices. The same goes for his characterization of early modern and modern thought, whose diversity is reduced to liberalism and positivism in his retelling. When he argues that "pluralism is better guaranteed by Christianity than by the Enlightenment," he gives voice to an entrenched but mistaken interpretation of the Enlightenment, which fails to grasp Herder (say) as a central figure in it.[20]

And while it's fair to say that Durkheim, Simmel, and Weber did have tenets that can be characterized as those of liberal individualism, they also had tenets that cut against that liberal individualism. Pace Milbank, they would be more accurately described as anti-positivist than positivist—concerned as each was with *Verstehen*, experience, meaning—while Milbank, analyzing the world through such teleological concepts as "late capitalism," might be said to ventriloquize a conceptual heritage he wants us to abjure. Yes, the classical sociologists did respond to the empirical evidence, and the felt reality, concerning the decline of traditional religious authority in their societies. But mostly, as we've seen, they also quarreled with crude versions of the secularization thesis; religion was too central to their understanding of society to be treated casually. Recall Simmel on the "fullness of being" enjoyed by the religious person: "the problem of religion today would be solved if people were to lead religious lives: that is, not lives which are lived 'with' religion, but lives that are carried out religiously, and which certainly are not carried out 'from' religion—that is, out of consideration for some object external to religious life."[21] In many respects, in fact, the classical sociologists were allies of social critics who complain about the crowding-out effects of scientism, technical control, and the cult of efficiency: these elders similarly doubted that a society where only such things prevailed would be viable. Still, Milbank is onto something when he writes, "We never question the idea that while 'religions' are problematic, the 'social' is obvious," and when he notes that "the emergence of the concept of the social must be located within the history of 'the secular.' " We needn't situate the social within the realm of revelation, as this advocate of Radical Orthodoxy does, to recognize the sometimes inharmonious intimacy between the concepts of secularity and of society.

The Cognitive Turn

RATIONAL CHOICES

The voices of Durkheim, Simmel, and Weber reverberate in our contemporary German thinkers' wranglings over society and secularity, and perhaps that isn't so surprising. When you're an attentive reader of these elder theorists—when your scholarly identity is, in part, shaped by their own projects—it becomes natural to situate your positions as dissenting from or concurring with them. You might think the situation would be very different when it comes to the quants and modelers of recent social science. Let me try to persuade you otherwise.

We might start with the economists and economically influenced sociologists who, over the past few decades, have sought to illuminate religion through rational-choice theory. That theory has long provided a basic framework for microeconomics; it assumes that individuals make decisions they believe will maximize their utility, given the constraints they face, and aims to explain and predict the behavior of actors (individuals, but also firms) in a variety of scenarios. In fact, the approach aligns with much of what Weber had to say about the savage's instrumental rationality, because this form of rationality was responsive to transactional utility (even if "ideal interests" could be included). Victorians referred to Tylor's "savage philosophers," because Tylor thought that the big question our ancestors grappled with was, What explains phenomena? Weber's focus was on savage *economists*, for whom the big question was, What do I get out of it?[22]

So what do social scientists get out of these methods—what can be done with them? The first move, typically, is to conceptualize the religious landscape as a competitive market in which various religious organizations (suppliers) compete for followers (consumers). You can view individuals as rational actors who choose their religious affiliations and levels of participation based on a cost-benefit analysis, opting for the religion or religious practices that offer them the greatest benefits (such as community, spiritual fulfillment, or salvation) at the lowest cost (time, money, or social standing). Perhaps you find that competition increases the quality and diversity of religious offerings. You might conclude that secularization in some societies (for example, parts of Europe) is not due to modernization per se but to the lack of religious competition, while other places, such as the United States, have higher levels of religious involvement because they have a highly competitive religious market. Perhaps religious pluralism, resulting from a free market of religion, can lead to higher overall religious participation because individuals are more likely to find a religious "product" that meets their needs.

Rational-choice models of religion have been deployed to explain other questions.[23] Why have more demanding creeds done better than less demanding ones? "Costly signaling" theory suggests that individuals who incur significant costs (participating in rituals, following dietary restrictions) more persuasively signal their commitment to the religion, which can have social benefits. "Religious capital"—your investment in your religion—can affect your level of attachment to it. It should be admitted that if the opposite had been the case, and we saw the membership of liberal and lenient denominations expanding, the model would explain that, too: lower costs of a good typically lead to increased consumption.

The best-known work in this area was done, in whole or part, by the industrious and prolific sociologist Rodney Stark; you could say his version achieved market dominance. Stark, along with collaborators such as William Sims Bainbridge, Roger Finke, and Laurence Iannaccone, advanced a model of religious development in which humans retain cultural products that seem to produce better results. Over time, the result is that religion, as the subtitle of one of Stark's books has it, "benefits everyone, including atheists." But not just any religion. Which religions produce good results? Ones that, in Stark's words, promulgate "images of gods as conscious, powerful, morally concerned beings."[24] In his view, successful religions, invoking such gods, contribute substantially to social cohesion, stability, and communal and individual well-being, community participation, and so on. In the past, he was convinced, societies have done better with religion, or the right religions, and he saw no reason why that historical pattern would change.

Stark, who died in 2022, was outspoken in denouncing "ancestor worship" in his discipline, and had little time for Durkheim and Weber. Inasmuch as Durkheim thought that rites and rituals were primary, and gods secondary, he had mistaken the force of God, or so Stark thought. Weber's "Protestant Ethic" thesis was all wrong, Stark argued just as strenuously: capitalism emerged in Catholic Europe, and when Weber later insisted that he was concerned only with "modern capitalism," he was rigging the game.

Take a closer look, though. Stark actually adopts Durkheim's notion of religion as creating moral communities—as promoting conformity to a moral order—albeit with the caveat that this is true not of religion as such but of the most successful religions. And though Weber, in particular, was a disciplinary idol that Stark wanted to smash, the shape of Stark's work was far more Weberian than was that of most ostensible Weberians; Stark, too, favored grand, century-scaling histories tracing civilizational careers. Picking up Joseph Needham's question, for example, Stark asks why the scientific revolution took place in the West and not China. His answer involves not only the general commitment of Christian theology to rationality but also a quality of striving that Christianity promoted. By contrast, traditional China, he says, promoted a sort of quietist adjustment to what was. Right or wrong, the analysis is notably close to Weber's.

"My disagreement with Weber is not about whether religious doctrines influenced the rise of the West," Stark admitted, "but *which* doctrines." He agrees with Weber that the "sanctification of work" mattered; his quarrel was specifically with what he saw as Weber's anti-Catholic prejudice. (Weber himself acknowledged that the asceticism he identified with Calvinism could be found in Catholic monasticism, Stark notes, so why did he brush this aside?) Methodologically, too, the adjacencies are apparent. The subjective rationality that Weber explored is a core concept for Stark; it's why he insisted he was offering what, in his paper on "The Micro Foundations of Religion," he called "a theory of religion based on reason and choice."

COGNITIVE SCIENCE GETS RELIGION

In Chapter 1, I touched on the cognitive science of religion—an approach that draws from cognitive, social, and evolutionary psychology in ways too enmeshed to be separable—and because it has emerged as a sizable program, I want to give it a fair amount of attention. Much recent work in this tradition shares Tylor's emphasis on belief but has also taken up a social dimension that Tylor had hurried past, informed by the sociology that developed in his wake. It appeals to the ways in which our individual psychologies were shaped by natural selection, but it can appeal as well to cultural evolution, with its very different logic, drawing on what Tylor, in his definition of culture, called the "capabilities and habits acquired by man as a member of society." As should become clear, my concern is not to affirm or debunk the hypotheses of cognitive science of religion (CSR to practitioners and critics), but to show how they resonate, in different ways, with arguments associated with the principals of my previous chapters.

In what has been called the Standard Model within the cognitive science of religion, a complex we may call religion may not be selected for directly but can be viewed as a byproduct of other psychological traits that proved adaptive.[25] Or, in Pascal Boyer's formulation, "We do not have the cultural concepts we have because they make sense or are useful, but because the way our brains are put together makes it very difficult not to build them."[26] Tylorian animism, as we saw, involves adopting an intentional stance toward the natural world. The Standard Model typically starts with a posited mechanism for this stance, often called an "agent detection device."

Evolutionary psychologists think that our brains are so designed that we respond to a wide range of experiences by attributing agency to something in the world. A compelling reason to be good at agent detection is the fact that we are social creatures, with friends and foes; and typically our agent detection devices are going to help us ascribe agency to actual agents. As the anthropologist Stewart Elliott Guthrie writes, "the most valuable interpretations usually are those that disclose the presence of whatever is most important to us. That usually is other humans." In the basic evolutionary picture, early hominids, like many primates, lived in groups; the advantages of doing so (increased protection from predators, say, and more efficient foraging) didn't require advanced cognitive traits; basic social instincts and behaviors could suffice, at least initially. Social cognition evolved in a stepwise and incremental way; creatures more attuned to social cues or with a rudimentary understanding of others' intentions had an advantage.

Guthrie, who broadly aligns himself with Tylor's intellectualism and focus on animism (although he doesn't accept Tylor's account of animism whole cloth), concludes that anthropomorphism, albeit by definition mistaken, is "reasonable and inevitable."[27] If you fail to detect an agent (whether a human enemy or a hungry bear), the costs are likely to be greater than if you detect an agent who isn't there. So researchers, invoking error-management theory, say that it's better if our agent detection is oversensitive than undersensitive—better to be prone to Type 1 errors (false positives) rather than Type 2 errors (false negatives). The result is that human beings have a "hyperactive agent detection device," a coinage that the psychologist Justin L. Barrett, drawing on Guthrie's argument, introduced.[28]

We understand agents, in turn, by applying to them a folk-psychological theory that supposes them to have beliefs, desires, and intentions that may be different from our own. Cognitive psychology calls this "theory of mind." Because human beings benefit from coordinating their behavior with others, a theory of mind can enhance individual survival. Now, the great foe of cooperation, in the vocabulary of game theory, is defection—people who take but don't give, who leave you in the lurch (defect), who can't be relied on, who try to take a free ride on your labors. A theory of mind is pretty successful in helping us predict and make sense of the behavior of others and ourselves; because we're equipped with it, the anthropologist Scott Atran argues, we're "wired to spot lurkers (and to seek protectors) almost anywhere." Having a theory of mind helps us to detect cheaters and find allies.[29] People thus get better at identifying the motivations of others, including their incentives to defect, and they are able, through language, to communicate to others the scandal of defection.

The result is that among creatures like us, the risks associated with defection are significantly higher than among social creatures with neither language nor theory of mind. Not only is the likelihood of detection high; its costs are high, too, since word of your defection can spread far beyond those who were able to witness or infer it. The costs of conformity will seem lower.

Our evolved minds may provide us with other tendencies and tropisms. One somewhat Tylorian argument is that mind-body dualism naturally arises from the theory of mind and tends to support religious ideas about nonmaterial spirits. (A person's mental states aren't directly observable; maybe they're immaterial, nonphysical entities?) Another argument, drawing support from work in child psychology, is that we're intuitively drawn to teleological explanations: explanations, even of the natural world, in terms of purposes. (Kids will say that mountains are for climbing.)[30] Over time, as hominid groups become more complex and as group members develop more sophisticated cognitive abilities, sociality and cognitive traits supportive of sociality arise in a reciprocal, co-evolutionary process. Enhanced cognitive abilities facilitate more complex social interactions, which in turn place further selective pressures on social cognition.

From this point, the Standard Model proceeds with explanations that chiefly involve cultural, rather than biological, evolution, granting that the two will continue to be interlinked in complex ways. Let's see how the model addresses the question of how stories about such supernatural agents get elaborated and transmitted.

One explanation comes from Joseph Henrich and Scott Atran, building on work by Boyer, Barrett, and others. It begins with the hypothesis—for which a great deal of cross-cultural evidence is enlisted—that we come into the world with predispositions to develop an intuitive ontology, a basic set of structures for thinking about the world around us. Beyond having theories of agency and of mind, human beings naturally classify the world into agents and nonagents, animals and plants, living and nonliving things. Flora and fauna are understood through a folk biology; nonliving things through a folk physics, and so on. Plants and birds and rocks all have characteristic doings.

But cultures may also develop the idea of an entity that violates some of these intuitive structures. Human beings are agents, which occupy space, and living things, which die. But ghosts, spirits, and angels violate these assumptions. They are, Henrich and Atran write, "agents that resemble us emotionally, intellectually, and physically except that they can move through solid objects and live forever."[31] Stories with small numbers of such violations—"minimally counterintuitive" representations—are easier to remember than those with none but also than stories with too many.[32] The thought is that paying attention to anomalies is a fitness-enhancing tendency, but that some reports are too far-fetched to credit. Folktales, which had to be remembered and passed on in oral cultures, often have entities with such minimal violations: a talking lion, a living mountain (although, to be sure, these are stories we don't necessarily believe).[33]

When we have cultural transmission, two developments are added: first, the accumulation of knowledge and the devising of concepts remote from our intuitive ontology, and second, the possibility that we will be misinformed by others. So, these authors argue, we should have evolved mechanisms aimed at testing belief against action before accepting the claims of others. When considering a proposition that people are urging on us, we'll take into account evidence of their success, skill, and prestige; we'll also pay attention to whether they seem committed to the proposition themselves.[34]

Once these mechanisms are in place, and the cues seem auspicious, we can learn and commit to counterintuitive propositions of the sort associated with religion. And counterintuitive beliefs associated with demanding rituals may have been easier to transmit to new learners, because such behavior signals that the existing adherents are genuinely committed to them (as costly-signaling theory would have it). In cultural evolution, those patterns of thought and action that are more likely to be repeated and transmitted across space and time have a better chance at replacing existing patterns of behavior.

The cognitive science of religion, as we've seen, started with a more or less Tylorian account of agency ascription and theory of mind (and even mind-body dualism), building on instrumentally rational inferences; then it swiftly extended itself through mechanisms helpful for cooperation and adaptive sociality. Aptly enough, Pascal Boyer, who describes himself as a cognitive anthropologist, eventually moved from writing books like *The Naturalness of Religious Ideas* and *Religion Explained* to creating a more general account: *Minds Make Society*. In even the minimal version of the Standard Model, then, the mechanisms that permit human sociality are mechanisms that conduce to religion. The complementary story, as we'll see, is that religions, or successful ones, conduce to sociality. In its stronger forms, the thesis is that if sociality is an existence condition for religion—if it is necessary for its emergence and its persistence—religion is an existence condition for society. Our ouroboros returns, as hungry as ever.

THE GREAT ENABLERS

The cognitive science of religion can be agnostic as to whether religions themselves benefit their members; durable religious forms simply have to have traits that favor their own survival. But influential accounts (including Henrich and Atran's) do connect religions—at least those that have survived and spread—to prosocial, group-beneficial norms: norms that increase cooperation and reduce conflict within a group. The successes of a group, in turn, are thought to facilitate the spread of the associated beliefs and customs, via "cultural group selection." (This may involve some combination of diffusion and conquest.) Prosocial norms typically encompass, though they can't be equated with, what we think of as moral norms.

The psychologist Ara Norenzayan has offered a particularly detailed account of religion's role in enabling large numbers of people to live together. That human beings went from *Gemeinschaften* to *Gesellschaften*—from small communities to huge but still cooperative societies—over the past twelve thousand years is, he says, a unique achievement of our mammalian species, but it's also a puzzle. Another puzzle, he says, is that most people on the planet belong to just a handful of religions, even though, by one estimate, there are ten thousand religions out there. Most religions fizzle out; a few become, well, market leaders. And the key to understanding their success, Norenzayan writes in *Big Gods: How Religion Transformed Cooperation and Conflict* (2013), is to understand how prosocial religions facilitate cooperation on a large scale. "Watched people are nice people," he writes.[35] So if naturally evolved religious intuitions happened to come up with powerful, punitive, all-seeing divine entities with morally interventionist inclinations? You'd have a group where everyone had a reason to behave in group-minded, prosocial ways. Rodney Stark, as we noted, similarly thought that religions promulgated a moral order insofar as their gods were powerful, active, and morally engaged. (He also commended Tylor for seeing that not *all* religions sustain the moral order.)[36]

The idea that a moralizing and punishment-dispensing supernatural entity can motivate us to adhere to the norms of a group is far from new. Simmel, you will recall, thought that moral norms represented the internalization of external compulsion, and, conversely, that religion represented the externalization of internal compulsion; our moral norms got intensified, psychologically, when we projected them onto God. Weber, too, saw that adherents to ethical salvation religions could conduct themselves in ways that were rational responses to, say, the prospect of hellfire.

So you don't need game theory to recognize the value of supernatural punishers. But it helps. As we know from the Prisoner's Dilemma, rational creatures pursuing their own individual advantage will often be unable to gain the benefits of cooperation. One way to encourage cooperation is to make the costs of defection very high. In the prisoner's dilemma, the offenders can both escape prison if they stick to a single story that exculpates them both. If either defects, however, the other will end up serving a long sentence. The cost of defection—the sentence given the prisoner who confesses and betrays his comrade—is worth it because the cost of loyalty is the risk of having that longer sentence imposed. But if you share a society with someone, you will face repeated prisoner's dilemmas. And once you have betrayed someone, they have reason not to rely on you next time. If you think you will regularly be in situations where you will need to trust one another, you can have a selfish motivation to take the path of cooperation—a motivation that's increased if you are likely to be punished for defection. And, a body of experimental research suggests, people are generally willing to punish someone they see as defecting from social norms, even if they are not themselves the victims of the defection, and even if the punishing makes them somewhat worse off. Mathematical models have also shown that such "altruistic punishment"—an inclination to punish norm-breaching even when it doesn't harm us personally—will entrench those norms and make it even more rewarding to cooperate.[37]

And what keeps people on the straight and narrow when they know that no other person is observing them—when there seems to be no one around in the moral quad? A belief in spiritual agents intent on delivering comeuppance. There are many proposals along these lines, varying in their details. One of them, which Norenzayan discusses and accepts in part, was made by Dominic Johnson and Jesse Bering, who elaborate on the ways that "the expectation and fear of supernatural punishment" (either in this world or in an afterlife, as via a "moralizing high god") solves the problem that it's costly to detect and punish cheaters.[38] Where Johnson and Bering part company with many other CSR theorists, including Norenzayan, is in rejecting "by-product" theory: this core feature of religion, as the two see it, was evolutionarily selected for. Norenzayan's view is that, culturally speaking, prosocial religions are like successful mutations. Some scientists, seconding Simmel, will just say that, as the neuroscientist Robert Sapolsky puts it, "a religion reflects the values of the culture that invented or adopted it" and "very effectively transmits those values." But unlike such theorists—and unlike Tylor—Johnson and Bering maintain that moral punishment is a universal feature of religions. Religions don't need to use the language of hellfire; in Hindu and Buddhist traditions, they say, retribution may arrive by way of karma and how you fare in reincarnation.[39] And so they think *all* religions will tend to be prosocial.

Still, the larger theory of the spirit patrol doesn't depend on whether it's a feature of all religions or specifically of successful religions; we can put aside the quasi-scholastic arguments about whether a belief in spiritual punishers is best seen as hardware, software, or firmware. The cutting edge of the "big gods" thesis is compatible with a range of views here. More relevant to our themes is the role that Norenzayan assigns to practices. "Displays of devotion and hard-to-fake commitments such as fasts, food taboos, and extravagant rituals further transmitted believers' sincere faith in these gods to others," writes Norenzayan, who also nods at Durkheim's collective effervescences. "Through these and other solidarity-promoting mechanisms, religions of Big Gods forged anonymous strangers into large, cohesive moral communities tied together with the sacred bonds of a common supernatural jurisdiction." Religions, as he sees it, bring together believing and belonging. "We don't have to choose between Hume and Durkheim," he writes, with Hume representing the intellectualism further developed by Tylor. What arise in these large supernatural jurisdictions are the moral tenets that Simmel (like some liberal theologians, such as Troeltsch) thought had gained force from universal religions. If we're all children of God, it's easier to treat even strangers as fictive kin. At the same time, the dynamic that Weber observed in the high-trust charismatic churches and sects he visited in the United States appears to be a crystallization and intensification of something that operates on a vast scale.

Some people will wonder whether the cognitive science of religion explains what they find important in religion; it certainly has a largely functionalist flavor. Let's reprise: the account explains how religious beliefs originate from our mental architecture (agent detection; mind-body dualism; teleology), takes up cultural transmissibility and memorability (via minimally counterintuitive concepts; rituals; institutions), and then considers how (in tandem with the formation of group identity) it may propagate prosocial, group-beneficial norms. The perspective here is resolutely exterior. It takes little notice of the "varieties of religious experience" that William James wrote about; it is deaf to tone and timbre. It does not tell us what religion means to the religious. The Standard Model has spun off secondary elaborations, to be sure, that try to explain, say, the category of the sacred or the existence of elevated emotion. But a mode of inquiry is bound to delimit its field of inquiry: wrenches like bolts. Unsurprisingly, the Standard Model operationalizes religion in a way that highlights aspects amenable to cognitive and evolutionary analysis; religion must be conceived in a way to support empirical investigation and theoretical development within a scientific framework. *These* beliefs, through *these* mechanisms of practice, produce *these* patterns of social behavior.

SCALING UP

Did religion really make society possible? The "big gods" thesis has been widely debated. On the one hand, Pascal Boyer and Nicolas Baumard maintain that large societies arose before moralized or prosocial religions, which (they maintain) appeared only after the Axial Age. Besides, didn't the Roman Empire, fortified by its military and fiscal efficiency, succeed without moralized religion, and didn't it collapse after it embraced one? On the other hand, Johnson disagrees with them all because he thinks even small gods (those of hunter-gatherers, and presumably our evolutionary ancestors) were prosocial. As for the Romans, he cites Polybius on the role of *deisidaimonia*, reverence for or fear of the gods: it was "what holds the Roman state together," Polybius claimed.[40] But however the theory fares, we've seen that its basic conceptual matrix is both Durkheimian—the creation of a moral community, sustained by ritual, is key—and neo-Tylorian: the beliefs (specifically in punishing, omniscient, moralizing deities) are primary. And it's all of a piece with Simmel's view that early religions amplified a group's socially beneficial norms.

What about the fact that Western and Northern Europe present us with high-trust, cooperative societies where levels of religious adherence seem particularly low? Johnson, like some of the critical sociologists discussed at the start of this chapter, thinks that this development is actually worrisome—that our overall social welfare is best sustained by religion. Norenzayan, borrowing a metaphor of Wittgenstein's, says that it's a matter of climbing a ladder and then kicking it away. In his view, secular societies are "really an outgrowth of prosocial religions."[41] The big monotheisms, by derogating false beliefs, got us used to the idea that we might be tempted by false beliefs, even as they shrank the role of supernatural activity to just the one God the Creator, who became increasingly abstract and noninterventionist. And, over time, when government comes to be seen as trustworthy, and plays a larger role in providing us with security, faith in institutions can supplant faith in the divine. Compare Weber's idea of how Western religion, itself progressively rationalized, eclipses everyday magic and drives rationalization.

One form of such rationalization is the secular study of religion. All our classical sociologists thought that within secularizing societies, something would play a role akin to religion; in Simmel's terms, religiosity wasn't going anywhere, but it didn't have to take the forms of religion as such. Insofar as our classical sociologists, in their various ways, were convinced that religion and society created each other, it's striking to see a powerful line of argument in the cognitive science of religion converging on this view. But it's also striking to see contemporary theorists reprise the debates among those classical sociologists—about the relative roles of belief, belonging, practice, rationality, affect. The tableau is almost Weberian: The old gods of social science rise from their graves, strive to gain power over our thought, and resume their battle among themselves.

Epilogue

ONE OF ANOTHER — DEFINITION AND DEFERENCE — THE CONCEPT IN THE DOCK — THE ACID OF REALITY — THE SEMANTICS OF SOCIAL KINDS — "RELIGION" AND ITS RATIONALES

ONE OF ANOTHER

At the start, I mentioned a set of social circumstances that brought me to think hard about the concept of religion. At the close, I should come clean about another. My great intellectual mentor, when I was an undergraduate, wasn't a person; it was a little society—a commune, really. Its members were known as the Epiphany Philosophers, and all shared a fascination with philosophy, science, and religion. The ripple effects of their gatherings were another illustration of a phenomenon we're now well-acquainted with. Those small societies our theorists of society created weren't an incidental development; there's something peculiarly generative about the right mixture of affirmation and argumentation.

The Epiphany Philosophers got going in the 1950s, with Margaret Masterman and her husband, Richard Bevan Braithwaite, at its center. By the time I showed up, Dorothy Emmet had joined them in a large house that was just around the corner from the Cambridge Language Research Unit, or CLRU, which Masterman had founded and still ran. Across the group's decades of existence, it can be hard to distinguish members from those who had merely spent time in its penumbra. But the "EPs," as they called themselves, had a journal, *Theoria to Theoria*—I was one of its editors for a few years—and its subtitle conveys the ethos: "an international journal of science, philosophy, and contemplative religion." Perhaps it isn't surprising that the group was important to Rowan Williams, the future archbishop of Canterbury, or to Mary Hesse, the great philosopher of science. More striking, especially today, is how many scientists—in particular, pioneers of computer science and artificial intelligence—passed through their portals.

But then Masterman herself did trailblazing work in computational linguistics, natural-language processing, and machine translation. All the while, she had to pilot her research center through the sporadic funding famines known as "AI winters," as belief in the cognitive capacities of machines waxed and waned among the grant-givers. Perhaps because she had been a student of Wittgenstein—her notes were an important part of the Wittgenstein compilation known as the "Blue Book"—she suspected that the challenges of word-sense disambiguation and the like weren't to be approached (as so many supposed) with a list of explicit rules. Doing her work without anything like the computational power and vast data sets we have now, she nonetheless prefigured the contemporary vector-based semantic networks that such resources have since made possible.[1] You could say that she had faith. Among her protégés were the computer scientists Yorick Wilks, who helped create one of the first AI chatbots; Karen Spärck Jones, whose information-retrieval techniques became part of the standard architecture for search engines; and Spärck Jones's husband, Roger Needham, who made breakthroughs in digital security protocols and helped lay the groundwork for distributed computing. ("Physics was made by God, but computer science was made by man," he once remarked.)

Masterman prized precision. Once, hospitalized for a few weeks after surgery, she read and reread Thomas Kuhn's *The Structure of Scientific Revolutions*, which popularized talk of paradigms. "On my counting, he uses 'paradigm' in not less than twenty-one different senses," she wrote in the paper that resulted, "possibly more, not less." (In response, Kuhn said that he "should now like some other phrase, perhaps 'disciplinary matrix' "; the term "paradigm" started to retreat from his work.)² But mysticism mattered to her, too, and however science and religion related, it should not be on meekly diplomatic terms. She despised mere politeness, in matters of life and intellect. "Put scientists and monastics together, and give them half a chance, and the scientists will uncontrollably make friends with the monastics; you won't be able to stop them," she once wrote. "And conversely monastics, if you give them half a chance, like scientists, and become easily attracted themselves to doing science. There is a certain tenacity and toughness, together with a strong vocational bent, in the scientist, which prevents them from being what Sisters, in particular, most dread: monastic hangers-on."[3]

Her husband, the mathematically gifted philosopher Richard Bevan Braithwaite, was something of an old-school positivist. "Now look here, I'm sorry," he'd preface some searing objection to an interlocutor's hidden lapse of logic. When he was made the Knightbridge Professor of Moral Philosophy at Cambridge he showed how game theory could be applied to moral problems, but he took even more pride in his long campaign to get the university to admit women on equal terms. Born a Quaker, he converted to Anglicanism and was baptized by the bishop of Ely, though only after contenting himself and the bishop that doing so was consistent with his nonbelief. In a lecture he gave in 1955, "An Empiricist's View of the Nature of Religious Belief," he argued that religious assertion was used as moral assertion, announcing "allegiance to a set of moral principles." This did not make him irreligious: "We are all social animals; we are all members one of another. What is profitable to one man in helping him to persevere in the way of life he has decided on may be helpful to another who is trying to follow a similar way of life."[4]

And then there was Dorothy Emmet, who had been one of positivism's most eloquent opponents. (To understand why there was nothing cultlike about the EPs, it helps to bear in mind their delight in argument.) In her youth, she had spent time tutoring unemployed Welsh miners, and was always—in our curious idiom—"socially conscious." Emmet had studied with Alfred North Whitehead at Harvard, immersed himself in his "process" philosophy ("process" contrasted with "substance": this was an approach that emphasized the dynamic nature of reality, seen as a shifting interconnection of events), and ended up running the philosophy department at the University of Manchester for a couple of decades. In a widely read volume titled *The Nature of Metaphysical Thinking*, she maintained that religion conveyed the sense that reality is other than our ideas of it; that "though we see the universe in the perspective of our minds, our minds are not its centre." And this perspective, it was clear to her, was also what sponsored a scientific approach to the world.

As for a scientific approach to society, humility was in order: it was unclear "what are the dominant ideas which are to express man's life in society." By the time we were prepared to undertake a new synthesis of knowledge, in fact, we may have learned that "the old style of synthesis in the grand manner is impossible." Epistemic humility also explained why empiricism could not crowd out metaphysics. "The word gives form to experience; it does not copy the structure of the real," she wrote. "But experience so informed itself arises out of interrelationships. To indicate the possibilities of such relationships and to bring them into conscious articulation is a distinctive task of metaphysical thinking."[5] *We are all members one of another*: she thought so, too.

Certainly the EPs were. Philosophy for them was a matter of arguing and agreeing and trying things out from new angles; it was also a matter of walking along bosky paths in the Norfolk countryside and drinking wine late into the evening. By the time I arrived, the CLRU had passed its prime; Dorothy and Richard had long since retired. And, like the Iris Murdoch characters they sometimes resembled, the EPs could be wonderfully dotty. (Richard would make unabashed reference to the "Braithwaite-Einstein theory of relativity," on the grounds that he was the one who had axiomatized it properly and made it logically rigorous.) And yet there was something magical about their omnivorous intellectual curiosity. Nothing was disciplinarily alien to them: physics, engineering, biology, linguistics, anthropology, theology. As a nineteen-year-old whom they'd welcomed into their circle, I was introduced to philosophy as not just an academic subject but a way of life. I'm almost tempted to say that I had found my religion. In truth, a hallmark of the EPs was that their taking religion seriously in a scientific era never devolved into defensiveness. They would have been appalled by the thought that religion should be hived off into its own mollycoddled magisterium, treated as sacrosanct, protected from secular exploration. They favored boats, not moats.

In the spirit of the EPs (I refer to the EPs as "them," but I suppose I was an EP, as well, junior division), I want to explore a perplexity that has surfaced at intervals throughout this book: is the existence of "religion" something that can be proved, or that must be taken on faith, or that should be discarded? I've already discussed a research program in the cognitive science of religion that proposes religion as a necessary condition for society, and we've heard from critics of secularity who raise the question of whether religion might be needed—individually, politically, socially—as a source of self-transcendence and of sustaining values. Our cognitive scientists see religion as having been a mechanism for the solidarity and cooperation that got society started; our interpretive social theorists think it may be needed for society's survival today. But it won't have escaped your notice that up to this point, I've bracketed the question of what they're talking about when they talk about religion. No longer. We're approaching the end of our journey. It's time to defer to Weber's stricture: "To define 'religion,' to say what it is, is not possible at the start of a presentation such as this. Definition can be attempted, if at all, only at the conclusion of the study."[6]

DEFINITION AND DEFERENCE

Within the cognitive science of religion, the question of definition is often something to whistle past. Atran and Henrich favor something like Tylor's minimum definition, writing, "Religious traditions center on supernatural agents, such as gods, angels, or ancestor spirits." (They add, "This includes religions such as Buddhism and Taoism, which doctrinally eschew personifying the supernatural, but whose adherents routinely worship an array of deities that behave in ways that violate our intuitive expectations about how the world works.")[7] Justin Barrett sounded more cautious in a 2007 paper: "Rather than specify what religion is and try to explain it in whole, scholars in this field have generally chosen to approach 'religion' in a piecemeal fashion, identifying human thought or behavioral patterns that might count as 'religious' and then trying to explain why those patterns are cross-culturally recurrent. If the explanations turn out to be part of a grander explanation of 'religion', so be it." He and other researchers wonder whether they can examine how universal cognitive tendencies manifest in various cultural contexts, without presupposing a unified category of religion. They debate whether progress in understanding the cognitive underpinnings of religious belief and behavior might be eased by focusing on more specific, empirically grounded phenomena, rather than relying on a broad and contested category.[8]

Related debates, as we've seen, have long been taking place among anthropologists and historians and members of religious studies departments. A few are straightforward "realists": they don't mind essentialist definitions because they think that "religion" is, ontologically, in perfectly good shape. Others are "critical realists," for whom socially constructed kinds of things can be metaphysically real. (There can be a true or false answer to the question of whether you're married.) Still others are nonrealists or "nominalists," who think that the category is, or could be, analytically valuable, even if it is a human-made imposition on social complexes with indeterminate boundaries.[9] And yes, some nonrealists, convinced that the concept does more harm than good, are "eliminativists," seeking to retire talk of religion, at least in scholarly contexts.

One popular move among religion scholars is to sidestep the whole "what's a religion" discussion by accepting that the notion is inherently vague and should be treated as what Wittgensteinians call a "family-resemblance" concept: each religion, like each member of a family, is, no doubt, like every other, in some respects, but there need be no distinctive characteristics they all share. "Why do we call something a 'number'?" Wittgenstein asked, but his answer had a general import. "Well, perhaps because it has a direct relationship with several things that have hitherto been called number; and this can be said to give an indirect relationship to other things we call the same name."[10] Some things we call religions lack a high God, or perhaps any gods; some posit no afterlife; some place little importance on ritual; and so forth.

But if we don't need a set of necessary and sufficient conditions, we needn't be flummoxed by such anomalies.

Many thinkers about religion (Norenzayan among them) have found this a useful approach; I have, too. Still, without some prior understanding of what a religion is, we'd have no way of deciding which points of resemblance are relevant—which ones resonate with the religion concept. Timothy Fitzgerald, for one, envisages this approach "defining religion into oblivion by making it indistinguishable from ideologies, worldviews, or symbolic systems in general."[11] An unconditioned acceptance of resemblances, such doubters say, would amount to the "chain migration" that immigration restrictionists like to conjure: semantic cousins letting in cousins letting in cousins, without end. One response involves augmenting, or refining, the approach with the "polythetic" strategy that biologists have applied to defining natural taxa. (This has been seen, variously, as an extension of the family-resemblance policy and an alternative to it.) You have a cluster of attributes, but you don't require that any candidate for the category have all of them.

The anthropologist Benson Saler—extending the family-resemblance and polythetic approach through the "prototype" theory associated with the cognitive psychologist Eleanor Rosch—writes that religion may be conceptualized "in terms of a pool of elements that more or less tend to occur together in the best exemplars of the category."[12] But, as in older polythetic accounts, we're left with the question of how many of the elements a religion must have. "A sufficient number," theorists tend to say. Such cluster concepts invite a lot of guesswork. Rodney Needham, in a 1975 paper on family-resemblance and polythetic approaches, wrote about a computer that could be programmed to handle up to fifteen hundred strains of bacteria, scoring each for two hundred traits. Later, Needham write, equably, "To take the word 'religion' very strictly, and to demand of it what we have no reason to think it can afford, would be self-defeating; so let us take it as we use it, and then try to establish what characteristic features give that use."[13] It's hard to avoid the thought that these approaches don't so much solve the issue of definition as defer or presuppose it.

THE CONCEPT IN THE DOCK

What about the eliminativist option? Some people—notably Wilfred Cantwell Smith—have sought to abolish "religion" for its own protection. Others, equally impassioned, want to do so in order to strike a blow against eurocentrism, imperialism, neocolonialism. But one can also worry, in a more detached way, that the category conflates so many distinct entities as to cast as much shadow as light. I've had this worry myself.

I mentioned, earlier, my own experience as a member of communities where the social common sense about the nonmaterial, agential world seemed categorically disjunct. In traditional parts of Asante, there wasn't any space between "Asante religion" and everyday life such that it made sense to hive off, into a separate domain, the richly textured set of beliefs people had concerning prayers, shrines, the nature of the soul, and so on. Why must those Asante beliefs be designated as religious—a concept that had long been alien to it? Thinking about why this was, I came, in my young adulthood, to a conclusion: when visitors from European Christendom arrived in other parts of the world, they asked: What do *they* have instead of Christianity? As Wilfred Cantwell Smith had complained, "the religious is that which has been called religious in the Western world, chiefly Christian and Jewish matters, and anything else on earth that can be shown to be comparable."[14]

Many religious scholars today are alert to the crypto-Christian or even crypto-Protestant ways in which the concept gets used. But so were our classical sociologists. For one thing, they had all read *Religion of the Semites*, in which William Robertson Smith had written eloquently on the topic. That doesn't mean they were liberated from the paradigm. When Weber took up, as a subject for religious sociology, Confucianism—which he mainly contrasted with the realm of the charismatic and priestly, since its literati sought to manage society not through extraordinary power but through a rational intellectual system—it was surely because in Chinese society over many millennia, Confucianism served some of the social functions of Christianity.

And plenty of patterns, in Asante and elsewhere, would have caught the eye of the early Christian ethnographers. What some people appeared to have instead of Christianity was what Durkheim called totemism, from the word "totem" that came into European languages from Ojibwa *odoodeman*, which means "family," but also "family mark" or emblem. Among American Indians, Aborigines, and many Africans, clans were associated with animals or plants. My own father belonged to one of eight Akan maternal descent groups, or matriclans, associated with the Bush Cow, known in our language as *Ekɔɔna*. And, of course, we had immaterial body-linked entities, related to life and consciousness. We had spirits (*abosom*) galore; we had a high God, Nyame, creator of all things, upholder of order; we had the earth goddess, Asase Yaa. That's what we had instead of Christianity, it would have been natural for Christian visitors to conclude.

But the disanalogies, in my view, went beyond the fact that Asante "religion" permeated everything, scarcely leaving a zone of secularity, and, again, had not been inclined to see itself as religion at all. There was also the social role that these putatively religious resources played in Asante. One of the Epiphany Philosophers, Dorothy Emmet, brought me an epiphany, fittingly enough, when she steered me, at age twenty, to the writings of the British social anthropologist Robin Horton. In "African Traditional Thought and Western Science," an essay published in two parts in 1967, Horton—who defiantly called himself "neo-Tylorian," and who had done extensive field work in West Africa—traced continuities as well as discontinuities between his titular subjects. Reading his essay clarified my cloudy unease. Because I discussed the argument at length in my book *In My Father's House*, more than three decades ago, I shall make short work of it here. But the key idea was that the role played by what people called traditional African religion was not so much that played by the (tamed and constricted) religions of the modern West; rather, traditional beliefs and procedures played cognitive and explanatory roles similar to science. They made sense of observable phenomena, and sought control over them, through posited forces that might not be directly observable.[15] (Horton also taught me to be on guard about the seeming generosity of "symbolic" interpretations, where we genially accommodate believers by denying that they actually mean what they say. That might tilt you against Durkheim.)

The beliefs and associated practices seen in traditional societies were—in ways Tylor saw and Weber affirmed—rational in their context. Like science, too, these "traditional religions" tend to legitimize certain forms of authority and social order. In traditional societies, priests or shamans may hold significant power, much as scientific experts do in Western societies. When I thought about everyday practices in my part of Asante, where problems and setbacks might be addressed through witchcraft, magic, and similar forms of intervention, Horton seemed to be onto something: what was sought from the old beliefs and practices was akin to what Westerners sought from science and technology. Many people in the communities I knew attended a Christian church (it helped them to be good), but when something important had to be set right, they used the tried-and-true (or tried-and-untrue) methods: oracles, shrines, spells, appeals to ancestors.

This picture poses some challenges to the theory of credences I mentioned in Chapter 1, for the make-believe model may draw too bright a line between credences and factual beliefs. From the inside, certainly, many supernatural beliefs don't obviously have the feel of an imagined stipulation.[16] And a commonsense explanation for why we don't present the gods or ancestors with requests that violate the basic laws of nature is that we've learned those requests are never granted, whereas less taxing requests sometimes seem to be. Still, even if you were persuaded, in some measure, of the "make-believe" picture, Horton's analogy might still hold up. The cognitive psychologist Alison Gopnik (whose work Van Leeuwen draws on) points to one suggestive connection. Children, she notes, pretend all the time—but after all, as you sit at home, almost every object around you was once imaginary. In the version of "theory theory" she helped devise, children are continually testing and revising their theories about the world.[17] Children and scientists are both exploring what's possible, in this account, because discovering truths about the world and inventing worlds are cognitively twinned.[18]

Horton was no relativist. Traditional religions, he argued, are more "closed" than scientific culture because they rely on a somewhat fixed set of spiritual or supernatural explanations that cannot be easily refuted or altered, although they will incorporate new elements over time. Western science, by contrast, is an "open" system characterized by its methodological reliance on empirical evidence, falsifiability, and the provisional nature of its theories. Still, Asante customs had cognitive and functional aspects that were better exemplified in modern scientific culture than in the mainstream religious institutions of Britain and Europe, or what Weber would have described as "rationalized" modern religious culture.

And so the old anthropological habit of separating discussions of religious institutions in particular places from scientific ones wasn't very helpful in understanding the traditional culture of Asante. Indeed, it isn't much help in understanding the historical development of European science. In the surely apocryphal story, Napoleon asked Pierre-Simon Laplace why his work on celestial mechanics made no mention of God, and Laplace replied, "Sir, I have no need of that hypothesis." The truth in that tale is that Laplace did spend a great deal of intellectual energy refuting the idea, which had been around since at least Newton, that God's intervention was necessary to guarantee the stability of the solar system.[19]

Something else struck me when I thought about the West African traditional beliefs I had some acquaintance with: a quality of localism. My father, as I say, lived in a world populated by the usual Asante spirits and spiritual ontologies. But when he visited friends in Sierra Leone, say, he expected that, just as the place he had traveled to had different people, it would have a different complement of local spirits. The history of Christianity is a history of universalizing a creed that entails an extensive concern about policing heresies. This concern is much less central to other things we call religions, especially, as you might expect, traditions that have no central authorities or no written documents. Chinua Achebe, the Nigerian novelist, once observed to me that he couldn't imagine his Igbo ancestors "traveling 4,000 miles to tell anybody their worship was wrong!"[20] In all these respects, the label "religion," derived from a Christian paradigm, could seem more occlusive than clarifying.

This localism was, at the same time, another disanalogy with science. Science aims to be a discourse that transcends local identities.

To offer a local metaphysics as its basis would produce a discourse that was not recognizable as a contribution to the cosmopolitan conversation of the sciences. (That is one reason that Soviet ideas of socialist science, which inspired Lysenko, or the even worse Nazi-inspired idea of a German science, belong somewhere in intellectual history but not in the history of the sciences.)[21] Still, given what was illuminated when we viewed traditional beliefs and practices through a lens other than that of religion, I had to wonder about the concept's global ambitions. A putative science of religion wasn't scientific if it was only valid on a local level; was it then itself a type of religion? Stopping short of such hyperbole, we could admit that, at the very least, we had been incautious about applying the template.

Many scholars in my cohort have reached similar conclusions. Over the past few generations, as we've seen, they have sought to rewind the history through which the concept of "religion" arose, as they've debated whether to modify it, qualify it, hold it with very long tongs, or jettison it. Yet when I immersed myself in the work of the classical sociologists who gave us our modern concept of religion, I was surprised at how alert they were to the way models can distort what they model.

Part of this reflected the neo-Kantian landscape of their intellectual era; but then even Comte had remarked that what we see depends on the theories we believe. Although critics of eurocentrism sometimes talk as if a view from nowhere were available, social knowledge and the socially situated knower can't be so neatly decoupled. It's naive to think that we could or should eject—or quarantine, as if taboo—every global social category with a culturally specific genealogy. (Windelband had a good point to make about what came to be called the genetic fallacy.) When we approach a society that is not our own, seeking to understand its thought and practices in a rigorous way, we will always have to begin with an enterprise of translation. Social science does well to start with *Verstehen*, understanding the conceptual world of those whose behavior we seek to explain. The sociology born of a Christian society will naturally use Christian concepts to try to make sense of non-Christian ones. That's no sin. But translation isn't just mapping concepts into concepts, it's triangulating both with reality. It's not simply a task, then; it's a process.

THE ACID OF REALITY

Our everyday language is papered with words spawned by theories that we've revised or abandoned. We should be neither melancholy nor sanguine about the fact that the Galenic medicine we've long discarded has secured for itself a sturdy lexical afterlife. But what philosophers call "referring expressions"—names or noun phrases that pick out certain objects or classes of objects, or aim to—aren't quite like that. A good deal of work at the intersection of the philosophy of language and the philosophy of science has gone into trying to clarify how theory-embedded categories or kind-terms refer to things out in the world. Let me return to the question of whether religion is, in some sense, real by exploring some easy cases of reference and then some harder ones.

Start with an example from the history of chemistry. What's an acid? When the word and concept first came into use, an acid was identified by its sour taste—*acidus* is Latin for "sour." In medieval times, acid was also known by its ability to dissolve metals, and to lose its attributes in the presence of substances known as alkalis. Then the great eighteenth-century scientist Antoine Lavoisier, often considered the father of modern chemistry, concluded that acids contained oxygen, and that the oxygen was responsible for their acidity. He was, as Humphry Davy soon showed, quite wrong about that. In the 1880s, Svante Arrhenius proposed a new definition of acids: An acid is a substance that dissociates in water to produce hydrogen ions (H^+). Half a century later, the modern definition arrived, by way of the Brønsted-Lowry model: an acid was a substance that could donate a proton (H^+) to another substance. The new definition expanded the range of chemicals that counted as acids. The Lewis model, hard on its heels, expanded it even further: it held that acids were chemical species (molecules or ions) that could accept a pair of electrons from another chemical species. The Lewis definition encompassed all the Brønsted-Lowry acids—they accept electron-pairs when they donate protons—and added some more candidates. None of this is controversial. Chemistry, as an institution, happily stipulates that acids are chemical species that donate protons or accept electron pairs.

Now, it was only in the twentieth-century that the very existence of things like atoms, molecules, and electrons gained widespread acceptance in the scientific community. But we also think that, by and large, late-eighteenth-century chemistry classified many acids and bases correctly, even if a lot of what it claimed about them was off-target. We think that when Lavoisier used the word "acid," he was nevertheless talking about what we call acids. In explaining why it seems proper to think that Lavoisier was referring to the things Brønsted and Lowry called proton donors—even though much of what he believed about acids is not true of proton donors—philosophers of science have borrowed ideas from the "causal theory of reference" in the philosophy of language.

The proposal is simple enough: if you want to know what object a word refers to, find the thing in the world that gives the best causal explanation of the central features of uses of that word. If you want to know what the name "Marie Curie" refers to, find the object in the world that is at the root of most of the causal chains that lead to remarks containing the expression "Marie Curie." With acids, because we believe that the stuff "out there" in the world that really accounted for the central features of Lavoisier's "acid talk" comprised acids, we concluded that he wasn't simply talking about something else or about nothing at all. Causal theories mean that we can still be referring to the same class of objects when our understanding of the class changes over time, and when the composition of the class shifts a little, too. Pluto can stop being a planet without shaking the foundations of "planet" talk.

By contrast, we know, say, that when early neurophysiologists (like Descartes) talked about "animal spirits" in the nerve fibers, they were referring to nothing at all: there is nothing we know of that can account for what they said about animal spirits; instead, there are truths about sodium pumps and lipid bilayers and synapses. There simply is no substance that was usually present when and only when the expression "animal spirits" was uttered and that behaves at all as they thought animal spirits behaved. The same goes for the seventeenth-century concept of phlogiston, which I mentioned in Chapter 1: this was an entity that every combustible substance supposedly contained and that was released in the course of burning. There just isn't anything that behaves like that.

Let's complicate things just a little. Joseph Priestley is conventionally said to have discovered oxygen, in 1774. Only, he thought that the substance he had isolated was "dephlogisticated air." A few years later, Lavoisier named the gas oxygen (Greek for "acid-producer") and showed that it was a necessary presence for combustion, thereby helping to bring down the curtain on phlogiston. Now, older "descriptive" theories of reference stipulate that a term's referent is specified by a description of some object, perhaps a cluster of attributes, and this approach could leave it unclear whether Priestley did discover oxygen, about which he believed so many false things. The causal approach clarifies the matter. Many things that Priestly believed about the substance he isolated were connected to actual features of oxygen. Nothing he believed about phlogiston was connected to actual features of a phlogiston-like substance.

Causal theories of reference help us distinguish between the misdescribed object and the nonexistent object. Many things, or classes of things, fall between these stools, however. With acids, we saw a changing definition that expanded the set of objects that earned the name "acid"—the term's "extension"—while preserving most objects that had previously been so designated. But sometimes it's hard to decide whether the unobservable entities that a scientific theory posits ought to be redefined or discarded. Throughout the nineteenth century, to take a much-discussed example, a lot of valuable work on light and what we now call radio waves presupposed the existence of a luminiferous ether, an unseen substrate, named in the seventeenth century, that was held to be present even in vacuums and through which light (and lightlike entities) traveled. In the 1860s, James Clerk Maxwell explored what he called "the electromagnetic field." Yet he never doubted the existence of the ether. Some philosophers of science think that ether, which was helpful to much successful theorizing, really referred to electromagnetic fields, and that we would have been justified in retaining ether and simply redefining it in terms of those fields.[22] Einstein himself, it has been noted, referred to the "ether" of electromagnetic fields, in early work, and later to the "relativized" ether that he thought was implied by general relativity. (Other philosophers wonder whether we will be talking about electromagnetic fields at all fifty years from now.)

THE SEMANTICS OF SOCIAL KINDS

So far, we've had cases about natural kinds, or putative natural kinds. Natural kinds are a privileged ontological caste, enjoying a straightforward mind-independent existence (or nonexistence). And what I've shown is that even in this realm, we can lack firm answers to questions about signification. The picture gains another dimension of complexity when we move to historical or social *abstracta*: "revolution," "bourgeoisie," "the state," "money," "recession," "eurocentrism," even "scientific theory." These things (which, for Durkheim, qualify as "social facts") are doubly the product of shared human activity—not only the activity of identifying and defining these categories but also the activity that, we believe, generated these categorized entities.[23] Today, philosophers of language often call them social kinds.

To talk of religion as a social kind isn't to say that it's in just as good shape, referentially speaking, as every other social kind; it's in worse shape than many. But it's also more consequential than many. It belongs to the subdomain of social kinds that living human beings apply to themselves. Oxygen is airily indifferent to whether we decide that "dephlogisticated air" refers to it; electromagnetism doesn't get charged up about whether it's the proper referent of "ether." The economics profession can define recessions and harmlessly identify them in historical periods innocent of the term; just as the people whom art historians categorize as Quattrocento artists wouldn't recognize one another under that name. But religion, as a folk category, is now part of the self-description of billions of people—and so scholars who want to use it as an analytic category might hesitate to make it unrecognizable to everyone else.

The point is that arguments over referring expressions have a special bite when it comes to social labels that can interact with, even create, what they label. Folklorists and ethnographers have sometimes distinguished between the "emic" and the "etic": the first is a standpoint that's internal to a community, using its own terms and concepts and self-understandings; the second adopts an external standpoint, and approaches a community with a set of disciplinary concepts that come from elsewhere. A native of a language has a command of its syntax but may not possess the concept "syntax." At the same time, the circulation of etic terms invariably influences emic ones. Give practitioners the concept of "capital" or "creed" and the etic becomes the emic; an outsider's term influences the insider's understanding of the world. Observation affects the observed.

The effects are especially significant when social identities are involved. Ian Hacking's model of "dynamic nominalism" focused our attention to this very issue; in what he called "looping effects," social identities and social categories interact—we change in response to being categorized, which, in turn, can modify the meaning of the category. The heavy drinker becomes an alcoholic, and then a recovering one. But if the term "dynamic nominalism" helpfully highlighted that process, it's a little misleading if you take the "nominalism" to contrast with realism. Hacking wasn't interested in that contrast ("the classes of individuals that come into being are real enough, in any plausible sense of the word," he says), and endorsed "dialectical realism" as an alternative description.[24] Being told that what you have is a religion can affect not just how you relate to it, but who you think you are.

Where does this leave our social scientists, interested in framing a field of inquiry and learning more about it? We could decide that religion doesn't need a unitary meaning. When I discuss the major Abrahamic religious traditions, I may want to cut against the assumptions people have and adopt a practice-centered approach. After all, the propositional content of the Nicene or Athanasian Creed is obscure and perhaps incoherent, but the act of avowing it can matter a lot. Focusing on practices, on the saying versus the said, can be helpful precisely because our synonyms for religion tend to be belief-centered: creed, faith, persuasion, confession. When I discuss the "traditional" thought of the Azande or the Nuer or the Asante, I may want to adopt a neo-Tylorian, belief-centered emphasis, to bring out features that people may not associate with religion of the modern Christian paradigm, and pull away from its "separate spheres" model. Neither emphasis is remotely exclusive; they relate to what features I'm trying to make visible.

The larger truth is that we negotiate the world with maps that approximate reality with various degrees of empirical adequacy. In ways I've explored in a previous book, which drew from Vaihinger's *The Philosophy of "As If,"* these are idealizations; and when we credit them with being "true enough," we should recognize that being approximately true is finally a special way of being false. We're justified in proceeding as if something false is true, however, so long as the resulting model is useful for some legitimate objective. Progress in the social and natural sciences is routinely secured through such provisional idealizations. We judge them by their fitness to their purposes.[25]

"RELIGION" AND ITS RATIONALES

Let's recall that Weber, who had read and caviled at Vaihinger's tome, proposed a similar strategy in explaining and defending the deployment of ideal types. In his famous "objectivity" essay, he mentioned a few such ideal types, including individualism, a city economy, imperialism, and church. When Weber wrote that the " 'essence' of religion is absolutely not our concern," he was writing as someone who strongly suspected it didn't have one.[26] According to Weber, ideal types were analytic concepts that scholars devised by accentuating, in a tendentious way, certain details from a particular point of view. What justified them, he said, wasn't that they corresponded to reality in any straightforward manner (we were to resist hypostasizing them); it was that they were fit for purpose. They performed work.

Nor could we do without them. "All knowledge of cultural reality," he argued in that objectivity essay, "is always knowledge from particular points of view." What is and isn't significant and relevant? That depends on the purposes and interests of your inquiry. I quoted from that essay in Chapter 4, but I didn't quote from its surprisingly lyrical, if wistful conclusion about the provisionality and perishability of all theorizing, all scholarship: "The light of the great cultural problems moves on. Then science too prepares to change its standpoint and its thinking apparatus and to view the streams of events from the heights of thought. It follows those stars which alone are able to give meaning and direction to its labors." Weber's moments of lyricism are especially moving because we know that they didn't come easily to him; they were wrung out of his soul.

If "religion" can still provide meaning and direction to our labors, what purposes does it serve? The answers can seem as plentiful as those stars. Civil-rights lawyers, legislators, and policymakers need to operationalize the concept for their specific purposes—maintaining a policy of religious freedom that strikes a balance between accommodation and nonestablishment, say, or protecting minorities from religious discrimination. To be a "faith-based organization" is to inhabit a particular political or legal status. Different scholars—sociologists, historians, psychologists, criminologists, from a range of intradisciplinary or interdisciplinary perspectives—will have their own distinctive interests. One scholar wants to explore the role of religion in the rehabilitation of criminal offenders; another wants to explore how religious affiliations affect charity, or prejudice, or suicide rates, or perhaps radicalization. Yet another wants to interrogate the methodologies her colleagues have employed. For clerics, the concept could relate to social support services, education, and charitable works. And for members of religious communities, the idea of religion could expand, or cabin, their ability to celebrate events that matter to them; to join a community of mutual care, to explore or solidify a worldview and a sense of the meaning of their existence. It can make them more (or less) tolerant; it can help them to resist forms of aggression or discrimination that target them as members of a religious group. Meanwhile, religious forms of solidarity can be directed against the secular scholar. Because religions are often the basis of social identities, scholars of religion have sometimes found themselves at odds with the people whose religions they study. In a book titled *Who Owns Religion?*, Laurie L. Patton has explored a series of such clashes: secular genealogies of doctrine can be offensive to their adherents, and the realm of scholarship is no longer hived off from the rest of the world.

Those who want to dissolve religion as a category also have their interests and purposes, often emancipatory ones. Yet it hasn't gone unnoticed that our eliminativists, the great Wilfred Cantwell Smith included, never quite manage to eliminate the term in their own work. "Critics deconstruct the concept of religion and then cheerfully continue to make use of it," Martin Riesebrodt tartly observed.[27] I cast no stones. I have written at length about the incoherence of the concept of "the West" and even of "culture": but, like the preacher of abstinence who enjoys an occasional tipple, I cannot quite manage without them, even as I muster the occasional apologetic wince. In any case, the notion that talk of religion can be dissolved by scholarly fiat is delusory. "Religion" has too many semantic stakeholders for that. For specific purposes, we may wish to naturalize or nominalize religion; we'll seldom go wrong by pluralizing it. That doesn't mean imposing pluralism on those averse to it; it does mean recognizing the multiplicity of ways in which religions overspill our categories.[28]

As the author of a monograph titled *For Truth in Semantics*, I am not likely to be accused of being indifferent to the alethic aspects of language and thought. The central idea in a sound theory of meaning is truth; I'm a realist in this way. But, as I noted in that book, I'm also a certain kind of pragmatist. "The essence of pragmatism," Frank Ramsey wrote, is that "the meaning of a sentence"—but let's say, rather, the content of beliefs—"is to be defined by reference to the actions to which asserting it would lead, or, more vaguely still, by its possible causes and effects."[29] To invoke causes and effects situates human believers in causal webs that stretch far away from us in time and space; but it entails, as well, that our concepts and categories are determined by social webs and intersecting circles in which we are mere nodes.

I propose, then, that we take seriously the religious term "observant." That's the word often used to describe religionists who focus on adherence to law and ritual in situations where such adherence cannot be taken for granted—Muslims, Jews, Sikhs, Hindus. The word, from the Latin *observare*, has had an interesting career in English; it first signified the quality of being scrupulous with respect to a law or custom and then acquired the meaning of paying close attention. Scholarship involves both valences—adherence to principles (of evidence and inference) and a discipline of noticing. That's one reason that Weber was so persuasive when he called scholarship a vocation, a *Beruf*, with the double resonances of the term. When, responding to this calling, we explore religions as social phenomena, we must be *observant*.

Our classical social theorists, whatever their failings and limitations, certainly were.

"All Faith is false, all Faith is true," Sir Richard Burton wrote, ventriloquizing a Sufi mystic. The same almost goes for definitions of religion. The legitimacy of our social concepts and categories is tested every day; the outcome depends on the ability to justify those social concepts through deliberation among the relevant stakeholders. As to what religion means, nobody gets to say; everybody gets a say. In our epistemologically fallen world, we start where we are, with the conceptual repertories that we have. We don't know where we will end up. Rationality, in ways I've explored elsewhere, is best conceived as an ideal, both in the sense that it's worth aiming for and in the sense that we can't realize it. What Weber called the "heights of thought" can be very high indeed, but also always earthbound—historically and socially situated, co-created by human beings who make one another and are made by one another. If religions embody social processes, so does the defining of religion and, indeed, of society. Today, they remain among those stars he invoked. They are—at least within the skies of our current configuration of knowledge—binary stars. As scholarly subjects, they may blink out; they may shine brighter. They will do so together.

And what of the things these categories aim to capture? Tylor, dreaming of a world swept clean of superstition, spoke of a second Reformation. Durkheim anticipated the ascent of a secular creed that drew from the Revolutionary trinity of liberty, fraternity, and equality and the catechisms of human rights. Simmel was convinced that religiosity, humanity's hermit crab, would simply come to crawl inside and inhabit new forms. Weber glimpsed a world prowled by a pantheon of contending gods, clashing value systems, fighting for followers. The point is, once more, that none of these theorists imagined secularity as the secularists typically imagine it, because they knew that lives lived together produced, and required, ecologies of transcendental meaning. And here Victorian prophets who worried about a world denuded of larger significance got it wrong; we have, if anything, a surplus of it. Gods in captivity can still breed, and brood, and bolster, and bully.

Today, amid countless forms of digital linkage, the social realm can expand to an unimaginable scale—and splinter into sharp, tiny shards. The human community has never seemed so vast nor so small, as our perceptions of the sacred hold us together and tear us apart. Recall Simmel's suggestion that religious belief wasn't believing *that* but believing *in*—akin to the human act of believing *in* some cherished other. Without the exercise of this capacity, he was certain, "society would disintegrate." Modern sociology arose in the wake of successive social crises caused by industrialization—forms of distress and danger known, in the nineteenth century, as "the social question," as if there might be just one. We have our own crises with their own causes, and they unleash stormy quarrels—infused with religious fervor—over the authority of experience, faith, and the things we hold sacred. As we collectively confront global perils on a small and fragile planet, many social questions have a claim to our attention. Among them is whether we can continue to believe in one another.

Acknowledgments

This book grew out of the 2016–2017 Dwight H. Terry lectures I gave at Yale University, and I'm grateful for those who invited me to give them and to the discussants I met there. But I have accumulated many debts that extend before that lectureship and since. Indeed, from the specific acknowledgments that appear in my notes, and sometimes in the main text, you will know that I have been writing about religion, on and off, for about five decades, and you will have read the names of some of those whose work has inspired my own. I have also spoken often about these issues: indeed, the first talk I ever gave as an assistant professor in the United States was one at Wesleyan on "Other People's Gods"; and I have given scores of talks on the subject since then, including, most recently, one of the 2021 Hempel Lectures at Princeton ("On the Invention of Religion"), and the Hans Blumenberg Professorship Lecture ("Ways of Belonging") at the University of Münster in the summer of 2024. I am appreciative of all those who invited me to give these talks, and the many in between, and to all those who engaged with them and thereby helped shape my ideas. I am deeply grateful to the students at NYU with whom I have conducted seminars on religion in New York, Abu Dhabi, and London over the past few years. And, as in all my work, I owe an infinite debt to daily conversations with my husband, Henry Finder, and to his countless suggestions about the versions of these arguments that he read with the eye of a brilliant editor and a careful and imaginative thinker.

I want to thank, as well, the two readers for Yale University Press whose criticisms strengthened and clarified my arguments. I'm grateful to Jean E. Thomson Black, who piloted this work through the publication process; to Julie Carlson, for her painstaking copyediting; to Graciela Galup, who designed the cover; and to all the others at the press who help make the transition from manuscript to book feel more than cosmetic (though, blessedly, *also* cosmetic). I have profited, as well, from the careful fact-checking of Shawn Harris and Emily Ulbricht, who bravely burrowed into the endnotes, helped verify references, and caught many small errors. Alas, I cannot promise that no other small mistakes—or, worse, large ones—persist. The responsibility for those remains mine alone, even as the thinking here grew from a shared enterprise—from traditions of inquiry, stretching across time and space, into how we human beings make sense of the cosmos and our bonds with one another.

Notes

A general comment about quotations: All italics are from the original work, and in keeping with the guidance of later editions of the *Chicago Manual of Style,* case-shifted letters—typically at the start of a quoted sentence—have not been bracketed.

INTRODUCTION

1. Quentin Skinner, "The Idea of a Cultural Lexicon," *Essays in Criticism* 29, no. 3 (July 1979): 205–224. On "religio" in classical Rome, see Wilfred Cantwell Smith, *The Meaning and End of Religion: A New Approach to the Religious Traditions of Mankind* (New York: Macmillan, 1963), 21, 27, 28, 29. Compare Pierre Hadot's argument that in the classical world, philosophy was a way of life that was, for some of its adherents, itself a form of religion. See Hadot, *Philosophy as a Way of Life: Spiritual Exercises from Socrates to Foucault*, trans. Michael Chase (Hoboken, NJ: Wiley-Blackwell, 1995); Augustine, *De Civitate Dei contra Paganos; The City of God against the Pagans*, ed. and trans. R. W. Dyson (Cambridge: Cambridge University Press, 1998); and cf. Brent Nongbri, *Before Religion* (New Haven: Yale University Press, 2013), 28, 32.

2. See Nongbri, *Before Religion*, 59–62. See also Fred Donner, "From Believers to Muslims: Confessional Self-Identity in the Early Islamic Community," *Al-Abhath* 50–51 (2002–2003), 9–53, 11, where Donner argues that *"the community of Believers was originally conceptualized independent of confessional identities."*

3. Baruch Spinoza to Peter Balling, July 20, 1664, in *Spinoza: The Letters*, trans. Samuel Shirley (Indianapolis: Hackett, 1995), 125–126. The dream has been widely discussed. See Michael A. Rosenthal, "The Black, Scabby Brazilian: Some Thoughts on Race and Early Modern Philosophy," *Philosophy & Social Criticism* 31, no. 2 (March 2005): 211–221; Willi Goetschel, "Spinoza's Dream," *Cambridge Journal of Postcolonial Literary Inquiry* 3, no. 1 (January 14, 2016): 39–54; Lewis S. Feuer, "The Dream of Benedict de Spinoza," *American Imago* 14, no. 3 (Fall 1957): 225–242.

4. Jonathan Z. Smith, *Relating Religion: Essays in the Study of Religion* (Chicago: University of Chicago Press, 2004), 181.

5. David Hume, *The Natural History of Religion*, sec. 6, para. 5, 7, in Hume, *Principal Writing on Religion Including Dialogues Concerning Natural Religion and the Natural History of Religion*, ed. J. C. A. Gaskin (New York: Oxford University Press, 1993), 155–156.

6. Gotthold Ephraim Lessing, "On the Origin of Revealed Religion," in *Lessing: Philosophical and Theological Writings*, ed. and trans. H. B. Nisbet (Cambridge: Cambridge University Press, 2005), "inner truth" (36), "new, eternal gospel" (238).

7. Wilfred Cantwell Smith writes, "The plural 'religions' . . . is impossible so long as one is thinking of something in men's hearts, such as piety, obedience, reverence, worship. (None of these words has a plural.) The plural arises—it becomes standard from the mid-seventeenth-century and commonplace in the eighteenth—when one contemplates from the outside, and abstracts, depersonalizes, and reifies the various systems of other people of which one does not oneself see the meaning or appreciate the point, let alone accept the validity." Smith, *Meaning and End of Religion*, 43. See also Jonathan Z. Smith, *Imagining Religion* (Chicago: University of Chicago Press, 1982), 104.

8. Friedrich Schleiermacher, *On Religion: Speeches to Its Cultured Despisers*, trans. and ed. Richard Crouter (Cambridge: Cambridge University Press, 1996), 22. Later editions included a footnote to the Second Speech, in which Schleiermacher complains about theologians who proceed as if Christianity were the highest form of knowledge, with the form and dignity of metaphysical speculation, and who insist that creeds like polytheism don't qualify as a religion in the way Christianity does. He rejects both suppositions, and says it is his aim to show "how even the most imperfect forms of religion are of the same kind." Schleiermacher, *Ueber die Religion: Reden an die Gebildeten unter ihren Verächtern*, 4th ed. (Berlin: G. Reimer, 1831), 121. (I've used a conventional translation of the title: a closer rendering would be "About Religion: Speeches to the Educated among Its Despisers," though it is true that *Bildung* has richer resonances than the English word "education.")

9. Schleiermacher's phrase "das schlechthinnige Abhängigkeitsgefühl"— which appeared in the second edition of his *Der christliche Glaube* (The Christian faith)—is usually rendered as such, though an argument has been made for the more punctilious "absolute feeling of dependency." Friedrich Schleiermacher, *Der christliche Glaube* (1830–1831), ed. Martin Redeker, 2 vols. (Berlin: Walter de Gruyter, 1960), vol. 1: 31, 33, 36, 41, 43, etc.

10. Schleiermacher, *On Religion*, 34, 123, 68.

11. We'll see that the neo-Platonic role of emanation could be recast in various ways, with Hegel's Absolute and the Geist replaced by other entities.

12. Ludwig Feuerbach, *The Essence of Christianity*, trans. Marian Evans from the 2nd German ed. (London: John Chapman, 1854), 196. In his "Preliminary Theses on the Reform of Philosophy" (1842/1843), Feuerbach wrote, "Der Anthropotheismus ist die selbstbewußte Religion—die Religion, die sich selbst versteht. Die Theologie dagegen negiert die Religion unter dem Scheine,

als wenn sie sie ponierte" (Anthropotheism is the self-aware religion—the religion that understands itself. Theology, on the other hand, negates religion under the pretense that it takes as given). Ludwig Feuerbach, "Vorläufige Thesen zur Reform der Philosophie," in *Philosophische Kritiken und Grundsätze, Sämmtliche Werke*, vol. 2 (Stuttgart: Fromanns Verlag, 1904), 237.

13. Karl Marx, "Theses über Feuerbach," *Marx-Engels-Werke*, vol. 3: *1845–46* (Berlin: Dietz Verlag, 1956), 6–7. Thesis 6: "Feuerbach löst das religiöse Wesen in das menschliche Wesen auf. Aber das menschliche Wesen ist kein dem einzelnen Individuum inwohnendes Abstraktum. In seiner Wirklichkeit ist es das ensemble der gesellschaftlichen Verhältnisse." Thesis 7: "Feuerbach sieht daher nicht, daß das 'religiöse Gemüt' selbst ein gesellschaftliches Produkt ist, und daß das abstrakte Individuum, das er analysiert, einer bestimmten Gesellschaftsform angehört."

14. "Die Kritik der Religion ist also im *Keim die Kritik des Jammertales*, dessen *Heiligenschein* die Religion ist." Karl Marx, "Zur Kritik der Hegelschen Rechtsphilosophie" (A contribution to the critique of Hegel's philosophy of right), *Deutsch-Französische Jahrbücher* (February 1844): 71–72.

15. J. S. Mill, *Auguste Comte and Positivism* (London: Trübner & Co., 1865), 153. He considered Comte's religion sans theology to be inordinately morally exigent: "The most prejudiced must admit that this religion without theology is not chargeable with relaxation of moral restraints. On the contrary, it prodigiously exaggerates them. It makes the same ethical mistake as the theory of Calvinism, that every act in life should be done for the glory of God, and that whatever is not a duty is a sin. It does not perceive that between the region of duty and that of sin there is an intermediate space, the region of positive worthiness. It is not good that persons should be bound, by other people's opinion, to do everything that they would deserve praise for doing. There is a standard of altruism to which all should be required to come up, and a degree beyond it which is not obligatory, but meritorious" (142–143). (Utilitarianism is usually assumed to lack, or reject, the concept of supererogation; this was not true of Mill's utilitarianism.) As a point of intellectual history, Mill also argued, near the start of the book, that it was Hume who first "conceived in its entire generality" the doctrine that the only knowledge available to us was knowledge of observable phenomena.

16. Thomas H. Huxley, "On the Physical Basis of Life," *Fortnightly Review* 5, n.s. (1869): 141.

17. Harriet Martineau, *Society in America* (New York: Saunders and Otley, 1837), vol 2: 343, 346, 341, 347.

18. Harriet Martineau, *The Positive Philosophy of Auguste Comte* (London: Trübner & Co., 1875), v.

19. Tomoko Masuzawa, *The Invention of World Religions* (Chicago: University of Chicago, 2005), 12–13, 32–33.

20. See Philip Almond, *The British Discovery of Buddhism* (Cambridge: Cambridge University Press, 1988); and Masuzawa, *Invention of World Religions*.

21. Sir Monier Monier-Williams, *Buddhism, in Its Connexion with Brahmanism and Hinduism, and in Its Contrast with Christianity* (London: John Murray, 1889), 537; Masuzawa, *Invention of World Religions*, 132; and cf. the story of how Gautama became a Christian saint, Saint Josaphat, in Donald S. Lopez Jr. and Peggy McCracken, *In Search of the Christian Buddha* (New York: W.W. Norton, 2014).
22. Leora Batnitzky, *How Judaism Became a Religion* (Princeton, NJ: Princeton University Press, 2011).
23. Mill, *Comte and Positivism*, 133; Herbert Spencer, *First Principles* (London: Williams & Nordate, 1867), 37.
24. F. Max Müller, *Introduction to the Science of Religion* (London: Longmans, Green, 1873), 17.
25. F. Max Müller, *Natural Religion* (London: Longmans, Green, 1889), 188. Tracing the term "religio," he concludes that it "began with the meaning of care, attention, reverence, awe; it then took the moral sense of scruple and conscience; and lastly became more and more exclusively applied to the inward feeling of reverence for the gods and to the outward manifestation of that reverence in worship and sacrifice" (39).
26. William James, *The Varieties of Religious Experience: A Study in Human Nature* (New York: Longmans, Green, 1903), 31, 53.
27. Émile Durkheim, *Les formes élémentaires de la vie religieuse* (Paris: Félix Alcan, 1912), 65.
28. Jane Ellen Harrison, *Themis: A Study of the Social Origins of Greek Religion* (Cambridge: Cambridge University Press, 1912), 29, 487. She continues—alluding to a definition ventured in 1898 by Émile Durkheim, with whom she is broadly sympathetic—"To think of religion as consisting in 'des croyances obligitoires connexes de pratiques définies' chills its very life-blood."
29. James H. Leuba, *A Psychological Study of Religion: Its Origin, Function, and Future* (New York: Macmillan, 1912), 23, 17.
30. Max Weber, "Religious Groups," in Weber, *Economy and Society*, ed. Guenther Roth and Claus Wittich; this essay trans. Ephraim Fischoff (1968; Berkeley: University of California Press, 1978), 399; Georg Simmel, "A Contribution to the Sociology of Religion [1898]," in Georg Simmel, *Essays on Religion*, ed. and trans. Horst Jürgen Helle with Ludwig Nieder (New Haven: Yale University Press, 1997), 101. "Vitzliputzli" was what the Germans called the Aztec god Huitzilopochtli, about whom Heine wrote a well-known poem.
31. Melford Spiro, "Religion: Problems of Definition and Explanation," in M. Banton, ed., *Anthropological Approaches to the Study of Religion* (London: Tavistock, 1966), 96.
32. Clifford Geertz, "Religion as a Cultural System," in Geertz, *The Interpretation of Cultures* (New York: Basic Books, 1973), 90.
33. Robert N. Bellah, "Religious Evolution," *American Sociological Review* 29, no. 3 (June 1964): 359. He offers the coupon-like caveat that this definition is "for limited purposes only."

34. "These four terms, taken together, express the collection of related symbols that make up a religious system," Catherine L. Albanese writes. Creeds are glossed as "explanations about the meaning of human life in the university"; codes are "rules that govern everyday behavior"; cultuses are *"rituals to act out the insights and understandings that are expressed in creeds and codes"*; communities are "groups of people either formally or informally bound together by the creed, code, and cultus they share." What's less clear is why this constitutes a "system of symbols." Catherine L. Albanese, *America: Religions and Religion* (Belmont, CA: Wadsworth, 1981), 8. The second set of C's come from Ara Norenzayan, "Why We Believe: Religion as a Human Universal," in *Human Morality and Sociality: Evolutionary and Comparative Perspective*, ed. Henrik Hogh-Olesen (London: Palgrave Macmillan, 2009), 59–60. In Norenzayan's view, "the core cognitive feature of religion—belief in supernatural agents, itself a byproduct of the naturally selected disposition for detecting agents—was further culturally transformed from counterintuitive agents to counterintuitive and morally concerned policing agents. This cultural innovation, along with costly commitment aided by ritual, made possible a novel social phenomenon—stable, large, cooperative moral communities of genetically unrelated individuals"(58).

35. Robin Dunbar, *How Religion Evolved* (New York: Oxford University Press, 2022), xvii; Daniel Dennett, *Breaking the Spell: Religion as a Natural Phenomenon* (New York: Viking, 2006), 9.

36. Cavasji in Rohinton Mistry, *Such a Long Journey* (Toronto: McClelland & Stewart, 1991), 87, 168, 331.

37. Martin Riesebrodt, *The Promise of Salvation*, trans. Steven Rendall (Chicago: University of Chicago Press, 2010), 19, 75. He elaborates: "The 'superhumanness' of these powers consists in the fact that influence or control over dimensions of individual or social human life and the natural environment is attributed to them—dimensions that are usually beyond direct human control. Religious practices normally consist in using culturally prescribed means to establish contact with these powers or to gain access to them. What contact or access means depends on the religious imagination concerned and on the social and cultural forms of accessibility." See also Christian Smith's version: religion is "a complex of culturally prescribed practices that are based on premises about the existence and nature of superhuman powers." In Christian Smith, *Religion: What It Is, How It Works, and Why It Matters* (Princeton, NJ: Princeton University Press, 2019), 3. Superhuman must, of course, be defined further: birds and fish and, indeed, microbes have powers beyond the human, and can affect our welfare. Arguments for preserving "religion" as a real category can be found in Kevin Schilbrack, "Religions: Are There Any?" *Journal of the American Academy of Religion* 78, no. 4 (December 20, 2010): 1113–1138. Schilbrack writes that he agrees that "the emergence of 'religion' as a category distinct from 'secular' is a modern rhetorical move that serves efforts to frame secular modernity as the good side of pairs such as evolved/primitive or rational/

superstitious," but notes that religion is a social kind and that there "is value in distinguishing between forms of life that are religious and those that are not." Schilbrack, "After We Deconstruct 'Religion,' Then What? A Case for Critical Realism," *Method and Theory in the Study of Religion* 25, no. 1 (January 2013): 108.

38. Talal Asad, *Genealogies of Religion* (Baltimore: John Hopkins Press, 1993). Martin Riesebrodt raises the analytical objection in these terms: "If religion always means something different in different contexts, how do the critics of the concept of religion know that what is different in each case still represents 'religion,' especially in societies that have no concept of religion? Either the phenomena present such great differences that a common concept for them cannot be justified and the concept of religion should be abandoned, or they represent only different forms of something that remains definable in terms of shared characteristics." Riesebrodt, *Promise of Salvation*, 11.

39. Smith, *Meaning and End of Religion*, 12. He argued that, by contrast, "structures of devotional practices, disciplines for cultivating religious virtues, and the evolution of moral sensibilities within changing historical circumstances" are real, not "mere linguistic forms." Talal Asad chided Smith for being "so obsessed with the danger of reification (making a word into a thing) that he is oblivious to the opposite danger (making a thing into a word)." See Talal Asad, "Reading a Modern Classic: W. C. Smith's *The Meaning and End of Religions*," in Hent de Vries and Samuel Weber, eds., *Religion and Media* (Stanford, CA: Stanford University Press, 2001), 142. But if Smith was an eliminativist, he was a faltering one. In a later book, he offers a sort-of definition of "the religious life of a people": "men's and women's orientations and aspirations, at their most intimate and profound, their societies' assumptions and cohesions, at their most subtle and pervasive; and much else." Smith, *Belief and History* (Charlottesville: University Press of Virginia, 1977), 1.

40. Russell T. McCutcheon, *Manufacturing Religion* (New York: Oxford University Press, 1997), 22.

41. Timothy Fitzerald, *The Ideology of Religious Studies* (New York: Oxford University Press, 2000), 4, xi, 8. He sees the construction of religion as a global object of study as part of the processes of imperialism, colonialism, and neocolonialism. (A skeptic could inquire whether the global concepts of imperialism, colonialism, and neocolonialism really have greater semantic stability and coherence.)

42. Gordon Lynch, *The Sacred in the Modern World: A Cultural Sociological Approach* (Oxford: Oxford University Press, 2012), 5.

43. David Dubuisson, *The Western Construction of Religion*, trans. William Sayers (Baltimore: Johns Hopkins University Press, 2003), 207–212. And see Dubuisson, *The Invention of Religion*, trans. Martha Cunninghan (Sheffield, UK: Equinox, 2019); Riesebrodt, *Promise of Salvation*, 6.

44. Jonathan Z. Smith, *Imagining Religion: From Babylon to Jonestown* (Chicago: University of Chicago Press, 1982): xi; and Jonathan Z. Smith,

Relating Religion: Essays in the Study of Religion (Chicago: University of Chicago, 2004), 194.

45. Adam Ferguson, *An Essay on the History of Civil Society*, ed. Fania Oz-Salzberger (Cambridge: Cambridge University Press, 1996), 10; John Millar, *Observations Concerning the Distinction of Ranks in Society* (1771); Adam Smith, *The Theory of Moral Sentiments*, pt. 3, ed. Knud Haakonssen (Cambridge: Cambridge University Press, 2002), 173; James Dunbar, *Essays on the History of Mankind in Rude and Cultivated Ages* (London: W. Strahan, T. Cadell, 1780), 17; Francis Hutcheson, *A Short Introduction to Moral Philosophy*, 3rd ed. (Glasgow: Robert & Andrew Foulis, 1764), 1:128; David Hume, "Of the Origin of Government," *Essays, Moral, Political, and Literary*, new ed., ed. T. H. Green and T. H. Grose (London: Longmans, Green, 1889), 1:113. I'm grateful to the insightful discussions of this intellectual epoch in, inter alia, Gladys Bryson, *Man and Society: The Scottish Inquiry of the Eighteenth Century* (Princeton, NJ: Princeton University Press, 1945); Christopher J. Berry, *The Social Theory of the Scottish Enlightenment* (Edinburgh: Edinburgh University Press, 1997); and Berry, *Essays on Hume, Smith and the Scottish Enlightenment* (Edinburgh: Edinburgh University Press, 2019).

46. Robert A. Nisbet, *The Sociological Tradition* (1966; New Brunswick, NJ: Transaction, 1993), 15.

47. Karl Marx, "Preface" to the "Critique of Political Economy" (1859), in Marx, *Later Political Writings*, ed. Terrell Carver (Cambridge: Cambridge University Press, 1996), 160.

48. Donald MacRae, *Max Weber* (London: Fontana, 1974), 17.

49. Herbert Spencer, *The Principles of Sociology*, vol. 1 (New York: Appleton, 1884), 43.

50. In *A Secular Age*, Charles Taylor writes that he will refer to the "social imaginary," and "the modern social imaginary," rather than social theory, in order to discuss the way "ordinary people 'imagine' their social surroundings," which may not be in theoretical terms, although he grants that "it very often happens that what starts off as theories held by a few people may come to infiltrate the social imaginary, first of elites perhaps, and then of the whole society." When that happens, "people take up, improvise, or are inducted into new practices. . . . Rather like Kant's notion of an abstract category being 'schematized' when it is applied to reality in space and time, the theory is schematized in the dense sphere of common practice." Thatcher's remark shows, through resistance, the established force of a theoretically informed social imaginary. Taylor, *A Secular Age* (Cambridge, MA: Harvard University Press, 2007), 171, 177.

51. They might have identified *others* in this way—"Kramo" is an old word for Muslim in our language.

52. Twi is the name of the language spoken in Asante. It is one of a family of dialects spoken in the wider world of Akan cultures in Ghana, and belongs to the wider group of Akan languages. Perhaps the first book to explore something called Asante religion was *Religion and Art in Asante*

(Oxford: Clarendon, 1927) by the British colonial anthropologist Captain Robert Sutherland Rattray. An earlier version of some of the observations made here and elsewhere in the book, especially in Chapter 5, appeared in Kwame Anthony Appiah, "Explaining Religion: Notes toward a Research Agenda," in Simon A. Levin, ed., *Games, Groups, and the Global Good* (Dordrecht: Springer, 2009), 195–206; and Kwame Anthony Appiah, "What Is a Science of Religion?" *Philosophy* 93, no. 4 (October 2018): 485–503.

CHAPTER 1. EDWARD BURNETT TYLOR

Beyond the specific debts signaled in the notes, let me flag a few general ones. The remarkable social anthropologist Robin Horton is the person who, many years ago, first introduced me to Tylor and the intellectualist tradition. And anybody interested in the history of anthropology must be grateful to the industry and acuity of George W. Stocking, whose scholarship remains an invaluable guide to Tylor (and to so many others). Sadly, Tylor has never been the subject of a biography, but I'm grateful for the scholarship and archival excavations of Timothy Larsen and Marjorie Wheeler-Barclay, both of whom have helped bring dimension to someone too long flattened by historical neglect.

1. In 1899, the much younger Franz Boas was the first professor of anthropology on the Columbia faculty (he had lectured there since 1896); a degree-granting department was established there in 1902. An intricate disciplinary history can be told through the career of such terms as ethnology, anthropology, cultural anthropology, and social anthropology.

2. Edward B. Tylor, *Primitive Culture: Researches into the Development of Mythology, Philosophy, Religion, Art, and Culture*, 2 vols. (London: John Murray, 1871), 1:1. I have discussed Tylor's contributions to the culture concept in Kwame Anthony Appiah, *The Lies That Bind* (New York: Liveright, 2018).

3. Camberwell became a metropolitan borough of London in 1900. Now it's part of Southwark.

4. R. R. Marett, *Tylor* (London: Chapman and Hall, 1936), 13.

5. Edward Burnett Tylor, *Anahuac; or, Mexico and the Mexicans, Ancient and Modern* (London: Longman, Green, Longman and Roberts, 1861), iii.

6. Timothy Larsen, *The Slain God: Anthropologists and the Christian Faith* (New York: Oxford University Press, 2014), 16.

7. Tylor, *Anahuac*, 80, 288, 289.

8. See R. R. Marett, *Tylor* (London: Chapman and Hall, 1936), 63. "When he published the *Researches* in 1865, he was evidently not prepared to embark on the vast subject of religious origins," Marett writes, and even though he goes on to discuss Tylor's account of magical thinking, he is somehow confident that it is not a story of religion. Cf. Larsen, *Slain God*, 18.

9. He adds, "This is indeed true to some extent among the higher nations, for no Greenlander or Kaffir ever mixed up his subjectivity with the evidence

of his senses into a more hopeless confusion than the modern spiritualist." As we'll see, an interest in such survivals and revivals is among his intellectual hallmarks. Edward Burnet [sic] Tylor, *Researches into the Early History of Mankind and the Development of Civilization* (London: John Murray, 1865), 5–6, 7–8.

10. Tylor, *Researches*, 3, 110, 112–113.

11. Tylor, *Researches*, 119–120, 150.

12. Tylor, *Primitive Culture*, 2nd ed. (London: John Murray, 1873), 1:477. Unless otherwise noted (as here), references to this book will be to the first edition.

13. Larsen, *Slain God*, 20.

14. Edward Burnett Tylor, "The Religion of Savages," *Fortnightly Review* 6 (August 15–December 1, 1866): 73, 74, 86.

15. Tylor, "Religion of Savages," 85, 84, 82.

16. Tylor, *Primitive Culture*, 1: 257.

17. At this point, "Cultur" and "Kultur" were normal orthographic variations; later in the century, the spelling was standardized to "Kultur." The lexicographer (and theologian) Joachim-Heinrich Campe, early in the nineteenth century, was among those who wished to purge German of foreign loan words, and to Germanize the spelling of those that remained. He also sought to replace "Katholik" with "Zwanggläubiger": forced believer. ("Protestanten" were described as "Freigläubige"—those who freely believed.) See German Historical Institute Washington, "Joachim Heinrich Campe on the Germanization of Foreign Words," online at German History Intersections, https://germanhistory-intersections.org/en/germanness/ghis:document-286. For "The thesis which I venture to sustain," see Tylor, *Primitive Culture*, 1:28. For a discussion of Tylor and the concept of culture, see Kwame Anthony Appiah, *The Lies That Bind* (New York: W.W. Norton, 2018), 189–211.

18. Rousseau's formulation appears in his *Essai sur l'origine des langues*, which was mainly written in the 1750s, although published only posthumously, in 1781. Ferguson's distinction appears in his *An Essay on the History of Civil Society* (Dublin: Boulter Grierson, 1767), 120. "Civilization," in the modern sense, is said to have been introduced in a 1757 book by the Marquis de Mirabeau. John Millar traced an evolution from savage nations through pastoralism and barbarism to agriculture, through improvements in commerce and civilization, with its distinctions of professions and ranks. Millar, *The Origin of the Distinction of Ranks* (1779; Carmel, IN: Liberty Fund, 2006), 26. Adam Smith, in his *Lectures on Jurisprudence* (1763), favored four stages: "1st, the Age of Hunters; 2dly, the Age of Shepherds; 3dly, the Age of Agriculture; and 4thly, the Age of Commerce." In *Ancient Society* (1877), Lewis Henry Morgan popularized the three-stage model of savagery/barbarism/civilization, which, in his account, came with further subdivisions. A further caveat must be entered about the term "evolution." Social evolutionism, of this sort, may have been invigorated by Charles Darwin's work, but, as should be obvious, it didn't depend on it. In fact, Darwin's grandfather,

Erasmus, writing in the eighteenth century, laid out an account of evolution in the natural world, complete with "common descent with modification," on the model of artificial selection. The principal novelty of Darwin's work wasn't the evolution part—he scarcely used the word "evolution"—but the specific mechanism of natural selection. Tylor himself mainly referred to the "development" of culture, not its evolution.

19. Tylor, *Primitive Culture*, 1:258.
20. Tylor, *Primitive Culture*, 2:21, 2:224, 1:387, 1:383.
21. Tylor, *Primitive Culture*, 1:385–386.
22. Marcel Mauss and Henri Humbert, "Esquisse d'une théorie générale de la magie," *L'Année sociologique* (vol. 7, 1902–1903; later published as vol. 1 of *Sociologie et anthropologie*). See Marcel Mauss, *Sociologie et anthropologie* (Paris: Presses universitaires de France, 1950). J. G. Frazer, in *The Golden Bough: A Study in Comparative Religion* (1890), had advanced a linear, tri-une account in which magic preceded religion, which preceded science. Magic—which he divided into the imitative and the contagious—involved an effort at manipulating the world directly; religion involved the intercessory enlistment of supernatural agents, via supplication and placation. Robert R. Marett—in *The Threshold of Religion* (London: Methuen, 1909), 29—deemed Frazer's views "too intellectualistic," for magic "is not merely an affair of misapplied ideas, but must be studied likewise on its emotional side."
23. Tylor, *Primitive Culture*, 2:10. Buddhism was a test case not because most people who revered the Buddha had no gods, but because some of them had no gods, and this was the form that had attracted scholarly attention in the West.
24. Lactantius, *The Divine Institutes*, bk. 2, ch. 14, in *The Fathers of the Church*, trans. Sister Mary Francis McDonald (Washington, DC: Catholic University of America Press, 1964), 154.
25. The passage continues: "One great element of religion, that moral element which among the higher nations forms its most vital part, is indeed little represented in the religion of the lower races." Tylor, *Primitive Culture*, 1:386.
26. Tylor, *Primitive Culture*, 1:411.
27. Tylor, *Primitive Culture*, 2:189, 2:142. In fact, Tylor thought that the classical theory of ideas grew from this conception of spirits. For an intellectual historian, this argument (expanding on observations ventured in his *Researches*) is among his most provocative claims: "To say that Democritus was an ancient Greek is to say that from his childhood he had looked on at the funeral ceremonies of his country, beholding the funeral sacrifices of garments and jewels and money and food and drink, rites which his mother and his nurse could tell him were performed in order that the phantasmal images of these objects might pass into the possession of forms shadowy like themselves, the souls of dead. Thus Democritus, seeking a solution of his great problem of the nature of thought, found it by simply decanting into his

metaphysics a surviving doctrine of primitive savage animism. This thought of the phantoms or souls of things, if simply modified to form a philosophical theory of perception, would then and there become his doctrine of Ideas. Nor does even this fully represent the closeness of union which connects the savage doctrine of flitting object-souls with the Epicurean philosophy. Lucretius actually makes the theory of film-like images of things (simulacra, membranæ) account both for the apparitions which come to men in dreams, and the images which impress their minds in thinking. So unbroken is the continuity of philosophic speculation from savage to cultured thought. Such are the debts which civilized philosophy owes to primitive animism." Tylor, *Primitive Culture*, 1:449–451.

28. John Milton, *Paradise Lost*, bk. 4, ll. 677–678, available at Poets.org, https://poets.org/poem/paradise-lost-book-iv-argument; Tylor, *Primitive Culture* 2:172.

29. Tylor, *Primitive Culture*, 1:500; Tylor, *Primitive Culture*, 2nd ed., 2:108.

30. Tylor, *Primitive Culture*, 2:45.

31. Daniel Dennett, *Intuition Pumps and Other Tools for Thinking* (New York: W.W. Norton, 2013), 78. He used the word "intentional" because that's the word philosophers use for states like beliefs and desires that are *about* the world.

32. David Hume, *The Natural History of Religion*, sec. 3, para. 2, in Hume, *Principal Writing on Religion including Dialogues Concerning Natural Religion and the Natural History of Religion*, ed. J. C. A. Gaskin (New York: Oxford University Press, 1993), 141.

33. Tylor, *Primitive Culture*, 1:361.

34. Tylor, *Primitive Culture*, 1:6.

35. The claim was made by G. S. Lang, then resident in Queensland; see Tylor, *Primitive Culture*, 1:378. Lang's nephew, the celebrated man of letters Andrew Lang, became an occasional critic of Tylor's work. Where Tylor thought monotheism emerged from polytheism, Lang—like a number of prior theorists—was inclined to see primitive polytheisms as "degenerations" of a preceding monotheism.

36. Tylor *Primitive Culture*, 1:378 .

37. Tylor *Primitive Culture*, 2:224.

38. Tylor *Primitive Culture*, 2:225.

39. Tylor *Primitive Culture*, 2:302.

40. "Si d'un côté, toute théorie positive doit nécessairement être fondée sur les observations, il est également sensible, d'un autre côté, que, pour se livrer à l'observation, notre esprit a besoin d'une théorie quelconque." Auguste Comte, *Cours de Philosophie Positive*, vol. 1 (Paris: Bachelier, 1830), 8.

41. Peter L. Berger, *The Sacred Canopy: Elements of a Sociological Theory of Religion* (New York: Anchor, 1969), 100.

42. Quoted in Timothy Larsen, *The Slain God: Anthropologists and the Christian Faith* (New York: Oxford University Press, 2014), 31.

43. See Robert H. Codrington, *The Melanesians: Studies in Their Anthropology and Folk-Lore* (Oxford: Clarendon, 1891), 118–120. Note that he had first circulated his findings in the 1870s. For a more recent, and disabused, perspective on the concept—which Lévi-Strauss dubbed a "floating signifier"—see Nicolas Maylan, *Mana: A History of a Western Category* (Leiden: Brill, 2017).

44. Robert R. Marett, *The Threshold of Religion*, 2nd ed. (London: Methuen, 1914), xxxi. This was a collection of eight essays previously published in 1909; I'm quoting from the preface of the revised edition. The first chapter, "Pre-Animistic Religion," was first published in *Folk-Lore* (June 1900): 162–182. "I believe that most anthropologists of repute would nowadays subscribe to the negative proposition that animism will not suffice as a 'minimum definition of religion,' " he writes (xxii). "Tylor's animism is too narrow, because too intellectualistic. Psychologically, religion involves more than thought, namely, feeling and will as well; and may manifest itself on its emotional side, even when ideation is vague." "Something wider than animism is needed," he explains, putting a finer point on it (2). Cf. Marett, "The Tabu-Mana Formula as a Minimum Definition of Religion," *Archiv für Religionswissenschaft* 12 (1909): 186–194.

45. "Pre-Animistic Religion," as reprinted in Marett, *Threshold of Religion* (1914 ed.), 28.

46. Max Müller, *Lectures on the Science of Language* (London: Longmans, Green, 1861), 11.

47. Müller took this up in another series of lectures, given in 1863, and published as a second series of the *Lectures on the Science of Language* (London: Longmans, Green, 1864), 501–506. (Several later revised editions followed.) He had previously discussed these mythologies in his *Comparative Mythology: An Essay* (London: George Routledge, 1856), 119–125. Marjorie Wheeler Barclay cites Andrew Lang as among the thesis's outspoken skeptics. Wheeler-Barclay, *The Science of Religion in Britain, 1860–1915* (Charlottesville: University of Virginia Press, 2010), 47.

48. Tylor, *Primitive Culture*, 1:271.

49. Marett, *Tylor*, 79. J. W. Burrow suggests that Tylor's critique of Müller's philological treatment of religion "threw open the subject of religion to anthropological treatment." Burrow, *Evolution and Society: A Study in Victorian Social Theory* (Cambridge: Cambridge University Press, 1966), 237.

50. Müller, "The Savage," *Living Age*, 5th ser., 49 (January–March 1885): 365.

51. Tylor, *Primitive Culture*, 2:330, 329.

52. My discussion here is much influenced by the work of Robin Horton, the great late-twentieth-century Tylorean philosopher-anthropologist, epitomized in his *Patterns of Thought in Africa and the West: Essays on Magic, Religion and Science* (Cambridge: Cambridge University Press, 1993). I'll return to Horton in this book's epilogue. See also the discussion of his work in chapter 6 of Kwame Anthony Appiah, *In My Father's House* (New York: Oxford University Press, 1992).

53. Tylor, *Primitive Culture*, 2:328.

54. Tylor, *Primitive Cultures*, 2:336–337.

55. See Robertson Smith's discussion of methods in *The Prophets of Israel and Their Place in Israel* (New York: Appleton, 1882), 17, and in his *The Old Testament in the Jewish Church* (New York: Appleton, 1882), 4–29; Thomas O. Beidelman, *W. Robertson Smith and the Sociological Study of Religion* (Chicago: University of Chicago Press, 1974), 23.

56. In a passage removed from later editions, Robertson Smith had ventured that Christ's sacrifice was presaged in this ancient rite: "That the God-man dies for His people, and that His death is their life, is an idea which was in some degree foreshadowed by the oldest mystical sacrifices. It was foreshadowed, indeed, in a very crude and materialist form, and without any of those ethical ideas which the Christian doctrine of the atonement derives from a profounder sense of sin and divine justice. And yet the voluntary death of the divine victim, which we have seen to be a conception not foreign to ancient sacrificial ritual, contained the germ of the deepest thought in the Christian doctrine: the thought that the Redeemer gives Himself for his people, that 'for their sakes He consecrates Himself that they also might be consecrated in truth.' " W. Robertson Smith, *Lectures on the Religion of the Semites* (New York: D. Appleton, 1889), 393.

57. Smith, *Lectures*, 16–19.

58. Smith, *Lectures*, 19.

59. Tylor, *Primitive Culture*, 1:11–12.

60. Max Müller, *Contributions to the Science of Mythology* (London: Longmans, Green, 1897), 2:448. He goes on, "Even the Greeks do not say much about faith, though they have the word." Edward Evans-Pritchard, *Nuer Religion* (Oxford: Clarendon, 1956), 9. (In an illustration of the intellectual intimacy of these discussions and debates, Evans-Pritchard seems to have been inducted into anthropology by Marett, who was a fellow at his Oxford college, Exeter.) Rodney Needham finds it significant that between Evans-Pritchard's field work among the Nuer in the 1930s and the publication of this book, Evans-Pritchard joined the Roman Catholic church. Needham, *Belief, Language, and Experience* (Chicago: University of Chicago Press, 1973), 24.

61. Needham, *Belief, Language, and Experience*, 188; Jean Pouillon, "Remarks on the Verb 'to Believe,' " in Michel Izard and Pierre Smith, eds., *Between Belief and Transgression: Structuralist Essays in Religion, History, and Myth*, trans. John Leavitt (Chicago: University of Chicago Press, 1982), 1–8, originally published as "*Remarques sur le verbe 'croire,'* " in Michel Izard and Pierre Smith, eds., *La fonction symbolique* (Paris: Gallimard, 1979), 43–51, 44 ("Ainsi est-ce, si l'on peut dire, l'incroyant qui croit que le croyant croit à l'existence de Dieu"). Against the background of Tylor's individualism, it should be noted that the meaning of beliefs can be supraindividual, in the

immediate respect that it can involve more than one believer. Hilary Putnam's famous "elms and experts" argument (even though he can't identify an elm reliably, he can talk about elms, because others have expertise about elms) points to one dimension of the sociality of belief.

62. Wilfred Cantwell Smith, *Belief and History* (Charlottesville: University Press of Virginia, 1977), v. In a lecture on "Characteristics of Religion," Rodney Needham maintains that "it is not a general characteristic of religions that their tenets are held to be true," citing a remark that it is hard to be heretical in India. Needham, *Circumstantial Deliveries* (Berkeley: University of California Press, 1981), 76.

63. Neil Van Leeuwen, *Religion as Make-Believe* (Cambridge, MA: Harvard University Press, 2023), 65–98. Credences do rest on factual beliefs: the fact that it's Sunday, that there are seats available in the left pew, that our crops will die if it doesn't rain. There could be no miracles without regular factual beliefs like these about what is normally possible. But credences are more compartmentalized and less penetrant. Whereas ordinary factual beliefs are always operative, we don't take credences as the basis of action in all contexts; we act as if they're true only at certain times and places. Van Leeuwen notes studies showing that people pray for things that could happen—they pray for cancer to go into remission, not for a limb to regrow; they pray for someone to change their mind, not for a hole in their boat to vanish. Factual beliefs are involuntary; religious ones, he thinks, tend to involve choice. And factual beliefs are vulnerable in a way that credences are not. (It's easy to establish that you were wrong to believe you had your keys on you, but how do you refute a dietary taboo?)

64. Tylor, *Primitive Culture*, 1:71–72.

65. Ted Chiang, "Hell Is the Absence of God," in Chiang, *Stories of Your Life and Others* (New York: Orb, 2002), 245–280.

66. David Hume, *An Enquiry Concerning Human Understanding and Other Writings*, ed. Stephen Buckle (Cambridge: Cambridge University Press, 2007), 113.

67. Tylor, *Primitive Culture*, 2:339.

68. Tylor, *Primitive Culture*, 2nd ed., 2:358–359.

69. Marett, *Threshold of Religion*, 1.

70. Stanley Tambiah, *Magic, Science, Religion, and the Scope of Rationality* (Cambridge: Cambridge University Press, 1990), 43.

71. Tylor, *Primitive Culture*, 2:326.

72. Tylor, *Primitive Culture*, 2:326. Again, talk of the "lower races" here referred to a people's stage of cultural development, not to their intrinsic capacities. (The term "race" included, but was not limited to, its modern sense.) Early in the first volume, he wrote with respect to survivals that "we may draw a picture where there shall be scarce a hand's breadth difference between an English ploughman and a negro of Central Africa," and immediately set aside "the question of race": "For the present purpose it appears both possible and desirable to eliminate considerations of hereditary varieties or

races of man, and to treat mankind as homogeneous in nature, though placed in different grades of civilization." Tylor, *Primitive Culture*, 1:6.

73. Tylor, *Primitive Culture*, 2:339.

74. Larsen, *Slain God*, 33; Tylor, *Primitive Culture*, 2:410. Despite Tylor's progressivism, he anticipated a cycle of intellectual backlash: "It may be that the increasing power and range of the scientific method, with its stringency of argument and constant check of fact, may start the world on a more steady and continuous course of progress than it has moved on heretofore. But if history is to repeat itself according to precedent, we must look forward to stiffer duller ages of traditionalists and commentators, when the great thinkers of our time will be appealed to as authorities by men who slavishly accept their tenets, yet cannot or dare not follow their methods through better evidence to higher ends. In either case, it is for those among us whose minds are set on the advancement of civilization, to make the most of present opportunities, that even when in future years progress is arrested, it may be arrested at the higher level" (2:410).

75. This discussion can be found in Lucien Lévy-Bruhl, *Les functions mentales dans les sociétés inférieures* (Paris: Félix Alcan, 1910), 93; and in the more catchily titled English version, *How Natives Think* (New York: Alfred A. Knopf, 1925), 90. Tylor, in an 1877 review of Herbert Spencer's *Principles of Sociology* (which, appearing the previous year, advanced his so-called ghost theory, one that had distinct commonalities with Tylor's animism), chided him for condescending to primitive man, wrongly supposing primitive minds to be "devoid of rational curiosity as to nature" and wrongly characterizing their worldview as inconsistent. Edward B. Tylor, "Mr. Spencer's Principles of Sociology," *Mind* 2, no. 6 (April 1877): 144. As we've seen, Tylor was inclined to stress the unity of mankind.

76. E. E. Evans-Pritchard, "Religion in Primitive Society," *Blackfriars* 34, no. 398 (May 1953): 215.

77. Edward Evans-Pritchard, *Theories of Primitive Religion* (Oxford: Clarendon, 1965), 24–26, 29. With respect to the notion that the savage confused real connections with ideal ones (the picture and the one pictured, say), he went on, "The error here was in not recognizing that the associations are social and not psychological stereotypes, and that they occur therefore only when evoked in specific ritual situations, which are also of limited duration."

78. Unsigned review, *The Examiner* (London), May 27, 1871, 536; Wheeler-Barclay, *Science of Religion*, 96.

79. Tylor, *Anthropology: An Introduction to the Study of Man* (London: Macmillan, 1881). Only in that book did he squarely and consistently embrace the savagery-barbarianism-civilization trinity.

80. Tylor, *Anthropology*, 408–409.

81. Wheeler-Barclay, *Science of Religion*, 80–82, 96. She suggests that Tylor's "reluctance to engage directly in antireligious polemics helped to obscure the sweeping nature of his arguments." One may wonder whether it

was obscured, even if some readers choose not to connect the densely aligned dots. Tylor did openly oppose the spiritualism that had become fashionable in certain Victorian circles, and, as she notes, thereby gained the enmity of Alfred R. Wallace, who had come to embrace it, and who inveighed in print against Tylor's "one-sidedness."

82. Larsen, *Slain God*, 27.
83. Marett, *Tylor*, 8.
84. Ethel M. Arnold, "Social Life in Oxford," *Harper's* 81 (July 1890), 251.
85. A. C. Haddon, "Sir E. B. Tylor, F.R.S.," *Nature* (January 11, 1917): 373. I'm drawing on biographical details that appear in George W. Stocking Jr., "Edward Burnett Tylor and the Mission of Primitive Man," in Stocking, *Delimiting Anthropology* (Madison: University of Wisconsin Press, 2001), 103–115; Larsen, *Slain God*, 13–37; and Alison Petch, "Edward Burnett Tylor (1832–1917)," an article that credits research by Megan Price and is available at https://web.prm.ox.ac.uk/sma/index.php/articles/article-index/335-edward-burnett-tylor-1832–1917.html.

CHAPTER 2. ÉMILE DURKHEIM

Marcel Fournier's biography is now the most comprehensive one and is indispensable, yet half a century has not dulled the keen observations found in Steven Luke's marvelous work of 1972. Note that I may not provide references for biographical details that are common to multiple sources.

1. Émile Durkheim, *Les formes élémentaires de la vie religieuse: Le système totémique en Australie* (Paris: Félix Alcan, 1912), 78, 81, 91. I'm not taking advantage of the work's fine published English translations only because, given the subject of this book, I wanted to be able to keep a particularly close eye on the original, and occasionally be able to capture a nicety relevant for my purposes at the sacrifice of felicity. (Perhaps "Elemental" would be preferable to "Elementary," in the title, but concessions must be made to custom.) The 1912 edition can be read here: https://archive.org/details/lesformeslmentai00durk/page/n7/mode/2up. I'll be referring to non-English books with standard English translations by their English titles.

2. "When the philosophers of the eighteenth-century treated religion as a vast error," Durkheim writes in the same passage, they could at least explain its persistence "by the interest of the priestly caste in deceiving the masses. But if the peoples themselves had crafted these erroneous systems of ideas at the same time as they were their dupes, how could this extraordinary deception perpetuate itself throughout the entire course of history?" Durkheim, *Les formes élémentaires*, 98–99.

3. Émile Durkheim, *Le Suicide: Étude de Sociologie* (Paris: Félix Alcan, 1897), published in English as *Suicide*, trans. John A. Spaulding and George Simpson (New York: Free Press, 1951), 160; Émile Durkheim, *De la division du travail social* (Paris: Félix Alcan, 1893); quoting from Durkheim, *The*

Division of Labour in Society, 2nd ed., ed. and intro. by Steven Lukes, trans. W. D. Halls (London: Palgrave Macmillan, 2013), 79.

4. See Steven Lukes, *Émile Durkheim: His Life and Works* (New York: Harper & Row, 1972), 46; and Marcel Fournier, *Émile Durkheim: A Biography*, trans. David Macey (Cambridge: Polity Press, 2013), 29.

5. Letter to the Directeur, *Revue neo-scolastique* (Louvain) 14 (1907): 612–614, translated as "Influences upon Durkheim's View of Sociology (1907)," in Durkheim, *The Rules of Sociological Method and Selected Texts on Sociology and Its Method*, 2d ed. and intro. by Steven Lukes, trans. W. D. Halls (New York: Free Press, 2013), 199.

6. Émile Durkheim (with Paul Fauconnet), "Sociology and the Social Sciences" (1903), in Durkheim, *The Rules of Sociological Method*, ed. Steven Lukes, trans. W. D. Halls (New York: Free Press, 1982). "Comte never conceived sociology to be anything but a speculative, complete entity, closely linked to general philosophy," Durkheim wrote. "According to him, only one society existed, the association of mankind in its totality; the various states represented only different moments in the history of that one society" (176, 180). Spencer, too, was in this unfortunate sense a mere philosopher: his "voluminous sociological work has hardly any other purpose than to show how the law of universal evolution is applied to societies" (48).

7. Lukes, *Émile Durkheim*, 54.

8. Émile Durkheim, "Review of Albert Schäffle, *Bau und Leben des Socialen Körpers* (2nd Edition)," *Revue Philosophique der Soziologie* 20 (1885): 627–634. Reprinted in Émile Durkheim, *Textes I: Éléments d'une théorie sociale*, ed. Victor Karády (Paris: Éditions de Minuit, 1975), 355–377.

9. Émile Durkheim, "La Science positive de la morale en Allemagne," *Revue philosophique*, in 1887; collected in Durkheim, *Ethics and the Sociology of Morals*, trans. Robert T. Hall (Buffalo: Prometheus Books, 1993), 97–100. Cf. Anthony Giddens, *Capitalism and Modern Social Theory: An Analysis of the Writings of Marx, Durkheim, and Max Weber* (Cambridge: Cambridge University Press, 1971), 70.

10. Émile Durkheim, "La Science positive de la morale en Allemagne," *Revue philosophique*, in 1887; collected (as "The Moral Philosophers: Wilhelm Wundt") in Durkheim, *Ethics and the Sociology of Morals*, trans. Robert T. Hall (Buffalo, NY: Prometheus, 1993), 93–94.

11. Durkheim, "The Moral Philosophers: Wilhelm Wundt," 95.

12. Émile Durkheim, "Les Études de Science Sociale," *Revue philosophique de la France et de l'étranger* 22 (July–December 1886): 61–80, at 68, 67, 69.

13. Émile Durkheim, "Les principes de 1789 et la sociologie," *Revue internationale de l'enseignement* 19 (1890): 450–455. An illuminating discussion can be found in Ernest Wallwork, "Durkheim's Early Sociology of Religion," *Sociological Analysis* 46, no. 3 (Autumn 1985): 201–217.

14. Alfred Fouillée, *La Science sociale contemporaine*, 2d ed. (Paris: Hachette, 1885), 385.

15. Jean-Marie Guyau, *L'Irréligion de l'avenir: Étude sociologique* (Paris: Félix Alcan, 1887), translated (anonymously) as *The Non-Religion of the Future: A Sociological Study* (New York: Henry Holt, 1897); Émile Durkheim, "Guyau, *L'Irreligion de l'avenir: étude de sociologie*," *Revue philosophique* 23 (1887): 299–311, translated and reprinted as "Review Guyau—*L'Irréligion de l'avenir, étude de sociologie*," in W. S. F. Pickering, ed. *Durkheim on Religion: A Selection of Readings with Bibliographies*, trans. Jacqueline Redding and W. S. F. Pickering (London: Routledge and Kegan Paul, 1975), 24–38. I also benefited from Anthony Giddens's still invaluable survey "Durkheim as a Review Critic," *Sociological Review* 18, no. 2 (July 1970), 171–196; and from Marco Orru, "The Ethics of Anomie: Jean Marie Guyau and Émile Durkheim," *British Journal of Sociology* 34, no. 4 (December 1983): 499–518.

16. Guyau, *L'Irréligion de l'avenir*, iii, iv.

17. Émile Durkheim, "Course in Social Science—Inaugural Lecture," trans. Neville Layne, in Ivan Strenski, ed., *Émile Durkheim* (London: Routledge, 2016), 231, 232.

18. Alfred Espinas, *Des sociétés animales*, 2d ed. (Paris: Germer Ballière, 1878), 10.

19. Werner Cahnman, ed., *Ferdinand Tonnies: A New Evaluation: Essays and Documents* (Leiden: E.J. Brill, 1973), 246. Without descending to Whorfianism, one can wonder whether the fact that German, unlike English and French, did not (routinely) deploy related terms for the adjective "social" and the noun "society," conduced to certain habits of mind. The distinction between *gesellschaftlich* and *sozial* is challenging to render.

20. "In contrasting organic to mechanical solidarity, Durkheim was consciously reversing the dichotomy between modern and traditional societies characteristic of German social thought, and Tönnies (as he read him) in particular," Steven Lukes writes. "His own distinction was partly a way of stressing the social differentiation of 'organized' societies, involving interdependent and multiplying specialized roles, beliefs and sentiments as opposed to the un-differentiated unity of uniform activities, beliefs and sentiments and rigid social control found in 'segmental' societies." Lukes, *Émile Durkheim*, 148. Though Fournier thinks Durkheim owed his congruent binary to Tönnies, there were similar binaries floating around—not just Spencer's division between "military" and "industrial" societies but also Marx and Engel's division between town and country.

21. The forces of social cohesion were, for the usual reasons, a subject of attention. Dominick LaCapra has noted that, owing to industrialization, in Durkheim's lifetime "the rate of change in France itself, especially in the concentration of industry, was probably more rapid than it had ever been, and its effects were quite perceptible to the sensitive observer. In fact, the unbalanced nature of the economic transformation in France exacerbated problems common to all industrial societies." LaCapra, *Émile Durkheim: Sociologist and Philosopher* (Ithaca, NY: Cornell University Press, 1972), 39.

22. Durkheim, *De la division du travail social*; Durkheim, *Division of Labour in Society*, 72. Robert Bellah argues, "Durkheim uses the word 'society' in ways closer to classical theology than to empirical science. It is not that Durkheim makes an empirical society into an idol. It is that he so elevates, purifies, and deepens the word 'society' that it can, not unworthily, take the place of the great word it supersedes." Robert N. Bellah, "Introduction," in *Émile Durkheim on Morality and Society: Selected Writings*, ed. Robert N. Bellah (Chicago: University of Chicago Press, 1973), x.

23. Durkheim, *Division of Labour in Society*, 106–107. Note that Hegel, in his lectures on the philosophy of religion (delivered between 1821 and 1831, and published posthumously in 1832, as well as in a substantially revised edition in 1840), had said that "natural religion" represented a unity of the political and religious knowledge; that, "universally speaking, religion and the foundation of the state are one and the same." Georg Wilhelm Friedrich Hegel, *Lectures on the Philosophy of Religion*, vol. 1: *Introduction and the Concept of Religion*, ed. Peter C. Hodgson, trans. R. F. Brown, P. C. Hodgson, and J. M. Stewart (Oxford: Clarendon, 2007), 452.

24. Durkheim, *Division of Labour in Society*, 128.

25. Durkheim, *Division of Labour in Society*, 131.

26. Durkheim, *Division of Labour in Society*, 132.

27. Durkheim, *Rules of Sociological Method*, 25, 67.

28. Durkheim, *Rules of Sociological Method*, 87, 113, 128, 151.

29. Durkheim, Letter to the Directeur, *Revue néo-scolastique*, November 8, 1907, reprinted in Simon Deploig, *Le conflit de la morale et de la sociologie* (Paris: Alcan, 1912), 393–413, quoting from the version published in Durkheim, *Rules of Sociological Method*, 259–260.

30. William Robertson Smith, *Lectures on the Religion of the Semites* (New York: D. Appleton, 1889), 33.

31. Translated and reprinted in Durkheim, "Concerning the Definition of Religious Phenomena," in Pickering, *Durkheim on Religion*, 74–99, 90.

32. Durkheim, "Concerning the Definition of Religious Phenomena," 91.

33. Durkheim, "Individualism and the Intellectuals," in Bellah, *Émile Durkheim on Morality and Society*, this selection trans. Mark Traugott, 43–57, 46.

34. Durkheim, "Individualism and the Intellectuals," 48, 49.

35. Durkheim (with Paul Fauconnet), "Sociology and the Social Sciences," in Durkheim, *Rules of Sociological Method*, 194.

36. "Le totem est, d'abord et avant tout, un nom, et comme nous le verrons, un emblème." Durkheim, *Les formes élémentaires*, 154.

37. Durkheim, *Les formes élémentaires*, 269.

38. Merriam-Webster suggests that the word corroboree derives from *garaabara* in Dharuk, an Australian Aboriginal language once spoken in the area around Sydney. (Its last native speaker apparently died in 1970.) See also "Dharuk," Ethnologue.com, at https://www.ethnologue.com/language/xdk.

39. "C'est donc dans ces milieux sociaux effervescents et de cette effervescence même que paraît être née l'idée religieuse." Durkheim, *Les formes élémentaires*, 313.

40. Cf. the discussion of Robertson Smith's influence on Durkheim in Edward Evans-Pritchard, *Theories of Primitive Religion* (Oxford: Clarendon, 1965), 56.

41. Durkheim, *Les formes élémentaires*, 3.

42. Durkheim, *Les formes élémentaires*, 50–51. (Note that the standard Presses Universitaires de France edition, 1968, p. 42, has "gnogmes" for "dogmes.")

43. Durkheim, *Les formes élémentaires*, 42–43.

44. Durkheim, *Les formes élémentaires*, 65. "Une religion est un système solidaire de croyances et de pratiques relatives à des choses sacrées, c'est-à-dire séparées, interdites, croyances et pratiques qui unissent en une même communauté morale, appelée Église, tous ceux qui y adherent."

45. B. K. Malinowski, "Review of *Les formes élémentaires* by Émile Durkheim," *Folk-lore* 24, no. 4 (1913): 525.

46. Durkheim, *Les formes élémentaires*, 322.

47. Émile Durkheim, "La Prohibition de l'inceste et ses origines," *Année sociologique* 1 (1898): 1–70.

48. Durkheim, *Les formes élémentaires*, 135.

49. Durkheim, *Les formes élémentaires*, 134fn.

50. Durkheim, *Les formes élémentaires*, 56. What Durkheim writes in this passage can't be exactly what he means, since what he writes literally is that rituals are rules. What is clear from his discussion of actual cases is that he means that rituals are governed by rules determining how one should behave in relation to the sacred, because the Aboriginal rituals he discusses always involve the treatment of sacred things.

51. Evans-Pritchard, *Theories of Primitive Religion*, 65.

52. Evans-Pritchard, *Theories of Primitive Religion*, 68, 55; Evans-Pritchard, *Nuer Religion* (Oxford: Clarendon, 1956), 313.

53. Émile Durkheim, "The Dualism of Human Nature and Its Social Conditions," *Durkheimian Studies / Études Durkheimiennes* (no translator identified) 11, n.s. (2005): 35–45, esp. 37–38, 42.

54. Alasdair MacIntyre, "Durkheim's Call to Order," *New York Review of Books* (March 7, 1974): 25–26.

55. Lukes, *Émile Durkheim*, 17–30.

56. Fournier, *Émile Durkheim*, 692–693.

57. Fournier, *Émile Durkheim*, 693, 698.

58. Fournier, *Émile Durkheim*, 698, 706.

CHAPTER 3. GEORG SIMMEL

Simmel awaits a full biography, but anyone who writes about him will be indebted to Klaus Christian Köhnke's *Der junge Simmel: In Theoriebeziehungen und sozialen Bewegungen*; and to the editorial exertions of Otthein and Angela Rammstedt, among others. Frederick C. Beiser's panoramic work on German thought from Leibnitz to, well, Simmel is unexampled, combining clarity with a polemical crackle that makes it a pleasure to read. Among specialists, I'm especially grateful for the scholarly and interpretive labors of David Frisby, Elizabeth Goodstein, and Volkhard Krech.

1. Klaus Christian Köhnke, "Lettres à L'éditeur: Murderous Attack upon Georg Simmel," *European Journal of Sociology / Archives Européennes de Sociologie* 24, no. 2 (November 1983): 349, quoting the evening edition, no. 510 of the *Königlich priviligierte Berlinische Zeitung* (November 1, 1886). Two other newspaper articles cited in Köhnke's *Der junge Simmel* (Berlin: Suhrkamp, 1996), 34, differ slightly in their description of the events. "*Die Psychologie des Geldes*" was delivered at a March 1889 colloquium of Gustav Schmoller's. See Elizabeth S. Goodstein, "Thinking at the Boundaries: Georg Simmel's Phenomenology of Disciplinarity," *The Germanic Review: Literature, Culture, Theory* 94, no. 2 (2019): 186.

2. "If sociology succeeds" is from David Frisby, *Georg Simmel*, rev. ed. (London: Routledge, 2002), 32. For "humanist version," see Horst Jürgen Helle, *Messages from Georg Simmel* (Leiden: Brill, 2013).

3. Chocolate is still sold under the Sarotti brand—which adopted a tray-holding blackamoor as a mascot in 1918, redesigned only in 2004 (!)—via Stollwerck GmbH. These biographical details can be found in Jörn Bohr, Gerald Hartung, Heike Koenig, and Tim-Florian Steinbach, eds., *Simmel-Handbuch: Leben—Werk—Wirkung* (Berlin: J.B. Metzler, 2021), 63; Michael Landmann, "Bausteine zur Biographie," in *Buch des Dankes an Georg Simmel: Briefe, Erinnerungen, Bibliographie*, ed. Kurt Gassen and Michael Landmann (1958; Berlin: Duncker & Humblot, 1993), 11–33; and W. S. F. Pickering, "Durkheim, the Arts, and the Moral Sword," in Alexander Riley, W. S. F. Pickering, and William Watts Miller, eds., *Durkheim, the Durkheimians, and the Arts* (New York: Berghahn, 2013), 49. Simmel's father seems to have been deficient as a businessman, and he gave up his shares in the confectionary business rather prematurely.

4. Klaus Christian Köhnke, *Der junge Simmel* (Berlin: Suhrkamp, 1996), 140, 141. In a 1907 letter to Edmund Husserl about the philosopher Oskar Ewald, né Friedländer, Simmel writes, "he has something of the feminine and blurred appearance and behavior that one often notices in Viennese Jews. But if I am not mistaken, this is only an upper layer, under which there is a strong and determined spiritual being." Köhnke, *Der junge Simmel*, 145.

5. Simmel writes to a Jewish correspondent, in 1897, "The idea that the Jews might wish to move to some non-European country and sever the thread that connects them to European culture is a utopia. . . . It is even worse if we ask ourselves whether the idea of [Theodor] Herzl and [Max] Nordau can be realized. . . . To begin the conscious construction of a state basically means to begin building a house that has no foundation from the roof down; it also means wanting to replace a longer-lasting collective

achievement of entire generations with individual and consequently very brief efforts of individual persons. To want to equate the immense sum of human achievement with the genius of two or three personalities actually means challenging an entire collective, means the greatest presumption. . . . From a historical point of view, such presumption is called a utopia, but in life one should rather call it a crime—of course an unconscious one—for even in an extremely conscious human being there is much, very much that is unconscious. Therefore, I cannot welcome the Zionist idea; therefore I do not believe in its success." S. Lozinskij, "Simmels Briefe zur jüdischen Frage," in Hannes Böhringer and Karlfried Gründer, eds., *Ästhetik und Soziologie um die Jahrhundertwende: Georg Simmel* (Frankfurt: Klostermann, 1976), 240–241. (This correspondence was published in a Russian translation in 1924 and, since the original was unavailable, it was translated back into German for the 1976 collection by Herbert and Maria Brauner.)

6. Horst J. Helle, *Messages from Georg Simmel* (Leiden: Brill, 2013), 184–185.

7. Robert R. Marrett complained that treating "folk" as the equivalent of society or community, as in the rendering "folk psychology," was "an outrage to the English language," which could not be excused by the plea that it "imperfectly echoes a German phrase of ambiguous import." Marrett, "Review of Wilhelm Wundt's *Elements of Folk Psychology*," *Folk-Lore* 27, no. 4 (December 1916): 441. (Note that it has been proposed, boldly, that *Volksgeist* could be rendered as "culture"; and Steinthal notably criticized E. B. Tylor's work on culture.) The "religious communities" line is quoted in Ivan Kalmar, "The *Völkerpsychologie* of Lazarus and Steinthal and the Modern Concept of Culture," *Journal of the History of Ideas* 48, no. 4 (October–December 1987): 671–690. The best guide to this terrain is now Egbert Klautke's study *The Mind of the Nation: Völkerpsychologie in Germany, 1851–1955* (New York: Berghahn, 2013).

8. Lazarus ("Is not a community . . . ?") is quoted in Frederick C. Beiser, *The German Historicist Tradition* (New York: Oxford University Press, 2011), 477, in a discussion drawing on Moritz Lazarus and Heymann Steinthal, "Einleitende Gedanken über Völkerpsychologie," *Zeitschrift für Völkerpsychologie und Sprachwissenschaft* 1 (1860): 1–73; "Einige synthetische Gedanken zur Völkerpsychologie," *Zeitschrift für Völkerpsychologie und Sprachwissenschaft* 3, no. 1 (1865), reprinted in Moritz Lazarus, *Grundzüge der Völkerpsychologie und Kulturwissenschaft*, ed. Klaus Christian Köhnke (Hamburg: Felix Meiner, 2003), 131–238; "Ueber das Verhältniß des Einzelnen zur Gesammtheit," in *Das Leben der Seele* (Berlin: Dümmler, 1883), 1:321–411, reprinted in Lazarus, *Grundzüge der Völkerpsychologie und Kulturwissenschaft*, 39–130. The "without recognizing" and "highest degree" passages can be found in "Einige synthetische Gedanken zur Völkerpsychologie," in Lazarus, *Grundzüge der Völkerpsychologie und Kulturwissenschaft*, 161, 162. Lazarus and Steinthal wavered in their disciplinary ambitions, as Klautke makes clear, sometimes denying that they saw *Völkerpsychologie* as more than an adjuvant to existing disciplines.

9. Moritz Lazarus, "Verdichtung des Denkens in der Geschichte. Ein Fragment," *Zeitschrift für Völkerpsychologie und Sprachwissenschaft* 2, no. 1 (1862): 54–62, reprinted in Moritz Lazarus, *Grundzüge der Völkerpsychologie und Kulturwissenschaft*, 27–38. "I will never forget" is quoted in David Frisby, *Simmel and Since* (London: Routledge, 1992), 20.

10. Dilthey, *Einleitung in die Geisteswissenschaften: Versuch einer Grundlegung für das Studium der Gesellschaft und der Geschichte* (Leipzig: Duncker & Humblot, 1883); in English as Dilthey, *Introduction to the Human Sciences: An Attempt to Lay a Foundation for the Study of Society and History,* trans. Ramon J. Betanzos (Detroit: Wayne State University Press, 1988). Ernst Mach, decrying a purported division between two kinds of scholarship in 1866, had used the adjective *humanistisch* for the kind that wasn't the natural sciences. "I must confess, I do not believe in this duality of science," Mach declared in an 1866 lecture. "I believe that this view will appear just as naive to a mature age as the lack of perspective in Egyptian painting appears to us." Ernst Mach, *Populär-wissenschaftliche Vorlesungen*, 3rd and exp. ed. (Leipzig: Johann Ambrosius Barth, 1903).

11. "*Religious life* is a state of affairs *bound up not only with mythical thought*, but with *metaphysics, and with self-reflection,*" Dilthey writes. "The characteristic feature of religious life is that it makes assertions in virtue of a different kind of conviction than scientific evidence is." Dilthey, *Introduction*, 158–159.

12. Dilthey, *Introduction*, 94. Unwary readers should be reminded to read "genetic" as an adjective deriving from "genesis," not "genes." A genetic explanation concerns origination.

13. Dilthey, *Introduction*, 141, 144, 127, 128. In notes Dilthey made in 1904–1905 while he was making preparations for a revised edition of the book, he distinguished Simmel's conception of sociology from the one earlier advanced by Comte and Spencer, and insists that he had preceded Simmel in characterizing "external organization of society as a special sphere in which, viewed psychologically, relations of dominance and dependence and community relations are operative. My view is different from Simmel's principally inasmuch as I cannot simply trace these combinatory forces to the psychical moments mentioned." What he rejects is a discipline that "tries to summarize everything which de facto occurs in human society in a *single* science." "Appendix: Supplementary Material from the Manuscripts," in Dilthey, *Introduction*, 333. (Later, Dilthey's "hermeneutic turn," in his final decade, was meant to evade the critiques made most forcefully by Edmund Husserl: a tactical retreat, of sorts.)

14. Gustav Schmoller, "Das Wesen der Arbeitsteilung und der sozialen Klassenbildung" [The nature of the division of labor and the formation of social classes], *Jahrbuch für Gesetzgebung, Verwaltung und Volkswirtschaft im Deutschen Reich* 14, no. 1 (1890): 45–105. The "social organ" is from Gustav Schmoller, *Grundriß der Allgemeinen Volkswirtschaftslehre. Erster Teil*, 2nd ed. (Berlin: Duncker & Humblot, 1908), 62. And see Heinz-Jürgen

Dahme, "Georg Simmel und Gustav Schmoller. Soziologie in Berlin um 1890. Für Otthein Rammstedt (1938–2020) in Dankbarkeit," *Simmel Studies* 24, no. 1 (2020). In an 1887 review essay, Durkheim linked Schmoller to notions of social consciousness and collective spirit. See "La Science positive de la morale en Allemagne," *Revue philosophique* (1887), published as *Ethics and the Sociology of Morals*, trans. Robert T. Hall (Buffalo: Prometheus, 1993), 66–67, 75. Durkheim's *Division of Labor in Society* made reference to Schmoller's subsequent work on the division of labor.

15. Klaus Christian Köhnke, "Four Concepts of Social Science at Berlin University: Dilthey, Lazarus, Schmoller and Simmel," in Michael Kaern, Bernard S. Phillips, and Robert S. Cohen, eds., *Georg Simmel and Contemporary Sociology* (Dordrecht: Kluwer, 1990), 99–107.

16. Mill thought that Auguste Comte's positivist philosophy, emphasizing empirical evidence, was essentially a re-introduction of a doctrine that Hume had elaborated in detail. Logical Positivism or Logical Empiricism, primarily associated with the Vienna circle in the early twentieth century, made much of the verification principle, asserting that a statement is meaningful only if it can be empirically verified or is analytically true. This movement sought to eliminate, or minimize, metaphysics and speculative philosophy, emphasizing logic and science as the means to knowledge. I think I know what it means to say that Moritz Schlick or A. J. Ayer was positivist in orientation. But in the past half-century, "positivism" has increasingly become a broad-spectrum term of derogation, often used with very little specificity. Rather as certain children are appalled when their carrots touch their peas, certain critics are appalled when social or cultural discussions touch on facts that are neither social nor cultural.

17. Simmel, *Über sociale Differenzierung: Sociologische und psychologische Untersuchungen* (Leipzig: Duncker und Humblot, 1890), 19. (The spelling "soziale" was not yet standard.) The model of intersecting circles appeared again in his *Soziologie* of 1908, and there are continuities with observations earlier made by Lazarus: "Within the great circle of society, smaller circles form, and ever narrower ones, down to the family. Now, these circles do not stand next to each other but intersect and touch each other in many ways. Thus, within society, there arises a highly intertwined relationship of connection and separation. Accordingly, the individual's participation in the overall spirit is also highly diverse in direction and intimacy, allowing for the immeasurable diversity of personal individualities." There are also discontinuities: Lazarus goes on to insist, "Not only his knowledge, but also his conscience, his feeling and his willing, his doing and his enjoying, his receiving and therefore also his creating, is predetermined by his birth at this point of overall spiritual development." Lazarus, *Grundzüge der Völkerpsychologie und Kulturwissenschaft*, 50–51.

18. A contrast in emphasis is not a clash in claims. In *The Division of Labor*, Durkheim remarks that individual differences tend to expand in advanced societies; that, as the presence of religion as such dwindles, the

individual becomes the object of a kind of religion; a cult of personal dignity arises. In *Le Suicide* (Paris: Félix Alcan, 1897), 382, he gives greater attention (as he will in his 1898 essay on "la religion de l'humanité") to the ways that individuality acquires a religious character: "Originally society is everything, the individual nothing.... But, bit by bit, things change. As societies grow in size and density, they become more complex, work is divided, individual differences multiply, and we see the moment approaching when the members of the same human group will have nothing in common, except that they are all people. In these conditions, it's inevitable that collective sentiment attaches with all its strength to the one unique object remaining to it, communicating, in so doing, an incomparable value. Since human personhood is the only thing that touches all hearts, since its glorification is the only goal that can be pursued, it is bound to acquire exceptional importance in everyone's eyes. It thus rises well above all human ends, taking on a religious character."

19. Simmel, *Über sociale Differenzierung*, 64.

20. Simmel, *Über sociale Differenzierung*, 129.

21. Simmel, *Über sociale Differenzierung*, 33.

22. Simmel, *Über sociale Differenzierung*, 97, 33. See my earlier note about this rendering of Schleiermacher's phrase.

23. The Caesar/Luther example appears in the second edition, in which Simmel writes further of the "intermediate zone in which a reproduction takes place" and posited "evolutionarily transmitted interpretive faculties," while cautioning that it was perhaps merely a "methodological fiction." "Phenomena occur as if this sort of latent correspondence between our minds and the minds of completely different persons really obtained. In this case, the hypothesis may be regarded as a symbolic expression of the as-yet-unknown energies that are actually responsible for the existence of these phenomena." Georg Simmel, *Die Probleme der Geschichtsphilosophie. Eine Erkenntnistheoretische Studie*, 2nd ed. (Leipzig: Duncker & Humblot, 1905), 57, 60, 61.

24. Georg Simmel, *Einleitung in die Moralwissenschaft: Eine Kritik der ethischen Grundbegriffe* (Berlin: Wilhelm Hertz, 1892–1893), 1:444. (Later facimile printings of this work were issued by J. G. Cotta.) I should mention that *Einleitung in die Moralwissenschaft* is sometimes referred to in English as *Introduction to Moral Science*, but this invites confusion with the term "moral sciences," in the usage popularized by William Whewell, J. S. Mill, and others, which encompasses psychology, philosophy, political economy, and more. Of course, "science," as I've mentioned, is itself a troublesome rendering of *Wissenschaft*.

25. Simmel, *Einleitung*, 1:69, 444, 445, 72. (Elsewhere, on 2:396, he alludes to the notion that the word "religion" derives from the Latin word *religere*, which means to bind or tie, suggesting that religion binds people to a higher power or to one another. It's a false etymology, he says, that speaks to something real.)

26. Simmel, *Einleitung*, 1:151.
27. Simmel, *Einleitung*, 1:445.
28. Simmel, *Einleitung*, 2:128–129; 1:445–446.
29. Simmel, *Einleitung*, 1:447–448.
30. Simmel, *Über sociale Differenzierung*, 81, 79.
31. Simmel, *Einleitung*, 2:22, 18.

32. In another early essay, "Notes about Spiritualism" ("Etwas vom Spiritismus," 1892), Simmel remarked on a new pervasion of scientific laws throughout society, but argued that "we, who are still in the midst of these things, still notice all sorts of countermovements and side currents. . . . we find the belief in the *spirits of deceased people* who have either returned to earth or have always been with us, and are able to communicate with us as to this and the next world through the mediation of persons with special gifts." Quoted in Jason Josephson-Storm, *The Myth of Disenchantment* (Chicago: University of Chicago Press, 2017). And see Taylor, *A Secular Age* (Cambridge, MA: Harvard University Press, 2007), 26.

33. Wilhelm Windelband, "Geschichte und Naturwissenschaft: Rede zum Antritt des Rektorats der Kaiser-Wilhelms-Universität Strassburg, gehalten am 1. Mai 1894," lecture, Kaiser-Wilhelms-Universität Strassburg, May 1, 1894. Psychologism, or *Psychologismus*—an effort to reduce logic, concepts, principles, structures of knowledge, and so on to mental phenomena or operations—arose as a charge because Dilthey could be read as reducing objective knowledge to subjective psychological processes. The charge of relativism arose because Dilthey's emphasis on understanding human phenomena within their historical and cultural contexts could be read as making truth and meaning contingent upon those specific historical or cultural contexts.

34. May 10, 1898, Letter to Heinrich Rickert, in *Buch des Dankes an Georg Simmel*, 94.

35. Heinrich Rickert, *Kulturwissenschaft und Naturwissenschaft: ein Vortrag* (Freiburg: Mohr, 1899). Husserl, notably, viewed the distinction between *Geist* and *Kultur*, in marking the disciplinary contrast with natural science, to be nothing more than a nomenclatural quibble. What mattered, he said, "was the radical ontological and phenomenological divisions to which the terminology was to be related." Husserl, *Natur und Geist: Vorlesungen Sommersemester 1919* (Dordrecht: Springer, 2002), 140. See also the discussion of Rickert's philosophy of value in Frederick C. Beiser, *The German Historicist Tradition* (New York: Oxford University Press, 2011), 393–439.

36. In Chapter 4, we'll see the influence of this line of thought on Max Weber. In Rickert's later work, notably the essay "Vom System der Werte" (On the system of values), *Logos* (1913) 4: 295–327, readable at https://www.gleichsatz.de/b-u-t/begin/rick11.html and reprinted in Heinrich Rickert, *Philosophische Aufsätze*, ed. R. A. Bast (Tübingen: Mohr-Siebeck, 1999), 73–106, and *Der System der Philosophie: Erster Teil: Allgemeine Grundlegung*

der Philosophie (Tübingen: Mohr, 1921), he correlated objective values with kinds of goods and an associated "subjective comportment" and worldview: for example, the objective value of beauty, the good of art, the subject comportment of intuition or *Anschauung*, the worldview of aestheticism. In the 1913 essay, he also introduces the concept of the "social-ethical" and puts it to work. A taste for binaries is apparent in his remarks about historical religions: "Yes, wherever one believes in a personal God, alongside whom the multitude of individual souls retains their independence, the decisive contrast to monism and pantheism emerges. Furthermore, historical religions are to be understood as structures in which elements from both types come together. For example, Christian mysticism can be understood as a hybrid form that combines personality values of social activity with pantheistic ideals of asocial contemplation."

37. Wolff credits an 1898 work by J. H. W. Stuckenberg with the coinage. See the discussion in Kurt. H. Wolff, "Introduction," in Wolff, ed. and trans., *The Sociology of Georg Simmel* (Glencoe, IL: Free Press, 1950), lxiii.

38. Georg Simmel, "The Problem of Sociology," *Annals of the American Academy of Political and Social Science* 6 (November 1895): 412, 422. (This article should not be confused with the excerpt of his *Soziologie* that ran under the same title in the *American Journal of Sociology* in 1909.)

39. Georg Simmel, "Zur Soziologie der Familie I," *Königlich Privilegierte Berlinische Zeitung (Vossische Zeitung)*, June 30, 1895 (Sunday suppl.), 26. And see the discussion in David Frisby, *Sociological Impressionism* (1981; London: Routledge, 2013).

40. Köhnke, *Der junge Simmel*, 377; Hans-Peter Müller and Tilman Reitz, eds. *Simmel-Handbuch: Befriffe, Haputwerke, Aktualität* (Berlin: Suhrkamp, 2018), 585–586; Frisby, *Sociological Impressionism*, 15.

41. Quoted in Köhnke, *Der junge Simmel*, 128.

42. Köhnke, *Der junge Simmel*, 20. See also the illuminating discussion in Martin Kusch, "The Sociology of Philosophical Canons: The Case of Georg Simmel," in Sandra Lapointe and Erich H. Reck, eds., *Historiography and the Formation of Philosophical Canons*, 1st ed. (London: Routledge, 2023), 97–117.

43. Heinrich Rickert to Emil Lask, July 13, 1902, in Köhnke, *Der junge Simmel*, 131. And see Kusch, "Sociology of Philosophical Canons."

44. Georg Simmel, *Briefe, 1880–1911, Gesamtausgabe* 22, ed. K. C. Köhnke (Frankfurt am Main: Suhrkamp, 2005); Köhnke, *Der junge Simmel*; Frisby, *Georg Simmel*, 14–15.

45. Margarete Susman, "Erinnerungen an Simmel," in *Buch des Danken an Georg Simmel*, 280–281.

46. Georg Simmel, "A Contribution to the Sociology of Religion," in Simmel, *Essays on Religion*, ed. and trans. Horst Jürgen Helle with Ludwig Nieder (New Haven: Yale University Press, 1997), 101, translating Georg Simmel, "Zur Soziologie der Religion," *Neue deutsche Rundschau* 9, nos. 1/2 (1898): 111–123. Simmel had absorbed Windelband's earlier warning against

conflating "genetic" and "critical" methods—about supposing (in the Nietzschean way) that an explanation of how values arose therefore undermined their validity. Simmel elsewhere suggested that Nietzsche had made this error. Windelband, "Kritische oder genetische Methode?" (1883), reprinted in Windelband, *Präludien: Aufsätze und Reden zur Philosophie und ihrer Geschichte* (Tübingen: Mohr-Siebeck, 1915), 2:99–135.

47. Simmel, "Contribution to the Sociology of Religion," 102, 103.
48. Simmel, "Contribution to the Sociology of Religion," 104.
49. Simmel, "Contribution to the Sociology of Religion," 107, 106.
50. Simmel, "Contribution to the Sociology of Religion," 108, 109.
51. Simmel, "Contribution to the Sociology of Religion," 111, 112.
52. Simmel, "Contribution to the Sociology of Religion," 113, 114, 115, 112; "the entire existing unity" appears in Georg Simmel, *Sociology: Inquiries into the Construction of Social Forms*, vol. 1, trans. and ed. Anthony J. Blasi, Anton K. Jacobs, and Mathew Kanjirathinkal (Leiden: Brill, 2009), 41. For the original German version, see Georg Simmel, *Soziologie: Untersuchungen über die Formen der Vergesellschaftung* (Leipzig: Verlag von Duncker & Humblot, 1908).
53. Simmel, "Contribution to the Sociology of Religion," 115.
54. Simmel, "The Problem of Religion Today [1911]," in Simmel, *Essays on Religion*, 8; Simmel, "Contribution to the Sociology of Religion," 119.
55. Simmel, "Contributions to the Epistemology of Religion," in Simmel, *Essays on Religion*, 122. Originally published as Georg Simmel, "Beiträge zur Erkenntnistheorie der Religion," *Zeitschrift für Philosophie und philosophische Kritik* 119 (1902): 11–22.
56. *Buch des Dankes an Georg Simmel*, 102–103.
57. Georg Simmel, "Religion," in Simmel, *Essays on Religion*, 203, 207, 208.
58. Simmel, "Religion," 159.
59. Simmel, "Religion," 210, 211, 204, 207, 202.
60. Ernst Troeltsch, "Zur modernen Religionsphilosophie," *Deutsche Literaturzeitung* 28 (1907): 838–841, at 841. (Cited in Kusch, "Sociology of Philosophical Canons.") Yet Troeltsch, in his 1912 *Social Teachings of the Christian Church (Die Soziallehren der christlichen Kirchen und Gruppen)*, developed this thesis further in his argument about universalism and individualism in the primitive church, in which "out of an absolute individualism there arises a universalism which is equally absolute. Both these aspects of the Gospel are based entirely upon religion; their support is the thought of the Holy Divine Will of Love, and they mutually aid each other quite logically. . . . The main thing we notice is the transformation of life-values and the emergence of a new ideal of humanity, arising out of the destruction of the militaristic and polytheistic nationalist and conquering states. The emphasis on the independence of personality in individuals and the universal idea of humanity is due to Monotheism. The ideal of a humanity based on spiritual freedom and fellowship, in which tyranny, law, war, and force

are unknown, was due to the development of a purified and deepened faith in God, which arose over against the polytheistic cults which sanctioned the existing social order with its basis of force. Although these new ideas were very similar, they gained acceptance in very different ways and their course of development was very varied. Finally, however, the underlying unity asserted itself and a new sociological and socio-political ideal arose. This ideal, which was the result of all these efforts and aspirations, maintained its intensity and independence over against the purely secular institutions which had arisen out of the struggle for existence and their legal modifications, even after they had lost their polytheistic sanction." Troeltsch, *Social Teachings* (New York: Macmillan, 1931), 1:57, 68.

61. Georg Simmel, "The Sociology of Secrecy and of Secret Societies," *American Journal of Sociology* 11, no. 4 (January 1906): 441–498, at 448, 450.

62. Simmel, *Sociology*, 1:163, 47, 46.

63. Quoted in *Buch des Dankes an Georg Simmel: Briefe, Erinnerungen, Bibliographie*, ed. Kurt Gassen and Michael Landmann (1958; Berlin: Duncker & Humbolt, 1993), 27.

64. Georg Simmel, "Fundamental Religious Ideas and Modern Science: An Inquiry [1909]," in Simmel, *Essays on Religion*, 6.

65. Georg Simmel, "The Sociology of Conflict," trans. A. W. Small, *American Journal of Sociology* 5, no. 4 (January 1904): 503–504.

66. Georg Simmel, "On the Concept and the Tragedy of Culture," in Simmel, *The Conflict in Modern Culture and Other Essays*, trans. Peter Etzkorn (New York: Teachers College Press, 1968), 30, 35; Simmel, "Religion," 209.

67. Simmel, "Contributions to the Epistemology of Religion," 121.

68. See Efraim Podoksik, "Neo-Kantianism and Georg Simmel's Interpretation of Kant," *Modern Intellectual History* 13, no. 3 (November 2016): 597–622; quoting the 3rd ed. (1913) of Simmel's *Kant*, collected in Georg Simmel, *Kant. Die Probleme der Geschichtsphilosophie*, vol. 9 of *Gesamtausgabe, 24 Bde.* (Frankfurt am Main: Suhrkamp, 1997), 62.

69. Wilhelm Dilthey, "Das Problem der Religion" (1911), reprinted in Wilhelm Dilthey, *Gesammelte Schriften, 6 Die geistige Welt: Einleitung in die Philosophie des Lebens* (Leipzig: Teubner, 1924), 288–305, at 304.

70. Margarete Susman, *Das Nah- und Fernsein des Fremden: Essays und Briefe* (Frankfurt: Jüdischer Verlag, 1992), 56.

71. Simmel, "The Problem of Religion Today," *Essays on Religion*, 16, 18, 17. In the original text of the last quote, Simmel is specifically referring to the "religious nature": he writes, "Die religiöse Natur steht niemals im Leeren, weil sie die Fülle in sich hat," in Georg Simmel, "Das Problem der Religiösen Lage," in Max Frischeisen-Köhler, ed., *Weltanschauung* (Berlin: Verlag Reichl & Co., 1911), 337, 338. See also Charles Taylor, *A Secular Age* (Cambridge, MA: Harvard University Press, 2007), 769.

72. Volkhard Krech, *Georg Simmels Religionstheorie* (Tübingen: Mohr Siebeck, 1998), 266.

73. Letter to Adolf Harnack, January 3, 1914, in *Buch des Dankes an Georg Simmel*, 82.

74. For intellectual historians, Nietzsche, Dilthey, and Simmel are all associated with *Lebensphilosophie*, but Beiser notes that Simmel was the only one of them who referred to himself as a *Lebensphilosoph*. The larger grouping is a retrospective one. See Frederick C. Beiser, *Philosophy of Life: German Lebensphilosophie, 1870–1920* (Oxford: Oxford University Press, 2023), 3.

75. Henri Bergson, *Creative Evolution*, trans. Arthur Mitchell (New York: Henry Holt, 1911), xxiii.

76. Henri Bergson, *Correspondances*, ed. André Robinet, Nelly Bruyère, Brigitte Sitbon-Peillon, and Suzanne Stern-Gillet (Paris: Presses Universitaires du France, 2002), 234.

77. Patrick Watier, "The War Writings of Georg Simmel," *Theory, Culture & Society* 8, no. 3 (1991): 219–233. And see Ralph Leck, "Simmel's Afterlife: Tropic Politics and the Culture of War," *New German Critique* 75 (Autumn 1998): 109–132.

78. *Buch des Dankes an Georg Simmel*, 133.

79. Georg Simmel, "The Conflict in Modern Culture," in Simmel, *The Conflict in Modern Culture and Other Essays*, trans. K. Peter Etzkorn (New York: Teachers College Press, 1968), 24, 25. Translated from Simmel, *Der Konflikt der modernen Kultur*, 2nd ed. (Munich: Dunker & Humblot, 1921).

80. I'm drawing from Margarete Susman, "Erinnerungen an Georg Simmel," in *Buch des Dankes an Georg Simmel*, 281–282; Käte Ledermann, "Esther in Freundschaft—zu ihren 50. Geburtstag und zwanzigjährigem Im-Lande-Sein," *Simmel Newsletter* 4, no. 1 (1994): 78–91; Richard Swedberg and Wendelin Reich, "Georg Simmel's Aphorisms," *Theory, Culture & Society* 27, no. 1 (2010): 26–27, 45–46.

81. Georg Simmel, *The View of Life*, trans. John A. Y. Andrews and Donald N. Levine (Chicago: University of Chicago Press, 2010), 54, 55. Originally published in German as *Lebensanschauung: Vier metaphysische Kapitel* (Duncker & Humblot, 1918).

82. Simmel, "Appendix: Journal Aphorisms," in Simmel, *View of Life*, 164.

83. Simmel, "Contributions to the Epistemology of Religion," 121.

84. Simmel, *The Conflict in Modern Culture and Other Essays*, ed. and trans. K. Peter Etzkorn (New York: Teachers College Press, 1968), 25; Donald N. Levine and Daniel Silver, "Introduction," in Simmel, *View of Life*, xxvii.

CHAPTER 4. MAX WEBER

The biographical and textual attention that Weber has received is oceanic. For much of the twentieth century, Americans seemed more devoted to his work than his compatriots were; his compatriots have caught up. The *Max Weber-Gesamtausgabe*, which was in the works for decades (the volumes have appeared from 1984 to 2020; preparations started much earlier), is an astonishing achievement: a team of dedicated scholars has annotated to a fare-thee-well almost every page Weber ever wrote. Weber has also been blessed with some remarkable biographers, not least Joachim Radkau, whose deeply researched, highly readable work is more than a thousand pages in the German original. (I have mainly restricted my references to the thoughtfully truncated English edition.) I've also benefited from the rich social history of Dirk Kaesler's equally immense and well-researched biography of 2014—and from Jürgen Kaube's comparatively svelte volume marking the same 150th anniversary, a work that is consistently shrewd and often witty. (Again, I may not provide citations for widely shared biographical information.) Peter Ghosh's *Max Weber and "The Protestant Ethic"* is exemplary in being both intellectually penetrating and textually punctilious. Given my interests in this chapter, I've found particular illumination in scholarship by Edith Hanke and Hartmann Tyrell.

1. Joachim Radkau, *Max Weber: A Biography*, trans. Patrick Camiller (Cambridge: Polity, 2009), 40. This volume is an abridged (though also supplemented) version of what was originally published as *Max Weber: Die Leidenschaft des Denkens* (Munich: Carl Hanser Verlag, 2005); Max Weber to Marianne Schitgner, January 16, 1893, in *Max Weber Gesamtausgabe*, part 2, vol. 2, ed. Horst Baier et al. (Tübingen: J.C.B. Mohr [Paul Siebeck], 1994), 302. Hereafter cited in the customary way as *MWG*, without date of publication but with section (*Abteilung*), volume (*Bande*), and, where indicated, part (*Teile*) numerically designated.

2. Letter to Helene Weber, written on July 8, 18, and 19, 1884, in *MWG* II/1:431. The "chasm" is from letter to Helene Weber, December 6, 1885, *MWG* II/2:569. And see Radkau, *Max Weber*, 41, 15, 17. The most detailed account of the parents' marriage can be found in Dirk Kaesler's biography; Max senior—Wilhelm Maximilian Weber—evaded his family's plans for a "cousin marriage" when he found the seventeen-year-old Helene, thus, as Kaesler notes, "establishing a union with the wealthy Hamburg branch of the Weber family." This isn't to say that the union was not a loving one; still, Kaesler detects "the self-confident stance of an ambitious social climber who seeks not only his own—and risky—path in professional politics but also diverges from a predetermined path of an arranged marriage." Dirk Kaesler, *Max Weber: Preuße, Denker, Muttersohn* (Munich: C.H. Beck, 2014), 88.

3. Max Weber to Alfred Weber, March 25, 1884, *MWG* II/1:405–406. (The counsel didn't quite take; Ernst Troeltsch later complained that Alfred disliked Christians.) The intellectual historian Peter Ghosh goes so far as to contend that the religious conception of religion found in Weber's *The Protestant Ethic* and other later work is essentially to be found in this letter, stressing the power of Christianity abstracted from specific religious belief. Peter Ghosh, *Max Weber and "The Protestant Ethic": Twin Histories* (Oxford: Oxford University Press, 2014), 93.

4. Historicism (or *Historismus*, which Ernst Troeltsch introduced as a categorical term in the modern sense) was, as we saw in the discussion of Simmel, a critique that became caught up in another critique: in a formula, it cured reification but courted relativism.

5. "*Sie* wollen 'persönliche' Bücher schreiben. *Ich* bin der Überzeugung, dass die persönliche Eigenart (die Sie ganz sicher in starkem Maße besitzen), immer dann und *nur* dann zum Ausdruck kommt, wenn sie *ungewollt* ist, hinter dem Buch und seiner Sachlichkeit zurücktritt." Max Weber to Werner Sombart, July 16, 1908, *MWG* II/5: 605. Cf. Ghosh, *Max Weber and "The Protestant Ethic*," 4.

6. As we'll see, the idea of the individual entity in history is conceptually fraught. The "historical individual" (*das historisches Individuum*) for Rickert, in a usage Weber evidently adopted, was any object we were conscious of as a particular thing. As we're told in the first installment of Rickert, *Die Grenzen der naturwissenschaftlichen Begriffsbildung* (Tübingen: J.C.B. Mohr [Paul Siebeck], 1896), 394: "The Italian renaissance is just as much a historical individual as Machiavelli, the Romantic school as much as Novalis." For Rickert, theory dissolved such individuals, and the challenge was that reality consisted of them. (See, e.g., Rickert, *Die Grenzen*, 236–241.) Weber himself thought that we needed constructs to come to grips with individuals. See also Wolfgang Schluchter's intricate discussion in *The Rise of Western Rationalism*, trans. Guenther Roth (Berkeley: University of California Press, 1981), 15–17.

7. Weber's *Doktorarbeit*, his *Habilitationsschrift*, and a commissioned study of the condition of farmworkers in Eastern Germany appeared in 1889, 1891, and 1892. The textual perplexities of his posthumous works are discussed, inter alia, in Friedrich H. Tenbruck, "The Problem of Thematic Unity in the Works of Max Weber," *British Journal of Sociology*, 31, no. 3, special issue (September 1980): 316–335; Wolfgang Schluchter, " 'Wirtschaft und Gesellschaft': Das Ende eines Mythos," in Schluchter, *Religion und Lebensführung* (Frankfurt am Main: Suhrkamp, 1988), 2:597–634; Wolfgang J. Mommsen, "Max Weber's 'Grand Sociology': The Origins and Composition of *Wirtschaft und Gesellschaft: Soziologie*," *History and Theory* 39, no. 3 (October 2000): 364–383; and Sam Whimster, "Translator's Note on Weber's 'Introduction to the Economic Ethics of the World Religions,' " *Max Weber Studies* 3, no. 1 (November 2002): 74–98.

8. Jürgen Kaube, *Max Weber: Ein Leben zwischen den Epochen* (Berlin: Rowoht, 2014), 64.

9. Weber had written "nur wenn man nicht mehr *kann*, darf man aufhören": see Max Weber to Helene Weber, January 24 and 25, 1886, *MWG* II/1:579, 580. Jürgen Kaube draws attention to this passage in his *Max Weber*, 427.

10. Max Weber to Alfred Weber, March 7, 1886, *MWG* II/1:590–594, quoting from 591–593. (The quote is from a poem of Goethe's, "Beherzigung.")

11. Max Weber, *Zur Geschichte der Handelgesellschaften im Mittelalter* (1889); published as *The History of Commercial Partnerships in the Middle Ages*, trans. Lutz Kaelber (Lanham, MD: Rowman & Littlefield, 2003).

12. Max Weber, *Die römische Agrargeschichte in ihrer Bedeutung für das Staats-und Privatrecht* (Stuttgart: F. Enke, 1891); available in English as *Roman Agrarian History and Its Significance for Public and State Law*, trans. Richard I. Frank (Claremont, CA: Regina Books, 2008).

13. "Das Graulen vor dem 'schwarzen Mann' liegt unsren Liberalen nun einmal im Blut und läßt sie in jedem Pastor eigentlich einen zum Heuchler mindestens veranlagten Menschen vermuthen." Max Weber to Marianne Schnitger, June 2, 1893, in *MWG* II/2:394.

14. See Paul Honigsheim, "Max Weber: His Religious and Ethical Background and Development," *Church History* 19, no. 4 (December 1950): 219–239.

15. Marianne Weber, *Max Weber: A Biography*, trans. Harry Zohn, reprint ed. (London: Routledge, 1988), 230–233; originally published in German as *Max Weber—ein Lebensbild* (Tübingen: Mohr Siebeck, 1926). I've slightly modified Zohn's translation. See also Joachim Radkau, *Max Weber*, 7.

16. Radkau, *Max Weber*, 147, 533.

17. Donald G. MacRae, *Max Weber* (New York: Viking, 1974), 30.

18. Weber's essay, or monograph, was published as "Roscher und Knies und die logischen Probleme der historischen Nationaloekonomie," and appeared in Schmoller's *Jahrbuch für Gesetzgebung, Verwaltung und Volkswirtschaft*. In English, it has been published as a separate book as *Roscher and Knies: The Logical Problem, of Historical Economics*, trans. Guy Oakes (New York: Free Press, 1975). I'll be quoting from a later version: Max Weber, "Roscher and Knies and the Logical Problems of Historical Economics," in Weber, *Collected Methodological Writings*, ed. Hans Henrik Bruun and Sam Whimster, trans. Hans Herik Bruun (London: Routledge, 2012); and see Kaube, *Max Weber*, 145, 149.

19. Weber, "Roscher and Knies," 12, 24, 29, 32, 14.

20. Weber, "Roscher and Knies," 10.

21. Weber, "Roscher and Knies," 21.

22. Weber, "Roscher and Knies," 22.

23. Guenther Roth, "Edgar Jaffé and Else von Richthofen in the Mirror of Newly Found Letters," *Max Weber Studies* 10, no. 2 (July 2010): 151–188.

24. Translated as " 'Objectivity' in Social Science and Social Policy" in *Max Weber on the Methodology of the Social Sciences*, trans. and ed. Edward A. Shils and Henry A. Finch (Glencoe, IL: Free Press, 1949), 49–50, 57, 71, 72. Simmel was not the first to talk of *Wirklichkeitswissenschaft*, but his particular usage was influential. See Simmel, *Die Probleme der Geschichtsphilosophie: Eine erkenntnistheoretische Studie* (Leipzig: Duncker & Humblot, 1892), 43. Heinrich Rickert used the term as far back as the first edition of the first part of his *Die Grenzen der naturwissenschaftlichen Begriffsbildung*, 255, 263, 265, 285, etc. Cf. Hans Henrik Bruun, *Science, Values, and Politics in Max Weber's*

Methodology, new exp. ed. (London: Routledge, 2007), 117, 129, disputing F. H. Tenbruck's suggestion that the term is a key to Weber's thought.

25. Weber, " 'Objectivity' in Social Science and Policy," 71.

26. Weber, " 'Objectivity' in Social Science and Policy," 71. Weber's last sentence here, in full: "The fate of an epoch which has eaten of the tree of knowledge is that it must know that we cannot learn the *meaning* of the world from the results of its analysis, be it ever so perfect; it must rather be in a position to create this meaning itself. It must recognize that general views of life and the universe can never be the products of increasing empirical knowledge, and that the highest ideals, which move us most forcefully, are always formed only in the struggle with other ideals which are just as sacred to others as ours are to us." ("Das Schicksal einer Kulturepoche, die vom Baum der Erkenntnis gegessen hat, ist es, wissen zu müssen, dass wir den *Sinn* des Weltgeschehens nicht aus dem noch so sehr vervollkommneten Ergebnis seiner Durchforschung ablesen können, sondern ihn selbst zu schaffen imstande sein müssen, dass 'Weltanschauungen' niemals *Produkt* fortschreitenden Erfahrungswissens sein können, und dass also die höchsten Ideale, die uns am mächtigsten bewegen, für alle Zeit nur im Kampf mit anderen Idealen sich auswirken, die anderen ebenso heilig sind, wie uns die unseren.") There are similarities with Habermas's thesis, from the 1960s, about "knowledge-constitutive interests."

27. Weber, " 'Objectivity' in Social Science and Social Policy," 90. There are notable similarities with the arguments developed by the neo-Kantian Hans Vaihinger, the first part of whose *Philosophy of As-If* (1911) was taken from his own 1877 *Habilitationsschrift*, "Logical Studies on Fictions. Part I: The Theory of Scientific Fictions." *Logische Untersuchungen. I. Teil: Die Lehre von der wissenschaftlichen Fiktion.*

28. Early copies of the *Archiv* issue containing the first part were available in late 1904, Peter Baehr and Gordon C. Wells tell us, but the issue really appeared in 1905. See "Editors' Introduction" in Max Weber, *The Protestant Ethic and the "Spirit" of Capitalism: And Other Writings*, ed. and trans. Peter Baehr and Gordon C. Wells (New York: Penguin, 2002), xliin1. Theirs is the sole full translation of the original version of *The Protestant Ethic* in English, and is the version I'll be quoting from. Talcott Parsons's 1930 rendering of the 1920 edition was the only version of the book available to English readers in the twentieth century. (Stephen Kalberg published a new translation of that text in 2001). Baehr and Wells, in their edition, do an excellent job of assessing the differences between the 1905 and the 1920 texts; an exhaustive concordance can be found in *Die protestantische Ethik und der 'Geist' des Kapitalismus*, ed. Klaus Lichtbau and Johannes Weiß (Weinheim: Beltz, 1993).

29. Thomas Nipperdey, "Max Weber, Protestantism, and the Context of the Debate around 1900," in *Weber's Protestant Ethic: Origins, Evidence, Contexts*, ed. Hartmut Lehmann and Guenther Roth (Cambridge: Cambridge University Press, 1987), 73–81, esp. 74–76.

30. For quotations in this paragraph and the next, see Weber, *Protestant Ethic*, 3–4.

31. Weber, *Protestant Ethic*, 9. Aristotle, *Nicomachean Ethics*, 1094b, 24–28, available online at the Perseus Catalog; see https://www.perseus.tufts.edu/hopper/text?doc=Perseus%3Atext%3A1999.01.0054%3Abekker+page%3D1094b%3Abekker+line%3D20.

32. Weber, *Protestant Ethic*, 70.

33. Weber, *Protestant Ethic*, 73.

34. Matthew 6:19, KJV.

35. Weber, *Protestant Ethic*, 117.

36. Weber, *Protestant Ethic*, 27, 144. By contrast, Weber argues, "religious *ideas*—as Calvinism demonstrates particularly well—are of *far* greater significance than someone like William James . . . is inclined to admit," citing James's *Varieties of Religious Experience*. (Although Weber's references to James are few, scholars tell us that Weber's copy of the German translation of *Varieties of Religious Experience* that appeared in 1910 was densely filigreed with scribbled notes.)

37. Georg Simmel, *The Philosophy of Money*, ed. David Frisby, 3rd ed., trans. Tom Bottomore and David Frisby (London: Routledge, 2004), 474.

38. A more obvious presence was Martin Offenbacher's statistical study *Konfession und soziale Schichtung: Eine Studie über die wirtschaftliche Lage der Katholiken und Protestanten in Baden* (*Denomination and Social Stratification: A Study of the Economic Situation of Catholics and Protestants in Baden*), a 1900 dissertation that Weber supervised. (Its results have since been disputed by statisticians.) Offenbacher had written that economic advancement came with the legitimization of the acquisitive drive (*Erwerbstrieb*) in the wake of Calvin. But Peter Ghosh plausibly conjectures that Weber was the offstage prompter behind the sentiment.

39. Weber, *Protestant Ethic*, 120, 121.

40. Years after the "Protestant Ethic" essays came out, Weber marveled that they had scarcely made mention of the "canonical prohibition on taking interest." Sombart himself pursued this thesis further in his 1911 essays "The Jews and Economic Life." (Jürgen Kaube astutely notes that an "antisemitic aroma" arises less from the specific claims than from the way Sombart wrote about them.) Veblen, in a review of Sombart's *Modern Capitalism*—see Thorstein Veblen, "Review of *Modern Capitalism*," *Journal of Political Economy* 11 (1903): 300–305—was puzzled that Sombart saw capitalism arising in Italy and Germany, rather than in Britain and the United States. Weber agreed with Veblen on this.

41. "Zweck einer kapitalistischen Stiefelfabrik ist niemals die Anfertigung von Stiefeln, sondern immer nur die Erzielung von Profit" is from Werner Sombart, *Der moderne Kapitalismus* (Leipzig: Duncker & Humblot, 1902), 51.

42. Albrecht Ritschi, *Die christliche Lehre von der Rechtfertigung und Versöhnung* (Bonn: Adolf Marcus, 1870–1874), also published as Ritschi,

The Christian Doctrine of Justification and Reconciliation trans. and ed. H. R. Mackintosh and A. B. Macaulay (Edinburgh: T.&T. Clark, 1902), 14, 27. "Justification"—a key element of Lutheran doctrine—refers to the act in which God expiates the sins of believers and declares them righteous through the imputation of Christ's righteousness; "reconciliation" is the restoration of the sinner's relationship to God, "adoption into the position of children," which again is a divine act achieved through Christ's sacrifice.

43. Weber's view of Lutheranism was decidedly less benign. In 1906, he wrote to a theologian acquaintance, "Lutheranism is for me, I do not deny it, in its *historical* forms the most terrible of terrors." Max Weber to Adolf Harnack, February 5, 1906: "das Luther*tum* ist für mich, ich leugne es nicht, in seinen *historischen* Erscheinungsformen der schrecklichste der Schrecken." *MWG* II/5:32.

44. Ritschl, *Christian Doctrine of Justification and Reconciliation*, 28.

45. Weber, *Protestant Ethic*, 75.

46. Max Weber, " 'Churches' and 'Sects' in North America (1906)," in Weber, *Protestant Ethic*, 206.

47. Martin Green says that Karl Jaspers later counseled Marianne to destroy the document. Martin Green, *The von Richthofen Sisters* (New York: Basic Books, 1974), 291. Weber described the *Protestant Ethic* as his "Hauptarbeit" in a letter to Rickert, June 14, 1904, *MWG* II/4:231.

48. Kaube, *Max Weber*, 282; Eberhard Demm, "Max and Alfred Weber and Their Female Entourage," *Max Weber Studies* 17, no. 1 (January 2017): 64–91, 70.

49. Max Weber to Marianne Weber, March 7, 1911. (She was off on a lecture tour.) *MWG* II/7.1:130. Radkau, *Max Weber*, 352–353, 366.

50. Radkau, *Max Weber*, 337.

51. Max Weber to Ferdinand Tönnies, February 19, 1909, in *MWG* II/6:65. The book he refers to is by Gertrud Simmel writing as Marie Luise Enckendorff, *Vom Sein und vom Haben der Seele: Aus einem Tagebuch* (Leipzig: Duncker & Humblot, 1906), or *On the Being and the Having of the Soul: From a Diary*, with the relevant passage on page 4. A tree develops from a seed that contains its form, she argues, but a tree that is damaged or constrained, though still perceptibly a tree, is "less of a tree, it corresponds more imperfectly to its own form and nature; it expresses not only itself but something foreign—and when the foreign overwhelms it, it exists no more. Thus our soul is like a tree that follows its law—that is, expresses itself—or that cannot unfold and withers. The duty of the tree is its form."

52. Friedrich Schleiermacher, *On Religion: Speeches to Its Cultured Despisers*, trans. and ed. Richard Crouter (Cambridge: Cambridge University Press, 1996), 30, 55. Radkau, *Max Weber*, 532, echoing Fredric Jameson's identification of a "curious" attitude that "combines something of the allure of a religiously fellow-travelling agnosticism with the secret inferiority longings of the impotent in matters of belief," in his "The Vanishing Mediator," *New German Critique* 1 (Winter 1973): 62; Kaube, *Max Weber*, 289; Max Weber to Marianne Weber, January 22, 1911, *MWG* II/7.1:58.

53. "Es könnte sogar sein, daß ich einer *bin*. Wie ich mehr in meinem Leben *geträumt* habe als man sich eigentlich erlauben darf, so bin ich auch nirgends *ganz* verläßlich daheim. Es ist, als könnte (und wollte) ich mich aus *allem* ebensowohl auch *ganz* zurückziehen." Eduard Baumgarten, *Max Weber: Werk und Person* (Tubingen: Mohr Siebeck, 1964), 677.

54. Sam Whimster, "Introduction to Weber, Ascona, and Anarchism," in Whimster, ed., *Max Weber and the Culture of Anarchy* (Houndmills, UK: Palgrave Macmillan, 1999), 10; Max Weber to Robert Wilbrandt, *MWG* II/8:165.

55. "Subjektiv zweckrational orientiertes und am objektiv Gültigen 'richtig' orientiertes ('richtigkeitsrationales') Handeln sind an sich gänzlich zweierlei. Dem Forscher kann ein von ihm zu erklärendes Handeln im höchsten Grade zweckrational, dabei aber an für ihn ganz ungültigen Annahmen des Handelnden orientiert erscheinen. An magischen Vorstellungen orientiertes Handeln beispielsweise ist subjektiv oft weit zweckrationaleren Charakters als irgendein nicht magisches 'religiöses' Sichverhalten, da die Religiosität ja gerade mit zunehmender Entzauberung der Welt zunehmend (subjektiv) zweckirrationalere Sinnbezogenheiten ('gesinnungshafte' oder mystische z.B.) anzunehmen genötigt ist." In Max Weber, "Über einige Kategorien der verstehenden Soziologie" *Logos* 4 (1913): 253–294; reprinted in *MWG* I/12:389–440, at 397. The essay was translated by Edith E. Graber as "Some Categories of Interpretive Sociology," *Sociological Quarterly* 22, no. 2 (Spring 1981): 151–180, at 154–155.

56. Weber, "Some Categories of Interpretive Sociology," 159, 160. This essay introduces *Gemeinschaftshandeln* and *Gesellschaftshandeln* (held to be equivalent to *Vergesellschaftetes Handeln*), without the broader category of *soziales Handeln* that stippled later work of Weber's.

57. Weber, "Some Categories of Interpretive Sociology," 158.

58. The word *Individualismus*, which gained currency in the mid-nineteenth century, was regularly used (including by Simmel) as a synonym for *Individualität*. Steven Lukes, "The Meanings of 'Individualism,' " *Journal of the History of Ideas* 32, no. 1 (January–March 1971): 45–66.

59. Georg Simmel, *Sociology: Inquiries into the Construction of Social Forms*, vol. 1, trans. and ed. Anthony J. Blasi, Anton K. Jacobs, and Mathew Kanjirathinkal (Leiden: Brill, 2009), 636–640; originally published in 1908 as *Soziologie: Untersuchungen uber die Formen der Vergesellschaftung*. "The individualism of equivalency, which is not from the outset a *contradictio in adjecto* only if under 'individualism' one understands independence and freedom not limited by any narrow social bond, and the individualism of inequality, which draws the consequence of that freedom on the basis of the infinite variety of human capabilities and thus makes them incompatible with equivalency—both of these forms of individualism are found in their basic opposition together at one point: that each one finds the possibility of its development in the measure in which the circle around the individual provides it the stimulus and material through its quantitative expansion of

the room for that purpose" (Simmel, *Sociology*, 640). Cf. Hartmann Tyrell, *"Religion" in der Soziologie Max Webers* (Weisbaden: Harrassowitz Verlag, 2014), xvi. With respect to Simmel's emphasis on the "interactive" nature of social relations (*Wechselwirkung*), Weber, in unpublished notes on Simmel, complained that this was too universal a phenomenon—in physics as in society—to carry much weight. See Weber, *Collected Methodological Writings*, 418–421.

60. "Stets ist (im Sinn unserer Terminologie) wertrationales Handeln ein Handeln nach 'Geboten' oder gemäß 'Forderungen,' die der Handelnde an sich gestellt glaubt" (Value-rational behavior [in the sense of our terminology] is always behavior according to "commandments" or in compliance with "demands" that the actor believes to be imposed on him.) "Soziologische Grundbegriffe, II: Begriff des sozialen Handelns," *MWG* 1:23, 176.

61. Rogers Brubaker, *The Limits of Rationality: An Essay on the Social and Moral Thought of Max Weber* (London: Routledge, 1984), 2, 36.

62. Max Weber to Paul Siebeck, December 30, 1913, in *MWG* II/8:449–450.

63. Max to Helene Weber, May 16, 1882, MWG II/1: 270–271; Eduard von Hartmann, *Die Selbstzersetzung des Christenthums und Die Religion der Zukunft* (Berlin: Carl Duncker's Verlag, 1873), 13. On law religions versus salvation religions, see Otto Pfleiderer, *Religionsphilosophie auf geschichtlicher Grundlage* (Berlin: G. Reimer, 1878), 725, 726. Pfleiderer had written at length on the rationalization of theology, and about how a universalist morality arose amid the evolution of religion. In his Gifford lectures of 1894, Pfleiderer said that "the family is the oldest religious community, and only as such did it become a moral fellowship." Paternal authority is grounded in the father's role of the "performer of the rites of domestic worship." The circle of moral obligation, in this primitive phase, is limited to the family. But in time, the narrow circle expands; civil society broadens as citizens are united through common obligation to the city's gods. There was no distinction to be drawn between religion and morality. Eventually, though, morality "advances unceasingly forward; its circles widen," while religion hews to custom, purveying old dogmas that are a "hindrance to the rational order of society." Priests desiccated morality into lists of prohibitions and commands, and, Pfleiderer goes on, "representatives of religious authority are accustomed only too easily to confound the interests of their class with the divine will." Against this "compulsion of priestly guardianship, the sound moral sense of man rightly rebelled." Still, Pfleiderer notes, these secularized forms of morality—eudaemonist, utilitarian—were the products of people with a Christian education. And how sustainable was that great principle of universal philanthropy without Christianity: people are not all so pleasing, and some will respond to our benefactions with ingratitude or malice. The ethic requires that we look not merely at the "common reality" before us, people as we see them, but at "the indestructible divine element" within them, and, Pfleiderer says, "how can one believe in the divine *in*

man without belief in the divine which is *superior* and *prior* to man?" Otto Pfleiderer, *Philosophy and Development of Religion, Being the Gifford Lectures Delivered before the University of Edinburgh*, 1894, vol. 1 (Edinburgh: William Blackwood and Sons, 1894), 38, 42, 45, 58, 62.

64. Hermann Siebeck, *Lehrbuch der Religionsphilosophie* (Tübingen: Mohr, 1893), 444 and 48–50; I'm indebted to the discussion of sources in Hans Kippenberg, *Discovering Religious History in the Modern Age*, trans. Barbara Harshav (Princeton, NJ: Princeton University Press, 2002), and in Edith Hanke, "Erlösungsreligionen," in Hans G. Kippenberg und Martin Riesebrodt, *Max Webers "Religionssystematik"* (Tübingen: Mohr Siebeck, 2001), 209–226, for leading me to this and other little-read texts.

65. Troeltsch, *Die Absolutheit des Christentums und die Religionsgeschichte*, based on a 1901 lecture and published in an expanded edition by Mohr in 1929, then as *The Absoluteness of Christianity and the History of Religions*, trans. David Reid (Richmond: John Knox Press, 1971), 109; discussed in Edith Hanke's essay, "Erlösungsreligionen." Some regarded salvation or redemptory religions as either too narrow or too broad a category. Cornelius P. Tiele, who became the incumbent of a new chair of history of religion at Leiden in 1877, objected that, taken strictly, only Pauline Christianity and certain Indian religions qualified; taken broadly—with salvation construed as a deliverance from evil—all religions did.

66. The monograph-length manuscript, which was never finished, was published in 1922 under the title "Religionssoziologie," in Johannes Winckelmann's edition of *Wirtschaft und Gesellschaft*; and now appears, as "Religiöse Gemeinchaften," in *MWG*, I/22.2:85–448. Max Weber, "Religious Groups," in *Economy and Society*, ed. Guenther Roth and Claus Wittich, vol. 1, trans. Ephraim Fischoff (Berkeley: University of California Press, 1978), 399.

67. Weber, "Religious Groups," 400.

68. Edward Burnett Tylor, *Primitive Culture* London: John Murray, 1871), 1:20, 21.

69. Max Weber to Hans Rickert, after July 3, 1913, *MWG* II/8:262; Weber, "Die Wirtschaftsethik der Weltreligionen: Einleitung," *MWG* 1/19:119.

70. Weber, "The Definition of Sociology and of Social Action," in Weber, *Economy and Society*, 1:22.

71. Weber, "Religious Groups," 401.

72. Weber, "Religious Groups," 400–401.

73. 1 Corinthians 12:8–10, KJV.

74. Max Weber to Dora Jellinek, June 9, 1910, *MWG* II/6:560. (Dora was George Jellinek's daughter, then twenty-two.) "If the Stefan George circle already bore all the hallmarks of a sect—including, by the way, the specific charisma of such a group—the nature and manner of the Maximin cult is simply absurd because, with all its might, it fails to convey anything about this redeemer incarnation that could make his divinity credible to anyone

other than those who knew him personally," Weber writes. (He's referring to cultic adoration, in George's circle and in George's writing, of the poet prodigy Maximilian Kronberger, known as "Maximin," who was around fourteen when he came to George's attention and was scarcely sixteen when he died.)

75. Weber, "Religious Groups," 403.
76. Tylor, *Primitive Culture*, 1:117–118, 120.
77. Weber, "Religious Groups," 406, 403. Weber writes: "Nicht die Persönlichkeit oder Unpersönlichkeit oder Überpersönlichkeit, 'übersinnlicher' Mächte ist das zunächst Spezifische dieser ganzen Entwicklung, sondern: daß jetzt nicht nur Dinge und Vorgänge eine Rolle im Leben spielen, die da sind und geschehen, sondern außerdem solche, welche und weil sie etwas, bedeuten." (Where Weber refers to things and events that now play a role in life because of what they mean, Fischoff's rendering, at 403, referring to "new experiences" playing this role, distorts the line.)
78. Weber, "Religious Groups," 405.
79. Weber, "Religious Groups," 408, 409, 554.
80. "Die Wirtschaftsethik der Weltreligionen: Religionssoziologische Skizzen: Einleitung," to provide its full original title, was written in 1913, and published in the *Archiv* in September 1915, vol. 41; it then appeared in Weber, *Gesammelte Aufsätze zur Religionssoziologie* vol. 1 (Tübingen: J.C.B. Mohr [Paul Siebeck], 1920), 237–275 (in a compilation prepared by Marianne Weber and Johannes Winckelmann); and it was published in English as "The Social Psychology of World Religions," in H. H. Gerth and C. Wright Mills, trans. and eds., *From Max Weber: Essays in Sociology* (New York: Oxford University Press, 1946), 267–301. Here's the passage in full: "Und wenn auch erst die rationalisierten Religionen in jene spezifisch-religiösen Handlungen neben der umittelbaren Aneignung des Heilsgutes eine metaphysische Bedeutung hineinlegten und so die Orgie zum 'Sakrament' sublimieren, so fehlte doch schon der primitivsten Orgie eine Sinndeutung keineswegs gänzlich." (And even if it was only the rationalized religions that attributed a metaphysical significance to those specifically religious actions alongside the immediate appropriation of the means of salvation, thereby sublimating the orgy into a "sacrament," it was nevertheless the case that even the most primitive orgy was by no means entirely devoid of interpretive meaning.)
81. Weber, "Religious Groups," 413.
82. Weber, "Religious Groups," 414.
83. Weber, "Religious Groups," 424.
84. See Dirk Kaesler, *Max Weber: Preuße, Denker, Muttersohn* (Munich: C.H. Beck, 2014), 670–674; Kaube, *Max Weber*, 294–301. The most detailed recounting of the episode launched by that incensing letter to the editor can be found in Joachim Radkau, *Max Weber: Die Leidenschaft des Denkens* (Munich: Carl Hanser Verlag, 2005), 633–642; the author removed it from the English edition. A paper war against the author of the letter, an odious antisemitic *völkisch* nationalist and philosopher who was later implicated in

the assassination of Walter Rathenau and was an admirer of Hitler, became redirected toward the ruin of a less worthy target: a colleague who taught journalism and had leaked to a Dresden journalist the story that Weber had declined a challenge to a duel and evaded the obligations of *Satisfaktionsfähigkeit* by citing ill health. "He only became unrestrained in the fight when it was no longer about Marianne's feminine honor," Radkau observes, "but about his own masculine honor: namely about his readiness to duel" (634).

85. Rudolf Von Ihering, *Law as a Means to an End*, trans. Isaac Husik (Boston: Boston Book Company, 1913), 87, originally published as *Der Zweck im Recht*, in two volumes (1877, 1883). Durkheim, in his youth, wrote about Ihering—also spelled Jhering—at some length.

86. Weber, "Religious Groups," 437, 438.

87. See Sam Whimster, "Translator's Note on Weber's 'Introduction to the Economic Ethics of the World Religions,' " *Max Weber Studies* 3, no. 1 (November 2002): 74–98.

88. Because this has become a famous metaphor, in various paraphrases, we might return to his language: "Interessen (materielle und ideelle), nicht: Ideen, beherrschen unmittelbar das Handeln der Menschen. Aber: die 'Weltbilder,' welche durch 'Ideen' geschaffen wurden, haben sehr oft als Weichensteller die Bahnen bestimmt, in denen die Dynamiken der Interessen das Handeln fortbewegte." From his 1913/1920 "Die Wirtschaftsethik der Weltreligionen. Vergleichende religionssoziologische Versuche. Eine Einleitung." *MWG* I/19:83–522, at 101.

89. Max Weber to Paul Siebeck, September 7, 1914, *MWG* II/8:787; Weber to Ferdinand Tönnies, October 15, 1914, MWG II/8:799; Weber to Helene Weber, September 4, 1915, *MWG* II/9:116.

90. Max Weber to Robert Michels, June 20, 1915: "daß nicht Senegalneger und Ghurkas, Russen und Sibiriaken unser Land betreten und unser Schicksal entscheiden." *MWG* II/9:66.

91. Max Weber to Mina Tobler, November 23, 1917, in *MWG* II/9:818. The edition's annotators plausibly see an allusion to "Iron Heinrich" in the Grimm brothers' fairytale "The Frog Prince." But Weber, as other letters indicate, was also arrested by the metal collars on bondsmen in Walter Scott's *Ivanhoe*.

92. When Weber's essay was republished in *Gesammelte Schriften* (1920), its title was slightly adjusted: "Zwischenbetrachtung: Theorie der Stufen und Richtungen religiöser Weltablehnung" ("Interim Consideration: Theory of the Stages and Directions of Religious World Rejection" would be a literal rendering). I will quote from the English version translated as "Religious Rejections of the World and Their Directions," in Hans H. Gerth and C. Wright Mills, trans. and eds., *From Max Weber: Essays in Sociology* (New York: Oxford University Press, 1946). Karl Jaspers to Else Jaffé, May 1967, is quoted in Radkau, *Max Weber*, 559.

93. Weber, "Religious Rejections," 332.

94. Weber, "Religious Rejections," 355.

95. Weber, "Religious Rejections," 334.

96. Weber, "Religious Rejections," 336.

97. Weber, "Religious Rejections," 342.

98. Weber, "Religious Rejections," 343, 344, 347, 349.

99. Max Weber, *The Religion of China*, trans. Hans H. Gerth (Glencoe, IL: Free Press, 1951), 27, 83–84, 205. (Note that while the *Archiv* version was "Konfuzianismus," "Konfuzianismus und Taoismus" was the title of the revised essay as published in *Gesammelte Aufsätze zur Religionssoziologie* of 1920.)

100. Weber, *Religion of China*, 242.

101. Weber, *Religion of China*, 196, 199.

102. Weber, *Religion of China*, 200; I have slightly modified Gerth's translation. ("Mandarin" was the conventional way of referring to the Chinese literati, using a Portuguese word borrowing from Sanskrit by way of Malay.)

103. Weber, *Religion of China*, 226.

104. Weber, *Religion of China*, 227.

105. Weber, *Religion of China*, 248.

106. Weber, *Religion of China*, 229.

107. Weber, *Religion of China*, 246, 235. Notice that we're approaching Wundt's discipline of *Völkerpsychologie* in these passages.

108. See, e.g., David L. Hall and Roger T. Ames, *Thinking through Confucius* (Albany: State University of New York Press, 1987); and Youngsun Back, "Confucian Heaven: Moral Economy and Contingency," *European Journal for Philosophy of Religion* 8, no. 1 (Spring 2016): 51–77. "The ubiquity of the concept of transcendence in the Western tradition has introduced into our conceptual inventory a host of disjunctive concepts—God and the world, being and not being, subject and object, mind and body, reality and appearance, good and evil, knowledge and ignorance, and so forth—which, although wholly inappropriate to the treatment of classical Chinese philosophy, nonetheless have seriously infected the language we have been forced to employ to articulate that philosophy," Hall and Ames write. "The mutual immanence of the primary elements of the Confucian cosmos—heaven, earth and man—precludes the use of the language of transcendence and therefore renders any sort of dualistic contrast pernicious." Hall and Ames, *Thinking through Confucius*, 17.

109. See, e.g., Joseph Needham, *The Grand Titration: Science and Society in East and West* (London: George Allen and Unwin, 1969).

110. Radkau, *Max Weber*, 466–468.

111. Max Weber, *Die Wirtschaftsethik der Weltreligionen: Hinduismus und Buddhismus*, *Archiv für Sozialwissenschaft und Sozialpolitik*, vol. 41, no. 3; vol. 42, nos. 2 and 3. It was published in English, in 1958, as Weber, *The Religion of India: The Sociology of Hinduism and Buddhism*, trans. and ed. Hans Gerth and Don Martindale (Glencoe, IL: Free Press, 1958).

112. Weber, *Religion of India*, 4, 7, 9.

113. Max Weber, "Introduction to the Economic Ethic of the World Religions" (*Die Wirtschaftsethik der Weltreligionen: Religionssoziologische Skizzen: Einleitung*), published as "The Social Psychology of World Religions," in Hans Gerth and C. Wright Mills, trans. and eds., *From Max Weber: Essays in Sociology* (New York: Oxford University Press, 1946), 269–270.

114. Weber, *Religion of India*, 149.

115. Weber, *Religion of India*, 166.

116. His first such outing was on August 1, 1916, in Nuremberg. He denied that the war, on the German side, had economic motivations, while insisting that German military strength drew from its industrial enterprise: "When Russian intellectuals say that our present Germany is no longer the Germany of Kant but a Germany of Krupp, we gladly accept this." See Radkau, *Max Weber: Die Leidenschaft des Denkens* (2005; Munich: Carl Hanser Verlag, 2020), 740–742; and the very detailed account in Hinnerk Bruhns, *Max Weber und der Erste Weltkrieg* (Tübingen: Mohr Siebeck, 2017), 35–50. Versions of the Nuremberg speech, as recorded by newspaper journalists, can be found in *MWG* I/15:648–689.

117. Max Weber, *Ancient Judaism*, trans. Hans H. Gerth and Don Martingale (New York: Free Press, 1952), 47. The contents of a handwritten manuscript from 1911 and 1913 ("Ethik und Mythik/rituelle Absonderung"), part of his investigations into the subject, can be found in *MWG* I/21.1:178–209.

118. Weber, *Ancient Judaism*, 244.

119. Weber, *Ancient Judaism*, 190, 191.

120. Weber, *Ancient Judaism*, 174.

121. Weber, *Ancient Judaism*, 112.

122. Weber, *Ancient Judaism*, 277.

123. Weber, *Ancient Judaism*, 382.

124. These cadences have been much discussed. "Es ist das Schicksal unserer Zeit, mit der ihr eigenen Rationalisierung Intellektualisierung, vor allem: Entzauberung der Welt, daß gerade die letzten und sublimsten Werte zurückgetreten sind aus der Öffentlichkeit, entweder in das hinterweltliche Reich mystischen Lebens oder in die Brüderlichkeit unmittelbarer Beziehungen der Einzelnen zueinander. Es ist weder zufällig, daß unsere höchste Kunst eine intime und keine monumentale ist, noch daß heute nur innerhalb der kleinsten Gemeinschaftskreise, von Mensch zu Mensch, im pianissimo, jenes Etwas pulsiert, das dem entspricht, was früher als prophetisches Pneuma in stürmischem Feuer durch die großen Gemeinden ging und sie zusammenschweißte. Versuchen wir, monumentale Kunstgesinnung zu erzwingen und zu 'erfinden,' dann entsteht ein so jämmerliches Mißgebilde wie in den vielen Denkmälern der letzten 20 Jahre. Versucht man, religiöse Neubildungen zu ergrübeln ohne neue, echte Prophetie, so entsteht im innerlichen Sinn etwas Ähnliches, was noch übler wirken muß. Und die Kathederprophetie wird vollends nur fanatische Sekten, aber nie eine echte Gemeinschaft schaffen. Wer dies Schicksal der Zeit nicht männlich ertragen kann, dem muß man sagen: Er kehre lieber, schweigend, ohne die übliche

öffentliche Renegatenreklame, sondern schlicht und einfach, in die weit und erbarmend geöffneten Arme der alten Kirchen zurück. Sie machen es ihm ja nicht schwer. Irgendwie hat er dabei—das ist unvermeidlich—das 'Opfer des Intellektes' zu bringen, so oder so. Wir werden ihn darum nicht schelten, wenn er es wirklich vermag. Denn ein solches Opfer des Intellekts zugunsten einer bedingungslosen religiösen Hingabe ist sittlich immerhin doch etwas anderes als jene Umgehung der schlichten intellektuellen Rechtschaffenheitspflicht, die eintritt, wenn man sich selbst nicht klar zu werden den Mut hat über die eigene letzte Stellungnahme, sondern diese Pflicht durch schwächliche Relativierung sich erleichtert." Max Weber "Wissenschaft als Beruf," 1919, *MWG* I/17:109–110; available at https://www.molnut.uni-kiel.de/pdfs/neues/2017/Max_Weber.pdf.

125. Weber is paraphrasing the first paragraph of the chapter on "Theism" from John Stuart Mill's "Three Essays on Religion" (London: Longmans, Green, Reader, and Dyer, 1874), 130: "There is the amplest historical evidence that the belief in Gods is immeasurably more natural to the human mind than the belief in one author and ruler of nature." In Weber's revised memorandum on "Value Freedom," he had written, more pointedly, "As old Mill has remarked, any empirical observation of these facts would make one realize that the only metaphysics that fits them is [that of] absolute polytheism." See Max Weber, "The Meaning of 'Value Freedom' in the Sociological and Economic Sciences," in Weber, *Collected Methodological Writings*, trans. Hans Henrik Bruun, ed. Hans Henrik Bruun and Sam Whimster (London: Routledge, 2012), 314, originally published as "Der Sinn der 'Wertfreiheit' der soziologischen und ökonomischen Wissenschaften," *Logos: Internationale Zeitschrift für Philosophie der Kultur 7* (1917). Goethe himself had averred, in a letter to Friedrich Jacobi (January 6, 1813), that "als Dichter und Künstler bin ich Polytheist"—"as a poet and artist, I am a polytheist." Cf. Richard Rorty's warm discussion of what he called romantic polytheism, with respect to Nietzsche, Mill, William James, and Dewey, in his "Pragmatism as Romantic Polytheism," in Rorty, *Philosophy as a Cultural Politics: Philosophical Papers*, vol. 4 (Cambridge: Cambridge University Press, 2007), 27–41.

126. Weber wrote, "Die alten vielen Götter, entzaubert und daher in Gestalt unpersönlicher Mächte, entsteigen ihren Gräbern, streben nach Gewalt über unser Leben und beginnen untereinander wieder ihren ewigen Kampf." Fredric Jameson saw, in such passages, a key to why Weber was so fascinated by religion: "for Weber the religious phenomenon is the very hypostasis of value in general, value seen from the outside by the man who no longer believes in any values and for whom such living belief has thus become a kind of mystery in the older ritualistic sense." Jameson, "Vanishing Mediator," 62.

127. Friedrich Wilhelm Graf, "Ernst Troeltsch's Evaluation of Max and Alfred Weber: Introduction and Translation of a Letter by Ernst Troeltsch to Heinrich Dietzel," *Max Weber Studies* 4, no. 1 (January 2004): 105.

128. Leo Strauss, *Natural Right and History* (Chicago: University of Chicago Press, 1953), 36, 42, 60–61, 73–74.

129. Radkau, *Max Weber*, 659; Weber, *Protestant Ethic*, 121.

130. Weber to Marianne, June 26, 1918, *MWG* II/10.1:205.

131. Max Weber, "Charismatic Authority," in *Economy and Society*, ed. Guenther Roth and Claus Wittich (Berkeley: University of California Press, 1978), 242. Eisner, like Jaffé, was a pacifist during the war, a position Weber described as involving "masochism" and "nauseating exhibitionism." Radkau, *Max Weber*, 502, 509–510. Kurt Eisner's biographer Bernhard Grau makes it clear that Jaffé was regarded by members of Eisner's inner circle as a useful if perhaps compromised figure, "a representative of the bourgeois intelligentsia" who wasn't so much a party politician as "the type of a mainly politically independent, and, in any case, undogmatic specialist minister." Bernhard Grau, *Kurt Eisner, 1867–1919: Eine Biographie* (Munich: C.H. Beck, 2001), 366.

132. Kaube, *Max Weber*, 405; Radkau, *Max Weber*, 542–543.

133. "Nach reiflicherem Studium des Thatbestandes verbessert": Max Weber to Else Jaffé, February 25, 1919, *MWG*, II/10:1, 483.

134. Kaesler, *Max Weber*, 887. (The historian in question, the medievalist Karl Kampe, pointedly noted in his diary that those who gathered for the farewell were "about two-thirds full or half-Jews.") Weber later praised Tobler for her selection of lieder: *MWG* II/10.2:803. Kaube, *Max Weber*, 400; Radkau, *Max Weber*, 529.

135. Fritz Ringer, *Max Weber: An Intellectual Biography* (Chicago: University of Chicago Press, 2004), 204; and Weber to Otto Neurath, October 4, 1919, in which Weber writes that he would "not shed a tear" for the prewar "free" capitalist conjuncture, *MWG* II/10:2, 799.

136. Peter Ghosh, "Political and Unpolitical Germany: Max Weber and Thomas Mann," *Internationales Archiv für Sozialgeschichte der deutschen Literatur* (2023), https://doi.org/10.1515/iasl-2023-0002.

137. "Lili's Tun erscheint mir immer sicherer als das *einzig* Berechtigte. Und: Schöne. Sie *glaubte* nun mal nicht an ihre Mutter-Qualifikation, *hielt* sich für ein 'Unglück' für die Kinder. Mit Recht oder, sicher, mit Unrecht: *wer* will da von 'Pflichten' sprechen? Und überhaupt! *Wer* hat das durchlebt? Es ist christliche Würdelosigkeit, das Leben *so* als 'Wert an sich' zu nehmen.' " (Lili's action seems to me ever more surely the only justified one. And: Beautiful. She just did not believe in her qualifications as a mother, considered herself a "disaster" for the children. And anyway! Who has lived through that? Whether rightly or, surely, wrongly: who will speak of "duties" here? And after all! Who has experienced that? It is Christian indignity to regard life as a "value in itself.") Max Weber to Mina Tobler, April 20, 1920, *MWG* II/10.2:1015.

138. Radkau, *Max Weber*, 539, 547–548; Kaube, *Max Weber*, 419.

139. Stephen Kalberg, "Max Weber's Types of Rationality: Cornerstones for the Analysis of Rationalization Processes in History," *American Journal of Sociology* 85, no. 5 (March 1980): 1146.

140. Max Weber, " 'Prefatory Remarks' to Collected Essays in the Sociology of Religion (1920)," in Weber, *The Protestant Ethic and the Spirit of Capitalism*, trans. Stephen Kalberg (London: Routledge, 2001), 149–164, 160. The Talcott Parsons translation, first published in 1930, used the essay as an introduction to *The Protestant Ethic*; in Kalberg's translation, it appears as an ancillary essay.

141. Weber, " 'Objectivity' in Social Science and Social Policy," 76.

142. Weber to Else Jaffé, September 7, 1919, *MWG* II/10.2:762; David J. Chalcraft, "Weber, Wagner, and Thoughts of Death," *Sociology* 27, no. 3 (August 1993): 437. Weber inserted, slightly awkwardly, the passage into the revised *Protestant Ethics*, though Chalcraft notes that Weber's quotation actually combines two separate lines of Siegmund's.

143. Max Weber to Else Jaffé, April 24, 1920, *MWG* II/10:2, 1030; Radkau, *Max Weber*, 534.

144. Peter Ghosh observes that for Weber, "modern men's adherence to values and orders was *both* plural and absolute—the fact of plurality did not lead to *pluralism*, to resignation or reduced commitment." Ghosh, *Max Weber and "The Protestant Ethic,"* 284.

145. Robert Musil, *The Man Without Qualities*, trans. Sophie Wilkins (New York: Knopf, 1995), 1:603. Musil studied at the University of Berlin from 1903 to 1908, where, Frisby tells us, he attended some of Simmel's lectures.

146. Kaube, *Max Weber*, 288; Guenther Roth, "Introduction to the Transaction Edition: Marianne Weber and Her Circle," in Marianne Weber, *Max Weber: A Biography*, trans. and ed. Harry Zohn (Piscataway, NJ: Transaction, 1988), xliii. Marianne died in 1954; Mina Tobler in 1967; and Else, who lived to be ninety-nine, in 1973.

147. I'm making what I think is a plausible inference. Marianne writes of how, on one day, he greeted the doctor with a bit from a comic Mozart aria ("Se vuol ballare"), his strong voice attesting to his health. But later, she says, "someone hears him sing another song: 'Dig me a little grave in the green heath." ("Grabt mir ein Gräbelein auf grüner Heide.") Marianne Weber, *Max Weber: Ein Lebensbild*, 3rd rev. ed. (Tübingen: Mohr Siebeck, 1984), 711. What Marianne quotes, secondhand, isn't a known song lyric. (I'm grateful to Michael Fischer and Johanna Ziemann of the Albert-Ludwigs-Universität Freiburg Zentrum für Populäre Kultur und Musik for checking it against their voluminous resources.) But in meaning it's a close approximation of Müller's lines "Grabt mir ein Grab im Wasen, / Deckt mich mit grünem Rasen." And the chance that a German music-lover such as Weber wouldn't be highly familiar with this Schubert song-cycle, D. 795, and with this specific song, is approximately zero.

CHAPTER 5. CRITICAL AND COGNITIVE TURNS

1. Hans Joas, *Do We Need Religion? On the Experience of Self-Transcendence*, trans. Alex Skinner (2008; London: Routledge, 2016), 7, 14.

2. Rudolf Otto, *The Idea of the Holy: An Inquiry into the Non-Rational Factor in the Idea of the Divine and Its Relation to the Rational*, trans. John W. Harvey (London: Oxford University Press, 1929; translated from the ninth edition of *Das Heilige*, originally published in 1917), e.g., 10–20; Simone Weil, *Gravity and Grace*, trans. Arthur Wills (New York: G.P. Putnam's, 1952), e.g., 90–96; and Iris Murdoch, *The Sovereignty of Good* (London: Routledge and Kegan Paul, 1970), 84; Joas, *Do We Need Religion?* 10.

3. Joas, *Do We Need Religion?*, 12, 13, 56.

4. Hans Joas, *The Power of the Sacred: An Alternative to the Narrative of Disenchantment*, trans. Alex Skinner (Oxford: Oxford University Press, 2021), 9. See also Hans Joas, *Faith as an Option: Possible Futures for Christianity*, trans. Alex Skinner (Stanford, CA: Stanford University Press, 2014). In the days of Bismarck, Eduard von Hartmann felt something similar: "The repulsive crudeness in the brutal present-day egoism of social democracy ultimately stems from the, admittedly innocent, loss of the old religious worldview, and can only be overcome at its root by regaining a new religious worldview." Hartmann, *Die Sozialen Kernfragen* (Leipzig: Wilhelm Friedrich, 1884), 171–172. That new religious worldview was, of course, to be a carefully engineered one.

5. Hartmut Rosa, *Resonance: A Sociology of Our Relationship to the World* (Cambridge: Polity, 2019), 286. Originally published as *Resonanz: Eine Soziologie Der Weltbeziehung* (Berlin: Suhrkamp, 2016).

6. Hartmut Rosa, *Demokratie Braucht Religion* (Munich: Kösel-Verlag, 2022), 54, 55–56, 74–75.

7. Jürgen Habermas, *Glauben und Wissen: Friedenspreis des Deutschen Buchhandels 2001* (Frankfurt: Suhrkamp, 2001), 22.

8. Habermas continues, "Philosophy has repeatedly learned through its encounters with religious traditions—and also, of course, with Muslim traditions—that it receives innovative impulses when it succeeds in freeing cognitive contents from their dogmatic encapsulation in the crucible of rational discourse. Kant and Hegel are the most influential examples of this. The encounters of many twentieth-century philosophers with a religious writer such as Kierkegaard, who thinks in postmetaphysical, but not post-Christian, terms, are also exemplary in this regard. . . . We cannot exclude that they involve semantic potentials capable of exercising an inspirational force on society as a whole as soon as they divulge their profane truth contents. In short, postmetaphysical thinking is prepared to learn from religion while at the same time remaining agnostic. It insists on the difference between the certainties of faith and publicly criticizable validity claims; but it eschews the rationalist presumption that it can itself decide which aspects of religious doctrines are rational and which irrational. The contents that reason appropriates through translation must not be lost for faith." Jürgen Habermas, *Between Naturalism and Religion*, trans. Ciaran Cronin (Cambridge: Polity Press, 2008), 142–143.

9. Habermas, *Between Naturalism and Religion*, 214. "The neutrality of state power vis-à-vis different worldviews, which guarantees equal individual

liberties for all citizens, is incompatible with the political generalization of a secularized world view. Secular citizens, in their role as citizens, may neither deny that religious worldviews are in principle capable of truth nor question the right of their devout fellow-citizens to couch their contributions to public discussion in religious language. Liberal political culture can even expect its secular citizens to take part in the efforts to translate relevant contributions from religious language into a publicly intelligible language" (112). The question of what counts as "publicly intelligible" invites difficulties that I won't get into.

10. Simmel, "Fundamental Religious Ideas and Modern Science: An Inquiry [1909]," in Simmel, *Essays on Religion*, ed. and trans. Horst Jürgen Helle with Ludwig Nieder (New Haven: Yale University Press, 1997), 6.

11. Ulrich Beck, *A God of One's Own: Religion's Capacity for Peace and Potential for Violence*, trans. Rodney Livingstone (Cambridge: Polity, 2010), "institutionalized individualization," "illiteracy" (86); "God of your own," "wellness" (153); "Amnesty International" (88). Originally published in German as *Der eigene Gott* (Frankfurt am Main: Suhrkamp Verlag, 2008).

12. Beck, *God of One's Own*, "second modernity" (44); "cosmopolitan religiosity" (59); "crazy patchwork" (140); "actually existing impurity" (136).

13. Beck, *God of One's Own*, 49, 152, 178.

14. John Milbank, *Theology and Social Theory: Beyond Secular Reason*, 2nd ed. (1990; Oxford: Blackwell, 2006), 52, 3.

15. Milbank, *Theology and Social Theory*, 9, 23–55.

16. Milbank, *Theology and Social Theory*, 17, 5, 6.

17. Leo Tolstoy, *The Destruction of Hell and Its Restoration*, trans. Tim Newcomb (N.p.: Newcomb Livraria Press, 2023), Kindle edition location 238.

18. Milbank, *Theology and Social Theory*, 66, 189, 66, 106.

19. Ernst Troeltsch, *The Social Teaching of the Christian Churches*, trans. Olive Wyon (1911/1912; New York: Macmillan, 1931), 1:68. (The book's original title, *Die Soziallehren der christlichen Kirschen und Gruppen* would be more precisely rendered *Social Teachings of the Christian Churches and Groups*.) Troeltsch's exploration of this ideal, with its amalgam of universalism and individualism, rewards attention: "Was this idea peculiar to the Christian Gospel, or were there similar movements in existence at the same time? It is quite clear that similar ideas were present among the later Stoics, especially those of Rome. . . . The doctrine of the Stoics was, primarily, a religious metaphysical doctrine, which arose out of the religious process of transformation which took place in late antiquity, and here also we have to do with a general sociological structure which has arisen out of a centre of religious thought. Its philosophical monotheism also led to a religious relation with humanity which was clearly opposed to the popular conception of religion in the ancient world. . . . The Law of Nature (an idea which was destined to play an extraordinary part in Christian theory) requires, on the one hand, conformity with the harmonious course of Nature, and the share

of the individual within the social system, and, on the other hand, a spirit of inner elevation above all these considerations, and the moral and religious freedom of the dignity of reason which is united with God, and is therefore far above being disturbed by any concrete external happenings in the world of time and sense. It is the duty of the will to learn to discern this Law of Nature, and through this knowledge to achieve the control of the external desires of sense, and also the inward dignity and purity of harmony between the will of man and the ordering of Providence, and thus through knowledge to attain the personality which is hidden in God. All this leads to a theory of individualism expressed in terms of the idea of religious and ethical personality, and also to its inevitably correlated idea of an equally (logical) universalism, which recognizes that all men are equally called to the same knowledge of God and which, in their common surrender to the Divine Law of Nature, unites them by an ethical bond" (64–65).

20. John Milbank, *The Future of Love* (Eugene, OR: Cascade Books, 2009), 170. I have touched on the cartographic debates over the Enlightenment and Counter-Enlightenment in Kwame Anthony Appiah, "Dialectics of Enlightenment," *New York Review of Books* (May 9, 2019): 37–41.

21. Georg Simmel, "Das Problem der Religiösen Lage," in *Weltanschauung*, ed. Max Frischeisen-Köhler (Berlin: Verlag Reichl & Co., 1911), 338, 337.

22. Max Weber, invoking ideal types and the value of methodological fictions, defended the "marginal" school of economics associated with Carl Menger and Eugen von Böhm-Bawerk, in his essay "Grenznutzlehrer und das 'psychophysische Grundgesetz,' " *Archiv für Sozialwissenschaft und Sozialpolitik* 29 (1908): 546–558; *MWG* I/12:115–133; Max Weber, "Marginal Utility Theory and 'The Fundamental Law of Psychophysics,' " trans. Louis Schneider, *Social Science Quarterly* 56, no. 1 (June 1975): 21–36.

23. See, for example, Michael McBride, "A Rational Choice Theory of Religious Authority," *Rationality and Society* 28, no. 4 (2016): 410–438; Rex Ahdar, "The Idea of 'Religious Markets,' " *International Journal of Law in Context* 2, no. 1 (2006): 49–65; Anthony Gill, *Rendering unto Caesar: The Catholic Church and State in Latin America* (Chicago: University of Chicago Press, 1998). The journalist Larry Witham surveyed the field in *Marketplace of the Gods: How Economics Explains Religion* (Oxford: Oxford University Press, 2010). There are relevant arguments, too, in George A. Akerlof and Rachel E. Kranton, *Identity Economics: How Our Identities Shape Our Work, Wages, and Well-Being* (Princeton, NJ: Princeton University Press, 2010).

24. Rodney Stark, "Religious Effects," in *Sociology of Religion: A Rodney Stark Reader*, ed. Dedong Wei and Zhifeng Zhong (Waco, TX: Baylor University Press, 2015), 111.

25. Contributions to this model—by authors who may nonetheless disagree on significant points—include work synopsized in such popular and scholarly books as Pascal Boyer, *Religion Explained* (New York: Basic Books, 2001); Scott Atran, *In Gods We Trust: The Evolutionary Landscape of Religion* (Oxford: Oxford University Press, 2002); Daniel Dennett, *Breaking the*

Spell: Religion as a Natural Phenomenon (New York: Viking, 2007); Justin L. Barrett, *Why Would Anyone Believe in God?* (Lanham, MD: AltaMira Press, 2004); and Ara Norenzayan, *Big Gods: How Religion Transformed Cooperation and Conflict* (Princeton, NJ: Princeton University Press, 2013). See also Benjamin Grant Purzycki, Joseph Henrich, and Ara Norenzayan, eds., *The Evolution of Religion and Morality*, vol. 1 (New York: Routledge, 2023); and Martin Lang, Benjamin Grant Purzycki, Joseph Henrich, and Ara Norenzayan, eds., *The Evolution of Religion and Morality*, vol. 2 (New York: Routledge, 2024). A useful overview, albeit a skeptical one, is provided by Russell Powell and Steve Clarke, "Religion as an Evolutionary Byproduct: A Critique of the Standard Model," *British Journal for the Philosophy of Science* 63, no. 3 (September 2012). (I'm bracketing influential work by David Sloan Wilson, because it involves controversial arguments about the unit of selection—in particular, the thesis that group selection applies at the genetic level—and most researchers think they "have no need of this hypothesis.")

26. Boyer, *Religion Explained*, 187.

27. Stewart Guthrie, *Faces in the Clouds: A New Theory of Religion* (New York: Oxford University Press, 1993), 3. Guthrie notes that the idea of invisibility is "based on broad experience: camouflaged animals are constantly becoming invisible to us." Furthermore, he argues that although sociability is inherent, "humanizing is not a mode of comfort seeking: 'When the night wind slams a door in a house in which we had thought ourselves alone, or taps something against our window, we may hear it as a human but feel queasy, not comforted. Dimly sighting an overloaded garbage can in a twilit alley, we may see it as a crouching mugger and feel a jolt of fear, not a glow of sociability. A patrolling soldier hears every snapping twig, every bush rustled by the wind, as the enemy and is set on edge, not set at ease" (74). He further observes that animals animate their world, noting "the cat sees fluttering leaves as prey, horses see blowing bags as threats, and dogs hear sirens as howls" (39).

28. Barrett, *Why Would Anyone Believe in God?*, 32. Some cognitive psychologists talk about a (hyperactive) agency detection *module*, but modularity—a view of cognition that involves separable domain-specific systems—is a contested research program in cognitive science. The virtue of "device" is that we can't take it very literally; it's a capacity we have, and we can be agnostic about the mental architecture behind it.

29. Atran, *In Gods We Trust*, 69. The term "theory of mind" was introduced in David Premack and Guy Woodruff, "Does the Chimpanzee Have a Theory of Mind? *Behavioral and Brain Sciences* 1, no. 4 (1978): 515–526. That humans have a theory of mind, tellingly, became perspicuous when considering another species. (Again, it's the "How's the water? *What* water?" problem.) In the vast subsequent literature, there have been disputes about how we do this: is it by applying an implicit theory and working out its consequences through unconscious reasoning, or do we run inner simulations, in which we discover imaginatively what we would do if we were in those

states and then assume that others will do likewise? We can remain agnostic about that issue. What's clear is that we successfully manage our relations because we recognize the mental life of others.

30. See Paul Bloom, *Descartes' Baby* (New York: Basic Books, 2004), 191–195, 203–204; and cf. Bloom, "Religion Is Natural," *Developmental Science* 10 (2007): 147–151; and Deborah Kelemen, "Are Children 'Intuitive Theists'? Reasoning about Purpose and Design in Nature," *Psychological Science* 15, no. 5 (May 2004): 295–301. Children between four and nine, she reports, have especially "promiscuous teleological intuitions": raining is what clouds are *for*. Other researchers say that even preschoolers distinguish between organisms and other entities, and are more likely to give teleological, rather than physical, explanations for traits in organisms. See Kostas Kampourakis, Eirini Palaiokrassa, Maria Papadopoulou, Vasiliki Pavlidi, and Myrto Argyropoulou, "Children's Intuitive Teleology: Shifting the Focus of Evolution Education Research," *Evolution: Education and Outreach* 5, suppl. 2 (2012): 279–291.

31. Joseph Henrich and Scott Atran, "The Evolution of Religion: How Cognitive By-Products, Adaptive Learning Heuristics, Ritual Displays, and Group Competition Generate Deep Commitments to Prosocial Religions," *Biological Theory* 5, no. 1 (2010): 18–30, at 20.

32. The thesis concerning the transmissibility of "minimally counterintuitive" concepts is developed, inter alia, in Pascal Boyer, "Cognitive Aspects of Religious Symbolism," in Boyer, ed., *Cognitive Aspects of Religious Symbolism* (Cambridge: Cambridge University Press, 1993), 4–47; Pascal Boyer, *The Naturalness of Religious Ideas: A Cognitive Theory of Religion* (Berkeley: University of California Press, 1994); and Justin L. Barrett and M. A. Nyhof, "Spreading Nonnatural Concepts," *Journal of Cognition and Culture* 1 (2001): 69–100.

33. It may be contingent, historically, which such stories acquire the status of religious belief and which do not. I shall continue to use the word "counterintuitive" to refer to concepts and beliefs that run against the intuitive systems of folk psychology, folk biology, and folk physics. But we should bear in mind that many such beliefs do not run counter to the educated intuitions of modern people, who derive their beliefs from developed sciences and religions.

34. Henrich and Atran, "Evolution of Religion," 22. Yet the game of basketball, say, extensively deploys nonverbal forms of misdirection—feints—that are not very costly.

35. Ara Norenzayan, *Big Gods* (Princeton, NJ: Princeton University Press, 2013); an earlier version of the argument was rehearsed in Ara Norenzayan and Azim .F. Shariff, "The Origin and Evolution of Religious Prosociality," *Science* 322 (2008): 58–62.

36. Max Weber, "Social Psychology of World Religions" (a.k.a. his *Einleitung*), in Hans Gerth and C. Wright Mills, trans. and eds., *From Max Weber: Essays in Sociology* (New York: Oxford University Press, 1946), 280; Rodney

Stark, "Gods, Ritual, and the Moral Order," *Journal for the Scientific Study of Religion* 40, no. 4 (2001): 619–636.

37. Robert Boyd and Peter J. Richerson, "Punishment Allows the Evolution of Cooperation (or Anything Else) in Sizable Groups," *Ethology and Sociobiology* 13, no. 3 (May 1992): 171–195. Readers who know about ultimatum games will be familiar with this idea. The locus classicus here is Ernst Fehr and Simon Gächter, "Altruistic Punishment in Humans," *Nature* 415 (2002): 137–140.

38. Dominic Johnson and Jesse Bering, "Hand of God, Mind of Man: Punishment and Cognition in the Evolution of Cooperation," *Evolutionary Psychology* 4, no. 1 (January–December 2006): 221. See also Dominic Johnson and Oliver Krüger, "The Good of Wrath: Supernatural Punishment and the Evolution of Cooperation," *Political Theology* 5, no. 2 (2004): 159–176. In *Big Gods*, 128–129, Norenzayan cites research indicating that societies facing water scarcity—where freeloading was a bigger problem—tended to propagate supernatural monitors, and notes that "one of the most culturally successful of all Big Gods, the God of Abraham, was originally a god of the desert." Norenzayan argues, against Johnson and Bering, that many small-scale communities don't have omniscient, moralizing gods like these (123–126); foraging societies often subject misconduct—such as brawling and murder—to social, but not supernatural disapproval. (He also agrees with Tylor about the separability of religions and morality.) Johnson, disputing Norenzayan, concurs with Simmel's statement that "in general every group constructs its God in such a way that He commands what it recognizes as socially beneficial." Group-beneficial practices, he stresses, need not be what we would consider moral. Van Leeuwen mentions the supernatural-punishers idea approvingly, but there's a challenge in reconciling either version of supernatural-punishers model with Van Leeuwen's: if your cognitive attitude toward the supernatural punishers is one of make-believe credences, readily suspended in many nonritual contexts, will it have the efficacy that Johnson, Bering, and Norenzayan ascribe to it?

39. Dominic Johnson, *God Is Watching You: How the Fear of God Makes Us Human* (Oxford: Oxford University Press, 2015), 4, 47–48. Robert Sapolsky, *Behave: The Biology of Humans at Our Best and Worst* (New York: Penguin, 2017), 305.

40. Johnson, *God Is Watching You*, 50; cf. Valerie Warrior, *Roman Religion* (Cambridge: Cambridge University Press, 2006), 50. *Deisidaimonia* was often thought of by the ancients as excessive.

41. Dominic Johnson writes, "there is at least some evidence that weaker religious beliefs, and weaker beliefs in supernatural punishment in particular, are associated with negative social outcomes," which is "precisely what the supernatural punishment theory would predict." In support of the thesis, he cites a study that ostensibly shows lower crime rates among countries where more people believe in hell than in heaven, retribution being a more powerful motivation than reward. Johnson, *God Is Watching You*, 218–220, citing Azim F. Shariff and Mijke Rhemtulla, "Divergent Effects of Beliefs in Heaven and Hell on National Crime Rates," *PLOS One* (June 19, 2012). But that reward is a milder incentive than punishment doesn't entail that the ratio should matter; perhaps what counts is that you strongly believe in hell and strong hell-believers tend to be strong heaven-believers, too. It should also be noted that the study is a tally of countries, so tiny Tuvalu has the same evidential weight as India or Nigeria (while Indonesia and Malaysia don't count at all; they were excluded because they lacked sufficient variance in heaven/hell belief); and certain crimes (for example, kidnapping) were excluded without explanation. In fact, substantial empirical evidence suggests that populations with relatively low levels of reported belief tend to have relatively low crime rates. For an overview of the literature, see Phil Zuckerman, "Atheism, Secularity, and Well-Being," *Sociology Compass* (Fall 2009). There are obvious confounders: wealthier and better educated populations tend to have lower rates of reported religious belief. In *God Is Watching You*, Johnson also cites Robert Barro and Rachel MacCleary, "Religion and Economic Growth across Countries," *American Sociological Review* 68 (October 2003): 760–791, suggesting a positive correlation between growth and the belief in heaven and well; but slights their finding that economic growth correlates negatively with church attendance, which could be taken as a proxy for strength of belief. In any case, a 2011 effort to test Barro and MacCleary's findings (which had used data from before 1992) against an updated data set failed to confirm them.

EPILOGUE

1. See the posthumous collection by Margaret Masterman, *Language, Cohesion, and Form*, ed. Yorick Wilks (Cambridge: Cambridge University Press, 2005). Masterman, who once programmed a computer to write haiku, also published three novels (including a mystery) in her twenties.

2. Margaret Masterman, "The Nature of a Paradigm," in *Criticism and the Growth of Knowledge: Proceedings of the International Colloquium in the Philosophy of Science, London, 1965*, vol. 4, ed. Imre Lakatos and Alan Musgrave (Cambridge: Cambridge University Press, 1970), 59–90, specifically 61. In his contribution to the volume, "Reflections on My Critics," Thomas Kuhn explained, " 'disciplinary' because it is common to the practitioners of a specified discipline; 'matrix,' because it consists of ordered elements which require individual specification" (271). In a later essay, Kuhn wrote that "if the term 'paradigm' is to be successfully explicated, scientific communities must first be recognized as having an independent existence," and apologized for having made "a paradigm seem like a quasi-mystical entity or property which, like charisma, transforms those infected by it." Kuhn, "Second Thoughts on Paradigms," *The Essential Tension* (Chicago: University of Chicago Press, 1977), 295.

3. Margaret Masterman, "Sketch of a Contemplation," in Dorothy Emmet and Rowan Williams, *Religious Explorations* (1989), 5, available at Epiphany Philosophers, http://epiphanyphilosophers.org/wp-content/uploads/2016/12/Full_RE_2.pdf. By "Sisters," she means nuns.

4. R. B. Braithwaite, *An Empiricist's View of the Nature of Religious Belief* (Cambridge: Cambridge University Press, 1955), 19, 33.

5. D. M. Emmet, *The Nature of Metaphysical Thinking* (London: Macmillan, 1945), 108, 219, 220, 227. The book went through multiple printings and editions over the ensuing years.

6. Weber, "Religious Groups," in pt. 2, vol. 1 of Weber, *Economy and Society*, ed. Guenther Roth and Claus Wittich (1968; Berkeley: University of California Press, 1978), 399.

7. Scott Atran and Joseph Henrich, "The Evolution of Religion: How Cognitive By-Products, Adaptive Learning Heuristics, Ritual Displays, and Group Competition Generate Deep Commitments to Prosocial Religion," *Biological Theory* 5, no. 1 (2010): 20.

8. Justin L. Barrett, "Cognitive Science of Religion: What Is It and Why Is It?" *Religion Compass* 1, no. 6 (September 2007): 768. A decade later, Barrett circled back to the problem in a published commentary. He recognized that, while botanists can freely call peas or cucumbers "fruit," researchers have felt pressure to square their use of "religion" with the folk uses of the term. Yet "the very fact that definitional agreement has not emerged after more than a century of prolonged scholarly attention by many different disciplines suggests, perhaps, that the concept *religion* is not particularly valuable for science." Justin L. Barrett, "Could We Advance the Science of Religion (Better) without the Concept of 'Religion'?," *Religion, Brain & Behavior* 7, no. 4 (2017): 282–283.

9. In a touchstone of radical nominalism, Georg Lichtenburg wrote, in one of his *Sudelbücher*, "Nature creates, not *genera* and *species*, but *individua*, and our shortsightedness has to seek out similarities so as to be able to retain in mind many things at the same time. These conceptions become more and more inaccurate the larger the families we invent for ourselves are." Georg Friedrich Lichtenberg, *The Waste Books*, trans. R. J. Hollingdale (1990; New York: New York Review Books, 2000), notebook A (1765–1770), epigraph 3, p. 3.

10. Ludwig Wittgenstein, *Philosophical Investigations*, trans. G. E. M. Armstrong, 4th ed. (Malden, MA: Blackwell, 2009), §67.

11. Ninian Smart, Benson Saler, Peter Byrne, and many others have appealed to the "family resemblance" strategy, although they elaborate it in different ways. Timothy Fitzgerald, *The Ideology of Religious Studies* (New York: Oxford University Press, 2000), 73.

12. "While all of the elements that we deem to pertain to the category religion are predictable of that category, not all of them are predictable of all the phenomena that various scholars regard as instantiations of religion." Benson Saler, *Conceptualizing Religion: Immanent Anthropologists, Transcendent*

Natives, and Unbounded Categories (Leiden: E.J. Brill, 1993), 225. The historical challenge, in his view, is to "transform a folk category into an analytic category that will facilitate transcultural research and understanding"—but he doubts that the challenge is any different from that posed by categories such as "the state" or "kinship."

13. In this paper, Rodney Needham took polythetic criteria as equivalent to the "family resemblance" strategy (as had Stephen Toulmin); most would distinguish them. Rodney Needham, "Polythetic Classification: Convergence and Consequences," *Man* n.s. 10, no. 3 (September 1975): 349–369. The "take it as we use it" approach appears in Needham, "Characteristics of Religion," in Needham, *Circumstantial Deliveries* (Berkeley: University of California Press, 1981), 73. He was effectively delivering a rejoinder to his critique of "belief."

14. Wilfred Cantwell Smith, "Methodology and the Study of Religion: Some Misgivings," in Robert Baird, ed., *Methodological Issues in Religious Studies* (Chico, CA: New Horizons Press, 1975), 26. I'm grateful to Seanan Fong for drawing this passage to my attention.

15. Robin Horton, "African Traditional Thought and Western Science, Part I," *Africa* 37, no. 1 (January 1967): 50–71, and "African Traditional Thought and Western Science, Part II," *Africa* 37, no. 2 (April 1967): 155–187. It also appears as a book chapter in Horton, *Patterns of Thought in Africa and the West* (Cambridge: Cambridge University Press, 1993), 197–258.

16. Van Leeuwen, discussing research, which he helped organize, concerning when people say they "think" something and when they say they "believe" something—marking an implicit distinction between factual and credal commitments—does concede that his Ghanaian respondents don't quite fit the pattern; the distinction for them seems more porous. See Neil Van Leeuwen, *Religion as Make-Believe* (Cambridge, MA: Harvard University Press, 2023), 138.

17. Alison Gopnik, "The Theory Theory as an Alternative to the Innateness Hypothesis," in L. M. Antony, ed., *Chomsky and His Critics* (Oxford: Blackwell, 2003), 238–254. And see Gopnik, "Finding Our Inner Scientist," *Daedalus* 133, no. 1 (2004): 21–28. The term "theory theory" was coined by Adam Morton in 1980.

18. Perhaps there's a hint in the connection between our very word invention and the Latin verb *invenire*, which usually means both discover and invent.

19. Laplace made many contributions to the mathematical problem of modeling the Newtonian dynamics of the solar system, although, disturbingly, his work did not prove what he thought. So far as I know, the question of whether the solar system is stable is still a mathematically open one. Weber, of course, had much to say about how European science was advanced by church-driven forms of rationality. More recently, much work in the history of science, attending (e.g.) to church patronage of scientific research and to the deep continuities between alchemistry and chemistry, has also debunked the science-versus-religion scheme.

20. Chinua Achebe. "Interview with Anthony Appiah, D. A. N. Jones and John Ryle," in (London) *Times Literary Supplement* (February 26, 1982), 209.

21. It has been argued that the progress of English mathematicians was hindered in the eighteenth century because, out of nationalist sentiment, they long persisted in using Newton's ungainly notion of fluents and fluxions for the operations of calculus, rather than Leibniz's easier and more algebraic notation (which we essentially use today). And modern Chinese physics could not have been helped when, during phases of the Cultural Revolution, Einstein and his theory of relativity was deemed taboo.

22. See Clyde L. Hardin and Alexander Rosenberg, "In Defense of Convergent Realism," *Philosophy of Science* 49, no. 4 (December 1982): 604–615. They argue: "if it is legitimate to say that the atomic theories of Dalton, J. J. Thomson, Bohr, and Schrödinger all refer, and refer to the same sort of entity, namely, the atom, then it is equally legitimate to say that the ether theories of Fresnel, MacCullagh, Maxwell and Lorentz all refer, and refer to the same entity, namely, the electromagnetic field" (611). Indeed, they note that Einstein referred to the field as "the ether" (614). See also Stathis Psillos, *Scientific Realism: How Science Tracks Truth* (London: Routledge, 2005). Enlisting an augmented "descriptive causal theory" of reference, Psillos thinks that what matters is that "the core causal description associated with the term 'electromagnetic field' takes up the core causal description associated with the term 'ether.' Maxwell's postulation of the electromagnetic field was, in essence, associated with the same sets of properties that had been associated with the postulation of the ether"(296). As to why ether was, in fact, abandoned by scientists, he argues that this issue is "ultimately sociological" (298).

23. "Natural kinds," a notion we owe to John Stuart Mill, has also come under scrutiny; some philosophers want us to give it up. But the distinction between natural and social kinds, including the ones I mention here, is pretty commonplace. Contemporary philosophers who think about social kinds, notably Ásta Kristjana Sveinsdóttir and Sally Haslanger, tend to think that they can be real and objective; Haslanger, in particular, argues that we can have social kinds without names for them.

24. Ian Hacking credited Bert Hansen with the phrase. The subjects of dynamic nominalism, or dialectical realism, "come into being by a dialectic between classification and who is classified," he writes. "Naming has real effects on people, and changes in people have real effects on subsequent classifications. In any event we are not concerned with an arid logical nominalism or a dogmatic realism." See Hacking, "Between Michel Foucault and Erving Goffman: Between Discourse in the Abstract and Face-to-Face Interaction," *Economy and Society* 33, no. 3 (August 2004): 279, 280.

25. See Kwame Anthony Appiah, *As If: Idealization and Ideals* (Cambridge, MA: Harvard University Press, 2017). I mentioned earlier Jürgen Habermas's notion of "knowledge-constitutive interests," which usefully provides another vantage. These knowledge-constitutive interests could be

technical interests, foremost in the empirical-analytical sciences and those of the engineer seeking to control natural processes. They could be practical interests, which clustered with the historical and hermeneutical forms of scholarship, the *Geisteswissenschaften*, aimed at modes of mutual understanding across cultures and eras. And they could be emancipatory interests, which clustered around the "critical social sciences" (including sociology, political theory, aspects of anthropology and social psychology), forms of inquiry that sought to understand social and political phenomena with an aim to envision possibilities of social transformation. It's a taxonomy that reflects a certain time and place—Frankfurt-school-adjacent German academia in the late 1960s—but the approach is broadly consonant with the way disciplines use idealizations.

26. "Allein wir haben es überhaupt nicht mit dem 'Wesen' der Religion, sondern mit den Bedingungen und Wirkungen einer bestimmten Art von Gemeinschaftshandeln zu tun." Weber, "Religiöse Gemeinschaften" (Typen religiöser Vergemeinschaftung), in *MWG* I/22.2:121.

27. Martin Riesebrodt, *The Promise of Salvation*, trans. Steven Rendall (Chicago: University of Chicago Press, 2010), 6.

28. For a discussion of pluralism and its difficulties, see Courtney Bender and Pamela E. Klassen, eds., *After Pluralism: Reimagining Religious Engagement* (New York: Columbia University Press, 2010). The editors write that their goal "is to examine the grounds on which religious difference is itself constructed as a problem that has pluralism as its solution." They see a possibly problematic connection between pluralism and unity, "between celebrating the plurality of religious diversity and organizing under the unity of the category of religion." In their view, "the doctrines and programs of pluralism that dominate contemporary academic and public conversations do not constitute a theory of understanding religious interactions as they take place in the world" (2, 5, 12). See also the discussion of "hard pluralism" in Kwame Anthony Appiah, *The Ethics of Identity* (Princeton, NJ: Princeton University Press, 2005), 71–78.

29. Frank P. Ramsey, "Facts and Propositions," *Proceedings of the Aristotelian Society, Supplementary Volume 7* (1927): 170.